A COMPLETE GUIDE

OREGON WINE COUNTRY

1ST EDITION

OREGON WINE COUNTRY

A Great Destination

Sherry L. Moore and Jeff Welsch

The Countryman Press
Woodstock, Vermont

OPPOSITE: *Pinot Noir fruit in full regalia.* Bill Miller

Dedicated to Sherry's mentors: Mary, Marlie, and Suzy, who showed me how to follow a dream.

Oregon Wine Country: A Great Destination

ISBN: 978-1-58157-123-3

Interior photographs by the author unless otherwise specified
Front covr photograph: Airlie Winery, Monmouth, OR, © Bill Miller, Allegory Commercial
Photography. To see more of Bill's work, please visit www.allegory-photo.com
Maps by Paul Woodward, © The Countryman Press
Book design by Bodenweber Design
Composition by Eugenie S. Delaney

Published by The Countryman Press, P.O. Box 748, Woodstock, VT 05091
Distributed by W. W. Norton & Company, Inc., 500 Fifth Avenue, New York, NY 10110
Printed in the United States of America

10 9 8 7 6 5 4 3 2 1

Recommended by *National Geographic Traveler* and *Travel + Leisure* magazines

A crisp and critical approach, for travelers who want to live like locals.—*USA Today*

Great Destinations™ guidebooks are known for their comprehensive, critical coverage of regions of extraordinary cultural interest and natural beauty. Each title in this series is continuously updated with each printing to ensure accurate and timely information. All the books contain more than one hundred photographs and maps.

THE ADIRONDACK BOOK

THE ALASKA PANHANDLE

ATLANTA

AUSTIN, SAN ANTONIO
  & THE TEXAS HILL COUNTRY

BALTIMORE, ANNAPOLIS & THE CHESAPEAKE BAY

THE BERKSHIRE BOOK

BIG SUR, MONTEREY BAY
  & GOLD COAST WINE COUNTRY

CAPE CANAVERAL, COCOA BEACH
  & FLORIDA'S SPACE COAST

THE CHARLESTON, SAVANNAH
  & COASTAL ISLANDS BOOK

THE COAST OF MAINE BOOK

COLORADO'S CLASSIC MOUNTAIN TOWNS

COSTA RICA: GREAT DESTINATIONS
  CENTRAL AMERICA

DOMINICAN REPUBLIC

THE FINGER LAKES BOOK

THE FOUR CORNERS REGION

GALVESTON, SOUTH PADRE ISLAND
  & THE TEXAS GULF COAST

GUATEMALA: GREAT DESTINATIONS
  CENTRAL AMERICA

THE HAMPTONS

HAWAII'S BIG ISLAND: GREAT DESTINATIONS
  HAWAII

HONOLULU & OAHU: GREAT DESTINATIONS
  HAWAII

THE JERSEY SHORE: ATLANTIC CITY TO CAPE MAY

KAUAI: GREAT DESTINATIONS HAWAII

LAKE TAHOE & RENO

LAS VEGAS

LOS CABOS & BAJA CALIFORNIA SUR:
  GREAT DESTINATIONS MEXICO

MAUI: GREAT DESTINATIONS HAWAII

MEMPHIS AND THE DELTA BLUES TRAIL

MICHIGAN'S UPPER PENINSULA

MONTREAL & QUEBEC CITY:
  GREAT DESTINATIONS CANADA

THE NANTUCKET BOOK

THE NAPA & SONOMA BOOK

NORTH CAROLINA'S OUTER BANKS
  & THE CRYSTAL COAST

NOVA SCOTIA & PRINCE EDWARD ISLAND

OAXACA: GREAT DESTINATIONS MEXICO

OREGON WINE COUNTRY

PALM BEACH, FORT LAUDERDALE, MIAMI
  & THE FLORIDA KEYS

PALM SPRINGS & DESERT RESORTS

PHILADELPHIA, BRANDYWINE VALLEY
  & BUCKS COUNTY

PHOENIX, SCOTTSDALE, SEDONA
  & CENTRAL ARIZONA

PLAYA DEL CARMEN, TULUM & THE RIVIERA MAYA:
  GREAT DESTINATIONS MEXICO

SALT LAKE CITY, PARK CITY, PROVO
  & UTAH'S HIGH COUNTRY RESORTS

SAN DIEGO & TIJUANA

SAN JUAN, VIEQUES & CULEBRA:
  GREAT DESTINATIONS PUERTO RICO

SAN MIGUEL DE ALLENDE & GUANAJUATO:
  GREAT DESTINATIONS MEXICO

THE SANTA FE & TAOS BOOK

THE SARASOTA, SANIBEL ISLAND & NAPLES BOOK

THE SEATTLE & VANCOUVER BOOK

THE SHENANDOAH VALLEY BOOK

TOURING EAST COAST WINE COUNTRY

TUCSON

VIRGINIA BEACH, RICHMOND
  & TIDEWATER VIRGINIA

WASHINGTON, D.C., AND NORTHERN VIRGINIA

YELLOWSTONE & GRAND TETON NATIONAL PARKS
  & JACKSON HOLE

YOSEMITE & THE SOUTHERN SIERRA NEVADA

The authors in this series are professional travel writers who have lived for many years in the regions they describe. Honest and painstakingly critical, full of information only a local can provide, Great Destinations guidebooks give you all the practical knowledge you need to enjoy the best of each region.

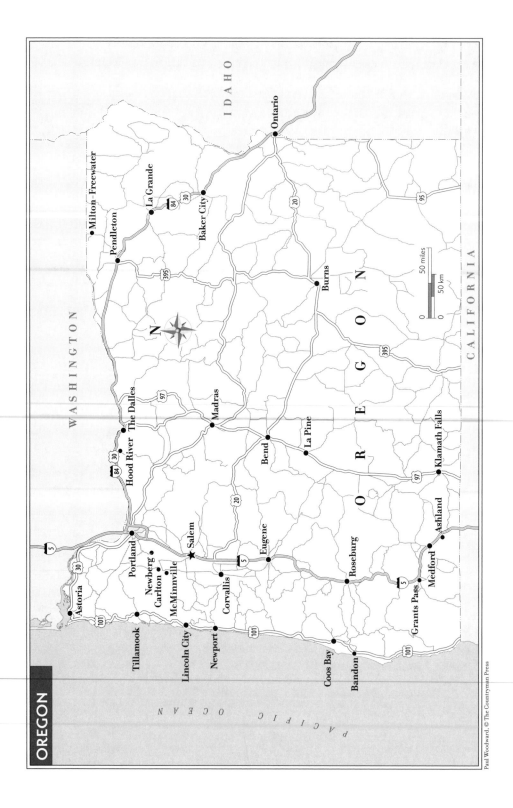

OREGON

WASHINGTON

IDAHO

OREGON

CALIFORNIA

PACIFIC OCEAN

Astoria
Portland
Tillamook
Newberg
Carlton
McMinnville
Lincoln City
Salem
Corvallis
Newport
Eugene
Roseburg
Coos Bay
Bandon
Grants Pass
Medford
Ashland
Klamath Falls
Hood River
The Dalles
Madras
Bend
La Pine
Burns
Pendleton
Milton–Freewater
La Grande
Baker City
Ontario

50 miles
50 km

Paul Woodward, © The Countryman Press

CONTENTS

Acknowledgments

It seems as if it took a village to raise this book. We are eternally grateful for the support of friends and family, and apologize if we don't mention you by name.

Special thanks to our friends John and Donna for chauffeuring us through wine country on a memorable Memorial Day weekend—especially to John, for his photography talents. Shout outs to Sherry's wine-buddy tasters Claire, Marilyn, Sharon, Kathy, Chantal, and Ann. Also to Camille, who lent her palate and sleuthing skills. Thanks to Sherry's parents, Dee and Martin Rotto, gracious hosts who drove us and shared little-known facts on Oregon history and geography.

A bubbly toast to Deb, for her wine knowledge and support, and Sissy, for sending positive energy and believing. Gratitude goes to our new friend and Realtor, Meri, who enthusiastically shared her insights. Also to tour guide Kim in Ashland, for his photos of southern Oregon. Sherry is also appreciative of coworkers Peg and Darcy for graciously excusing absences, both physical and mental, while finishing this project.

This book could not have happened without the help of hundreds of vintners and winemakers who were patient in answering our questions—many while in the midst of crush. Their dedication, passion, and earnest pursuit of perfection make it possible for fans like us to revel in their success and enjoy the fruits of their labors, vintage after vintage.

Finally, thanks to the folks at Countryman Press—Lisa Sacks, Kim Grant, Doug Yeager, and Kermit Hummel—for their guidance and patience.

Sherry L. Moore and Jeff Welsch

FOREWORD

When I think about the evolution of Oregon's wine industry, I'm in awe. In the early 1980s, there were about 30 wineries in Oregon. That's when a small group of my family, friends, and college fraternity brothers had the ambitious notion of buying a piece of land in the fertile Willamette Valley and trying our hand at growing grapes.

Turns out we weren't alone. Word was starting to get out that Oregon is a pretty good place to grow vinifera. Many others with visions of burgeoning clusters of Pinot Noir thriving in the cool climes of western Oregon established vineyards at the same time. The Willamette Valley was leading the way, but other areas such as the Rogue, Umpqua, and Columbia valleys were also planting vineyards.

When we harvested our first crop in 1985, it didn't take long to discover that we were about to get hit right between the eyes with the old "supply and demand" adage: Big supply, low demand! We either couldn't get enough money for the fruit we grew or we couldn't sell it at all. So, like many of the other growers who were sitting on mounds of grapes with nowhere to go, we decided to start our own winery. We called ours Eola Hills Wine Cellars.

In this endeavor, out timing couldn't have been better. An interesting phenomenon coincided with this early period in the state's wine industry: The consumer was starting to notice Oregon wines—particularly Pinot Noir. And it wasn't just our local consumers. Oregon wines were gaining worldwide recognition. It wasn't long before the "supply and demand" scenario had completely reversed itself and demand was outstripping supply!

In the years since, the Oregon wine industry has exploded. Those 30 wineries of the early '80s became more than two hundred by the year 2000. They have continued to expand to nearly four hundred wineries in the state, with no end in sight. And the reputation of Oregon as a premium wine-producing area has become firmly affixed internationally.

The growing wine scene has begged for a comprehensive guide that captures the essence of Oregon, our wines, and our wine country. *Oregon Wine Country: A Great Destination* does just that with an effort that goes beyond the traditional guidebook formula. The two longtime Oregonians who authored this insightful book provide the insiders' knowledge you'll need for ideal wine touring.

When I first got to know Jeff Welsch, we were bicycling through Oregon Wine Country. He was the sports editor of the Corvallis newspaper and an excellent sports writer. It didn't take long to figure out this guy was pretty passionate about topics that interested him. Soon it was obvious he was an excellent writer—period!

I came to know his wife, Sherry, through her work at a nearby winery. She was also the wine buyer at my local food cooperative, where she periodically featured Eola Hills wines at her weekly tastings. Her knowledge and sensible approach to wine and the industry makes the consumer feel comfortable and excited to taste the Oregon experience.

Jeff and Sherry have a unique perspective on what sets this down-to-earth industry apart. In this book they leave no stone unturned, from the heart of wine country in the Willamette Valley to the loneliest winery in the nether reaches of the eastern mountains. They have gone to exhaustive lengths to include each winery currently operating and open to the public, along with where to eat, sleep, play, and absorb Oregon through a wine lens. They share with readers an understanding that comes only from exploring every corner of the state, for business and for pleasure.

To get the most out of your touring in Oregon Wine Country, this is the only book you will need.

Welcome . . . we're glad you're here!

Tom Huggins, General Manager
Eola Hills Wine Cellars

From right to left, Tom, Bill, and Jim Huggins at Wolf Hill Vineyard, one of Eola Hills Wine Cellar's four "estate" vineyards.

The Way This Book Works

This book is about wineries. If that seems obvious, consider that most books on Oregon wine include Washington as well. Other books on the subject choose a select group of wineries, usually the most renowned, and devote the rest of their space to photographs. *Great Destinations: Oregon Wine Country* is for people who want to know about *all* of the wineries in this diverse state, along with where to eat, sleep, and recreate.

We have strived to describe all of Oregon's wineries, with or without official tasting rooms, including those only open by appointment. In most cases, "by appointment" means a vintner is small, has other jobs, or just can't consistently staff a tasting room. Don't let it deter you or cause you to cross a winery off your list. Think of it as calling before you visit to make sure someone is home.

You will find as much detailed information as we could squeeze into these pages. What you won't find is critiques—a few personal notes and favorites, but no ratings. Our reasoning is simple. Wine drinkers have a wide array of subjective tastes. Personal preference prevails. We've tried to encapsulate what each winery stands for or embodies in a few sentences. We also give you names, numbers, hours of operation, a list of wines produced, and special features. We have done our utmost to make information as current as possible, but be advised that the industry changes rapidly. Doors open, doors close. Hours fluctuate. Changes were made for the book as late as March 2010.

Along with the licensed wineries as of press time, this book provides overviews of key communities. These are places we've written about, simply enjoyed, or resided in during our 30 years in Oregon. We hope our insiders' knowledge will help define your tour and allow you to make the most of your time. We've included attractions, recreation, and special events that we think a wine tourist would find appealing.

Our book is arranged on the assumption that touring begins in Portland. We begin with listings at the northern end of the Willamette Valley and continue south, concluding with the least toured—but no less interesting—regions of the state. Though the Columbia Gorge is chapter 8, it's 30 minutes east of Portland, so you might choose to divert there for a day or two. Touring the entire Willamette Valley could easily take weeks.

We have listed wineries in proposed touring orders. They are intended to be in geographical order for touring efficiency—a bit of a trick, especially in the Willamette Valley. After all, Mother Nature did not lay out these volcanic coastal mountains in a convenient grid. Some backtracking will be required. If at the end of the day you are still searching for that certain wine from a bottle you enjoyed, you can look it up in the alphabetical listing in the index. Be sure to check off your winery visits in our Great Grape Destinations list in Appendix C.

Lodging and dining establishments are alphabetized within each area. We chose a select, diverse few we thought would appeal to wine enthusiasts. With lodging, the highest rate is typically for a premium room during peak season (usually Memorial Day weekend through autumn) and the lowest generally represents a standard room, off-season rate.

Lodging

$75 or less = Inexpensive
$75 to 125 = Moderate
$126 to 199 = Expensive
$200 and above = Very Expensive

Restaurants and wine bars were chosen based largely on their emphasis of Oregon and/or Northwest wines. Dining prices are based on the cost of an average single entrée.

Dining

$10 or less = Inexpensive
$11 to $20 = Moderate
$21 to $30 = Expensive
$30 and above = Very Expensive

One of the favorite pastimes in Oregon Wine Country is wine-related events, which take place throughout the year. In our Festival and Events appendix (A) we have included festivities that have a long history and/or are likely to be repeated. We don't guarantee weather, but what's a little mist when your fingers are wrapped around a clear stem and your nose is warmed by the fragrant esters of a world-class wine? For current information, check the Oregon Wine Advisory Board's Web site. Or pick up a copy of the thoroughly readable *Oregon Wine Press* before setting out on your journey. *OWP* also has an extensive events calendar at www.oregonwinepress.com/calendar.

Wine touring in Oregon requires an adventurous spirit and a leisurely pace. The Oregon Department of Transportation's ubiquitous blue-and-white wine signs are helpful, but sometimes disappear. Country roads can be tricky. We suggest checking Web sites for directions, plugging in a GPS, or simply calling—folks are more than happy to guide you in to their tasting rooms.

Whether you're a dedicated vino-phile or an eager novice, this book should provide you with all the requisite information to help you explore a state we will forever hold near and dear. We invite you to select your destination, peruse the chapter, and follow your palate. Then settle back into savoring all the flavors of Oregon—one winery, one restaurant, and one celebration at a time!

Introduction

From the time Meriwether Lewis and William Clark arrived at Fort Clatsop on the Pacific Ocean in 1805, followed shortly by legions of settlers in Conestoga wagons, Oregon has embodied a hardy pioneer spirit. So it is with its grape growers, winemakers, and wines.

At first blush, Oregon might not *seem* like wine country, even though grapes were planted here by the first settlers as far back as the 1840s. Perhaps that's why it wasn't until two full centuries after viticulture took root in neighboring California that the wine industry became even a modest contributor to Oregon's economy.

After all, it rains in Oregon. A lot. In the lush western valleys and coastal areas, the steady drizzle typically starts in October and doesn't let up until the Fourth of July. As with those first settlers who searched for the end of the Oregon Trail, fortitude and a resolute nature are required to survive and thrive. With grapes, this means a varietal that doesn't mind getting a little ruddy, a grape that looks at the cold, gray skies and says "bring it on." It means a vine that likes to wrap roots around rocks in uneven, seemingly inhospitable soils, and mischievously threaten to run amok like undisciplined children on the long, warm days of summer.

Turns out Oregon and Pinot Noir were made for each other. In the four decades since David Lett and other wine pioneers planted the fickle grape in the Dundee Hills, the state has become world-renowned for this complex, challenging wine that manifests itself differently from vineyard to vineyard. In 1979 Oregon Pinot burst onto the world scene when Lett flabbergasted the French by whipping their Burgundies in blind tastings with his Eyrie Vineyards South Block Reserve.

In hindsight, the success should come as no surprise, given that Oregon straddles the 45th Parallel, just like several famed European producing regions: France's Alsace, Bordeaux, and, of course, Burgundy. The Willamette Valley's climate is most reminiscent of Burgundy. It just took someone with the savvy and determination to see the improbable vision through.

Pinot Noir is Oregon's signature grape, but this state of salt-of-the-earth pioneers has its share of success with other red and white varietals—72 and counting as of 2009. Although vinifera takes up the majority of vineyard space, Oregon is not too proud to claim award-winning wines produced from hybrids. Many have had success with Maréchal Foch, named for the French World War I general, because it is a hardy early ripener and resistant to frost—an all-too-common spring occurrence in the late spring or early fall. Raising grapes can be a heart-stopping business.

Riches from the land and the sea are nonetheless abundant, and nothing stimulates the palate or the imagination like Oregon foods paired with its wines. The state is a bountiful basket of epicurean and wine delights. You can feast on fresh Dungeness crab paired with an Old World–style Riesling, savor a caught-that-day halibut matched with a Burgundian-style Chardonnay, or enjoy grilled Pacific salmon and wild mushrooms served with an

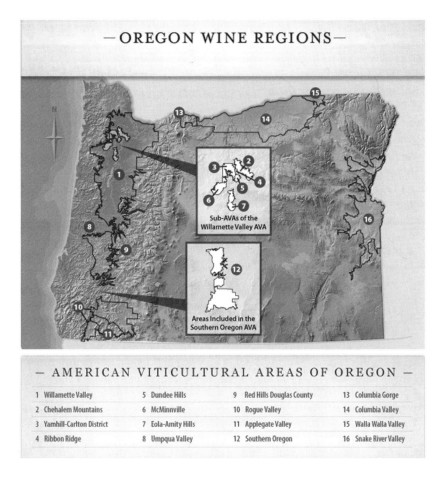

—OREGON WINE REGIONS—

Sub-AVAs of the
Willamette Valley AVA

Areas Included in the
Southern Oregon AVA

— AMERICAN VITICULTURAL AREAS OF OREGON —

1	Willamette Valley	5	Dundee Hills	9	Red Hills Douglas County	13	Columbia Gorge
2	Chehalem Mountains	6	McMinnville	10	Rogue Valley	14	Columbia Valley
3	Yamhill-Carlton District	7	Eola-Amity Hills	11	Applegate Valley	15	Walla Walla Valley
4	Ribbon Ridge	8	Umpqua Valley	12	Southern Oregon	16	Snake River Valley

out-of-this-world Pinot. Finish a summer meal with juicy, hand-picked peaches drenched in Muscat Ottonel, or pass around an artisan cheese made in the Willamette or Rogue Valley, paired with a sparkling Blanc de Blanc or Pinot Noir port. As Oregonians can readily attest, life doesn't get much better.

Part of Oregon's wine intrigue is the diversity of its regions. Within the borders of a state that's about one-third the size of France, grapes are able to grow the in cool, damp and rocky foothills of the Coastal Range, the warm forests of the Rogue and Umpqua river valleys, and the arid high deserts of the Columbia Plateau. Within each region, terroir can be dramatically different mere miles apart.

Oregon's nearly 800 vineyards, spread among 16 approved wine-growing regions (American Viticultural Areas, or AVAs), are more diverse than even those of California, which has nine times as many wineries. Once virtually ignored, Oregon now has 17,400 acres planted in grapes and boasts nearly four hundred wineries. More than 1.5 million cases are produced every year, making wine a $200 million industry annually on sales alone—third in the United States. Wine tourism sweetens the state's coffers by another $100 million every year. From their humble post-Prohibition beginnings, essentially in

1961, Oregon grapes and wines have become one of the state's most important agricultural commodities.

Yet for the most part, the industry folks have maintained their collective brand as down-to-earth neighbors who hold themselves to the highest of standards. Often as not, you'll find the winemaker, owner, or vineyard manager—often the same person—pouring behind the counter, ready to share his or her passion with any inquisitor. Wine novices intimidated by the headiness of such places as Napa Valley will feel comfortable and welcome in nearly every Oregon winery. There are exceptions. You will come across ostentatious estates with extravagant facilities and pretentious tasting rooms. But even the highest of the highbrows will be inviting—they need to sell wine, too. You'll find the diversity makes for better touring.

Oregon wine touring has become a booming pastime. Buses, limos, and tour vans are available, taking the stress out of finding your way to the out-of-the-way and allowing maximum tasting pleasure (See Appendix B). Perhaps a bittersweet sign of Oregon's emergence on the international scene and a loss of innocence: most wineries now charge a tasting fee. Most are nominal, some are donated, and others are earmarked to specific causes, but you can be certain all fees are a drop in the bin toward the expense poured into the product.

Oregon's wine industry continues to demand transparency and ethics from itself. What you see in and on the bottle is what you get. When the label states that the vintage or fruit is from a specific appellation such as the Columbia Gorge, at least 95 percent of the wine is just that. When the label states the varietal, such as Pinot Noir, a minimum of 90 percent of the wine inside the bottle is just that. Some southern Oregon AVAs are granted leniency to match the federal minimum of 75 percent.

While on a wine tour, it's important to remember a few simple rules of etiquette. Heavy perfume or cologne can interfere with tasting and elicit frowns of disapproval. Don't feel compelled to drink the entire sample. Too many tastes add up and will limit your experience later in the day—especially if you're driving. Spitting is allowed and even encouraged.

Picnicking and wine touring go hand in hand.   John Baker

It is also customary to make a purchase, especially if samples are complimentary and the server has spent substantial time with you.

Though winery and tasting room locations are often challenging to find, blue-and-white roadside signs help point the way. Our suggestion is to check the Oregon Wine Advisory Board's Web site for guidance, and follow the tabs under "Experience Wine Country" for fairly accurate maps. Or just point your car in the general direction of your desired route and see where you end up. There's a great deal to discover along the way. By the way, Oregon is one of two states where it's illegal to pump your own gas, so you won't ruin your "nose" with fuel odors on your hands and clothes.

When you're finished with a day of tasting worldly wines and meeting contagiously passionate people, you'll find plenty of fine eating establishments and comfortable beds in a wide array of settings. Bed-and-breakfasts, lodges, cabins, and chain motels are readily available—unless it's a traditional Oregon wine holiday such as Memorial Day or Thanksgiving weekend. The crowds can be overwhelming at those times, but the experience exhilarating and memorable.

Memorial Day weekend signals the onset of summer. New releases are ready for a grand opening and there's almost a Mardi Gras atmosphere. Wine tourists hire limos and tour buses en masse or gather in groups to caravan. Tasting rooms usually closed are abuzz with activity. The events are as diverse as Oregon, ranging from rowdy country music and Cuban dance lessons to refined classical art and barrel sampling. Wines are paired with specialty foods, from local cheeses and picnic fare to the catered and exotic. Memorial Day is a time wineries put their best feet forward, and all hands are on deck to ensure a good time is had by all.

The other celebratory season is the Friday, Saturday, and Sunday after Thanksgiving. The crush is complete, the leaves have turned or fallen, and the mood is festive but slightly more subdued. This weekend is more about open houses, food pairing, and holiday gift buying. It's also a time for visiting family members and friends to see what this wine-country thing is all about. Another trend: Wineries are opening their doors the weekend before Thanksgiving as a pre-holiday opportunity to secure wines for upcoming entertaining. Of late, Labor Day weekend has become a contender in the race for prime touring time.

An added bonus to Oregon wine country: no sales tax. You'll have extra dollars to indulge in more bottles or cases. An exception to that rule is for lodging. As is the case in most states catering to tourists, Oregon does have a room tax.

Today, even in a staggering economy—Oregon's unemployment rate was above 10 percent in 2009—optimism prevails. The number of wineries is still increasing, by about a dozen a year. Vineyards are popping up in places nobody could have imagined. Wine bars, shops, and tasting rooms are sprouting in likely and unlikely locations, and there's no end in sight. For many dreamers of vines, wines, and wineries, Oregon Wine Country truly is the Eden at the end of the trail.

1

History and Terroir

Down to Earth

Call it *Bottle Shock,* Oregon-style.

In 1979, a fledgling Oregon vintner named David Lett was invited to submit a red wine for a blind tasting against the haughty French in a competition called the Gault Millau French Wine Olympiades. Next to the aristocratic French, German, and Italian winemakers, Lett was a dirt-under-the-fingernails farmer who had this crazy notion that great wine could be made in cool, wet, blustery Oregon.

What happened next turned the wine world, well, *Sideways.*

A mere three years after a California winery stunned the French with a winning Chardonnay, a bottle of Lett's wine finished among the top 10 Burgundies in a field of more than 330. He orchestrated his own shocker with grapes nurtured in the unheralded northern Willamette Valley. Even more stunning, the state had won with perhaps the world's most revered wine—made from a fickle, petulant, and occasionally ornery cool-climate grape that has confounded some of the industry's most accomplished vintners.

Pinot Noir.

Lett achieved this landmark success with his Eyrie Vineyards South Block Pinot less than a decade after departing his native California to start anew in Oregon. He came despite warnings from colleagues in the University of California–Davis oenology department that he was nuts. Within 15 years of the arrival of Lett and other wine pioneers, Oregon suddenly was a major wine player, and the industry's growth in the three decades since has been phenomenal. Today, Oregon is at close to 400 wineries and counting. Where once the Willamette Valley was the sole bastion of winemaking, now vineyards have been carved out of fir forests, desert steppes, and old orchards as far south as Ashland, as far east as Ontario, and in places even those early pioneers never would've imagined. Nearly 2 million cases of Oregon wine are sold annually in what has become a $200 million industry.

Not that some of Oregon's early vintners would have been so shocked.

As far back as the 1820s, fur trappers planted grapes at French Prairie, just northeast of modern-day Salem. A half-century later, entrepreneurs Henderson Luelling and Ernest Reuter planted vines in the Willamette Valley—the former favoring the American varietal

OPPOSITE: *Springtime in Oregon Wine Country blooms in many hues.*   John Baker

Concord, the latter recognizing the potential of cool-climate wine grapes. Reuter was especially interested in a grape from France's Burgundy region: Pinot Noir.

While Reuter also grew Pinot Blanc, Riesling, and Gewürztraminer on David Hill, west of Forest Grove, other dreamers had already begun experimenting with viticulture in the arid eastern end of the Columbia Gorge and the California-esque Umpqua and Rogue valleys of southern Oregon. In fact, though the Willamette Valley is the epicenter of Oregon wine today, the state's first official winery, Valley View, was started in 1851 by Peter Britt in Jacksonville, near Medford. The state even enjoyed some mild national and international fame—Reuter is said to have won a gold medal at the 1904 St. Louis World's Fair. Then, in 1914, it all ended.

Prohibition forced winemakers to tear out their grapes or go broke. Many simply closed up and left their vines. Others replanted hazelnut, apple, pear, or cherry orchards. A few made legal fruit wines during the two decades of Prohibition, and others started anew when the ban was lifted, producing wines for the military. One, Honeywood Winery just outside of Salem, began making fruit wines in 1933 and today makes both fruit- and vinifera-based wines. It is Oregon's oldest continuously running winery.

The state's contemporary wine history really began in 1961, when another refugee from U.C. Davis, Richard Sommer, planted Riesling and four other cool-climate varietals near Roseburg. Sommer provided training for the next wave of Oregon wine pioneers and, in 1968, produced the state's first Pinot Noir from his HillCrest Vineyards.

Rainy days are common in Oregon Wine Country, but so are rainbows. Courtesy Trinity Vineyards

The Legacy of Papa Pinot

Early in 1965, a 25-year-old University of California–Davis graduate with a pioneering spirit hopped in a modern-day Conestoga wagon—a pickup truck and trailer—and headed for his own Eden at the end of the Oregon Trail.

Just like those who had come to the Willamette Valley more than a century before, David Lett had a vision. Unlike those early arrivals who coveted the agricultural potential of western Oregon's lush hillsides and valleys, Lett was going it alone.

In Lett's figurative rearview mirror was the dentistry career his parents wanted for him, viticulture professors who said it couldn't be done, and colleagues who thought he'd lost his mind. In his literal rearview mirror was his uncle's horse trailer and three thousand grapevine cuttings destined for this bold, cold new world.

Lett was driven by a love for the petulant Pinot Noir grape and a lust for a challenge. Having spent time at wineries in the comparable Burgundy region of France, he was certain that somewhere in the hill country south of Portland awaited the perfect Pinot patch, where he would find a harmonic convergence of mild winters, warm summers, cool nights, and rich soils—a place where a hardworking, easily agitated grape would thrive.

His mission was to find it.

Lett rooted his young vines in a leased rye field just outside Corvallis and continued north. He poked around both sides of the valley, first eyeing the eastern foothills of the Cascade Range before settling on a 20-acre hillside site amid hazelnut orchards, Douglas firs, and oaks about 30 miles southwest of Portland.

At the time, the Red Hills of Dundee Hills were just another pastoral picture on a Willamette Valley postcard. Lett and his new bride, Diana, paid $9,000 for their acreage. On their honeymoon, they planted the valley's first Pinot Noir, the United States' first Pinot Gris, and four other varietals.

Thus begins the story of The Eyrie Vineyards and the dedicated, congenial, and sometimes crusty man whose handiwork would earn him the moniker "Papa Pinot"—a nod not only to his place in history but also to his resemblance to the writer Ernest "Papa" Hemingway. Within nine years of producing his first Pinot Noir in an abandoned turkey-processing plant in McMinnville, Lett's South Block Reserve crashed the European-dominated top 10 in France's Wine Olympiades.

But Lett's efforts didn't end there. He was an organic farmer before organic farming became trendy, a meticulous sort with a European ethos who finessed and massaged his wines in a tireless pursuit of quality over quantity. He also was instrumental in the novel land-use planning credited with saving Oregon farmland and countryside from urban sprawl. Always there to lend a hand to those who respected the art of making beautiful wine, he was a cofounder of the Oregon Winegrowers Association and helped bring the International Pinot Noir Celebration to McMinnville.

Though he never sought it, his fame grew until his death at age 69 in the autumn of 2008, after which he was eulogized by industry giants and the *New York Times*.

Full-scale immigration began four years after Sommer. The first was Charles Coury, a meteorologist who in 1965 planted Pinot Noir and Alsatian varietals on the same hill where Reuter had succeeded a century earlier.

After Lett's arrival to the area in the mid-1960s, he was followed in short order in the early 1970s by names now synonymous with what is now called the Oregon Story:

Adelsheim, Ponzi, Erath, and others. These learned people from diverse backgrounds became self-proclaimed hippies of the dirt and reveled in the challenge, bonded by a collective naïveté, adventurous spirit, and a drive to prove wrong the naysayers back home.

The Oregon Story is a bit of lore that wine enthusiasts here can recite at the pop of a cork. Less than a year after the Wine Olympiades, a French winemaker named Robert Drouhin orchestrated a rematch to determine whether Eyrie's success was a fluke. This time, Lett's Pinot Noir finished second by two-tenths of a point to Drouhin's Chambelle-Musigny.

If Lett's achievements in France weren't proof that he and his colleagues weren't loony, then consider: Seven years after their perception-altering showdown in France, the Drouhin family purchased land in the Red Hills and opened a winery. In classic Oregon style, it was Lett and fellow pioneer David Adelsheim who helped their former competitor find the perfect piece of Pinot land.

TERROIR

Terroir is a French word generally meaning "a sense of place." In wine terms, it's about geology, topography, and climate.

Oregon's wine story really begins millions of years ago, with the evolution of the state's terroir. Of the three geologic phenomena that shaped the state, one has been a slow grind over millions of years, one a single cataclysmic moment, and the last either a lone event or a repeat covering thousands of years.

Oregon rests on the stationary Continental Plate, but just offshore under the Pacific Ocean is the restless Juan de Fuca Plate, grinding like a wheel cog at a geologic snail's pace. When the Juan de Fuca's forward motion is halted and inevitably springs free, the result is earthquakes. When it has moved relatively smoothly, it has scraped soils off the ocean bottom and added on to a coastline that once was near present-day Idaho.

This activity is all part of the tumultuous Pacific Ring of Fire, which produced a powerful series of planet-altering super-volcano eruptions about 20 million years ago in present-day eastern Oregon. The resulting Columbia River Basalt Flows covered much of the state. They are seen today in the dramatic coastal capes and in such hills as Dundee.

The final piece to the geologic puzzle was placed about 15,000 years ago, when a giant ice dam on the Clark Fork River in western Montana burst, and sent a 2,000-foot-deep lake rushing across eastern Washington, through the Columbia Gorge and up the river valleys—as far as present-day Eugene. Whether it was one event or a series of dam collapses is still debated, but the result of the Missoula Floods was silt as deep as 150 feet in the north Willamette Valley. It is because of these rich soils that the valley is one of the great agricultural regions in America.

As you tour the Willamette Valley, you'll hear winemakers talk lovingly about two types of soil: Jory and Willakenzie. Jory arrived courtesy of the volcanic eruption, and Willakenzie is the result of the colliding plates (the Missoula Flood silts are not thought of as great wine-growing soils). Differing soils can be a ridge apart, a vineyard apart, or even a block apart. And only the trained eye or palate can tell: With their reddish hues and clay feel, they look virtually the same. The Dundee, Salem, and Eola hills are Jory flows, while Willakenzie soils tend to be on the west side of the valley.

Yet as similar as they are in appearance, these soils produce dramatically different

Pinots. Wines from the Jory soils tend to be fruitier; wines from Willakenzie are more intense and tannic.

Naturally, the distinctions are not always so simple, thanks to the two other major components of terroir: climate and topography.

By and large, Oregon is renowned for its rain, though that's an over-generalization. Much of the rain falls on the coast and in the Willamette Valley, but even in the valley moisture is rare between the Fourth of July and mid-October. Southern Oregon is warmer and drier, à la northern California, and many grape-growing areas of eastern Oregon are as arid and nearly as hot as Tucson, Arizona, often requiring irrigation.

No place epitomizes these differences more than the Columbia Gorge, which touts its "World of Wine in 40 Miles." Nearly every grape from A (Albariño) to Z (Zinfandel) is grown in this scenic chasm through the Cascade Range. The west end is damp, cool, and blustery Pinot country; the east is hot and dry, the way Syrah likes it.

Farther south, the Mediterranean climes are renowned for wines familiar to California growers. The aptly named "100 Valleys of the Umpqua" region around Roseburg could easily boast "A World of Microclimates in 40 Miles" due to harmonic convergences of climate and topography.

Of course, Oregon's signature grape, Pinot Noir, loves the dramatic temperature ranges of the Willamette Valley, yet from ridge to ridge diverse microclimates exist. One might be a sultry Coast Range rain shadow where marine air is a nonfactor, another the eastern end of a river corridor that brings cool Pacific breezes in the summer. One might be a south-facing slope with relentless sun at 1,000 feet, another facing east with partial exposure at 500 feet. Some parts of the Chehalem Mountains receive 60 inches of rain per year, others 35. No wonder there are six American Viticulture Association (AVA) appellations in the 150-mile Willamette Valley alone.

The upshot: No two wineries, no two vineyards, and no two wines of the same variety and vintage are exactly alike.

It's all part of the charm and intrigue of this fascinating place called Oregon Wine Country.

2

Willamette Valley North

Where Pinot Prevails

Mention Oregon Wine Country to vino aficionados, and images of the Red Hills, Ribbon Ridge, and the undulating Chehalem Mountains invariably come to mind, along with the requisite tasting parlors and boutiques.

Vineyards and wineries have sprung up seemingly everywhere since the first wave of wine pioneers arrived in the 1960s. The resulting phenomenon is a change in the rural scenery and character of small towns unlike any Oregonians ever would've imagined a few short decades ago.

Portland has always been one of America's freshest and friendliest large cities—a laid-back version of Seattle, complete with latte-sipping, bicycle-pedaling, Subaru-driving, Air America–listening, jeans-and-Nike-wearing residents. Today, the serene agricultural towns just southwest of the City of Roses have blossomed as well, giving other rural communities around the state an understandable case of Pinot envy.

These towns mostly embrace their newly acquired fame, taking advantage of the traffic and interest. Throughout the year, the sounds of chatter and music, the aroma of gourmet fare and wine-filled barrels, and the joy and pride on vintners' faces blend into one satisfying sigh of pleasure for those of us lucky enough to be here.

GETTING HERE AND AROUND

Transportation begins and ends in Portland, which has a busy international airport served by every major airline. The Willamette Valley is bisected north-to-south by I-5, but most of the area's wineries are on winding, two-lane roads through hinterlands, which merely adds to the charm of a day of wine touring. A notable exception is OR 99W (OR 99 splits in Portland and rejoins at Junction City, creating two highways with the same number). Once ideal for carefree Sunday drives, 99W between Portland and McMinnville has become an all-day traffic jam—thanks largely to the booming wine industry.

For those who want that leisurely pace, take US 26 west through the Sunset Hills past Beaverton to the Forest Grove exit. Work your way south on OR 47 through Gaston, Yamhill, and Carlton, then on toward Dundee and Newberg if you wish.

OPPOSITE: *Barrels share space on crowded holiday weekends and provide ambiance and aroma.*   John Baker

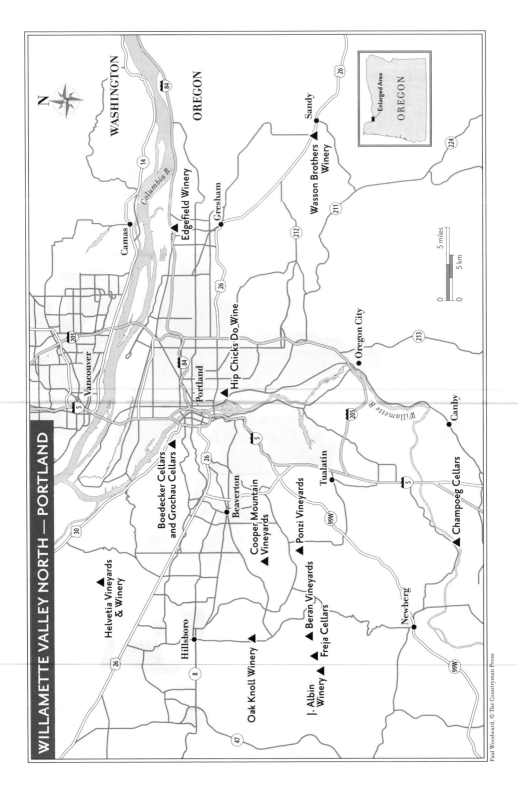

WILLAMETTE VALLEY NORTH — PORTLAND

WASHINGTON

OREGON

Columbia R.

Camas

Vancouver

14

84

205

5

30

Edgefield Winery

Gresham

26

84

Portland

Hip Chicks Do Wine

Boedecker Cellars
and Grochau Cellars

26

5

Beaverton

Cooper Mountain
Vineyards

Ponzi Vineyards

Tualatin

205

Willamette R.

Oregon City

213

Canby

Champoeg Cellars

99W

5

Helvetia Vineyards
& Winery

Hillsboro

8

26

Oak Knoll Winery

J. Albin
Winery

Freja Cellars

Beran Vineyards

47

Newberg

99W

Wasson Brothers
Winery

Sandy

26

211

212

224

Enlarged Area

OREGON

5 miles

5 km

0

0

Paul Woodward, © The Countryman Press

Lucky wine tasters get a tour of a vineyard in the north Willamette Valley. John Baker

PORTLAND AREA (WILLAMETTE VALLEY AVA)

River City, Rose City, Stumptown, or PDX—whatever the affectionate tag, Portland is a metropolis like no other. It is a big city with a small-town persona, its soul defined not by its sprawling suburbs but by its vibrant heart.

Portlanders aren't trendy; they're trend-setters. The metropolitan area's million-plus citizens are progressive, proud, and relish their individualism. Their style is casual and outdoorsy with a brush of grunge, wrapped in a layer of sophistication tinged with an air of slight indifference—friendly enough, but not overly so. Men with manicures and manbags, women in sweatshirts and heels, dogs decked in couture or mud . . . it all fits. The term "metrosexual" was probably born here. All things local, regional, sustainable, and gourmet are the norm.

The whole ethos of Portlanders is that they know they have it good and they wallow, swallow, and embrace every bit, sip, and bite of it. They also defend it. A city that once allowed the Willamette River to catch on fire has become a fierce river- and land-keeper. In 1973, the state's leaders had the foresight to create urban-growth boundaries protecting rural lands just outside the city limits. Oregon also was one of the first states to require deposits on bottle returns; the city even has a nickel deposit on plastic water bottles. Going green isn't a badge of honor here—it's a way of life.

Thousands of fleece-clad cyclists commute to work, their task made easier by miles of bike lanes and European-style traffic signals that accommodate drivers, walkers, and pedalers. Parks are a priority here. In the West Hills above the city, Washington Park is a woodsy complex of museums, gardens, and a zoo. Its extensive trail system for runners, hikers, mountain bikers, and horseback riders amid towering Douglas firs sets Portland apart from every major city in the country.

The city is defined by four quadrants of distinctive neighborhoods within districts, each with unique personality and flair: the boutique-ish Northwest, gentrified Northeast, old-money and alternative Southeast, and the urban Southwest, where ubiquitous condos intermingle with upscale homes overlooking the city. They are divided roughly by the Willamette River south to north and eclectic Burnside Avenue east to west.

Northwest Portland is a mixture of old shabby and new chic, personified by the recently established Pearl District and its culinary cutting edge. Once decaying, Northeast Portland now is a fashionable bastion of comfortable old homes with contemporary facelifts, an area where rusted iron rings once used to tie horses are still affixed to curbs. Southeast is a blend of cultures—and likes it that way.

Southwest Portland is essentially downtown, from which the city pulse is strongest. And of late, a newer "fifth quadrant" has arrived on the scene: North Portland is home to the respected working-class, lunch-pail folks who make the busy ports on the Willamette and Columbia rivers hum.

Each of these quadrants have communities within the community, many defined by commercial cores of shopping, dining, and grocery stores that limit trips into the city—and limit traffic at the same time. Most of these districts revolve around a restaurant, café, bar, or bakery that feeds Portland's energy.

Portland is a food, wine, microbrew, and spirits Mecca whose chefs, brewmasters, and bartenders are regionally, nationally, and internationally renowned. Its restaurants and nightspots are often featured in such national media as the Food Network, *Food & Wine,* and *Wine Spectator.* Creative chefs thrive on the abundance of fresh and locally raised, cap-tured, or cultivated fare, ranging from berries to bovines, grains to greens, nuts to 'sh-rooms, seafood to spirits, artisan cheeses, pork, lamb . . . even emu. What isn't provided, they handcraft with what they have or can get in fair trade. The motto in nearly every restaurant listed below is "farm to fork"—utilizing these fresh, local, seasonal, organic, and sustainable ingredients. Sysco trucks needn't apply.

Naturally, this pride of origin carries over to the area's vineyards and wine production. The city stays in tune with the wineries, connecting them to the food. The *Oregonian*'s Food Day section (Wednesdays) lists many an event, tasting, or class with Oregon vino as its centerpiece. Portland's wine bars, tapas bars, bottle shops, tasting rooms, and hundreds of restaurants know how to make the most of what's nearby. This is all to your benefit: you don't have to travel far for a most memorable experience.

Wineries in the Portland Area

Wine touring around Portland covers the gamut, from an urban industrial zone to classic country estates scattered throughout the hills, mostly southwest of the city. Starting from Portland International Airport, go downtown first to the three wineries in two warehouse districts, and then literally head for the hills of Aloha, Hillsboro, and Beaverton.

Hitting the two wineries on the east side will require some backtracking, but Wasson and Edgefield are so unique they're worth the effort. Wasson makes many fruit wines and Edgefield is part of a restored poor-farm complex in the busy suburbs. In fact, you might want to make it your last stop before catching a flight home at nearby PDX.

PORTLAND
HIP CHICKS DO WINE

503-234-3790
www.hipchicksdowine.com
4510 SE 23rd Avenue
Tasting Room: Daily 11–6
Fee: $5 for seven wines, $3 for three limited-production wines
Owners/Winemakers: Laurie Lewis and Renee Neely
Wines: Muscat, Pinot Gris, Cabernet Franc, Malbec, Pinot Noir, Syrah, red and white blends
Cases: 4,000
Special Features: Tours and classes for private parties, classes on wine and cheese pairing, and an intro to sensory evaluation called "Name that Aroma"

The original Hip Chicks label and logo are purely playful, which accurately depicts the style of two fun and hip gals, Laurie and Renee. (The female figures on the label resemble the team, just a tad.) The dynamic duo makes wines that are friendly, fruit-forward, and meant to drink now, no waiting necessary. Known for their Belly Button wine (a Pinot Gris and Muscat blend), they also produce serious wines. Their target market is Gen Xers, but you can find older folk who think their wine just fine, too. They're tricky to find, like playing "Where's Waldo?" Don't hesitate to call for directions.

BOEDECKER CELLARS

503-288-7752
www.boedeckercellars.com
2621 NW 30th Avenue
Tasting room: Fri. 2–7, Sat.–Sun. 1–5, and by appointment
Fee: $5
Owners/Winemakers: Stewart Boedecker and Athena Pappas
Wines: Chardonnay, Pinot Gris, Pinot Noir
Cases: 3,000
Special Features: Jointly owned facilities with Grochau Cellars, one of a few wineries actually in Portland

Stewart and Athena, self-described as opinionated and argumentative, do everything from bin to bottle. With high acclaim from *Wine & Spirits* and *Wine Spectator*, this confident couple came onto the scene like gangbusters in 2003 with their winery across from the Pyramid/McTarnahan Brewery. Their big, structured wines have been well received, "making all the work worth it," Boedecker says. Their wines tend to sell out, so it's best to get on their release party lists or check bottle shops in the state.

GROCHAU CELLARS

503-522-2455
www.gcwines.com
2621 NW 30th Avenue
Tasting: By appointment only
Fee: Complimentary
Owners: John and Kerri Grochau
Winemaker: John Grochau
Wines: Sauvignon Blanc, Pinot Noir, Tempranillo, Syrah
Cases: 3,000
Special Features: Jointly owned facilities with Boedecker Cellars

"Don't screw it up" is the motto, minimal handling is the method. John spent many a day serving and selling wine on the other side of the bottling line, most notably for 13 years at Higgins in Portland. He wanted to learn the craft, so he spent time at Erath, in Sonoma, and under the tutelage of Doug Tunnell at Brick House. John's respectful and noninterventionist approach brings forth wines that reflect the terroir of the select vineyards with which he works. Try not to miss his annual Cuvée des Amis (friends' blend), which is a best-of-the-vintage barrel blend of Pinot Noir. The name was selected to honor the vineyard friends who helped with his first vintage in 2001.

For the Best in Small, It's the Indie

The old axiom "Good things come in small packages" certainly rings true at the annual Portland Indie Wine Festival, where each May some 40 of the state's top artisan producers are invited to an intimate urban venue to showcase their winners. This is a festival for the serious wine drinker who appreciates talking chalk, soils, and terroir with a winemaker in a farmer's-market setting. You'll find a wide range of independent vintners, from the elegant to the countrified, all eager to share a passion for their avocation.

Think of it as the Best in Show, Small Producer category (under 2,500 cases). The Indie is the only juried festival in Oregon, meaning a panel of acclaimed wine judges selects the participants through blind tastings. The competition is stiff. Only one in four entrants earns a coveted table at the Indie. And the judges apparently know of what they sip—as an attendee, you won't find a disappointing taste in the bunch.

The small-is-beautiful motto reigns with food as well. Paired with these exquisite wines are diminutive appetizer plates prepared by up-and-coming chefs who rub shoulders with some of Portland's culinary icons. The tables are lavish and abundant, a foodie's nirvana.

While Pinot certainly takes center stage at the Indie, you'll find all of Oregon well represented. Producers hail from as close as next door to as far as the Applegate Valley.

The $75 fee might seem steep, but imagine the time and energy you'd expend visiting a fraction of these wineries. Many don't even have tasting rooms or regular public hours.

To put an extravagant exclamation mark on your weekend, start with the Producers Dinner on Friday night. Along with a stellar meal, you'll have exclusive access to Indie library wines and sold-out vintages. It's further proof that while the emphasis is on small, for Oregon the Indie Wine Festival is definitely big-time.

HELVETIA VINEYARDS & WINERY

503-647-7596
www.helvetiawinery.com
22485 NW Yungen Road
Tasting Room: Summer, Fri.–Sun. 12–5;
winter, Sat.–Sun. 12–5, and by appointment
Fee: $2, refunded with purchase
Owners: John Platt and Elizabeth Furse
Winemaker: John Platt
Wines: Chardonnay, Gewürztraminer, Pinot Gris, rosé, Pinot Noir
Cases: 1,500
Special Features: Picnic area under a canopy

Welcome to Oregon's original Dundee Hills. Before Prohibition, the rural side of the West Hills above Portland was the hub of the state's tiny wine industry. Helvetia is the last vestige of this little-known slice of history. Swiss immigrant Jacob Yungen's century-old home is still there and serves as the winery's visitor center, where you can see his original wine-making equipment. Platt and Furse have been growing grapes here since the late 1980s and opened the winery in 1996—in the middle of Furse's tenure in the U.S. House of Representatives. Platt is also a lawyer and activist immersed in issues involving Native American water rights.

ALOHA

COOPER MOUNTAIN VINEYARDS

503-649-0027
www.coopermountainwine.com
9480 SW Grabhorn Road
Tasting Room: Daily 12–5
Fee: $5, refunded with three-bottle purchase

Owner: Robert J. Gross
Winemaker: Gilles de Domingo
Wines: Chardonnay, Pinot Blanc, Pinot
Gris, Tocai Friulano, Pinot Noir, Malbec
Cases: 18,000
Special Features: NSA (no sulphites added)
Pinot, year-round picnic area.

In a state known for its eco-friendly,
organic, and biodynamic winemaking, this
is where it all began. In 1990, under the
direction of Gross, a homeopath and
acupuncturist, Cooper Mountain went
down the natural path. Twelve years later,
after attaining organic and biodynamic status—the first winery in the Pacific
Northwest to be certified biodynamic—the
wines are well known on the health-food
wine shelves. Aside from some good-for-
you wines, such as the popular experiment
of Tocai Fruilano (a dry white with origins
in northeast Italy), Cooper Mountain also
makes Apicio, an Italian balsamic vinegar.
Their artisan, barrel-aged vinegar is only
available in the tasting room and you have
to remember to ask for a sample, preferably
after going through their tasty wine lineup.

*Mount Hood looms like a sentinel over downtown
Portland.* U.S. Geological Survey

BEAVERTON
PONZI VINEYARDS
503-628-1227
www.ponziwines.com
14,665 SW Winery Lane
Tasting Room: Daily 10–5
Fee: $10 for three to five wines
Owners: Dick and Nancy Ponzi
Winemaker: Luisa Ponzi
Wines: Arneis, Chardonnay, Pinot Blanc,
Pinot Gris, Dolcetto, Pinot Noir, dessert
wine
Cases: 11,500
Special Features: Also has tasting bar in
Dundee

The Ponzi name is synonymous with the
Oregon wine industry—microbrews too, for
that matter, as they also founded
Bridgeport Brewing Company (no longer

theirs). The inception of the family vineyards and winery came in 1970, making
Dick and Nancy among the state's wine pioneers. Ponzi is now under the direction of a
second generation: daughter Luisa is winemaker, and siblings Maria and Michel are
in charge of marketing and operations. Not
one to rest on his laurels, Dick just completed his dream project: a state-of-the-art
winemaking facility called Collina del
Sogno (Dream Hill). Environmentally and
grape-processing friendly, their site also
has a young vineyard of Pinot Noir, Pinot
Gris, and Dijon-clone Chardonnay.
Working from 120 total acres of sustainable
and LIVE-certified vineyard, Ponzi wines
are well made and widely distributed.

HILLSBORO
OAK KNOLL WINERY
503-648-8198
www.oakknollwinery.com
29700 SW Burkhalter Road
Tasting Room: Daily 11–5 (extended in
summer)
Fee: $5
Owner: Kopri Inc.
Winemaker: Jeff Herinckx
Wines: Niagara, Gewürztraminer,
Chardonnay, Müller Thurgau, Pinot Gris,

Riesling, Cabernet Sauvignon, Pinot Noir, fruit wines
Cases: 32,000
Special Features: Picnic area with Wi-Fi, wine accessories for sale

When Ron and Marjorie Vuylsteke opened Oak Knoll in 1970, it was the third winery in the state and first in Washington County. They were famous for their fruit wines, particularly the Blák Bèrree (Belgian for "blackberry") and Niagara, the hybrid some stubborn farmers grew legally during Prohibition. By the late 1970s, one out of every three bottles of wine sold in Oregon came from Oak Knoll. Today, they make some of Oregon's more traditional wines, including a reputable Pinot Noir, but they've come full circle. After 20 years, they are making the Blák Bèrree once again, and their hottest seller is the Niagara. There's a flavor at Oak Knoll to suit just about everyone in your party.

BERAN VINEYARDS
503-628-1298
www.beranvineyards.com
30088 SW Egger Road
Tasting Room: Memorial Day and Thanksgiving weekends, and by appointment
Fee: Complimentary
Owners: Bill and Sharon Beran
Winemaker: Bill Beran
Wines: Pinot Noir
Cases: 2,000
Special Features: Donations during holiday open houses go to Community Action of Washington County.

Family, family, family: Everywhere we looked in the converted dairy barn's upstairs tasting room on a busy Memorial Day weekend, we found a family member ready and eager to talk about Beran wines. And friends: It takes plenty of enthusiastic volunteer labor for the Beran production,

Beran's tasting room is in a remodeled dairy barn on a hilltop near Portland.   John Baker

which has evolved grandly from a hobby. The Berans once only sold their grapes, but in 1997 tried their hand at the world of small-production estate Pinot Noir. They love to wax poetic over the subtle differences between the Pommard and the Dijon-clone Pinot. We were undecided as to the best, so we took home one of each.

FREJA CELLARS

503-628-0337
www.frejacellars.com
16691 SW McFee Place
Tasting Room: Memorial Day, Thanksgiving, and Labor Day weekends, and by appointment
Fee: $10
Owner/Winemaker: William Gianopolus
Wines: Pinot Noir, rosé
Cases: 2,000

Gianopolus, who is a little less approachable than his wines and his friendly neighbors the Berans, only grows and makes Pinot Noir. "Willy" takes his labor-intensive winemaking seriously, stating that he resides firmly in the Burgundian camp and eschewing big, bold, new-world Pinots.

J. ALBIN WINERY

503-628-2986
www.laurelvineyard.com
19495 Vista Hill Drive
Tasting Room: Memorial Day and Thanksgiving weekends, and by appointment
Fee: $5
Owners: John and Lynn Albin
Winemaker: John "J." Albin
Wines: Pinot Gris, rosé, Pinot Noir, sparkling wines, dessert wine
Cases: 2,000

John Albin, until recently the executive winemaker at King Estate, has known what he wanted to do with his life since he was 10 years old. He attended U.C. Davis to support his vision, and then followed the footsteps of David Lett and other wine pioneers

to Oregon, a great place to raise grapes and kids. He and Lynn planted a small plot (Laurel Vineyard) of Pinot Noir back in 1981, so his personal label has older vines in the newly declared Chehalem Mountain AVA to work with. They are a true family operation, enlisting the help of their teenage sons to do the grunt work—including hand-labeling. They tell the boys it's learning the trade by immersion. John Albin has an earned reputation for making balanced wines with loads of finesse.

TROUTDALE
EDGEFIELD WINERY

503-665-2992
www.mcmenamins.com
2126 SW Halsey Street
Tasting Room: Daily 12–10 (check for winter hours)
Fee: $4 for flight of five wines
Owners: Mike and Brian McMenamin
Winemaker: Davis Palmer
Wines: Chardonnay, Pinot Gris, Riesling, Viognier, rosé, Pinot Noir, Merlot, Cabernet Sauvignon, Zinfandel, Syrah, red and white blends, sparkling wine, dessert wines, port
Cases: 20,000
Special Features: Tours can be arranged in advance, local art, live music most evenings inside or outside, several restaurants, part of the Edgefield lodging complex

McMenamin's is known for crafting beer, but in 1990 the brothers branched out into wine. They have improved through the years and offer a diverse assortment. The Black Rabbit red—a mostly Bordeaux blend of Cabernet Sauvignon and Merlot with a dash of Syrah, Grenache, or whatever Davis chooses from year to year—is a big seller. On the property is a three-acre decorative vineyard of Pinot Gris, which supplies the Poor Farm label—another people-pleasing wine. It could be the wine or it could be the colorful portraits on the bottle portraying former residents. We like both.

Vineyards can be found in surprising places around Portland.   Courtesy McMenamin's

WASSON BROTHERS WINERY
503-668-3124
17020 Ruben Lane
www.wassonwine.com
Tasting Room: Daily 9–5
Fee: Complimentary
Owners/Winemakers: John and Jim Wasson
Wines: Chardonnay, Gewurztraminer, Niagara, Muscat, Riesling, Pinot Noir, berry wines, sparkling wines
Cases: 3,500
Special Features: Gift shop

The oldest winery in Clackamas County likes to describe itself as "In a glass by itself." It is well off the beaten wine path, in orchard and nursery country between Portland and the Columbia Gorge. Be sure to try the Niagara, Wasson Brothers' top-selling wine, made from a cousin of the more renowned Concord grape. The Wassons are known for their berry wines, the drink of choice for rural locals. And if you're looking to get into the Oregon wine business, this might be the place: Wasson Brothers was still for sale in February 2010.

CHAMPOEG WINE CELLARS
503-678-2144
www.champoegwine.com
10375 Champoeg Road NE
Tasting Room: Memorial Day and Thanksgiving weekends, and by appointment
Fee: Varies by event
Wines: Chardonnay, Gewürztraminer, Pinot Blanc, Pinot Gris, Riesling, Pinot Noir
Cases: 250
Special Features: Picnic area, gift shop, winery tours

La Butte, which rises above the French Prairie north of Salem, was once considered the wine capital of the Oregon Territory—at least by the grape growers who lived there. Now, a teeny winery with a hands-on operation lives here. When they are open, you can view how wine is made from windows looking into the winery. The name Champoeg is Indian for "fields of camas bulbs," a favorite medicinal bulb of the natives.

Lodging in the Portland Area

PORTLAND
HEATHMAN HOTEL/MARBLE BAR
503-241-4100 or 800-551-0011
www.heathmanhotel.com
1001 SW Broadway Avenue
Rates: $149–229
Special Features: Complimentary regional wine tasting on Thursdays, Wi-Fi and work desk, 24-hour room service, pet-friendly floor, disability-accessible rooms

Following the Euro-luxury-boutique model, this historic (1927) 10-story building in the heart of the city puts shopping, dining, and window browsing at your feet. The Heathman is known for exemplary guest services and luxury accoutrements, including its signature "Art of Sleep"—three bed types (feather, pillow-top, Tempur-pedic), accompanied by fluffy bathrobes and slippers. The old landmark recently underwent a $4 million green renovation. A wine-tasting package is offered: one night of deluxe accommodations, a bottle of Oregon Pinot Noir, complimentary valet parking, personal concierge assistance for touring in the Willamette Valley, and the latest issue of *Wine Spectator*—all for $224–264. The restaurant and bar share a huge cellar, with more than 600 wines from 20 worldwide regions (with an emphasis on Oregon and France), and the largest champagne collection in the state. Look for Jeff Groh's annual dueling sommeliers event.

THE GOVERNOR
503-224-3400
614 SW 11th Avenue
www.governorhotel.com
Rates: $239–389
Special Features: Access to downtown, catering, Starbucks in lobby

Perhaps no Portland hotel merges history and luxury like The Governor. Built in 1909 and designed by Oregon's first state architect, it has such an aura that numerous movies have been filmed inside and outside

The Amazing McMenamin's McStory

In the early 1970s, brothers Brian and Mike McMenamin sensed a gap between Oregonians' increasingly progressive tastes and the scarcity of places to enjoy them. Starting with the reclamation of a dank, smoky bar in southeast Portland, the two have built a $70 million empire around fun and funky lodging, dining, and imbibing.

Among the 55-and-counting McMenamin's (www.mcmenamins.com) renovations are an abandoned school, a shuttered church, and a former roadhouse on a mountain pass. But best known is Edgefield Manor, a 38-acre European-style village just outside Portland. Once the Multnomah County Poor Farm, the dilapidated collection of buildings has been converted into colorful accommodations with walls painted with Oregon history by local artists. Edgefield also features a winery, distillery, restaurants, spa, and a theater pub where visitors can enjoy a burger and beer or, better yet, glass of Syrah while taking in a flick.

The lively ambiance, historic surroundings, and proximity to wineries make McMenamin's a favorite stop for tourists and locals seeking unusual, all-inclusive entertainment or a romantic getaway.

It's true that the Brew's Brothers are better known for their handcrafted beers and their distilled spirits than their wine labels, yet a map shows their various locations in Oregon and Washington are strikingly close to wine country. Coincidence? We think not.

its ornate and dramatically lit walls. The hotel is now on the National Register of Historic Places. Contributing to the luxury component are completely remodeled rooms and penthouse suites that afford panoramic views of the city.

HOTEL VINTAGE PLAZA

800-263-2305
www.vintageplaza.com
422 SW Broadway Avenue
Rates: $199–470
Special Features: "Mind. Body. Spa." programs

A multi-million-dollar revitalization of this wine-centric hotel has uncorked a new look and offers a fresh taste of Oregon. The Vintage Plaza blends old-world hospitality and new-world luxury at affordable rates. Indeed, as the Vintage Plaza is quick to boast, *Travel & Leisure* magazine rates it among the top 10 hotels nationally with rooms for $250 or less. A commitment to Oregon's wine industry makes these accommodations especially appealing. The rooms are named after wineries and many have special decor tied to a namesake winery. Local wines are poured in the lobby from 5 to 6 every evening.

TROUTDALE
MCMENAMIN'S EDGEFIELD

Owners: McMenamin Brothers
503-669-5226
www.mcmenamins.com
2126 SW Halsey Avenue
Rates: $30–175
Special Features: Winery and tasting room, microbrew theater pub, distillery, pool hall, a menagerie of restaurants and bars, nightly music, two par-3 pitch-and-putt pub courses, concerts

Edgefield is McMenamins' signature project. Beginning in 1990, the brothers purchased the 74-acre grounds, which in 1911 began as the Multnomah County Poor Farm. Over the years, the farm closed down and the Georgian Revival–style building became a nursing home. Today, the manicured grounds, orchards, and gardens feature a plethora of interesting activities, culinary and otherwise. The halls are a step back into history, with compelling murals painted by various local artists telling the unique history of the property. Rooms in the old manor run the gamut from suites with private baths to hostel-style bunks with lockers for $30. Edgefield has an annual two-day Celebration of Syrah that includes a silent auction that funds medical insurance for seasonal vineyard workers.

McMenamin's Edgefield Manor, in Troutdale, was once the county's poor farm. Courtesy McMenamin's

Dining in the Portland Area

Dining in Portland is a destination vacation all unto itself. Again, we've focused on the consistently cream-of-the-crop within a range of style and cuisine that emphasize Oregon wine. There are some nationally recognized and iconic establishments that didn't make the cut simply because of their wine list, not their reputation.

Oregon's down economy took a toll on eating establishments that were once the talk of the town. One shocker: Caprial's Westmoreland Kitchen, which had a show on Oregon Public Broadcasting and conducted popular cooking classes, closed its doors in August 2009.

PORTLAND
BLUEHOUR
503-226-3394
www.bluehouronline.com
250 NW 13th Avenue
Open: Mon.–Sat. 11:30 AM–close
Price: Expensive
Credit Cards: Yes
Special Features: Happy hour with half-price bar menu 4:30–6:30 daily

Located in the once-gritty industrial innards of the city, now revamped into the high-rent Pearl District, Bluehour is sophisticated elegance for the see-and-be-seen scene. Here you also see one of the best happy hours in the city for interesting small plates (fried olives, bruschetta, grilled veggie sandwiches, and a not-so-small, freshly ground local beef burger on ciabatta) at small prices. Fine dining from chef and co-owner Kenny Biambalvo can be spendy but satisfying, with Oregon wines by the bottle as prolific as designer-clad diners. After gorging on almost every item from the bar menu (love the fried olives with an Oregon Sauvignon Blanc), we've replicated a few for home entertaining—warmed chèvre in marinara sauce is the hands-down fave.

BEAST
503-841-6968
www.beastpdx.com
5425 NE 30th Avenue
Open: Wed.–Sat. dinner seatings 6 and 8:45, Sun. brunch seatings 10 and 12

Price: Expensive
Credit Cards: Yes
Special Features: Six-course prix fixe meal with attention to meat; everything made in the kitchen, right down to crackers and charcuterie

We'd be remiss not to mention Beast, even though Oregon wine is not a priority here. Renowned chef Naomi Pomeroy has always walked on the near side of fresh and innovative. Sherry first came across her when Ripe, her catering company, worked a vineyard wedding. Pomeroy and her former husband were dabbling in the "family supper" theme and went on to build a solid reputation and small empire of Portland restaurants. A divorce and a few hard lessons later, Clarklewis and Gotham Tavern are defunct and Pomeroy's on her own at Beast. Everything she prepares is memorable and served on two communal tables in a room about the size of your average home dining room. There is a wine option and each careful selection is meant to match the course. Dinner is $52 per person, plus an additional $35 for six wines. If you BYOB, be prepared for a $30 corkage fee—per bottle.

CAFÉ CASTAGNA
503-231-9959
www.castagnarestaurant.com
1758 SE Hawthorne Boulevard
Open: Daily 5 P.M.–close, Tues.–Sat. 11:30 A.M.–2 P.M.
Price: Moderate

Credit Cards: Yes
Special Features: Late-night bar menu
(beginning at 9:45) features such small
plates as steak or fish bites, prime-rib dip,
fried oysters, and shrimp, each for $2.25

Café Castagna is a spinoff from the grown-
up version (Castagna) next door. The café
has quite a menu, mixing the usual and the
unusual. Soup is always impressive and the
butter-lettuce salad, which looks like an
open flower blossom, is superb. A favorite
is the rail-thin crusted pizza, dusted with
criminis or tomatoes and basil. The famed
burger is a best bet, served with house
pickles and a stack of thin and crispy *frites*
that will bring you back for more. Oregon
and Northwest wines are well represented,
especially reds by the bottle.

THE FARM CAFÉ

503-736-3276
www.thefarmcafe.com
10 SE Seventh Avenue
Open: Daily 5–11:30
Prices: Moderate
Credit Cards: Yes
Special Features: Happy hour 5–6:30
Mon.–Fri. with half-off appetizers and
wines by the glass; sustainable and locally
sourced ingredients (purveyors listed
on Web site) including wine, beer, and
spirits

The menu at The Farm leans distinctly to
the left of meat. Appetizers you'll resist
sharing because they're so tasty: the baked
brie served with seasonal fresh fruit;
roasted hazelnuts (with a dash of Tabasco
and pinch of brown sugar), and the farmhouse cheese ball. They all pair well with a
glass of Oregon wine, and could easily comprise your entire meal. But there's more:
many-cheese stuffed ravioli, flame-seared
halibut, grilled corn and smoky blue
risotto, and the city's best veggie burger. It's
a great after-the-show place. The restored

Victorian home has three separate personalities. Start in granny's parlor with dark
heavy curtains, dripping chandelier,
crammed tables, and all the noise of a large
family dinner. Wind your way to the back
through the narrow hallway to find a new-
age bar with a sassy mixologist shaking her
cocktails and holding court. Adjacent is the
airy and spacious outside patio, a favorite
place to pick up the city vibes.

HIGGINS RESTAURANT & BAR

503-222-9070
www.higgins.ypguides.net
1239 SW Broadway Avenue
Open: Mon.–Fri. 11:30 A.M.–12 A.M.,
Sat.–Sun. 4 P.M.–12 A.M.
Price: Moderate to expensive
Credit Cards: Yes
Special Features: Bistro menu served daily
in the bar

At Higgins, practically an institution in
Portland, you will find "cuisine truly rooted
in Northwest soil" and a long-time support
of regenerative farming techniques.
Owner/chef Greg Higgins, an avid organic
gardener, began showing extraordinary
culinary skills when he was a youngster in
Eden, New York, influenced by recipes of
Fannie Farmer. Higgins's serious commitment to connecting food to source is evident in a Northwest-French-Italian medley
menu and his work with Portland Chef's
Collaborative. Three levels of tables and
detailed lighting bathe both plates and diners in a good shine. The open kitchen
design allows Higgins to see the pleasure
of his patrons, while the large windows
behind expose him to the street traffic,
ensuring nothing funky is going on behind
the skillet. Save room for his famed
desserts. Higgins has several Oregon
wines by the glass, and an all-Oregon white
and red list to complement his seasonal
menu.

A stellar lineup of Oregon wines adds to the decor at many restaurants. Courtesy Joel Palmer House

KEN'S ARTISAN PIZZA

503-517-9951
www.kenartisan.com
304 SE 28th Avenue
Open: Tues.-Sat. 5–10 P.M.
Price: Moderate
Credit Cards: Yes
Special Features: No reservations accepted, so come early or late; bicycle parking

Co-founder Ken Forkish and co-owner/chef Alan Maniscalco have just what you need to fill the void on a gray, wet day in Oregon: handcrafted pizza and local wine. Across the street at Ken's bakery, well known in the P-zone for artisan-baked yums, pizza was originally served on Monday nights. It was so popular that he had to open the pizzeria. The pies are fast-fired in the wood oven, dressed in seasonal and standard toppings with just the right amount of cheese on a blistered, chewy crust. Add a bottle of Oregon vino and the fog will lift. The restaurant only seats 55, with an additional 20 at the bar. Interior furnishings aren't fancy, but a bank of sliding windows leaves you feeling as if you're a part of the neighborhood. The selection of Oregon wines by the glass or bottle is solid.

MERIWETHER'S

503-228-1520
www.meriwethersnw.com
2601 NW Vaughn Street
Open: Mon.–Fri. 11:30–3 and 5–10, Sat.–Sun. 8 A.M.–10 P.M.
Price: Expensive
Credit Cards: Yes
Special Features: Off-the-menu brunch on weekends, Sunday Supper featuring meals prepared from the restaurant's hearth and family-style seating, events facility at the farm

Meriwether's is an island of casual but upscale dining in a sea of industrial warehouses, with "Farm to Table" as its credo. Their 18-acre Skyline Farm outside Portland includes five acres of produce grown specifically for the restaurant—

everything from roots and legumes to egg-plant and tomatoes along with the usual assortment of lettuce, herbs, and flowers. In 2008, the farm produced 8,000 pounds of produce for their own use. What they don't grow they get from local suppliers, including beef, pork, lamb, seafood, and fish. They're known for exquisite patio dining, available even in winter thanks to panels of overhead heaters. Meriwether's lists more than 50 Pinot Noirs by the bottle, arranged according to AVA, and 21 other Oregon wines. The building was part of the 1905 Portland Expo and framed photos depict the grand event.

MOTHER'S BISTRO & BAR

503-464-1122
www.mothersbistro.com
212 SW Stark Street
Open: Tues.–Fri. 7–2:30, Sat.–Sun. 9-2:30; Tues.–Thurs. 5:30–9 and Fri.–Sat. 5–10
Credit Cards: Yes
Special Features: Breakfast served until 2:30 P.M., M.O.M. (Mother of the Month) program with recipes provided by chosen mothers, happy hour Tues.–Fri. 3–6

When preparing for a day (and evening) of wine tasting, it's sound advice to fill up on some calorie-laden food. Although Mother's serves healthy choices such as a tofu and portobello scramble and Bill Clinton's omelet (loaded with veggies and garlic), we'd suggest the breakfast nachos or maybe the wild salmon hash. Better yet, try the homemade buttermilk biscuits and country sausage gravy. But someone has to order the corn flake–crunchy cinnamon French toast. Even better than the creative choices are the prices—small wonder that Mother's was chosen one of America's top restaurant bargains by *Food & Wine*. Wines, listed by glass and bottle, are weighted toward Oregon and Washington, all carefully selected. Some of Oregon's more obscure producers make the list and prices

are within the working family's budget. Five dessert wines by the glass are a sweet treat. The Velvet Lounge bar, with dangling chandeliers and gilded mirrors, offers a different menu. Reservations are strongly advised, or come as early as 7 A.M. or after 1 P.M. for best seating chances—the place is always packed.

NAVARRE

503-232-3555
www.navarreportland.blogspot.com
10 NE 28th Street
Open: Mon.–Thurs. 4:30–10:30, Fri. 11 A.M.–11:30 P.M., Sat. 9:30 A.M.–11:30 P.M., Sun. 9:30 A.M.–10:30 P.M.
Price: Moderate
Credit Cards: Yes
Special Features: More than 75 wines by the glass, mostly reds

Navarre is unique even by Stumptown standards. Braving the new food front in 2001, chef—and now happily sole proprietor—John Taboada sources 90 percent of his ingredients from one CSA (Community Supported Agriculture group): 47th Avenue Farms. On any given day, the specials—written on a mirror hanging under the handmade oak counter—reflect that morning's arrivals and the inspiration brought with them. Inside—about the size of a broom closet with a one-seater (toilet)—Mason jars full of preserved produce for future fits of culinary genius are stacked on utility shelving. Small plates of rustic Basque, Italian, or Northwest cuisine mean no fuss with presentation, no leaning towers or coulis swirled into a border, and no poetic descriptions. Menu items are one- or two-word labels, leaving options open. Check off what you'd like—either small or large plates—on a paper list, turn it in, and hope for the best. Add an all-Oregon wine component and you're set for a beyond-unique culinary outing. Named the *Oregonian*'s 2009 restaurant of the year for its innovative, simply stated, and forward-thinking style, Navarre has become an even busier place. Come early and grab an outside table on a good day—although the street traffic is noticeable, you'll have interesting people-watching.

PALEY'S PLACE BISTRO & BAR

503-243-2403
www.paleysplace.net
1204 NW 21st Street
Open: Daily 5:30 P.M.–close
Price: Expensive
Credit Cards: Yes
Special Features: Wednesday flight nights (featuring more international than local wine), heaters for front-porch and patio seating

Chef/owner Vitaly Paley has been waving his whisk for more than 14 years in the same location, actually an old Victorian home in a northwest neighborhood complete with family photos on the wall (Paley's suppliers and purveyors). The cuisine is naturally eco-sensitive and creative, combining Northwest and French garnished with an East Coast attitude. (Jeff starts to salivate whenever he thinks of their famed steak tartare.) They are also known for their sweetbreads, escargot simmered with marrow, and the oh-so-hard-to-resist chocolate soufflé cake. The Paley burger is created with ground-to-order organic Kobe beef on a house-made brioche bun and served with pickled veggies and kitchen-made ketchup. The antithesis of noisy and clamorous, Paley's has a style that's intimate, homey, and yet still sophisticated. They have a healthy mix of Oregon wines from boutiques to big producers.

PARK KITCHEN

503-223-7275
www.parkkitchen.com
422 NW Eighth Avenue
Open: Mon.–Fri. 11:30–2 and 5–9, Sat. 5–9

Price: Expensive
Credit Cards: Yes
Special Features: Patio dining in spring, summer, and fall; five-course wine dinners

Executive chef Scott Dolich has built a solid reputation in a just a few years with a restaurant he named for the Park Blocks section of town. Today, the Park Kitchen is among the upper echelon of dining experiences in Portland. Of course, the menu reflects the bounty available in this loaded state, coated in Mediterranean and American inspiration. How about house-made hotdogs or a New York–style Reuben—with brisket replaced by duck confit? Flavors run a full spectrum here and dishes are arranged by small and large, hot or cold, allowing you to put together a custom meal sure to surprise and suffice. Signature dishes: classic chickpea fries with squash ketchup, and flank-steak salad with Oregon blue cheese and sherried red onions. Park Kitchen has at least 30 Oregon and Washington wines from which to choose.

RINGSIDE STEAKHOUSE

503-223-1513
www.ringsidesteakhouse.com
2165 West Burnside Avenue
Open: Mon.–Fri. 11:30–2:30 and 5–12, Sat. 5–12, Sun. 4–11:30
Price: Expensive
Credit Cards: Yes
Special Features: Three-course dinner for $35 daily, late-night menu.

The original Chicago-style steakhouse, with its white-shirt-and-bowtie waiters and Sinatra-style clubhouse ambiance, has been bustling since 1944. It was a high school date-night joint a generation or two ago. Back then, it was all about the steak, with maybe one chicken entrée. Today, the choices have expanded to grilled lamb, salmon, and halibut, with classic sides such as creamed corn or spinach casserole. A bone-in ribeye still takes center stage; a supporting role goes to the famous hand-battered, thick-cut onion rings served with a French dressing and bleu cheese dipping sauce. The nifty wine list has many Oregon Pinots and glass pours of red or white. A second location for Ringside is at Glendoveer Golf Course, 14,021 NE Glisan Avenue.

VERITABLE QUANDARY

503-227-7342
www.veritablequandary.com
1220 SW First Avenue
Open: Daily 5–10, Mon.–Fri. 11:30–3
Price: Moderate to expensive
Credit Cards: Yes
Special Features: Garden patio dining literally in the heart of the city; late-night bar menu; menus posted close to daily on Web site

The VQ is a Portland landmark and has been around at least as long as we've been old enough to drink. It has maintained its Old Town charm with its polished dark-wood, aged-brick interior and shoebox size—but has added enough updates to keep it as fresh as the ingredients. Popular at lunch for its burger (beef and veggie), the restaurant has an intriguing dinner menu that changes according to available seasonal ingredients. Signature entrées that don't rotate off the menu are the veal osso bucco and New York strip. We prefer to make a meal of appetizers—dates stuffed with Marcona almonds and chèvre and wrapped in bacon and a bowl of seafood stew or green chile soup works. Brunch at VQ is all about the eggs Benedict, which begins with an English muffin (a chef's family recipe) packed with butter. Thanks to the expertise of Nicole Rocco, VQ is the recipient of the *Wine Spectator* Award of Excellence nine years and counting. You'll find at least four or five red and white glass pours from Oregon producers, and 50 or more by the bottle. One last tip: Remember to order dessert first. The chocolate Nocello (hazelnut liqueur) soufflé is baked to order and perfection takes time.

WILDWOOD

503-248-9663
www.wildwoodrestaurant.com
1221 NW 21st Avenue
Open: Mon.–Sat. 11:30–2:30, 5:30–close
Price: Expensive
Credit Cards: Yes
Special Features: Menu changes daily, winemaker dinners

Even though famed cofounder Cory Scrieber has moved on, Wildwood remains a champion for cooking from the source. Dustin Clark has provided his own imprint, keeping with the original intent on making the most of fresh, mostly Oregon-sourced ingredients. Shellfish, fish, and wild game are a must here, as are the mushrooms. An open-to-viewing kitchen embraced in earthy tones and wood set the scene for a touch of special. Oregon wines are still prominent, but the list has expanded to a more international selection. For Sherry, Wildwood conjures up memories of a summer shopping trips to northwest Portland punctuated by a late lunch and glass of wine with her mother on the street-front patio.

Wine Bars in the Portland Area

As with our dining selections, we highlight places—from simple to complex, hip to chic, or just fun—that focus their wine pours on Oregon, or at least the Pacific Northwest. Portland has numerous wine bars, but these are the places we like to frequent in a city that plays the game of one-upmanship like no other.

ALU WINE BAR

503-262-9463
www.aluwinebar.com

2831 NE MLK Jr. Boulevard
Open: Wed.–Mon. 5–12
Special Features: Patio

In the vein of reuse, reduce, and recycle, new owners (as of May 2009) Jeff Vejr and Susan Killoranon kept the name and expensive sign from the previous owner, who when renovating used recycled aluminum siding for the exterior. The name and logo come from the Netherlands, where they can be found on recyclable aluminum cans. What wasn't recycled was the menu. Wanting a fresh concept, Alu uses icons on the menu to symbolize purveyors that are sustainable, biodynamic, small estate, women-owned etc., allowing you to choose by your favorite affiliation(s). You'll find house specialties, such as smoked duck, sausage, and prosciutto, that meld well with an Oregon red. Adult beverages also are local, sustainable, and/or organic. The wine menu is world-inclusive, but the Oregon choices feature smaller producers. The owners grow the herbs, cure the meats, pickle the veggies, and take great care to meet self-imposed high standards. They claim to be the only establishment of their kind in all of foodie-driven Portland. As Vejr puts it, here you can "geek out in a comfortable, unpretentious setting."

BAR AVIGNON

503-517-0808
www.baravignon.com
2138 SE Division Street
Open: Daily 4 P.M.–close
Special Features: Happy hour 4–6 with $4 menu items and $5 wines by the glass

Wildwood's Randy Goodman and wife, Nancy Hunt, have put together a best-of-the-best wine bar in an "Everyone knows your name" setting. When you walk in, you'll find yourself sighing, dropping your shoulders, and settling into re-lax-ation mode. All of the menu items are prepared with love—grilled paninis, croquettes, and charcuterie. But the smoked trout crostini does it for us. You will also find more than twenty affordable wine selections by the glass, heavy on the Oregon side. We can't forget to mention the Dagoba (Oregon) chocolate cake with bourbon caramel sauce and *the* best crème brûlée ever. Named a "Best Value Wine Bar" by *Food & Wine,* Avignon also uses Portland distilled spirits in their cocktails and has local beer on tap.

LIVING ROOM THEATERS

971-222-2010
www.livingroomtheaters.com
341 SW 10th Avenue
Open: Movies begin around noon and run roughly until midnight
Special Features: Free Wi-Fi, HD digital projection, special prices Mon.–Tues.

Dinner and a movie? *And* a glass of Pinot? You can have it all in one place, and a footstool to boot. This classy, eco-friendly, theater–wine bar combo in the Pearl District features art and foreign films in full sensory mode. Reasonably priced tapas, pizzas, paninis, and desserts (chocolate cake is a must) along with wine and beer are served on real plates in the naturally lighted bistro-café dining area or in one of six smallish theaters. The theater seats are Barcalounger-comfortable, with handy cup and plate holders. To accommodate the under-21 crowd, alcohol is served in theaters only during late afternoon and evening showtimes. Current films are listed on the Web site, and reservations can be made on the day of show only. Live jazz in the lounge is another added attraction on weekends.

NOBLE ROT

503-233-1999
www.noblerotpdx.com
1111 East Burnside, fourth floor
Open: Mon.-Thurs. 5–11, Fri.–Sat. 5–12

Special Features: Happy Hour Mon.–Fri. 5–6, late night menu daily starting at 10

Noble Rot is back in its original digs, but on the top floor of this east-side retrofitted building. Co-owner and chef Leather Storrs mixes it up with American comfort food such as a cheeseburger and fries (substitute with the addictive onion rings), mac and cheese, and more typical wine fare. If you can get past the unappetizing name, you'll find flavorful and labor-intensive charcuterie on the Rot Meat Plate. A must-try is the famous onion tart. Local and seasonal ingredients drive the rest of the plates. The wine list is about half Oregon, half elsewhere, and the atmosphere cosmopolitan and crowded. The new space (as of 2009) is LEED Platinum certified and has a 3,000-foot rooftop garden that produces year-round and provides penthouse skyline views with seating.

OREGON WINES ON BROADWAY

503-228-4655
www.oregonwinesonbroadway.com
515 SW Broadway
Open: Mon.–Sat. 12–8
Special Features: Second Thursday of the month, 5–8 P.M., complimentary sampling often poured by a local vintner or winemaker

A narrow, compact bar for the suits, residents, and downtown shoppers lacks stuffiness or airs and is a place to begin (or end) your thirst for knowledge on Oregon wines. With up to 30 open bottles of Pinot alone, you can compare and contrast to your heart's content with sample sizes. If you settle on a favorite, you can order a glass or purchase bottles to go. A few nibbles can also be found, but the focus is on the state's fruits from the vine, although the owner (and servers) also have an affinity for French champagne. The only downer: service can be lacking for non-regulars.

PIX PATISSERIE

503-282-6539
www.pixpatisserie.com
3901 North Williams and 3402 SE Division
Open: Mon.–Thurs. 8 A.M.–12 A.M., Fri.–Sat. 8 A.M.–2 A.M., Sun. 9 A.M.–12 A.M.
Special Features: Movie night at the North Williams location with black-and-white films projected on the red velvet wall

Cheryl Wakerhauser, nicknamed Pix, deals in edible art. Using chocolate as her primary canvas and blending texture, flavor, and design, she concocts the best sweet treats your mouth will ever meet. You could say the treats are too pretty to eat, but don't let all that work stop you. While it's not technically a wine bar, wine is served—some from Oregon—late into the night. You'll be happy as a Pacific clam that you found Pix. There is a southeast location with different hours (and closed Monday) at 3402 SE Division (503-232-4407).

POUR WINE BAR & BISTRO

503-288-7687
www.pourwinebar.com
755 NE Broadway Avenue
Open: Mon.–Thur. 4:30–11, Fri.–Sat. 4:30–close
Special Features: "Poor Hour" has $3 wines, $2 beers, and $2 food items Mon.–Sat., 4:30–6:30

Robert Volz may seem quirky, but he's a man with a plan . . . or two. While cruising his neighborhood on a vintage motor scooter, he saw the empty building of his dreams and thought: wine bar! The unlikely location has lines to match the wines. The interior design is based on the work of midcentury Finnish-American architect Eero Saarinen. Curves throughout the interior are also meant to complement the Saarinen-style chairs that Volz scored from a 1950s cruise ship and remind us of the Jetsons' space-age home. Volz makes all the small plates behind the bar with the aid of an amped-up hot plate of sorts, and intends for the limited menu to pair with his hand-picked Oregon wines by the glass. Plans for expanding the bar are in the works, and might even include a bona fide kitchen.

THIRST WINE BAR & BISTRO

503-295-2747
www.thirstbistro.com
0315 SW Montgomery Street, Suite 340
Open: Tues.–Sun. 3 P.M.–close
Special Features: "Thirsty Tuesday" tastings 5:30–7:30 on select Tuesdays; located in River Place Esplanade with riverside seating

If your thirst runs to the Pacific Northwest in terms of wine or distilled spirits, this spot has the quench for you. Almost exclusively Oregon and Washington wines by the taste, glass, or bottle, many from smaller, boutique wineries, can be enjoyed riverside, indoors or out. Food runs from light fare to more substantial meals, and Thirst is dedicated to using local, organic, or natural ingredients in their regional cuisine. It's a notch above the usual. Do not walk away without tasting the handmade truffles concocted with clever combinations like wasabi ginger or blood orange and nutmeg. Thirst, anchored on the riverfront, has large window views that give the sense of being rocked by the gentle waves of the Willamette. What better way to take in the Oregon wine experience?

VINO PARADISO

503-295-9536
www.vinoparadiso.com
417 NW 10th Avenue
Open: Tues.–Sat. 4–11, Sun. 3–9
Special Features: Wine dinners, classes, retail sales, art gallery, ample street parking

Vino Paradiso, located in the slick Pearl District, is more restaurant than wine bar and sets a tone for the swanky and sophisticated. Still, the expanded small plates and more substantial entrees fall under the $20 mark and are more than stellar. The cellar and wine list is international, running the gamut from meek to wild. It frequently garners *Wine Spectator*'s Award of Excellence. High priority is given to Oregon red wines, particularly Pinot Noir, with some attention going to the whites. There is also an ever-changing wine-by-the flight menu consisting of select Oregon and elsewhere producers. High marks from *Sunset* magazine confirm this as a preferred choice for a wine-and-dine experience. Reservations recommended.

Attractions in the Portland Area

So much to choose from, so little time. A traveler could get lost for several days in Portland and never run out of things to do. This is a book about wine country, and so the idea is to head for the hills. But before you do, here are a few stops worth including on your itinerary.

Given that Portland has the well-deserved moniker "City of Roses," start with a trip to the pretty West Hills overlooking downtown. **Washington Park** is 400 acres of woods and trails minutes from the city's heart. The centerpiece is the **Oregon Zoo** (503-226-1561, 4001 SW Canyon Rd.), which houses everything from regional animals to international land and sea critters. The zoo also stages a summer concert series featuring big-name entertainment. Also in Washington Park, the **International Rose Test Garden** (503-823-3636) is a vivid display of more than seven thousand roses. Just a short walk from the rose gardens is the **Portland Japanese Garden** (503-223-1321), a verdant 5½-acre sanctuary that paints five garden portraits of Japan. The 185-acre **Hoyt Arboretum** (503-865-8733, 4000 SW Fairview Blvd.) features more than a thousand species of plants from every

Splendid views come at no charge while touring wineries. John Baker

corner of the planet. It's on a ridge barely two miles from downtown. Free summer concerts have been offered in the amphitheater for two weeks in August since 1908.

Down on the user-friendly Portland waterfront, take a cruise past the downtown skyline and enjoy memorable brunch, lunch, and dinner cuisine on the **Portland Spirit** (503-224-3900), which plies the busy waters of the Willamette. Across from downtown on the river, you'll notice a submarine docked in front of a giant building. That's the **Oregon Museum of Science and Industry** (503-797-4000), a.k.a OMSI, which offers a wide array of fascinating exhibits that appeals to young and old alike, including the submarine and a planetarium.

The city is just big enough to have one major-league sports franchise, and so emotions run deep for the NBA's **Portland Trail Blazers** (503-797-9619). When the team is winning and the players are staying out of trouble, tickets are at a premium and the atmosphere at the Rose Garden can be much like a college game. For a different type of cultural experience, the **Laurelhurst Theater** (503-232-5511, 2735 E. Burnside), built in 1923, has four screens and charges $3 across the board for independent and classic films. If you prefer a live performance in a luxurious setting, the **Portland Center for the Performing Arts** (503-248-4335, 1111 SW Broadway Ave.) brings top-level entertainers and performers to the Arlene Schnitzer Keller Auditorium and other theaters.

In the city's heart, **Powell's Books** (503-228-4651, 1005 W. Burnside) has been a Portland icon since 1971. With more than 1 million titles, it is the largest independent new-and-used bookseller in the world. After you've made a few selections, take a brisk walk to **Pioneer Square Park** (503-223-1613, 701 SW Sixth Ave.), affectionately known as Portland's Living Room. Something is always happening there.

You can get a snapshot of a mid-1800s world with a **Portland Underground** (503-774-4522, 226 NW Davis St.) tour that is both above and below ground. On this 2½-hour jaunt, which includes Chinatown and Old Town, you'll go underground to see where inebriated men were shanghaied into slavery and other tawdry affairs conducted. And before you take off for wine country, get a bird's-eye look at this beautiful city from the **Portland Aerial Tram** (503-494-8283, 3303 SW Bond Ave.), which connects the South Waterfront neighborhood along the Willamette River with the Oregon Health and Science University in the West Hills. The 3,300-foot ride takes three minutes.

Recreation in the Portland Area

Portlanders like to spend as little time in their cars as possible, whether it's to work or play at one of the city's seven-hundred-plus parks and recreation sites. Indeed, the Rose City surely is one of the most bicycle-friendly metropolitan areas in the nation. You can **rent a bike** on the Eastbank Esplanade and take off in any direction.

A favorite locale for cyclists, mountain bikers, hikers, horseback riders, and runners alike is the 30-mile Wildwood Trail in **Forest Park** (503-823-7529), an extraordinary 5,000-acre urban forest with more than 70 miles of wide single-track trails and fire roads. Forest Park is the largest natural forested area within an urban area in the United States.

Portland residents don't have to wait until the snow flies to ski. Mount Hood, visible from nearly every nook of town, has enough snow on its glaciers for year-round schussing at **Mt. Hood Ski Bowl** (503-222-2695). Mt. Hood Ski Bowl also has the largest terrain in the state for night skiing, more than 600 acres. Many skiers head to **Mt. Hood Meadows** (503-337-2217), a little farther east, for slightly better powder, smaller crowds, and the most skiable terrain on the mountain. Mt. Hood Meadows also offers cross-country skiing. Smaller ski areas on the mountain include **Cooper Spur** (541-352-7803), **Timberline** (503-272-3158), and the oldest ski area on the mountain, **Summit** (503-272-0256), which began operations in 1927. Summit has an adjoining area called **Snow Bunny** for snow tubing.

Shopping in the Portland Area

If you make only one shopping stop downtown, make it the **Portland Saturday Market** (503-222-6072), which touts itself as the nation's largest open-air arts and crafts fair and market. The name notwithstanding, this lively and eclectic blend of vendors and performers from around the globe also shows their prodigious wares on Sundays as well from March through December. Portland's shopping is largely divided into districts. The trendy and busy **Nob Hill** area in the near northwest part of town appeals to sophisticated urbanites with its microbreweries, sidewalk cafés, hip coffee shacks, and boutiques. The **Pearl District** in the once-blighted warehouse district along the Willamette River is more on the fashionable side with its galleries, antique stores, coffee shops, and upscale restaurants amid townhouses, lofts, and urban condos. The Pearl epitomizes Oregon's progressive and creative persona, and has been a national bellwether for urban reclamation projects. Aligning with its residents, the **Hawthorne** section of southeast Portland tends more toward counterculture with its pubs, cafés, and distinctly local shops. It's worth shopping in this large area just to people-watch.

Wine Shopping in the Portland Area

Great wine shops are all over Portland. Here are a few to look for: **Great Wine Buys** (503-287-2897, 1515 NE Broadway Ave.) has more than 700 wines, including more than two hundred from Oregon, and offers Friday and Saturday night tastings, food-pairing advice and wine classes. At **Korkage Wine Shop** (503-293-3146, 6351 SW Capitol Highway), the mission is to sell good wine for $25 or less. Thursday night tastings (6-8 P.M.) are $10 and somewhat raucous. Bring your own food or buy a cheese plate. **The Vintner's Cellar** (503-558-9463, 15711 SE Happy Valley Town Center Dr.) has everything you need if you've got the notion to see your name on a label. It is four easy steps from the first visit to fame and glory six to eight weeks later. Labeled as Oregon's only micro-winery, this is the ultra experience for anyone who wants to get a feel for actual winemaking. Meanwhile, the finer things in life can be found and taken home for your hedonistic moods at **Pearl Specialty Market & Spirits** (503-477-8604, 900 NW Lovejoy St., No. 140), where your wine tastes can be complemented with cheeses, chocolate, mixers and even a good cigar. Looking for solid value? **Square Deal Wine Company** (503-226-9463, NW Thurman St.) is a bottle shop that has its own Oregon label: Real Wine. They pride themselves in grab and go wine sourced from small Oregon vineyards.

Information

Travel Portland Information Center, 503-275-8355 or 877-678-5263, 701 SW Sixth Ave., www.travelportland.com

Washington County Visitors Association (Beaverton), 503-644-5555 or 800-537-3149, 11000 SW Stratus St., suite 170, www.visitwashingtoncountyoregon.com

NEWBERG AREA
(RIBBON RIDGE AND CHEHALEM MOUNTAIN AVAs)

How's this for irony: One of the wine hubs of the northern Willamette Valley was until quite recently a "dry" town, meaning alcohol was verboten. Newberg was founded as a Friends Church (Quaker) community in 1889 and is home to George Fox University, a four-year evangelical Christian college where even undergraduates of legal drinking age are required to abstain.

The town of 22,600 has loosened its fundamentalist mores over the years, but is still in its adolescence in terms of re-defining itself as a community. Its otherwise sleepy downtown with an old fashioned barbershop pole and a few eateries is bisected by the perpetual traffic jam that is OR 99W. The edge of town has the strip-mall aura neighboring communities have avoided. In an effort to build on the local wine economy, there are four tasting rooms downtown sandwiched between a few art galleries. The city has organized a First Friday art walk designed to get people onto the streets.

Newberg's main claim to celebrity fame is that President Herbert Hoover spent much of his boyhood here. About 90 percent of the world's hazelnut crop is produced here as well. Newberg is a town sitting on tons of potential. We await its arrival.

Wineries in the Newberg Area

On a map, Oregon's smallest appellation—less than eight square miles—appears to be an island surrounded by three of the state's behemoths: Dundee, Chehalem, and Yamhill-Carlton. In person, Ribbon Ridge is an oak- and fir-bathed peninsula protruding southward from the lush Chehalem Mountains, rising 700 feet above the green farms and pastures of the Chehalem River Valley.

Distinguishing Ribbon Ridge from its renowned neighbor appellations isn't just the fine, volcanic, marine-sediment Willakenzie soils, which are similar to Yamhill-Carlton's to the west. Nor is it merely the slightly warmer climate, which allows for an earlier

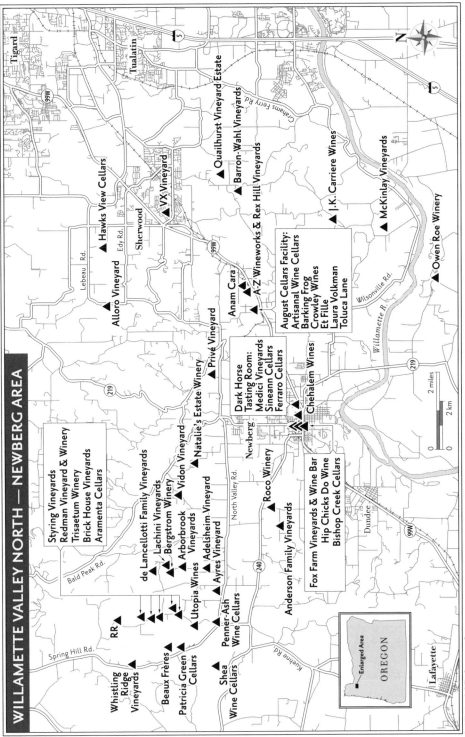

WILLAMETTE VALLEY NORTH — NEWBERG AREA

Paul Woodward. © The Countryman Press

Styring Vineyards
Redman Vineyard & Winery
Trisaetum Winery
Brick House Vineyards
Aramenta Cellars

de Lancellotti Family Vineyards
Lachini Vineyards
Bergstrom Winery
Vidon Vineyard
Arborbrook Vineyards
Adelsheim Vineyard
Ayres Vineyard
Natalie's Estate Winery

Whistling Ridge Vineyards
RR
Beaux Frères
Patricia Green Cellars
Shea Wine Cellars
Utopia Wines
Penner-Ash Wine Cellars

Anderson Family Vineyards
Roco Winery

Fox Farm Vineyards & Wine Bar
Hip Chicks Do Wine
Bishop Creek Cellars

Dark Horse Tasting Room:
Medici Vineyards
Sineann Cellars
Ferraro Cellars

Chehalem Wines

Newberg

Hawks View Cellars

Alloro Vineyard

Sherwood

VX Vineyard

Quailhurst Vineyard Estate

Barron-Wahl Vineyards

A-Z Wineworks & Rex Hill Vineyards

Anam Cara

Privé Vineyard

August Cellars Facility:
Artisanal Wine Cellars
Barking Frog
Crowley Wines
Et Fille
Laura Volkman
Toluca Lane

J.K. Carriere Wines

McKinlay Vineyards

Owen Roe Winery

Tigard

Tualatin

Lebeau Rd.

Edy Rd.

Bald Peak Rd.

Spring Hill Rd.

North Valley Rd.

Kuehne Rd.

Grahams Ferry Rd.

Wilsonville Rd.

Willamette R.

Dundee

Lafayette

OREGON

Enlarged Area

2 miles

2 km

growing season. Ribbon Ridge is also thought to be an elite club of winemakers. Grown here almost exclusively are Pinot Noir, Pinot Gris, and Chardonnay.

The larger Chehalem Mountain AVA is also a sub-appellation of the entire Willamette Valley, yet much larger—20 miles long and 5 miles wide, with more than 30 wineries. The Chehalem has such dramatic differences in elevation, precipitation, and temperatures that Pinot Noir harvests can be separated by as much as three weeks.

Think of the wineries around Newberg as in three pods: scattered wineries with Sherwood addresses, a cluster within walking distance in downtown Newberg, and the fabled Chehalem Mountain group to the northwest. In Newberg, we suggest parking at the Chehalem facility and walking up the one-way street to the other three downtown wineries.

If you're coming from Portland on OR 99W, you'll hit Sherwood first; if you're coming off the Sip 47 route from Yamhill or Carlton, you'll reach the cluster in the Ribbon Ridge and Chehalem AVAs. If you end your tour on Ribbon Ridge, you'll be in position to spend the night around Carlton.

SHERWOOD

HAWKS VIEW CELLARS

503-625-1591

www.hawksviewcellars.com

20210 SW Conzelmann Road

Tasting Room: By appointment only

Fee: $10

Owner/Winemaker: John A. Kemp

Wines: Pinot Gris, Riesling, Chardonnay, Pinot Noir

Cases: 1,250

Special Features: Private and corporate events, holiday parties

The focus at Hawks View is on their estate Pinot Noir and Pinot Gris, which is evident in the results: *Portland Monthly* rated the 2007 Pinot Noir the third-best Oregon wine in any category (the Pinot Gris was 19th). Hawks View does get grapes from Oregon and California for small productions of the Chardonnay and Riesling. The Kemp family uses LIVE practices in their Chehalem Mountains AVA vineyard. An elegant tasting room features a fireplace and three-sided views of the vineyards.

ALLORO VINEYARD

503-625-1978

www.allorovineyard.com

22075 SW Lebeau Road

Tasting Room: Memorial Day and Thanksgiving weekends, and by appointment

Fee: $10

Owner: David Nemarnik

Winemaker: Don Kautzner

Wines: Chardonnay, Muscat, Pinot Noir

Cases: 1,500

Special Features: Special events

The winery is located on Laurel Ridge amid Laurel Vineyard, thus the name: Alloro is Italian for Laurel. And you can certainly see the Italian touches in the decidedly Mediterranean facility. Owner David Nemarnik is, naturally, Italian and fondly remembers his grandfather's wine press. Alloro's vineyard is LIVE-certified.

VX VINEYARD

503-538-9895

www.vxvineyard.com

8000 NE Parrish Road

Tasting Room: May–Sept., Sat.–Sun. 12–5, Thanksgiving weekend, and by appointment

Fee: $1 per taste

Owners: Hall Family

Winemaker: Jason Silva

Wines: Pinot Gris, Pinot Blanc, Pinot Noir

Cases: 700

Special Features: Roasted or chocolate-covered hazelnuts grown on the farm available for purchase; viewing and picnic area near the Willamette River

If you're looking for a mini wilderness retreat to fit into your wine touring, follow the signs to the end of Parrish Road. Keep going and you'll find yourself on Willamette Farms, a working farm in the Hall family dating to the mid-1800s. In 2000, they put in vineyards and had their first production in 2003. Along with resident wildlife, there are nursery stock, orchards, boarded horses, and firewood for sale on these 200 acres bordering the Willamette River. The Vircingetorix (pronounced "*vur*-sin-jet-u-riks") on the label refers to an ancient Gallic chieftain who was known to spare the vineyards during his rebellion against Caesar's Roman rule.

QUAILHURST VINEYARD ESTATE

509-427-5132
www.quailhurstwines.com
16031 SW Pleasant Hill Road
Tasting Room: Memorial, Labor Day and Thanksgiving, and by appointment
Fee: $20 for flight of wines and tour of winery and equestrian center
Owners: Marvin and Deborah Hausman
Winemaker: Joe Dobbes
Wines: Rosé, Pinot Noir, dessert wines
Cases: 400
Special Features: Equestrian facility and Japanese gardens.

Coming to Quailhurst isn't just a visit, it's an event. The vineyard shares space with an equestrian facility and exquisite Japanese gardens, which were planted in the 1930s. When you come, chances are you'll also get some pearls of wisdom from owner Marvin Hausman, a doctor who understands as well as anybody in the industry the benefits of red wine in a healthy diet. As a bonus on your tour, you might catch some of Quailhurst's expert trainers working with horses to hone their skills for dressage competitions.

BARRON-WAHL VINEYARDS

503-625-7886
www.barronwahl.com
27015 SW Ladd Hill Road
Tasting Room: May–Nov., Sat.–Sun. 11–4, by appointment for parties of 10 or more
Fee: $5 per tasting, waived with purchase
Owners: Gordon Barron and Bill Wahl
Winemaker: Joe Dobbes
Wines: Pinot Noir
Cases: 3,000
Special Features: Special-events facility for parties up to 75

Even if your tastes aren't for Pinot Noir, the drive to Barron-Wahl is worth it for outstanding views. Though many Oregon wineries can claim Mount Hood and Mount Jefferson in the distance, Barron-Wahl is one of the few that boasts the volatile Mount St. Helens as well. Drink it all in from this onetime peony farm atop Parrett Mountain. Though Pinot is the only Barron-Wahl product, there are five different local wines in a large tasting room that's reminiscent of a trendy downtown Portland eatery. With their first vintage in 2006, Barron-Wahl took a bronze at the Oregon state wine competition.

MCKINLAY VINEYARDS

503-625-2534
7120 NE Earlwood Road
Tasting Room: Thanksgiving weekend and by appointment
Fee: Complimentary
Owner/Winemaker: Matt Kinne
Wines: Pinot Noir
Cases: 1,000

Matt Kinne's great-grandad George Angus McKinlay gave sermons at the Zena church on his day of rest after tending to his hazelnuts, prunes, and cherries on the east side of the Eola Hills northwest of Salem. Three generations later, the harmonic convergence between farming and spirituality is made again in a 32-acre vineyard on Parrett

Mountain, where the family legacy has continued with Pinot Noir since 1995. Kinne and his wife, Holly, live in a modest home in the middle of their vineyard two miles from Sherwood, and he makes his wine in a cellar below the house.

J.K. CARRIERE WINES

503-554-0721
www.jkcarriere.com
995 NE Parrett Mountain Road
Tasting Room: Mar.–Oct., Fri.–Sat. 11–3, and holiday weekends
Fee: $10, refunded with three-bottle purchase
Owner/Winemaker: Jim Prosser
Wines: Chardonnay, Pinot Noir
Cases: 2,600

A sparkling new winery and tasting room coupled with new plantings of Pinot Noir are the big news at J. K. Carriere. The Prossers are now firmly entrenched on 40 acres on the southeast flanks of Parrett Mountain—quite an upgrade from the old hazelnut barn about three miles away that once served as tasting room. The focus here, on the southernmost peak in the Chehalem Mountains, is on a classic Pinot Noir, with sharp acidity and graceful tannins. Winemaker Jim Prosser is one of a select group in Oregon whose experience includes not only France but Australia and New Zealand as well.

OWEN ROE WINERY

503-678-6514
www.owenroe.com
8400 Champoeg Road NE
Tasting Room: Tues.–Sat. 1–4 and by appointment
Fee: Complimentary
Owner/Winemaker: David O'Reilly
Wines: Riesling, Chardonnay, Pinot Gris, Cabernet franc, Cabernet Sauvignon, Pinot Noir, Syrah, red and white blends
Cases: 60,000

Special Features: O'Reilly is the second (value) label

If you're yearning for a bucolic setting amid lush rows of grapes or an upscale tasting room, Owen Roe isn't the place. Located across the Willamette River, the winery is set in a more centralized location because grapes are coming in from many a vineyard, all from Oregon or Washington. That doesn't make the setting any less festive. An appointment at Owen Roe means a complimentary tour of the facility and a tasting of five to seven wines in the barrel room. Come during harvest or crush and they'll be happy to let you watch the process. The winery is named for a politically active seventeenth-century Irishman named Owen Roe O'Reilly, and the wines have achieved cult status.

ANAM CARA

503-537-9150
www.anamcaracellars.com
22222 SW Nicholas View Drive
Tasting Room: Major holiday weekends
Fee: $20, refunded with purchase
Owners: Nicholas and Sheila Nicholas
Winemaker: Aron Hess
Wines: Riesling, Gewürztraminer, rosé, Pinot Noir
Cases: 2,000
Special Features: Educational tours for small groups

Distinct Anam Cara has created a buzz, catching the attention of *Wine Spectator* and the *Wine Advocate* with ratings of 90 and above for their estate Pinot. Nick and Sheila couldn't be happier with their life in paradise, where they say they love to sit on the deck and watch the grapes grow. Enthusiasts that they are, they also enjoy teaching others how the whole thing works, and welcome tours. Their wines are in many of the wine-centric eating establishments throughout the state. It could be due in part to Nick's 25 years of history in the restaurant biz, where he says a big part of his heart still lies. "Friend of my soul" is the English translation for the winery's Celtic name.

A-Z WINEWORKS & REX HILL VINEYARDS

503-538-0666
www.rexhill.com
30835 North Highway 99W
Tasting Room: Summer, daily 10–5, winter 11–5
Fee: $10 for five wines
Owners/Winemakers: Bill and Debra Hatcher, Sam Tannahill, Cheryl Francis, Gregg Popovich
Wines: Under Rex Hill label—Pinot Gris, Chardonnay, Pinot Noir; under A–Z labels—Pinot Blanc, Pinot Gris, Chardonnay, Riesling, rosé, red blend; under Francis Tannahill label—Gewürztraminer, Pinot Noir, Grenache, Syrah, red blends, dessert wines; under William Hatcher label—Pinot Noir
Cases: 120,000
Special Features: Extensive, cultivated gardens perfect for impromptu or planned picnicking; wine-education classes; events facility

A complex family tree of new owners means A–Z/Rex Hill is now the second largest winery in Oregon, behind Eugene's King Estate. Originally purchased in 1982 by Paul Hart and Jan Jacobsen, now the Hatcher family (A–Z) and a few other investors own the name, facility, and vineyards. Rex Hill has been *Wine & Spirits* Winery of the Year more than once and led the way in pulling the Portland crowd

A–Z/Rex Hill is now the second-largest winery in Oregon.

Courtesy Rex Hill Winery

out of the city and onto to their gorgeous grounds, which have served as a gateway to Willamette Valley wine country. The tasting room at Rex Hill has many enticing areas brimming with old-world charm and about as many activity options: private tastings, group gatherings, and wine classes. Or you can just belly up to the bar and chat up the savvy pourer du jour.

AUGUST CELLARS FACILITY

503-554-6766
www.augustcellars.com
14,000 NE Quarry Road
Tasting Room: May–Oct., daily 11–5, Nov.–Apr., Fri.–Sun. 11–5
Fee: Complimentary
Owner: Clarence Shaad family
Winemaker: Jim Schaad
Wines: Chardonnay, Gewürztraminer, Riesling, Maréchal Foch, Pinot Noir
Cases: 4,000
Special Features: If you're lucky, farmstead goat cheese made just up the driveway will be out for sampling.

A stone's throw from busy OR 99W, yet worlds away from the commotion, is a working winery for August Cellars and six other small producers. In the parking area outside the new green building, a water feature gently sends a cascading stream over river rock. Green leafy plants and wispy ornamental trees commune, creating a soothing wrapper for the incubating wine inside—all hidden among the forest. You can see why these winemakers love to come to work. The Schaad family (pronounced "shod") has farmed these 42 acres on Chehalem Mountain since 1942 and currently grow English walnuts, Italian prunes, and 13 acres of Pinot Noir. The two grandsons of patriarch Clarence Shaad run the place. Jim makes the wine and Tom runs the operation and facilities. They have a nice touch with the French-American hybrid Maréchal Foch.

Once inside August Cellars, you might catch a glimpse through glass-paned doors of one of the many winemakers that craft their wares at the state-of-the-art, eco-friendly facility. On weekends the tenants pour, but not all wines made here are open for tasting. It's best to call ahead and make appointments with specific wineries.

ARTISANAL WINE CELLARS

503-537-2094
Owners: Tom and Patricia Feller
Winemaker: Tom Feller
Wines: Viognier, Pinot Blanc, Pinot Noir, Gamay Noir, Tempranillo, red blend
Cases: 1,500

According to wife Patricia, Tom Feller has been fermenting things as long as she's known him. He was a home brewer for years and decided that if he was going to live in Oregon, he should be making wine. He took classes at Chemeketa and in 2005 made the big jump. Supplemental labor comes from their two college-aged kids, whom they "force" to work for them.

BARKING FROG

503-702-5029
Owners: Ron and Cindy Helbig
Winemaker: Ron Helbig
See description under Wineries in the Carlton Area, where Barking Frog has a tasting room.

CROWLEY WINES

971-645-3547
www.crowleywines.com
Owner/Winemaker: Tyson Crowley
Wines: Chardonnay, Pinot Noir
Cases: 1,500

Grapes for Tyson Crowley's Chardonnay come from vines almost 40 years old in the coveted Maresh Vineyard. Crowley is definitely in the old-world camp for his standout Pinot Noir, and it's reasonably priced at around $30. The keyhole on the label is a replication of the one on Tyson's grandfather's cigar box. If you join the Crowley e-mail list, you can

Reusing barrels is an art form at many Oregon wineries. John Baker

find out about special events staged on the big weekends and at other times. A winery of their own is in the works.

ET FILLE

503-853-5836
Owner: Howard Mozeico
Winemakers: Howard and Jessica Mozeico
Wines: Viognier, Pinot Noir, rosé
Cases: 2,500
Special Features: Private tastings in their barrel room by appointment

We found a few new favorites at the 2009 Indie Festival. Our first choice was Howard and daughter Jessica's beguiling and elegant Pinot Noir. Second and third were their Rosé of Pinot and their Viognier done in stainless without residual sugar, which we tasted in their cubicle at August Cellars. Howard, a self-taught amateur turned pro, and Jessica are both control freaks and close buddies—a good thing since they both have a hand in the winery work. As long as she listens to him, Howard says, "it works great." They do have to alternate music, as she listens to rock and he likes classical. They must be in tune, because their wines sing. *Et fille* is French for "and daughter."

LAURA VOLKMAN

503-806-4047
www.volkmanvineyards.com
Fee: $10, waived with case purchase
Owner/Winemaker: Laura Volkman
Wines: Chardonnay, Pinot Noir
Cases: 300

Volkman's watercolor label of the lady in red viewing her vineyard bears a distinct likeness to Laura. Owner, grower, and winemaker, she does it all with help from her husband, kids, friends, and dog named Bella. The Bella

Chardonnay, with its light oak treatment, is simply divine and worth the search. Her Pinots are winning high praise (91 from *Wine Spectator*) and are more old-world in style.

TOLUCA LANE

971-241-7728
www.tolucalane.com
Owners/Winemakers: Geoffrey and Lane Crowther
Wines: Pinot Noir
Cases: 400

This vineyard on Three Trees Lane outside of Amity was cleared of scrub trees and blackberry thickets and lovingly planted in Pinot clones by the hands of Geoffrey and partner Lane. Both had former careers, he as a lawyer, she as a Cordon Bleu–trained chef who managed the testing kitchen for *Bon Appetit.* But both wanted to live their dream. Low yields from the estate vineyard, minimalist techniques, and old-world style combine to define their style. The "Oregundian" Pinot goes for around $30. Buy it by the case, especially the Three Trees Lane Pinot, which is made only when the vintage is just right.

CHEHALEM WINES

503-538-4700
www.chehalemwines.com
106 South Center Street
Tasting Room: Daily 11–5 most of the year
Tasting fee: $5–$10 per flight
Owners: Harry Peterson-Nedry, Bill and Cathy Stoller
Winemaker: Harry Peterson-Nedry
Wines: Pinot Blanc, Pinot Gris, Chardonnay, Riesling, Pinot Noir, Cerise, Grüner Veltliner, red blend
Cases: 20,000
Special Features: Wine-bar tasting room with large art and a few tables

Harry Peterson-Nedry's name and finger-prints are all over Oregon wine history. He's politically active in the industry and wrote the petition that defined the tiny Ribbon Ridge AVA. Experimental in spirit, he was one of the first to go "no oak" with his INOX Chardonnay. Harry defines his style as a partnership with nature and technology. His wines command a high price and earn it. His Pinots often score above 90 with *Spectator,* and for that matter, so do his whites. Chehalem's tasting room is new (2008) and was opened to reach a broader audience; it also serves as anchor for Newberg as a wine destination.

FOX FARM VINEYARDS & WINE BAR

503-538-8466
www.foxfarmvineyards.com
602 East First Street
Tasting Room: Summer, Mon.–Thurs. 12–8, Fri.–Sat. 12–10, check for winter hours
Fee: $7 for six wines
Owners: Thomas Ratcliff and David Fish
Winemaker: Joe Dobbes, Jr.
Wines: Pinot Gris, Pinot Noir, Syrah
Cases: 700
Special Features: Other boutique wines represented; flights change weekly; private tastings or wine dinners for up to 20 in back room

Two serious oenophiles met at Pinot Camp and said, "Let's grow grapes and make wine." Enter David's wife, Desiree, the hospitality director, and the blend is complete. Taste their small-production wines or purchase obscure and rare vintages of other wines that can also be tasted for a fee. Fox Farm is a Dundee winery, but enjoys the best of both worlds with ease of accessibility in this downtown location.

HIP CHICKS DO WINE

503-234-554-5800
www.hipchicksdowine.com
602B East First Street

Tasting Room: Summer, daily 12–7, check for winter hours
Fee: $7 for six wines, including logo glass
Special Features: This is a second tasting room for Hip Chicks' Portland winery (see Wineries in the Portland Area), which prides itself on being a snob-free zone

BISHOP CREEK CELLARS

503-487-6934
www.bishopcreekcellars.com
614 East First Street
Tasting Room: Wed.–Sun. 1–7, extended hours in summer
Fee: $8–10
Owners: Reuel Fish and shareholders
Winemaker: Jeremy Saville
Wines: Pinot Gris, Pinot Noir, red blends
Cases: 1,000
Special Features: Participates in First Friday receptions for local artists, 5–9; Yappy Hour for dogs and owners last Wed. of the month, 5–9

Reuel Fish, principle shareholder behind Bishop Creek, is so passionate about wine that he became a certified sommelier just for fun. Bishop Creek's vineyards, 15 acres of primo soils in the Yamhill Carlton AVA, were planted in 1998, providing some precious old-vine fruit for their bottlings. About half of their grapes are sold to big names in the state. The Bishop Creek brand stays focused on Pinot Gris and Pinot Noir—what they grow and know best. The current winemaker has been vineyard manager for over nine years and knows his vines. The inviting tasting room maintains the integrity of old-town Newberg with its brick-wall structure, exposed piping, and original hardwood floors. It also embraces the community by sponsoring and displaying local art. When we visited, painted barrel tops and stave furniture provided whimsical character and color.

You can sample the flavors of three wineries at the Dark Horse Tasting Room. Courtesy Dark Horse Tasting Room

DARK HORSE TASTING ROOM

503-538-2427
1505 Portland Road (OR 99W)
Tasting Room: Summer, daily 11–5, check
for winter hours
Fee: $10, refunded with purchase
Special Features: An array of 10 to 12 open
bottles from three producers

Though the blue highway sign says MEDICI
VINEYARDS TASTING ROOM, it's really the Dark
Horse Tasting Room, an outlet bar of sorts
for Medici, Sineann, and Ferraro Cellars.
Wines for tasting are from all three producers, usually including Sauvignon Blanc,
Pinot Gris, Riesling, Pinot Noir, Cabernet
Sauvignon, Merlot, Zinfandel, and many
more. Medici and Sineann wines are made
by Peter Rosback, with Sineann being
Rosback's own baby. Dick Ferraro also
crafts his line at the Medici facility. The
Dark Horse sports a European feel with
warm colors, a few tables, and the obligatory long, dark wooden bar situated on a
laurel wood floor, which was taken from
Medici's property.

MEDICI VINEYARDS

503-538-9668
28005 NE Bell Road
Owners: Hal and Dotty Medici
Winemaker: Peter Rosback
Wines: Pinot Noir
Cases: 1,600
Special Features: Vintage pinots

Medici is known for old-vine Pinot
(planted in 1976) and vintage Pinots that
have 3-4 years of bottle aging before
release. They open at the vineyard for
big holiday weekends and throw a great
party.

SINEANN CELLARS

503-341-2698
www.sineann.com
Owner/Winemaker: Peter Rosback
Wines: Pinot Gris, Riesling,

Gewürztraminer, Pinot Noir, Zinfandel, Cabernet Sauvignon, Merlot, red blends, ice wine, port-style wine
Cases: 10,000

Join the choir and sing the praises of Rosback's wines. He creates and crafts for so many other wineries, but these are his pride and joy. His dessert wines are unforgettable. The Precious has residual sugar reaching the 50-percent mark and begs for strong cheese, a cozy fire, and/or a sublime sunset. Some of Sineann's wines ("shu-*nay*-un") are small-production and extremely popular, so stock up when you can.

FERRARO CELLARS

503-758-0557
www.ferrarocellar.com
Owners: Dick and Mary Ferraro
Winemaker: Dick Ferraro
Wines: Cabernet Sauvignon, Merlot, Zinfandel, red blend
Cases: 400
Special Features: Reasonably priced wines (low $20s)

Dick grew up in an Italian immigrant family in Walla Walla. In the '40s and '50s, Dick's grandfather was a broker of sorts for the area habitants wanting to make their own wine (mostly Zinfandel and Moscato). He put together orders for California grapes, and Dick remembers unloading them from the railcars and storing them in the root cellar along with the sausage, cured meats, breads, and pastries made by his grandmother. All that grape and wine imprinting lit a spark for Dick and his own family; they started Ferraro Cellars in 2002. Ferraro's wines are sourced from the Columbia Valley, where he and his family reside. Try the Mista Rosso Cab/Merlot blend.

ROCO WINERY

503-538-7625
www.rocowines.com
13260 NE Red Hills Drive
Tasting Room: Memorial Day and Thanksgiving weekends, and by appointment
Fee: Varies
Owners: Rollin and Corby Soles
Winemaker: Rollin Soles
Wines: Chardonnay, Pinot Noir
Cases: 1,000
Special Features: Wine-related merchandise

Rollin Soles has a sense of humor, a sense of history, and a better sense of wine. Soles and his wife, Corby, who took the first two letters of both their names ("Ro" and "Co") to christen their winery, call their vineyard Wits' End. As for history, the logo is an artist's rendition of a petroglyph rescued from the Columbia River before The Dalles Dam was constructed. Soles is a part of history as well: He was instrumental in the startup and success of Argyle Winery. The Soles opened a 10,000-square-foot winery in the Dundee Hills in 2009, just in time for Thanksgiving weekend.

ANDERSON FAMILY VINEYARDS

503-554-5541
20120 NE Herring Lane
Tasting Room: Memorial and Thanksgiving weekends, and by appointment
Fee: Varies
Owners: Cliff and Allison Anderson
Winemaker: Cliff Anderson
Wines: Pinot Gris, Chardonnay, Pinot Noir
Cases: 1,250
Special Features: Personalized tours

There are views, and then there are *views*. At Anderson Family vineyards and winery, you'll literally feel on top of the world, with an unobstructed 360-degree panorama of the Dundee Hills. A circular driveway surrounds a stately Douglas fir at the top, where the winery and tasting room are in a three-bay garage. Once a cow pasture on an ancient rockslide, the hill now provides "Steep slopes, deep roots and intense flavors." The Anderson niche is Pinot Noir and a Dijon Chardonnay made half in oak and half in stainless steel. Many of the organically farmed grapes are sold to a Who's Who list of neighbors. Cliff Anderson, who started fermenting juices under his bed when he was 16, loves to show people around.

PRIVÉ VINEYARD

503-554-0464
www.privevineyard.com
28155 NE Bell Road
Tasting Room: Private invitation only
Owners: Mark and Tina Hammond
Winemaker: Tina Hammond
Wines: Pinot Noir, Malbec, Cabernet Franc, red blends
Cases: 750
Special Features: If you're privy, you may find their Oregon Pinot at select wine shops and restaurants; sign up for their newsletter for locations

What do you do when demand outweighs supply? Start a customer list and limit purchases to one case per customer. Don't fret: If you jump on Privé's Web site, join the mailing list, and buy the value Pinot or the Bordeaux blend, the following year you have a chance at the estate premium Pinot (only 250 cases made). You'll also be included in invitation-only events hosted throughout the year. The Hammonds have created a "private winery" mystique and most of their vintages are sold before bottling. Tina has an enology degree from the Northwest Viticulture Center and has been crafting since 2001. Mark handles the vineyard.

NATALIE'S ESTATE WINERY

503-807-5008
www.nataliesestatewinery.com
16825 NE Chehalem Drive
Tasting Room: Memorial Day, Labor Day, and Thanksgiving weekends, and by appointment
Fee: $10
Owners: Boyd and Cassandra Teegarden
Winemaker: Boyd Teegarden
Wines: Chardonnay, Viognier, Pinot Noir, Syrah, Merlot, Cabernet Sauvignon, Sangiovese, Zinfandel, Meritage, red blend
Cases: 2,500

For Montanans, Natalie's Estate resonates because their Rock Horse Chardonnay is one of the best available in Big Sky country. The tasting room at Natalie's Estate feels like a tree-house chalet in a vine-maple and Douglas-fir grove. With its antler chandelier and river-rock fireplace, it's more of a country retreat. The Teegardens opened their winery in 1999, but they weren't novices. Boyd worked for Ernest & Julio Gallo's wholesaler in the Portland area. The winery is named for the Teegardens' daughter, who was a year old when they bought their land on the eastern end of the Chehalem Mountains.

VIDON VINEYARD

503-538-4092
www.vidonvineyard.com
17425 NE Hillside Drive
Tasting Room: Sat.–Sun. 12–5 and by appointment
Fee: $10
Owners: Don and Vicki Hagee
Winemaker: Don Hagee
Wines: Chardonnay, Pinot Gris, Pinot Noir
Cases: 1,000
Special Features: Open houses on major holiday weekends are events, accompanied by music and specialty local foods like handmade chocolates made with their Pinot Noir.

Vidon is abuzz with activity on Memorial Day weekend. John Baker

Vicky and Don put their heads and names together to form the winery at Vidon ("vee-*don*"). Don is a one-man show doing the wine thing, including clearing the property of debris, planting his sustainable vineyard on Chehalem Mountain, and making wine in his energy-efficient facility. He likes to say he picked a lot of rocks and dirt from under his toenails. Vicki has an outside job to support his expensive hobby. They're doing something right, as validated by the long lines to taste his Pinot Noir at the 2009 Indie Festival. Their 20-acre vineyard and winery exude something special and is one of those places that say "stay a while." Minimal intervention, indigenous fermentation, and few or no additions mark Vidon's style. It all works very well.

DE LANCELLOTTI FAMILY VINEYARDS

503-554-6802
www.delancellottifamilyvineyards.com

18405 NE Calkins Lane
Tasting Room: Weekend before Thanksgiving, and by appointment
Fee: $10
Owners: Paul and Kendall de Lancellotti
Winemaker: Paul de Lancellotti
Wines: Pinot Noir
Cases: 400
Special Features: The de Lancellotis are also co-owners of the Inn at Red Hills, a 20-room boutique hotel that includes Farm to Fork Restaurant and Press Wine Bar

Kendall comes with a wine pedigree: she is a Bergström, sister to winemaker Josh. In fact, the de Lancellottis are part owners of the Bergström family winery next door, and Josh Bergström has helped Paul make some of de Lancellotti's Pinot Noir. The de Lancellottis' young and biodynamic vineyard (2001), as well as label, is separate. Small-production estate Pinot is the only wine for the family—and with a 92 from *Wine Advocate,* they know how to produce.

BERGSTRÖM WINERY

503-554-0468 or 503-554-0463
www.bergstromwines.com
18215 NE Calkins Lane
Tasting Room: Daily 10–4
Fee: $20
Owner: Bergström family
Winemaker: Josh Bergström
Wines: Chardonnay, Gewürztrzminer, Riesling, Pinot Noir
Cases: 10,000
Special Features: Outdoor seating

Bergström's wines are nationally and even internationally acclaimed—a remarkable feat given that the family entered the business almost by chance. Family patriarch

John Bergström grew up on a small farm in Sweden, but after arriving in Oregon as a teenager he studied to become a surgeon in Portland. For retirement he bought 15 acres on the flanks of the Chehalem Mountains, and didn't think much about grapes until some area winemakers, recognizing the potential of the property, pitched the idea. The rest, as they say, is history. Son Josh developed an affinity for wine, studied in France, and has returned to established himself as one of the elite Pinot producers.

LACHINI VINEYARDS

503-864-4553
www.lachinivineyards.com
18225 Calkins Lane
Tasting Room: By appointment only
Fee: $20, refunded with purchase

Lachini began producing single-vineyard Pinot Noir in 2001. John Baker

Owners: Marianne and Ron Lachini
Winemaker: Laurant Montalieu
Wines: Pinot Gris, Cabernet Sauvignon,
Pinot Noir, dessert wine
Cases: 4,500
Special Features: Transitioning to organic
and biodynamic farming

What began with a modest Pinot Noir harvest on 45 acres in 2001 has gradually evolved into a full-bore operation producing highly regarded and priced wines. The Lachinis were set to break ground on a new winery in 2009. With his Italian family heritage, Ron is big on wines—and the media are big on Lachini wines, which have scored 90 and higher from both *Wine Spectator* and *Wine Enthusiast*. Lachini also scores high on the eco-meter: They are LIVE and Salmon-Safe certified.

ARBORBROOK VINEYARDS
503-538-0959
www.arberbrookwines.com
17770 NE Calkins Lane
Tasting Room: Mon. and Thurs.–Fri., 11–4,
Sat.–Sun. 11–5, and by appointment
Fee: $10, refunded with purchase
Owners: Dave and Mary Hansen
Winemaker: Laurent Montalieu
Wines: Pinot Gris, Pinot Noir
Cases: 2,200
Special Features: Tours available

Ten acres of producing vineyards surround Dave and Mary's life, and Mary's Arabian horses. While Mary tended her horses, the couple dreamed of growing and making wine. The tasting room, once the drying room for the hazelnuts and walnuts grown here, is a tastefully converted 1940s barn. Arborbrook is a family affair—young daughter Sydney and Dave's son Brendan get their hands dirty, too. Memorial Day and Thanksgiving weekends have the added "wow" factor of being catered by Red Hills Provincial of Dundee.

ADELSHEIM VINEYARD
503-538-3652
www.adelsheim.com
16800 NE Calkins Lane
Tasting Room: Wed.–Sun. 11–4
Fee: $15
Owners: David and Ginny Adelsheim and
Jack and Lynn Loacker
Winemaker: Dave Paige
Wines: Chardonnay, Pinot Blanc, Pinot
Gris, Auxerrois, Pinot Noir, Syrah, rosé
Cases: 45,000
Special Features: Tours led by bright and informative thirtysomethings; tasting room is an experience for novices and the experienced alike

Ginny and David Adelsheim were forerunners in the "new wine country," now the established and touted Chehalem Mountain AVA, when they planted their 15-acre vineyard in 1972. A few vines and wines later, the name still resonates with pedigree and history. New in 2009 is the carefully designed castle-like winery and tasting room. Even though the somewhat cold exterior seems foreboding, the congenial and professional staff makes you feel comfortable. During a Memorial Day weekend tour, we found the setup to be highly organized, educational, and, of course, the wines primo. Buy their small-lot Pinots and Auxerrois (an Alsatian white) at the tasting room; chances are they won't be found elsewhere.

AYRES VINEYARD
503-538-7450
www.ayresvineyard.com
17971 NE Lewis Rogers Lane
Tasting Room: Memorial Day and
Thanksgiving weekends, and by appointment
Fee: $10, refunded with purchase
Owners: Don and Carol McClure and Brad
and Kathleen McElroy
Winemaker: Brad McElroy

Adelsheim has an opulent new winery and tasting room near Newberg. John Baker

Wines: Pinot Blanc, Pinot Noir
Cases: 1,800

McElroy, who learned under Veronique Drouhin, lives on the property along with fellow owners Don and Carol McClure, the designated greeters. The winery is under the main house, 12 feet below the ground. Ayres practices sustainable agriculture, giving the wines, as McElroy puts it, "a soul."

PENNER-ASH WINE CELLARS

503-554-5545
www.pennerash.com
15771 NE Ribbon Ridge Road
Tasting Room: Wed.–Sun. 11–5 and by appointment
Fee: $5–15
Owners: Ron and Lynn Penner-Ash
Winemaker: Lynn Penner-Ash
Wines: Viognier, Riesling, rosé, Pinot Noir, Syrah, red blend

Cases: 9,500
Special Features: Beautiful grounds with picnic area

Lynn Penner-Ash was part of an early elite group of women winemakers in Oregon, getting her start as winemaker at Rex Hill in the late 1980s. In 2000, she started her own label. Their winery sits atop a hill overlooking Newberg, with volcanic Mount Hood and Mount Jefferson as snowcapped backdrops. The tasting room, built in 2005 with locally sourced materials, was featured in the September 2009 issue of *Sunset* as a place to visit for views and wine. The elegant Willamette Valley Pinot Noir is their hottest seller.

PATRICIA GREEN CELLARS

503-554-0821
www.patriciagreencellars.com
15225 NE North Valley Road

Tasting Room: By appointment only
Fee: $20, partially refunded with purchase
Owner/Winemaker Jim and Patty Green
Wines: Sauvignon Blanc, Pinot Noir
Cases: 11,000
Special Features: An educational tour usually comes with your tasting.

Patricia Green is a firm believer in, and early advocate of, single-vineyard Pinots. Her vineyard-designate Pinot Noirs are highly coveted, and she has a devoted following for her Sauvignon Blanc (supplies are limited). For all their status, the Greens are definitely mom and pop. They're known for their wine, not their sign—two wine barrels and a small sandwich board at the mailbox beckon visitors to the winery and 12-acre vineyard. The Greens bought an existing winery and all the rusting equipment that came with it. When we were there, the tasting-room setup featured two wine barrels and a Costco folding table.

Clearly they are more focused on substance than style: Their Pinots, ranging from barnyardy and mushroomy to fruity, are stored and spend considerable time in world-class Cadus oak barrels.

BEAUX FRÈRES

503-537-1137
www.beauxfreres.com
15155 NE North Valley Road
Tasting Room: Memorial Day, weekend before Thanksgiving (call to confirm), and by appointment
Fee: $15
Owners: Michael Etzel, Robert Parker Jr., and Robert Roy
Winemaker: Michael Etzel
Wines: Pinot Noir
Cases: 4,500
Special Features: Appointment includes a personal tour followed by a tasting.

There's no architecture or fluffy pillows

Beaux Frères' simple tasting room belies its reputation. Jeff Welsch here—just substantial Pinot Noir. The tasting setup is simple and unpretentious in a corner of the winery, belying the fame and origins of Beaux Frères. Michael Etzel convinced his brother-in-law, Robert Parker Jr. (creator of the *Wine Advocate*), to go in on a former pig and dairy farm in prime Pinot country in 1986. Michael and family planted the vines, worked in the industry, and eventually, with the addition of partner Roby Roy, built the winery. The simple colored-pencil drawing of vineyard rows on the label also sends a message: "We're just a small and goofy winery." Hardly! Beaux Frères strives for old-world style, using high concentrations of natural CO_2 instead of sulfur to preserve the wines, so be sure to decant and aerate to allow the wine to fully open. For the record, Parker does not review Beaux Frères wines in his publication.

WHISTLING RIDGE VINEYARDS
503-554-8991
www.whistlingridgevineyards.com
14551 NE North Valley Road
Tasting Room: Apr.–Nov., Sat.–Sun. 11–4, and by appointment
Fee: $5 for four wines
Owners: Richard Alvord and Patricia L. Gustafson
Winemaker: Marcus Goodfellow
Wines: Pinot Gris, Pinot Noir
Cases: 250

Whistling Ridge is one of the tiniest producers in the tiniest AVA. Alvord and Gustafson cultivated their 15 acres in 1990 after moving from Lake Oswego. For a small vineyard they grow many varietals, starting with Oregon mainstays Chardonnay, Pinot Noir, and Pinot Gris. In addition, and "for experimentation and fun," Gustafson says, they also grow Gewürztraminer, Riesling, Muscat, Pinot Blanc, and a unique grape called Schönburger, a product of Germany and a cousin of the Pinot Noir.

RR (RIBBON RIDGE)
503-706-9277
www.ribbonridgewinery.com
21080 NE Ribbon Ridge Road
Tasting Room: at Chehalem
Owner: Harry Peterson-Nedry
Winemakers: Harry Peterson-Nedry and Wynne Peterson-Nedry
Wines: Pinot Noir
Cases: 600

Harry started his wine career and reputation on Ribbon Ridge, which was recently named an AVA with his help. He has 164 acres of vineyards, and from the oldest vines (planted in 1980) comes superstar Pinot. In Harry's own words, it's more masculine than the Chehalem Pinot Noir he and his daughter, Wynne, also make. It is poured only by request at the Chehalem tasting room. The name was changed to RR out of respect for the Ribbon Ridge AVA designation, and to try to clear up any confusion. RR, Chehalem, and Stoller are sister wineries. Chehalem is the mothership and owned equally by Peterson-Nedry and the Stollers. Each also has a separate winery: Harry's is RR, and Bill and Cathy have Stoller.

STYRING VINEYARDS
503-866-6741
www.styringvineyards.com
19960 NE Ribbon Ridge Road
Tasting Room: Memorial Day and Thanksgiving weekends, and by appointment in summer
Fee: $5
Owners: Kelly and Steve Styring
Winemaker: Steve Styring
Wines: Chardonnay, Riesling, Pinot Gris, Chardonnay, Pinot Noir, port-style and dessert wines
Cases: 1,000
Special Features: Tasting room in Carlton

The Styrings make organic wines they love to drink from varietals that "love it here as much as we do." They call Pinot their passion, Riesling their whimsy, and dessert wines their bliss. Styring has 40 acres on Ribbon Ridge, on which 10½ acres are in cultivation.

REDMAN VINEYARD & WINERY

503-554-1290
www.redmanwines.com
18975 NE Ribbon Ridge Road
Tasting Room: Memorial Day, Labor Day, and Thanksgiving weekends, and by appointment
Fee: $10
Owner: Cathy Redman
Winemaker: TBA
Wines: Chardonnay, Barbera, Pinot Noir, Tempranillo, red blend
Cases: 750
Special Features: Winery tours

Bill and Cathy Redman found their 30-acre patch of paradise on Ribbon Ridge in 2004, harvested a final batch of hazelnuts, tore out the orchard, and planted their first vineyard—a dream a quarter-century in the making. Then tragedy struck the family when Bill died in March 2009 after battling cancer for six months. As is customary, the close-knit family of wine folks in the area pitched in to ensure that harvest, crush, and production would go on as scheduled. In Redman's honor, take home a bottle of Bill's Blend, the Pinot Noir/Barbera mix he created for special meals at home. Bill's Blend is $50 and only 100 cases were to be produced.

TRISAETUM WINERY

503-538-9898
www.trisaetum.com
18401 Ribbon Ridge Road
Tasting Room: Thurs.–Sun. 11–4 and by appointment
Fee: $10–15, refunded with purchase
Owners: James and Andrea Frey
Winemakers: James Frey and Greg McClellan

Wines: Riesling, Pinot Noir
Cases: 4,000
Special Features: Winery tours, art gallery, patio

Were it not for a freak summer snowstorm, James and Andrea Frey might be rangers in Yosemite National Park or naturalists in Arizona. Instead, forced into Plan B on their honeymoon, they drove right past snowed-in Yosemite and ended up in Napa Valley. You can guess the rest of the story. In 2005, they found their perfect parcel on Ribbon Ridge, where they planted six Pinot Noir clones along with two Riesling clones. Since then, they have been producing reputable selections of both, with a big assist from fellow winemaker Josh Bergström. While at Trisaetum, you'll want to wander amid the 1,500 square feet of photos and oil paintings by winemaker James Frey. The winery's name? The Freys' children are Tristan and Tatum.

BRICK HOUSE VINEYARDS

503-538-5136
www.brickhousewines.com
18200 Lewis Rogers Lane
Tasting Room: Memorial Day and Thanksgiving weekends, and Fri.–Sat. by appointment in summer
Fee: $10, refunded with purchase
Owners: Doug Tunnell and Melissa Mills
Winemaker: Doug Tunnell
Wines: Chardonnay, Gamay Noir, Pinot Noir
Cases: 8,000
Special Features: Certified organic and biodynamic.

Set amid peaceful hazelnut orchards on Ribbon Ridge, Brick House couldn't be more starkly juxtaposed with owner Doug Tunnell's previous life as a Middle East war correspondent for CBS Radio. The Oregon native has found his calling in the vineyard, where he's one of the few in the state to grow Gamay Noir—a grape he grew fond of during a reporting stint in France. Gamay Noir is best known today as the varietal from Beaujolais, and his is widely considered the best of its kind in Oregon.

ARAMENTA CELLARS
503-538-7230
www.aramentacellars.com
17979 NE Lewis Rogers Lane
Tasting Room: Daily 10:30–5
Fee: $10 for 5 wines, refunded with six-bottle purchase
Owners: Ed and Darlene Looney
Winemaker: Ed Looney
Wines: Chardonnay, Pinot Noir, red blend
Cases: 1,200
Special Features: Guest studio for one or two people on the property ($190/night), overlooking pond and vineyard

The moniker might sound a bit stuffy, but in fact Aramenta—named for Darlene's aunt—is as homespun as it gets on Ribbon Ridge. Ed Looney was once a tool-and-die maker, so he knows how to fix things in the vineyard. Aside from some memorable wines, Aramenta also offers a pastoral setting and atmosphere that'll lure you in for a spell. If you buy enough wine, or the Looneys like you enough, they might invite you to cast a fly to the trout lazing in their picturesque pond.

UTOPIA WINES
503-298-7841
www.utopiawine.com
17445 NE Ribbon Ridge Road
Tasting Room: Sat.–Sun. 10–5 and by appointment
Fee: $5, applied to purchase
Owner/Winemaker: Daniel Warnshuis
Wines: Pinot Noir
Cases: 550
Special Features: Tasting room is at the vineyard.

Truly dedicated to the site, Daniel Warnshuis ("warn-sice," rhymes with *nice*)

firmly believes wine begins and ends in the vineyard. His 17 acres of LIVE-certified acres on Ribbon Ridge have 11 different clones of Pinot planted for maximum diversity—a major factor in creating complexity in his finished wine. Ancient technique, no cutting of corners, and the use of only fruit from his vines complete the utopian package. To taste is to realize that he knows what he's doing. Warnshuis happily gives tours so he can talk about a favorite subject: his philosophy on Pinot Noir.

SHEA WINE CELLARS
503-241-6527
www.sheawinecellars.com
12321 NE Highway 240
Tasting Room: Memorial Day and Thanksgiving weekends, and by appointment in summer
Fee: $10
Owners: Dick and Deirdre Shea
Winemaker: Drew Voit
Wines: Chardonnay, Pinot Noir
Cases: 5,000
Special Features: Wines are self-distributed in 20 states

Even before Dick and Deirdre Shea began making their own high-end Pinot Noir and Chardonnay, the Sheas' grapes were highly coveted by Oregon vintners. The 200-acre vineyard has provided big-name wineries with extraordinary fruit since the late 1980s, and those in the know still genuflect at the vineyard gates and mention the name at the drop of a cork. Some of Oregon's most storied producers, among them Ken Wright and Josh Bergström, have put "Shea" on their labels. In the mid-1990s, Shea Vineyards evolved into Shea Wine Cellars because, as Dick Shea puts it, "We decided to create our own expression." Their outstanding Chardonnay is a Dijon clone; only a few hundred cases are produced annually.

Lodging in the Newberg Area

THE ALLISON INN & SPA
Owners: Ken and Joan Austin
503-554-2525
www.theallison.com
2525 Allison Lane
Rates: $295–1,100
Special Features: Fireplace, balcony with
view, and concierge service with all rooms;
restaurant, bar, and in-room dining;
indoor pool and spa pools; ADA and hear-
ing-impaired rooms; pet-friendly; wed-
ding/event facility

Is Oregon Wine Country ready for this?
Winemakers will emphatically say, "Yes!"
Residents of this once-sleepy town are
watching with a more cautious eye. The
Allison is a world-class destination resort
with 85 luxurious guest rooms, including
20 astounding suites. It is poised to trans-
form little ol' Newberg, a town few tourists
have pointed to on a map and said, "That's
where I want to go!" To say that the Allison
has luxurious accommodations with
supreme guest services is yet an under-
statement. Think Four Seasons on steroids.
Joan and Ken Austin, owners of a successful
dental equipment business, are well known
for their philanthropy in the Newberg community. There's even an elementary school
named for Joan. The Austins' hope is that
the Allison will not only draw tourists from
around the world—all able and willing to
drop some dollars into the community—but
that it will also make a small dent in
Oregon's burgeoning unemployment rate.
More than 1,000 hopefuls showed up for
160 job openings at the Allison in 2009.

AVELLAN INN
Owner: Patt Gheith
503-537-9161
www.avellaninn.com
16900 NE Highway 240
Rates: $125–155

Special Features: "Breakfast, Bed and
Biscuit" program for canine travel compan-
ions; a lethal chocolate mousse

Since she lives amid an Oregon nirvana of
13 acres of berries and orchard, it's no surprise that the results of foraging forays
show up in many of the five-course breakfasts prepared and served by new owner
Patt Gheith. Sink your teeth into homemade granola and seasonal fruit crepes
topped with cinnamon whipped cream.
Under the always-room-for-dessert philosophy, you won't be able to resist the
frozen granita concoctions of blackberry
Riesling, blueberry Merlot, and raspberry
Beaujolais. Patt and Scully (her Rhodesian
Ridgeback) have run the inn since 2007 and
are in the process of creating a modern
converted-barn decor they can call their
own. Children and dogs are welcome. In
addition to the two rooms Avellan currently
has, a rental cottage is in the works.

CHEHALEM RIDGE B&B
503-538-3474
www.chehalemridge.com
28700 NE Mountain Top Road
Rates: $120–170
Special Features: Three rooms have private
balconies overlooking the valley

Literally perched on a hill overlooking the
valley and vineyards, Chehalem Ridge
reminds us of an ornate birdhouse. That
could be intentional, because Kristin and
Curt Fintel are bird lovers. Four contemporary rooms, all with private baths, provide a
sense of peace and serenity. The views of
the Willamette Valley and Coast Range are
terrific, and they're offered at no charge
along with a full gourmet breakfast.

THE DREAMGIVER'S INN
Owners: Linda Kesler and Kristen Hardy
503-625-1476
www.dreamgiversinn.com
7150 NE Earlwood Road

Rates: $179–199
Special Features: Cushy bathrobes, cushioned window seats for reading, breakfast served on the deck, coffee and tea throughout the day

Complete your vision quest for the perfect Pinot at this tastefully appointed inn. The red-and-white colonial-style home boasts four Pottery Barn–style rooms named Trust, Grace, Courage, and Faith. Kesler and Hardy became business partners over a shared dream to present hospitality in a pampered way. They do it well, with heart and added touches such as bottled water and snacks, dinner reservations, and wine touring suggestions. They also have the advantage of proximity to a new winery (Terra Vina) one mile away.

LIONS GATE INN
Owner: Loni Parrish
503-476-2211
www.distinctivedestination.net
401 North Howard Street
Rates: $150–200
Special Features: Part of a three-unit group in wine country called Distinctive Destinations

Lions Gate is a meticulously renovated 1911 Craftsman home with four bedroom suites, within walking distance of Newberg's only highly recommended fine-dining restaurant. A careful combination of earth-friendly additions (green mattresses, solar panels, tank-less hot water) and restored original works (fir floors, cabinets, doors, trim) make for dramatic and distinct environs. The four suites are named for the seasons, and the colors match accordingly. Owner Loni Parrish is an interesting story in that she feels a deep connection to her community and the "mature structures" that comprise her town. She has made it a personal mission to rejuvenate and stimulate her local economy. Lion's Gate and two other vacation rentals are the beginnings of her small, eco-friendly, and employee-friendly empire, Distinctive Destinations.

SPRINGBROOK HAZELNUT FARM
Owners: Charles and Ellen McClure
503-538-4606 or 800-793-8528
www.nutfarm.com
30295 North Highway 99W
Rates: $225
Special Features: No TV or phone, heirloom rose garden, swimming pool, tennis court

Sometimes you feel like a nut, sometimes you feel like you're on the nut farm. The nut in this instance is the famed Oregon hazelnut, and you will find accommodations among the nuts to be most inviting, peaceful, and historic. All the buildings on the 70-acre grounds are listed historic landmarks. Accommodations are in the former carriage house and the original farm cottage. All are restored to maintain some of their original persona. Breakfast is served in the main house, which is filled with family antiques, Turkish rugs, a grand piano, and a contemporary collection of Oregon art.

UNIVERSITY HOUSE OF NEWBERG
Owners: Leigh and David Wellikoff
503-538-8438
www.universityhousenewberg.com
401 North Meridian Street
Rates: $150–250
Special Features: Hot tub, airport shuttle (PDX) by reservation

Ever dream of that picture-perfect two-story house with a white picket fence? The University House is it, and you're free to wander within most of the 2,100 square feet of restored historic home. Guests have the three-bedroom, two-bath house to themselves, including a fully equipped kitchen in case you have a hankering to whip up breakfast or a late-night snack. A two-night minimum on weekends and holidays is required.

VINEROOST

503-625-2534
www.vineroost.com
6950 NE Earlwood Road
Owners: Holly and Matt Kinne
Rates: $150–200 per night for entire house
Credit Cards: Yes
Special Features: McKinlay Estate Winery
next door; wine library

Situated among 12 acres of McKinlay
Vineyards Pinot Noir in the Chehalem AVA,
this wine-country charmer is a welcome
respite that can be rented by the day, week,
or month—about how long it could take to
tour every winery in the Willamette Valley.
With three bedrooms, the home can sleep
up to eight people and features many
amenities, including a large outdoor living
space. Children and pre-approved pets are
welcome. An extensive vegetable garden
and Nubian and La Manchia goats grace the
grounds.

Dining in the Newberg Area

For all the lodging options in the Newberg area, it is remarkably devoid of good eateries,
which is a fairly reliable indicator of a town doing some searching for a soul or purpose.
Most people (even tasting-room staffs) opt to bring their own lunch or head to Dundee.
There is one bright spot on the horizon: a long-standing deli and coffee house
(Underground Café) with new owners and a new ambition to tie into the wine country sur-
rounding them.

THE PAINTED LADY

503-538-3850
www.thepaintedladyrestaurant.com
210 South College Street
Open: Wed.–Sun. 5–10
Price: Expensive ($60 four courses, $100
with wine pairing)
Credit Cards: Yes
Special Features: Victorian house lovingly
and vibrantly restored by the owners

The husband-and-wife team of Allen Routt
and Jessica Bagley combine their culinary
training, world travels, and experience to
bring you a memorable dining encounter.
Classic appetizers, salads, entrées, and
desserts have a contemporary flair and uti-
lize Oregon's bounty of seafood, local
meats, produce, and fruit. They have a *Wine
Spectator* Award–winning wine list that
blends Oregon offerings with many familiar
California and imported labels. Wines by
the glass range from $9 to $15, and there
are usually 20 or more Oregon Pinots by the
bottle for $47–$160. The restaurant's name
refers to the movement—begun in San
Francisco—that requires exterior paint of
three or more contrasting colors on
Victorian or Edwardian homes to make the
most of frills and flourishes.

UNDERGROUND CAFÉ COFFEEHOUSE

503-554-1843
www.undergroundcafeandcoffeehouse.com
1002 Springbrook Drive (Safeway Shopping
Center)
Owners: Martin and Janet Bleck
Open: Mon.-Thurs. 6:30 A.M.–8:30 P.M.,
Fri. 6:30 A.M.–11 P.M., Sat. 7 A.M.–10 P.M.,
Sun. 8 A.M.–7 P.M.
Price: Inexpensive to moderate
Credit Cards: Yes
Special Features: Picnic box lunches; cus-
tom catering; small plates and live music on
Friday night

Martin and Janet Bleck left the demanding
schedules of their formal food–oriented
lives in Florida for a little peace and quiet
in Oregon Wine Country. They got the
wine-country part, but not the slower pace.
Breakfast burritos, signature sandwiches,
wraps, salads, and amazing soups all show
an experienced hand and creativity. Of

course, they also serve coffee drinks and sensational smoothies. They pour only local beer and neighborhood wines, from bubbly to dessert. Their local hazelnut brittle is nicknamed "crack" because it's so addictive. In the future look for more live music, theme nights, and a dinner menu from the Blecks, who seem to need little sleep.

JORY RESTAURANT & BAR

503-554-2526
www.theallison.com
2525 Allison Lane
Open: Mon.–Sat. 6:30–10 A.M. and 11:30–2, Thurs. 5:30–9, Fri.–Sat. 5:30–10, Sun. 10–2 and 5:30–9.,
Price: Very expensive
Credit Cards: Yes
Special Features: Located at Allison Resort and Spa; bar/lounge; private Chef's Table next to kitchen, outdoor dining, private rooms, personal wine permitted with corkage fee

The Allison calls their dining experience a "Culinary Program," the first hint that you are entering the realm of something special, perhaps even snobby. Although it's jaw-droppingly gorgeous, Jory somehow avoids pretension and is comfortably chic. Easy on the eyes—if not necessarily on the credit card—it's the hottest thing going in these parts. Choose from three-, four-, or five-course dinners accompanied by pairing suggestions. For that celebratory life occasion, consider the Chef's Table, where up to seven guests partake in an exclusive dinner prepared by chef Nathan Lockwood front and center of the kitchen. The wine menu is balanced, with local and world wines, and carefully crafted to be educational without being daunting.

Attractions in the Newberg Area

The **Hoover-Minthorn House** (503-538-6629, 115 South River St.) is first on the list of any tourist activity in Newberg. The 31st president lived in this house as a child with his aunt and uncle, John and Laura Minthorn, from 1885 to 1891. The bedroom furniture Hoover used remains in this white Italianate home, which is on the National Register of Historic Places.

The Willamette River draws the attention of hikers, bicyclists, historians, and picnickers at the popular **Champoeg State Heritage Area** (503-678-1649), seven miles east of Newberg. The site of Oregon's first provisional government in 1843, Champoeg is 615 acres of forests, meadows, wetlands, trails, picnic areas, campsites, and special historical events. For a different type of nostalgic experience, pack a picnic with a bottle of wine and check out what's playing at the **99W Drive-In Theatre** (503-538-2738) on a Friday, Saturday, or Sunday night. The drive-in, one of the few in Oregon, has been showing first-run movies since 1953.

As scenic as the Willamette Valley is, rare is the spot in the heart of wine country where you can see the Big Five volcanoes in the area: Washington's Mount Rainier, Mount St. Helen's, and Mount Adams and Oregon's Mount Hood and Mount Jefferson. While you're touring wine country, be sure to take a drive up Bald Peak Road to 1,629-foot **Bald Peak State Scenic Viewpoint** (800-551-6949) and drink in the best views in the entire valley.

Recreation in the Newberg Area

For a serene bird's-eye view of wine country, glide above the countryside in a hot-air balloon with **Vista Balloon Adventures** (503-625-7385, 23324 SW Sherk Ave.) in Sherwood or **Pacific Peaks Balloons** (503-590-5250, 16065 SW Barrington) in Tigard. Vista offers wine flights over Yamhill County vineyards that include a catered brunch for $189. If you want a day on the links between winery-hopping, **Chehalem Glenn Golf Course** (503-538-5800, 4501 East Fernwood Rd.) in Newberg is a picturesque and reasonably challenging course.

Shopping in the Newberg Area

Newberg's search for an identity outside the church is playing catch-up in this arena, too, though **White Collectibles and Fine China** (503-538-7421, 620 East First St.) has an interesting array of dinnerware. **The Big Red Barn** (503-554-1560, 17330 NE Highway 240) takes a fresh look at country living, with old and new treasures, Christmas ornaments, wine fixtures (but no wine), and Northwest food items congregating in a century-old dairy barn.

Information

Chehalem Valley Chamber of Commerce, 503-538-2014, 415 East Sheridan, www.chehalemvalley.org

Dundee/Dayton Area (Dundee Hills AVA)

If Yamhill County is the heart of Oregon Wine Country, then Dundee is its soul. Actually, this unassuming little town likes to think of itself as the "Heart and Soil" of the famed Red Hills. Dundee, named for a town in Scotland, was known first for prunes and then for hazelnuts. Then Papa Pinot came along with 3,000 young Pinot vines in 1965.

In the four decades since, this once-rural community has become downright chic. Most people are here for the wine, restaurants, and popular Sunday farmer's market that features local fruits, hazelnuts, produce, and artisans' works.

Part of the allure is that these slopes overlook the town of Dundee, literally a one-stop-light blip on the road where old buildings and rough roads show signs of its other agricultural past. The future for Dundee is coming—two or three luxury inns are on the landscape. However, two destination wine restaurants (Tina's and Red Hills) have been here almost from the beginning.

Wineries around Dundee and Dayton (Dundee Hills AVA)

The Dundee Hills are Oregon's Côte d'Or—Slopes of Gold. The key to the area's Pinot success lies in its climate and southeast-facing slopes. Erosion from these north–south hills created ideal terrain for Pinot Noir. Because of the Coast Range rain shadow, moisture is limited to about 35 inches per year, most of it coming during the winter, long after a glorious growing season and harvest. Frost is rare. There are about 50 vineyards covering 1,200 acres, predominately growing Pinot Noir, Pinot Gris and a bit of Chardonnay. Many of these famous wineries have Dayton addresses but are definitely part of the Dundee AVA.

An interesting place in Dundee is the 12th & Maple Wine Company, one of the largest custom-crush facilities in Oregon. Head winemaker Aron Hess and two assistants make wine for nearly two dozen grape growers in the area.

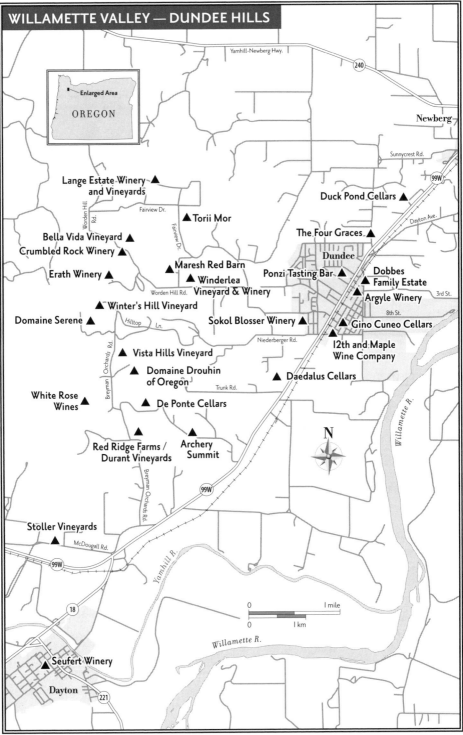

WILLAMETTE VALLEY — DUNDEE HILLS

Yamhill-Newberg Hwy.

240

Newberg

Sunnycrest Rd.

OREGON

Enlarged Area

99W

Lange Estate Winery ▲
and Vineyards

Fairview Dr.

Duck Pond Cellars ▲

Dayton Ave.

▲ Torii Mor

The Four Graces ▲

Bella Vida Vineyard ▲

Dundee

Crumbled Rock Winery ▲

▲ Maresh Red Barn

Ponzi Tasting Bar ▲

Dobbes
Family Estate

Erath Winery ▲

▲ Winderlea
Vineyard & Winery

Worden Hill Rd.

▲ Argyle Winery

3rd St.

▲ Winter's Hill Vineyard

8th St.

Domaine Serene ▲

Hilltop   Ln.

Sokol Blosser Winery ▲

▲ Gino Cuneo Cellars

Niederberger Rd.

▲ 12th and Maple
Wine Company

▲ Vista Hills Vineyard

▲ Domaine Drouhin
of Oregon

Trunk Rd.

▲ Daedalus Cellars

White Rose
Wines ▲

▲ De Ponte Cellars

Willamette R.

N

▲
Red Ridge Farms /
Durant Vineyards

▲
Archery
Summit

99W

Stoller Vineyards
▲

McDougall Rd.

99W

18

0   1 mile

0   1 km

Yamhill R.

Willamette R.

▲ Seufert Winery

Dayton

221

Paul Woodward. © The Countryman Press

Pinot Noir blankets the gentle hillsides at Bella Vida Vineyard. Steven Whiteside

DUNDEE

DUCK POND CELLARS

503-538-3199 or 800-437-3213
www.duckpondcellars.com
23145 Highway 99W
Tasting Room: May–Sept., daily 10–5,
Oct.–Apr. daily 11–5
Fee: Complimentary for five wines; $5 for
additional wines, waived with purchase
Owners: Fries and Jenkins families
Winemaker: Mark Chargin
Wines: Gewürztrmainer, Pinot Gris,
Riesling, Cabernet Sauvignon, Merlot,
Pinot Noir, Syrah, Sangiovese, port, dessert
wine
Cases: 100,000
Special Features: Tours by appointment for
groups up to 100, extensive patio and deck
area, large gift shop, RV and bus parking

Owned by the same two families since 1993,
Duck Pond is known for making drinkable
wines at affordable prices. Their friendly
and festive tasting room is an event in itself
and is especially suited for a gathering of
friends or family. The gift shop is loaded
with everything from house wares and wine
accessories to apparel, gourmet food and
non-wine specialty beverages. Here you can
also find and taste their other wines from
Washington's Columbia Valley under the
Desert Winds label.

THE FOUR GRACES

800-245-2950
www.thefourgraces.com
9605 NE Fox Farm Road
Tasting Room: Daily 10–5, closed major
holidays
Fee: $10 for five wines
Owners: Steve and Paula Black
Winemaker: Laurent Montalieu
Wines: Pinot Blanc, Pinot Gris, Pinot Noir
Cases: 15,000

The 110-acre Black Family Vineyard is
carefully groomed and tended, and utilizes
controlled yields for higher-quality grapes.
It also provides one of the most stunning
settings for tasting in the Red Hills. The

four graces are Steve and Paula's grown daughters, and the vineyard designates reflect their personalities. The reserve is named for the girls' brother, Nicholas, the keeper of the four graces.

DOBBES FAMILY ESTATE

503-538-1141 or 800-566-8143
www.dobbesfamilyestate.com
240 SE Fifth Street
Tasting Room: Daily 11–6
Fee: Complimentary; $10 for reserve wines, refunded with $50 purchase
Owner/Winemaker: Joe Dobbes Jr.
Wines: Pinot Gris, Viognier, Pinot Noir, Syrah
Cases: 5,000
Special Features: Outdoor patio.

Joe Dobbes Jr. just might be the most prolific winemaker in Oregon. Don't let those 5,000 cases sway you; that's just for the Dobbes Family Estate label. In all, Dobbes produces well over 60,000 cases a year for a stable of 11 wineries that love having his name attached to their labels. Under his own label, Dobbes has both high-end and value wines. His top wines are balanced and sensual. His popular By Joe label speaks to the lunch-pail, hard-hat, working folks. Under Dobbes Family Estate wines, he does 8–10 Pinots—no two of which taste the same. The Viognier isn't too shabby, either; Oprah Winfrey touted it in June 2009. The compact but attractive tasting room, with a water feature and gardens, is feng shui with a Pacific Northwest tint, and is staffed by pros in the know. Joe's father, Joe Dobbes Sr., formerly owned Marquam Hill, now AlexEli.

PONZI TASTING BAR

503-554-1500
www.ponziwines.com
100 SW Seventh Street
Tasting Room: Daily 11–5
Fee: $2–8 per taste, $8–12 per flight

Joe Dobbes Jr. is one of Oregon's most prolific winemakers.   Courtesy Joe Dobbes Family Estate

Special Features: Gift items and food products, three to five guest wines featured each week, Oregon beer on tap

This is a second tasting room for Ponzi. You can taste other select Oregon wines as well, by the sample, glass, or bottle. Ponzi has a great location in the heart of Dundee, but service is sketchy. The winery is in Beaverton (see Portland wineries).

ARGYLE WINERY
503-538-8520 or 888-427-4953
www.argylewinery.com
691 Highway 99W
Tasting Room: Daily 11–5, closed major holidays
Fee: $2.50 per taste, $10 per flight
Owners: Brian Croser and Rollin Soles
Winemaker: Rollin Soles
Wines: Chardonnay, Riesling, Pinot Noir, sparkling wines, dessert wine
Cases: 55,000
Special Features: Picnic area.

Argyle is situated in an old Victorian farmhouse in the heart of the town of Dundee, so naturally Pinot Noir is on the list. But that isn't what sets Argyle apart from its brethren scattered amid the Red Hills. No, this winery is renowned for its meticulously crafted sparkling wines using Oregon Chardonnay and Pinot Noir, made gently and one bottle at a time by legendary winemaker Rollin Soles. Argyle also boasts two of the better names for a wine: Nuthouse and Spirithouse, the former because the production room once stored hazelnuts and the latter for a friendly ghost supposedly haunting the winery, which once served as Dundee's city hall. We twist the cork off their bubbly often.

GINO CUNEO CELLARS
503-949-1992
www.ginocuneocellars.com
1242 Maple Street
Tasting Room: None

Owner/Winemaker: Gino Cuneo
Wines: Nebbiolo, Rosato, Sangiovese, specialty wines
Cases: 2,500

Founder of Cuneo Cellars (now Cana's Feast), the congenial Gino knows how to land on his feet. After a disagreement among investors, Cuneo found himself in a position to start fresh and focus on his first love, Italian wines. Under the label Tre Nova, he's sourcing fruit from eastern Washington and making sensational varietals at a custom crush facility in Dundee—a virtual winery setup. And he's doing something not done anywhere else in the state, possibly in any state. Using Sangivoese, Barbera, and Nebbiolo, he's making an Appassimento, Amarone-style, which involves drying the grapes. As for sampling, you'll have to catch him holiday weekends at 12th and Maple.

SOKOL BLOSSER WINERY
503-864-2282 or 800-582-6668
www.sokolblosser.com
5000 Sokol Blosser Lane
Tasting Room: Daily 10–4
Fee: $5–15, depending on wines open
Owners: Bill and Susan Sokol Blosser
Winemaker: Russ Rosner
Wines: Pinot Gris, Pinot Noir, red and white blends
Cases: 85,000
Special Features: Picnic area, deck, special events facility

On any list of big wine names in Oregon, Sokol Blosser is at the top with many of its venerable neighbors. Bill Blosser was at the forefront of vineyard development in the Red Hills. Susan has always been and continues to be a leader in the environmental arena. In 2002, Sokol Blosser's 900-barrel cellar, built partially underground with wildflowers on the roof, was the first winery building in the U.S. to be LEED-certified. Their 1971 vineyard is certified

Holiday cheer fills the renovated tasting room at Sokol Blosser. Courtesy Sokol Blosser Winery

organic and they use 50 percent biodiesel fuel in their tractors. Susan is particularly in tune with the rhythms of the planet; she has given frequent speeches about the impacts of climate change on the wine industry, and the winery's goal is to be carbon-neutral. While they take stewardship seriously, they have their playful side with regular fun events. They also produce a "party in the bottle" white named Evolution with up to 11 varietals in the mix.

DAEDALUS CELLARS

503-538-4400
www.daedaluscellars.com
990 North Highway 99W
Tasting Room: Wed.–Sun. 11–5 and by appointment
Fee: $5
Ownesr: Aron Hess and Pam Walden
Winemaker: Aron Hess
Wines: Chardonnay, Grüner Veltliner, Pinot Gris, Riesling, Pinot Noir, red and white blends
Cases: 3,500
Special Features: Pickup parties for the wine club

Pronounced "*day*-da-lus," this winery is named for a James Joyce character in Greek mythology. Owners Aron Hess and Pam Walden met in France in the mid-1990s and have shared a wine bond ever since. Their first Pinot Noir came from a vineyard in the Columbia Gorge in 2000; they continue to make wine from a variety of Oregon sources. Of late, Daedalus has focused more on grapes from the Dundee Hills area, and the couple planted their own vineyard in 2008. The winery has some unique offerings, including the Grüner Veltliner from a vineyard in the Eola Hills. A second label, called Jezebel, features eccentric red and white blends.

WINDERLEA VINEYARD & WINERY

503-554-5900
www.winderlea.com
8905 NE Worden Hill Road
Tasting Room: Fri.–Sun. 11–4 and by appointment
Fee: $10
Owners: Bill Sweat and Donna Morris
Winemaker: Robert E. Brittan
Wines: Chardonnay, Pinot Noir

Oregon Wine Country by the Numbers

1,748,282: Cases of Oregon wine sold in 2008

34,700: Tons of grapes harvested in 2008

19,300: Total Oregon acres planted in grapes

17,571: Tons of Pinot Noir harvested in 2008

15,000: Years ago the Missoula Flood deposited rich soils in western Oregon

11,210: Acres planted in Pinot Noir

2,736: Acres planted in Pinot Gris

1,008: Acres planted in Chardonnay

856: Number of Oregon vineyards in 2008

777: Acres planted in Riesling

627: Acres planted in Cabernet Sauvignon

395: Number of Oregon wineries in 2008

200: Wineries in the Willamette Valley

80: Percent of Oregonians living within 20 miles of the Willamette River

72: Total varietals grown in Oregon

25: Wineries in the Dundee Hills AVA

16: AVAs in the state

15: Varietals that comprise 97 percent of the grapes produced

5: Number of bonded Oregon wineries in 1970

3: U.S. ranking for number of wineries per state

1: Place that can call itself Oregon Wine Country

Cases: 1,600

Special Features: Tasting fee donated to !Salud¡, three-course lunch on Friday in summer, events facility with commercial kitchen

These husband-and-wife owners are serious tasters from the East Coast who had an early crush for Pinot. They found the right winemaker in Brittan, who produces splendid Pinot and is also known for his Chablis-style Chardonnay. His goal: to make elegant, feminine and sensual food-friendly wines while practicing sustainable agriculture. Winderlea uses solar and passive-solar energy, and is working toward biodynamic certification.

MARESH RED BARN

503-537-1098

www.vineyardretreat.com

9325 NE Worden Hill Road

Tasting Room: Mar.–Dec., Wed.–Sun. 11–5

Fee: $5

Owners: Jim and Loie Maresh

Winemaker: Jim Maresh

Wines: Chardonnay, Pinot Gris, Riesling, Sauvignon Blanc, Pinot Noir

Cases: 1,000

Special Features: Maresh Red Hill Vineyard Retreat available for rent

A stroll through the family vineyard takes you to the tasting room in a highly visible and iconic red barn. Martha Maresh, daughter of Jim, likes to tell the story of Dick Erath coming up their driveway and telling them they had the best vineyard location for Pinot Noir, bar none. So in 1969 they planted their first vines. Maresh grapes are used by several wineries, some of which you can taste in the barn tasting room along with their bottling.

TORII MOR

503-538-2279

www.toriimorwinery.com

18325 NE Fairview Drive

Tasting Room: Daily 11–5

Fee: $10 for five reds, $5 for three whites

Owners: Donald and Margie Olson

Winemaker: Jacques Tardy

Wines: Chardonnay, Pinot Blanc, Pinot Gris, Pinot Noir, port

Cases: 15,000

Special Features: Stunning Japanese gardens and serene setting; Web site has many tantalizing recipes matched to their wines

The name loosely translates to "gates to the earth," and Don and Margie believe that Pinot Noir more than any other grape is the gateway to the earth. With Tardy, a native fifth-generation Burgundian winemaker, at the helm, Torii Mor's wines are heavily earthy and exquisitely crafted. Early wine-maker Patricia Green raised recognition to the label with exceptional vineyard-designate Pinots.

LANGE ESTATE WINERY & VINEYARDS

503-538-6476
www.langewinery.com
18380 NE Buena Vista Drive
Tasting Room: Daily 11–5
Fee: $10 for five wines
Owners: Don and Wendy Lange
Winemaker: Don Lange and Jesse Lange
Wines: Chardonnay, Pinot Gris, Pinot Noir, Tempranillo
Cases: 15,000
Special Features: Dog-friendly

The Langes have been on the scene since their first vintage in 1987, when they pro-duced a barrel-fermented Pinot Gris that Don labeled a "benchmark bottling" for his approach. Lange started by concentrating on Pinot Gris, Chardonnay, and vineyard designate Pinot Noirs, and has stayed close to his origins. Both Don and Jesse are avid fly anglers, which explains the prominent tribute to dry flies on most of their labels.

BELLA VIDA VINEYARD

503-538-9821
www.bellavida.com
9380 NE Worden Hill Road
Tasting Room: Fri.–Mon. 11–5
Fee: $5 for four wines
Owners: Steven and Allison Whiteside
Winemaker: Jacques Tardy, Jay Somers, and Brian O'Donnell
Wines: Pinot Noir, white blend
Cases: 550
Special Features: Winemakers' series

Call it the *Iron Chef* of winemaking, with the secret ingredient being fruit from the same Red Hills vineyard: one vineyard, one vin-tage, three winemakers. Since 2002, Steven

A Japanese theme flows through Torii Mor's tasting room and grounds. Courtesy Torii Mor Winery

Whiteside has been determined to take a scientific approach toward producing distinct Pinots. Jacques Tardy (Torii Mor) does the Burgundian thing with highly structured wines meant for laying down. Jay Somers (J. Christopher) is known for minimal intervention with his Pinots, letting the fruit speak for itself. Brian O'Donnell is more new-worldish, with a balanced Pinot that's ready to drink from the get-go. The Whitesides have their own production, created by one of the trio of lucky makers.

CRUMBLED ROCK WINERY

503-537-9682
www.crumbledrockwines.com
9485 NE Worden Hill Road
Tasting Room: May–Nov., Sat.–Sun. 11–5, or by appointment
Fee: Complimentary
Owners: Gerard Koschal and Julia Staigers
Winemaker: Gerard Koschal
Wines: Pinot Noir
Cases: 800
Special Features: Patio

First, the name: Owner and winemaker Gerard Koschal is a retired geologist. The reference is to the famed soils of Juliard Vineyard, which served Dundee-area winemakers well for 20 years before Koschal began making his own Pinot Noir (first release 2007). The tasting room doesn't look like much from the road, but once you're up the driveway and the vineyards unfold before you, with the Cascades serving as backdrop, you'll be glad you stopped. "We have one wine, no tasting fee, and a great view—and it tastes better outside," co-owner Julia Staigers says.

ERATH WINERY

800-539-9463
www.erath.com
9409 NE Worden Hill Road
Tasting Room: Daily 11–5
Fee: Complimentary first flight; $15 for two

flights of Pinot and winemakers' specials
Owner: Ste. Michelle Wine Estates
Winemaker: Gary Horner
Wines: Gewürztraminer, Pinot Blanc, Pinot Gris, Riesling, Dolcetto, Pinot Noir, dessert wines
Cases: 160,000
Special Features: Winery and vineyard tours

The state's largest Pinot Noir producer recently etched its place in Oregon wine history—dubiously, in the minds of purists—by becoming the first winery in the state to sell out to the corporate model. In the spring of 2006, publicly traded Ste. Michelle Wine Estates in Woodinville, Washington, purchased Erath, which was opened in 1967 by Cal Knudsen and Dick Erath, one of those pioneering expatriates from U.C. Davis. Some would say it's just another step, along with palatial wineries and stiff tasting fees, in the Napa-tization of Oregon. On the other hand, many Oregon winery owners were gratified that Erath was sold to a Northwest company, and Erath himself said he scrutinized would-be purchasers carefully. Erath is another one of those must-stops for the taste of history, and certainly they continue to produce reliable wines.

DAYTON
WINTER'S HILL VINEYARD

503-864-4538
www.wintershillwine.com
6451 Hilltop Lane
Tasting Room: May–Nov., daily 12–5, Dec.–Apr., Fri.–Mon. 12–5
Fee: $10–12, partially refundable depending on purchase
Owners: Peter and Emily Gladhart, Russell and Delphine Gladhart
Winemaker: Delphine Gladhart
Wines: Pinot Blanc, Pinot Gris, early Muscat, late harvest Pinot Gris, white blend, rosé, Pinot Noir, dessert wine
Cases: 3,000
Special Features: Vineyard and winery tours by appointment

Armed with a firm belief in their vineyard and a huge work ethic, Peter and Emily Gladhart would bring their bottles of pride and joy south to Friday afternoon tastings at First Alternative Co-op in Corvallis, ready to share their passion. You can share it as well in a calming relatively new tasting room highlighted by wrought-iron hinges on the cellar door from the family homestead. It's a meaningful place to the Gladharts, so it's named after her parents, who tended cherry and prune orchards on the acreage. The 150-acre property (35 in grapes) features a birding trail and, along with Stoller and Domaine Drouhin, is a stop for horseback tours run by Wine Country Farm.

DOMAINE SERENE

503-864-4600
www.domaineserene.com
6555 NE Hilltop Lane
Tasting Room: Wed.–Mon. 11–4
Fee: $15
Owners: Ken and Grace Evenstad
Winemaker: M. Eleni "Leni" Papadakis
Wines: Chardonnay, Viognier, Pinot Noir, Syrah
Cases: 20,000
Special Features: Private tours and tastings Mon.–Fri. by appointment ($40 per person, maximum 10)

The California-style complex at Domaine Serene features a clay tile roof and terracotta stucco exterior that matches the style of their Pinot: evocative, bold, and plenty oaky. With marble floors and granite tabletops, Domaine Serene feels on the formal side, much like a French wine estate. On Serene's domaine, they grow Chardonnay and Pinot Noir, the grape that lured them to Oregon more than two decades ago. However, they also do a non-estate Syrah and Viognier. Domaine Serene was a founding member of the Oregon Chardonnay Alliance and imports

Burgundian clones of the grape in a never-ending quest for perfection. They also have their Rock Block label for blockbuster Rhône wines. The old glove factory in Carlton still sports the faded name Rock Block.

VISTA HILLS VINEYARD

503-864-3200
www.vistahillsvineyard.com
6475 Hilltop Lane
Tasting Room: Daily 12–5
Fee: $10, refundable with purchase
Owners: John and Nancy McClintock
Winemaker: Varies
Wines: Pinot Gris, Pinot Noir
Cases: 1,000
Special Features: Viewing deck overlooking Willamette Valley and Coast Range.

They say you might feel as if you're in a treehouse at the appropriately named Vista Hills, where the west-facing tasting room is perched at the crest of a hill and is surrounded by towering Douglas fir and white oak trees. The wood-framed building offers a window to stunning views as well as the production facility on the lower level. Instead of having one winemaker, Vista Hills uses seven of the biggest names in the area to produce premium wines. Oregon's wet winters can get tiresome, so the McClintocks escape to Kona, Hawaii, where they grow coffee and cacao on five acres.

DOMAINE DROUHIN OF OREGON

503-864-2700
www.domainedrouhin.com
6750 NE Breyman Orchards Road
Tasting Room: Wed.–Sun. 11–4
Fee: $10 for three wines, refunded with $100 purchase
Owner: Domaine Drouhin
Winemaker: Veronique Drouhin
Wines: Chardonnay, Pinot Noir
Cases: 18,000
Special Features: Two private tours daily by

appointment; special tasting the Saturday before Thanksgiving; outdoor patio; horse-back tours

Maison Joseph Drouhin has been a promi-nent wine name in Beaunne, France, since the late 1880s. But it was a third-generation Drouhin, Robert, who took a look at David Lett's accomplishments at Eyrie and deter-mined that Oregon, not California, was a more likely place to grow the prince of Burgundy—Pinot Noir. Daughter Veronique has been making the wine since 1988, a year after the Drouhins landed in Oregon. Their current facility, with the tasting room above the production facility, was com-pleted in 1989. The Laurène Pinot, named after Veronique's oldest daughter, is the flagship wine that has earned national and international acclaim.

WHITE ROSE WINES
503-864-2328
www.whiterosewines.com
6250 Hilltop Lane
Tasting Room: Apr.–Nov., daily 11–5, Dec.–Mar. by appointment only
Fee: $7–15
Owner: Greg Sanders
Winemaker: Jesus Guillen Jr.
Wines: Pinot Noir
Cases: 2,500
Special Features: Winery tours

If a word can paint a thousand pictures, this place only needs three: *mythical, mystical,* and *magical.* The labels are mythical (they feature a dragon), the grounds mystical, and the wine magical. But pictures work, too, which might explain why White Rose tells its story in photos on its Web site. Words struggle to do the setting justice. This state-of-the-art winery is dressed in lavender gardens—not a rose in sight, white or otherwise—that provide a gentle, layered skirting of terrace overlooking the valley. The tasting room is understated and small,

so take a long, mesmerizing look around the grounds.

DE PONTE CELLARS
503-864-3698
www.depontecellars.com
17545 Archery Summit Road
Tasting Room: 11–5 daily
Fee: $10, refunded with $100 purchase
Owners: Fred and Shirley Baldwin
Winemaker: Isabelle Dutaratre
Wines: Pinot Noir
Cases: 3,000

De Ponte is a family-run 20-acre estate vineyard, winery, and tasting room sur-rounded by old-growth vines. Pull up a chair and feel almost like family in the smart-looking tasting room and sample the handiwork of Burgundian winemaker Dutaratre. There's a subtle style around here that emits an aura of premium qual-ity—the wines do their own marketing.

RED RIDGE FARMS/DURANT VINEYARDS
503-864-8502
www.redridgefarms.com
5510 NE Breyman Orchard Road
Tasting Room: Memorial Day and Thanksgiving weekends, last weekend of each month, and by appointment
Fee: $5
Owners: Penny and Ken Durant
Winemakers: Joe Dobbes and guest wine-makers
Wines: Pinot Gris, Chardonnay, Pinot Noir
Cases: 400
Special Features: Lodging, picnics wel-comed, complimentary estate olive-oil tasting, gift shop

Sherry's friend Camille (a.k.a. Sleuth) introduced us to Red Ridge Farms on one of our Memorial Day weekend treks. She is enamored with the place because it has everything she loves in one location: exotic and native plants, herbs, trees, gardening supplies, art and trinkets, and estate olive oil from 15 acres of Spanish olive trees and 60 acres of vineyard planted more than 30 years ago. All of this is wrapped in bucolic views—impressive. The estate vineyards supply the grapes for small-lot wines made by high-profile winemakers. There's also an alluring guest suite that sleeps two, complete with living room, bedroom, bath, kitchen, and dining room. The front deck, with Adirondack chairs, takes in the sur-rounding vista.

ARCHERY SUMMIT

503-864-4300
www.archerysummit.com
18599 NE Archery Summit Road
Tasting Room: Daily 10–4
Fee: $15 for four Pinots (sharing is OK)

Owner: Crimson Wine Group
Winemaker: Anna Matzinger
Wines: Pinot Noir
Cases: 12,000
Special Features: Two hour-long tours daily by appointment, 10:30–2 ($25 per person)

Among revered wineries in the Dundee Hills, Archery Summit is in rarified air with the best. Some of its mystique is history— the innovative Gary Andrus founded Archery Summit in its spectacular setting in 1993. Some of it is the winery's extraor-dinary cave system for aging wines, so extensive that they needed a mining permit to excavate the hillside marine basalt. Some 600 barrels are stored in natural tempera-tures, requiring no energy. Mostly, though, Archery Summit is famed for producing some of the top Pinot Noirs in a state where the competition is fierce. Full-bodied

Archery Summit offers tours of their renowned caves beneath the winery. Courtesy Archery Summit

Pinots, from five estate vineyards where sustainable farming is practiced, are coveted nationally. Young winemaker Anna Matzinger has picked up where Andrus left off. The tasting room is surprisingly small for such a big-name winery, so large groups should call ahead.

STOLLER VINEYARDS

503-864-3404
16161 NE McDougall Road
www.stollervineyards.com
Tasting Room: Daily 11–5
Fee: $10, refunded with six-bottle purchase
Owners: Bill and Cathy Stoller
Winemaker: Melissa Burr
Wines: Chardonnay, rosé, Pinot Noir
Cases: 10,000
Special Features: Cottage and Wine Farm House lodging is available year-round

Once a turkey farm (which explains the bird on the family crest), Stoller Vineyards is 176 acres of mostly Pinot Noir set amid 373 rolling, pastoral acres. Bill and Cathy Stoller, who also are co-owners of Chehalem, have made a concerted effort to work with the rhythms of the land. Stoller was the first winery in the country to be LEED Gold certified, thanks to such innovative techniques as wastewater reclamation and energy-efficient heating and cooling, including solar panels.

SEUFERT WINERY

503-709-1255
www.seufertwinery.com
415 Ferry Street
Tasting Room: Sat.–Sun. 12–5 and Memorial Day and Thanksgiving weekends
Fee: Complimentary
Owner/Winemaker: Jim Seufert
Wines: Pinot Noir, Syrah, Dolcetto, white blend, dessert wine
Cases: 2,000
Special Features: Pinot comparisons

This is a great place to test your Pinot palate. Jim Seufert makes single-vineyard Pinots from several sub-AVAs in the Willamette Valley, each from varying soil and farming conditions. For instance, the Pinot from Coleman Vineyard, in the McMinnville AVA, is assertive, spicy, and more tannic than the Pinot from the Vista Hills Vineyard, in the Dundee Hills AVA, which is fruitier, softer, and earthier. The facility is an unpretentious warehouse across the street from Dayton's city hall, where, Seufert says, "If you show up late you won't be kicked out." Seufert is a fourth-generation Oregonian who discovered his wine passions while traveling the world, and decided his native state was an idyllic place to fulfill his destiny.

Note: Two other small Dundee/Dayton wineries to keep an eye on are Aubichon and Le Cadeau, which share space in Dundee. Neither has tasting-room hours, but you can visit and taste at 459 SW Ninth Street by calling for an appointment.

Lodging in the Dundee/ Dayton Area

DUNDEE

BLACK WALNUT INN & VINEYARD

Owners: Karen and Neal Utz
503-429-4114 or 866-429-4114
www.blackwalnut-inn.com
9600 NE Worden Hill Road
Special Features: Special packages including golf, spa, helicopter rides to private winery tours; Italian-style, afternoon pick-me-ups daily 5:30–6:30

Setting the spoil-yourself standard for luxurious lodging—enough to attract the eye and rating of *Wine Spectator*—the Black Walnut Inn lives up to its reputation. With nine tastefully appointed suites, all with balcony and soaking tub accompanied by plush robes, the Tuscan-style villa has an authentically peaceful, old-world charm. Yet it remains true to its Oregon roots.

"Two gentlemen on the hill" offer elegant B&B accommodations at Dundee Manor.   Courtesy Dundee Manor

After painstakingly caring for the old and forgotten walnut trees, owners Karen and Neal could think of no better tribute than naming their inn after them. With a setting literally on top of 42 acres, even the world-liest of travelers will find the location jaw-dropping. The Utzs planted 13 acres of their prime vineyard property in Pinot Noir, and their first harvest was in 2007—from which 99 cases of wine fill their shelves. Even though Karen jokes that the sucking sound you hear is the vineyard draining their checking account, they still plan to plant more grapes, probably more Pinot. The rotating seasonal breakfast menu gives four sensational choices. House-made sausage from a local pork farmer is a new addition.

DUNDEE MANOR B&B

503-554-1945
www.Dundeemanor.com
8380 NE Worden Hill Road
Rates $175–250
Special Features: Wine getaway packages, special-event rentals

Hosts Brad and David, two sophisticated and worldly gentlemen, share both their home, a 1908 four-square Edwardian estate, and a "passion for excellence." They offer the ultimate in concierge service—from winery tours to tee times, dinner reservations to massage, and more. Their experienced palates and lust for fine food show on every designer breakfast plate, accompanied by candlelight and soft music. The grounds are a manicured marvel, and just beyond the brick- and iron-gated entrance, rocking chairs beckon from the front porch. There are four impeccable rooms with global themes. Children 12 and older are welcome.

THE INN AT RED HILLS

503-538-7666
www.innatredhills.com
1410 North Highway 99W
Rates: $195–375
Special Features: Farm to Fork deli, take-out, and restaurant; Press Wine Bar and Bottle Shop with small retail section of

wine and gourmet foods; outside seating with gas fireplace; vineyard walks

Owners Dustin Wyant and Kendall Bergström are following an old-world travel tradition of finding a comfortable bed, food, and gathering spot at the same site. The boutique hotel offers 20 units above the restaurant and Press Wine Bar, which emphasizes small-lot Oregon wines. The Euro-inspired concept is to create a village within one building, ensuring that your every wine-country need—except the vineyard—is under one roof. Bergström and Wyant put careful planning into retrofitting an old bank building. They utilized local labor, landscapers, artists, food purveyors, and supply companies. They also have raised the bar on sustainable business practices overseen by Paul de Lancellotti, director of education and sustainability. The mercantile area features 30 Oregon cheeses and specialty foods, and a wall behind the deli case literally stocked floor to ceiling with unique wines. "We carry what others can't" is the motto. The restaurant is casual, the lodging eco-luxe. And did we mention the individually designed rooms, and serene surrounding spaces? Simply divine.

VINEYARD RIDGE

503-476-2211
www.distinctivedestination.net
4,000 Fairview Drive
Rates: Mon.–Thurs. $325 (three-night minimum), Fri.–Sun. $425 (two-night minimum), weekly $2,000 (Fri.–Fri.)
Special Features: Deck overlooking the famed Red Hills

Vineyard Ridge is one of three properties operated by Distinctive Destinations. The large, comfortable home with a fireplace sits high above town and offers a panoramic view of the Pinot kingdom. If you want to be close to the Dundee action, but far enough away for some serenity, this is your place.

DAYTON
WINE COUNTRY FARM B&B AND CELLARS

Owner: Joan Davenport
800-261-3446 or 503-864-3446
www.winecountryfarm.com
6855 Breyman Orchards Road
Rates: $150–225
Special Features: Tasting room; horseback or carriage tours of estate and vineyard; children 12 and over welcome

The Wine Country Farm is a country charmer squeezed between two Domaines: Drouhin and Serene. Innkeeper Joan Davenport had a vision for the top of her newly acquired world, and now her hard work has borne fruit. The main house has six rooms and three suites, all with panoramic views. Vineyard tours on horseback are available for guests or others wanting a higher experience. Davenport's vineyard produces premium grapes, and the casual on-site tasting room is open daily during the summer and fall, on weekends during the winter and spring (depending on special events). Wine Country Farm is listed in the book *1,000 Places To See Before You Die.*

Dining in the Dundee/Dayton Area

There's no sense listing farm-fresh food and regional cuisine as special features in each of the dining options below, as they are the norm in Dundee. You can't go wrong with any of the three choices. In fact, they should exceed your expectations for dining off OR 99W.

DUNDEE
DUNDEE BISTRO

503-554-1650
www.dundeebistro.com
100A SW Seventh Street
Open: Daily 11:30–9
Price: Moderate
Credit Cards: Yes

Oregon chanterelles pair well with earthy Pinot Noir.

Special Features: Semi-covered patio dining

Chef and co-owner Jason Stoller Smith is all about the local food scene. This exceedingly popular restaurant offers intimate dining for large crowds and a small, personal bar. The Northwest meets Italy at the Dundee Bistro, where the tables are chrome and black with white linens. A new menu is printed twice a day, for lunch and dinner, working off what's available locally. Some of the more popular dishes include hand-made pappardelle pasta, hand-tossed pizzas, and truffle fries. Whole Hog

Wednesdays in the summer are a hoot—so popular they roast two whole pigs.

FARM TO FORK

503-538-7970
www.farmtoforkdundee.com
1410 North Highway 99W
Open: Daily 7–11, 11:30–3, 5 p.m.–close
Credit Cards: Yes
Special Features: Patio dining with gas fireplace; bakery/deli open daily from 6 A.M. for pastries and coffee; wine bar open daily from 4 P.M.

Delicacies begin to fill the case bright and early, and Farm to Fork stays open into the evening for your late-night snack, your next day's lunch, or just a nibble to get by. Such baked goods as stuffed croissants, tortes, and truffles are created by pastry chef Connie Paskavan, who is trained in French baking. There are several venues to enjoy food from your fork or fingers: deli to go or stay, a wine bar, private sit-down tables, and a community table in the back for meeting new friends. It's all meant to flow, without rigid lines for what or where you choose to eat.

RED HILLS PROVINCIAL DINING

503-538-8224
www.redhillsdining.com
276 Highway 99W
Open: Tues.–Sun. 5–9

Operated since 1992 by owner/chef team Richard and Nancy Gherts, Red Hills has long been a favorite of the wine-and-dine crowd. The restaurant is in a 1920s bungalow and sits just off the highway enough that you might miss it if you aren't paying attention. Slow food is taken seriously here, so don't go if you have something else to do the same evening. Sit back, savor, repeat. And save room for the hand-made desserts and ice cream in several intriguing flavors, such as lavender.

TINA'S RESTAURANT
503-538-8880
www.tinasdundee.com
760 Highway 99W
Open: Tues.–Fri. 11:30–2, daily 5–close
Special Features: Phone reservations a
must; popular recipes on Web site

Tina's is a tiny, stylish bistro where the best
wines of the valley can be found, quite possibly along with the winemakers who made
them. The two inviting and compact rooms
seat about 50. Menu ingredients are farm-
fresh, local, and usually organic. The self-
taught chef team of Tina and David Bergen
believes cuisine happens fast when working
with the freshest food possible, so they let
the food speak for itself—and speak it does!
We spent a memorable evening here,
thanks to the generosity of Sherry's brother
and sister-in-law.

DAYTON
JOEL PALMER HOUSE
503-864-2995
www.joelpalmerhouse.com
600 Ferry Street
Open: Tues.–Sat. 5–9
Price: Moderate to Expensive
Credit Cards: Yes

Special Features: Located in former home
of pioneer Joel Palmer

If you can only afford one extravagant meal
during your tour of Oregon Wine Country,
make it the Joel Palmer House. Jack and
Heidi Czarnecki bought the historic two-
story home with a vision for a restaurant
unlike any other, and they have succeeded.
Though the Czarneckis have always relied
upon locally produced ingredients—with an
assist from international foods—the signature ingredient is mushrooms:
chanterelles, morels, porcinis . . . earthy
morsels in almost every dish. The wild-
mushroom soup is from a 70-year-old
family recipe. Even in dessert you will find
fungi: The crème brûlée recipe integrates
candy-cap mushrooms. How particular is
Jack? He required his son, Chris, to
apprentice for three years before turning
the kitchen over to him in 2009. While Jack
continues to hunt for wild 'shrooms, Chris
has added his own creative touches. The
best bet: Chris's Mushroom Madness Menu
($75). Service is impeccable and friendly,
the atmosphere downright charming. Great
pains are taken to pair an entrée with an
Oregon wine.

Attractions in the Dundee/Dayton Area Area
The reason to come to Dundee is wineries and restaurants. The Dundee Bistro and Carlton
Farms offer a chance to pig out with **Whole Hog Wednesdays** (503-554-1650, 100-A SW
Seventh Street). Dundee Bistro chef Jason Stoller Smith barbecues a whole hog or two, and
prepares traditional sides, all for a mere $15.

Recreation in the Dundee/Dayton Area
Combine walking and sipping with Mark DeLong's **Dundee Hills Walking Wine Tour**
(503-789-7629; $85), a six-mile jaunt that allows you take in the vineyards in full sensory
mode. Pick up the pace a little with the **Red Hills Wine Country Classic** fun runs, 5K and
10K courses through wine country every September. Cap off your run with sparkling wine
from Argyle at Billick Park.

Shopping in the Dundee/Dayton Area
Naturally, even the farmers and other artisans around Dundee combine their produce and
wares with wine. The **Dundee Farmers Market** (503-835-0500) takes place every Sunday

in the summers at the Dundee Bistro/Ponzi Wine Bar parking lot. A place to get locally produced meats every day except Sunday is the **Riteway Meat Company** (503-538-4655, 892 Highway 99W), famed for its custom-made five-foot pepperonis and beef jerky. At **The Dapper Frog** (503-538-4747, 110 SW Seventh St.), you can find a wide assortment of artistic gifts, including vases, bowls, teaware, and, well, frogs.

Information

Dundee Hills Winegrowers Association, 503-864-4300, www.dundeehills.org

Willamette Valley Wineries Association, 503-646-2985, www.willamettewines.com

3

WILLAMETTE VALLEY ROUTE 47

Get Your Sips . . . on Route 47

After watching the Dundee and McMinnville areas steal much of the Willamette Valley wine thunder for years, exasperated winemakers along a largely forgotten corridor just to the west finally waved their hands frantically and said, "Hey, psst, over here—we make some pretty good wine, too!"

Such was the genesis of what is now known as the Sip 47 Wine Route, which is equal parts marketing tool and geographic distinction. The consortium of businesses along OR 47 refers to the area as "The Road Less Traveled," with good reason. Unlike the perpetual traffic jam on OR 99W, the Old Newberg Highway is classic Sunday-drive material, making for some lonely afternoons for the makers of some exceptional wines.

OR 47 in its entirety runs north–south from Clatskanie on the Columbia River through a slice of the Coast Range to the pastoral countryside northeast of McMinnville. But the increasingly popular Sip 47 Wine Route comprises the gentle 20-mile drive between Forest Grove and the burgeoning wine hub of Carlton.

GETTING HERE AND AROUND

The predominant way to enjoy Sip 47 is to start on the north end in Forest Grove and head south. The fastest and easiest way to do this from Portland is to take the Sunset Highway (US 26) west past North Plains to the OR 6 exit. That will connect you with OR 47 about seven miles north of Forest Grove. Turn left and continue into Forest Grove—the beginning of your Sip 47 journey.

FOREST GROVE AREA

Despite its proximity to burgeoning Portland, Forest Grove has managed to keep its literal (25 miles) and figurative distance from the state's largest city—though it is home to its fair share of commuters.

OPPOSITE: *Lenne's hilltop perch near Yamhill offers splendid views in every direction.* Sherry L. Moore

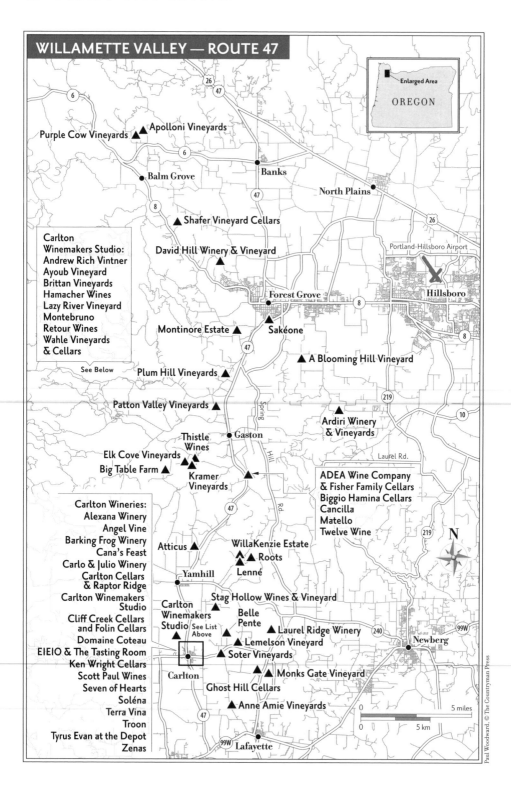

WILLAMETTE VALLEY — ROUTE 47

Enlarged Area

OREGON

6

26
47

Purple Cow Vineyards ▲ ▲ Apolloni Vineyards

6

Balm Grove

Banks

North Plains

47

8

26

▲ Shafer Vineyard Cellars

Portland-Hillsboro Airport

David Hill Winery & Vineyard
▲

Carlton
Winemakers Studio:
Andrew Rich Vintner
Ayoub Vineyard
Brittan Vineyards
Hamacher Wines
Lazy River Vineyard
Montebruno
Retour Wines
Wahle Vineyards
& Cellars

Forest Grove

8

Hillsboro

Montinore Estate ▲   Sakéone

8

47

▲ A Blooming Hill Vineyard

See Below

219

Plum Hill Vineyards ▲

10

Patton Valley Vineyards ▲

Spring

▲ Ardiri Winery
& Vineyards

Thistle
Wines   ● Gaston

Hill

Laurel Rd.

Elk Cove Vineyards ▲

Big Table Farm ▲ ▲ ▲
Kramer
Vineyards   ▲

Rd.

ADEA Wine Company
& Fisher Family Cellars
Biggio Hamina Cellars
Cancilla
Matello
Twelve Wine

219

Carlton Wineries:
Alexana Winery
Angel Vine
Barking Frog Winery
Cana's Feast
Carlo & Julio Winery
Carlton Cellars
& Raptor Ridge
Carlton Winemakers
Studio
Cliff Creek Cellars
and Folin Cellars
Domaine Coteau
EIEIO & The Tasting Room
Ken Wright Cellars
Scott Paul Wines
Seven of Hearts
Soléna
Terra Vina
Troon
Tyrus Evan at the Depot
Zenas

47

N

Atticus ▲

WillaKenzie Estate
▲ ▲ Roots

● Yamhill   Lenné

Stag Hollow Wines & Vineyard
▲

Carlton
Winemakers
Studio   See List
Above

Belle
Pente

▲ Laurel Ridge Winery

240

99W

▲ Lemelson Vineyard   Newberg

▲ Soter Vineyards

Carlton

▲ ▲ Monks Gate Vineyard

Ghost Hill Cellars

▲ Anne Amie Vineyards

0   5 miles

47

0   5 km

99W   Lafayette

Paul Woodward. © The Countryman Press

This American flag–flying town of 21,000 is near the marshy headwaters of the Tualatin River and is the last community of notable size between Portland and the coast on US 26. Though orchards, nurseries, and farmlands dominate now, the large stand of oak trees for which the community is named remains on the campus of Pacific University, a private four-year liberal-arts college.

Forest Grove has done an admirable job of staying connected to its history. There are 10 homes on the National Register of Historic Places, and the McMenamins Grand Lodge is a restored Masonic Lodge and orphanage that elicits visions of another era. Nurseries and well-worn farms immediately surround the town, and clear-cuts in the distant Coast Range make the mountains look like they got a bad haircut.

More than 20 wineries call this stretch home, and for all the relative anonymity of the region, there are some big guns and historic vineyards in the Pinot Noir and Chardonnay worlds here.

Wineries in the Forest Grove Area

The Sip 47 wine route actually begins northwest of Forest Grove off OR 6, also known as NW Wilson River Highway. From Portland, take US 26 (Sunset Highway) west to Banks and the OR 6 exit. Continue west to begin your tour at Apolloni and Purple Cow wineries.

FOREST GROVE
APOLLONI VINEYARDS
503-359-3606 or 503-330-5946
www.apolloni.com
14135 NW Timmerman Road
Tasting Room: Mar.–Dec., Fri.–Sun. 12–5
Fee: $5, refunded with purchase
Owners: Alfredo and Laurine Apolloni
Winemaker: Alfredo Apolloni
Wines: Pinot Blanc, Pinot Gris, Chardonnay, Viognier, rosé, Pinot Noir, red blend, dessert wine
Cases: 1,000
Special Features: Picnic area in a pleasantly off-the-beaten-path vineyard handles large groups with advance notice

Alfredo Apolloni grew up in a winemaking region of northern Italy and his wine label—which features a sixteenth-century family crest in the label—reflects his heritage. The whites, all done in stainless steel (no oak), are clean and crisp with bright acidity. The reds are masterfully crafted, including an estate Pinot that's barrel-aged in 30 to 40 percent new oak. The affable tasting-room staff makes this a pleasurable stop for the wine and the company, and you won't want to miss the Super Tuscan red blend.

PURPLE COW VINEYARDS
503-330-0991
www.purplecowvineyards.com
52720 NW Wilson School Road
Tasting Room: Sat. 11–5 and by appointment
Fee: $5
Owner/Winemaker: Jon Armstrong
Wines: Muscat, Pinot Noir, Maréchal Foch, Tempranillo
Cases: 750

Think you've seen every kind of tasting room imaginable? Think again. Here, tasting takes place in the narrow entryway of the Armstrongs' small home. Jon says he's working on a proper tasting room, but the current setup has its charms. In a highly competitive world, Purple Cow has found a niche with wines that are a little different. The off-dry Muscat is a find! Stop by and you're likely to get an extensive education in winemaking, if you're interested. "A winery for wine nerds" is how the good-natured Jon describes Purple Cow. As for the colored bovine spots on the label, the name comes from an imaginary friend of the Armstrongs' young daughter.

SHAFER VINEYARD CELLARS
503-357-6604
www.shafervineyardcellars.com
6200 NW Gales Creek Road
Tasting Room: Apr.–Dec., Thurs.–Mon. 11–5
Fee: Complimentary
Owners: Harvey and Miki Shafer
Winemaker: Harvey Shafer
Wines: Müller Thurgau, Pinot Gris, Gewürztraminer, Riesling, Chardonnay, Pinot Blanc, blush, Pinot Noir, port-style and sparkling wines
Cases: 20,000
Special Features: Year-round shopping in Miki's Santa Shop

The cute front of the tasting room, with its small porch and garden furniture, doesn't prepare you for what's behind the door. A warehouse-sized room filled with Christmas ornaments, decorations, and tchotchkes to fill anyone's stocking adds extra incentive to visit. The Shafers have been making wine for three decades, after planting grapes on their 70 acres in 1973.

DAVID HILL WINERY & VINEYARD
503-992-8545
www.davidhillwinery.com
46350 NW David Hill Road
Tasting Room: Daily 12–5
Fee: Complimentary, $1 per taste for reserves
Owners: Milan and Jean Stoyanov
Winemaker: Jason Bull
Wines: Pinot Gris, Riesling, Chardonnay, Gewürztraminer, Pinot Blanc, Pinot Noir, red and white blends, ports
Cases: 10,000

Special Features: Picnic area, wedding and events facility

Some of the first grapes ever planted in Oregon were rooted here in 1883, when it was known as Reuter's Farm. The farmhouse in which Reuter lived now serves as the tasting room for David Hill Winery, which had its beginnings in 1965 when early wine pioneer Charles Coury planted wine grapes. David Hill is known, not surprisingly, for its Farmhouse Red and Farmhouse White, both exceptional values. The setting is also renowned for its splendid views of rolling landscapes that regularly serve as a backdrop for weddings and other major events; both *Sunset* and *Home & Garden* magazines have touted it as one of the finest anywhere for nuptials. Working at David Hill has given winemaker Jason Bull the opportunity to expand his reach and create his own label: Zimri Cellars (500 cases). Bull eventually hopes to convert a barn on his Zimri Drive property in Newberg into his own winery.

MONTINORE ESTATE
503-359-5012
www.montinore.com
3663 SW Dilley Road
Tasting Room: Daily 11–5
Fee: $5 for five wines
Owner: Marchesi family
Winemakers: John Lundy and Stephen Webber
Wines: Riesling, Pinot Gris, Müller Thurgau, Gewürztraminer, Pinot Noir, Merlot, Syrah, port-style and dessert wines
Cases: 36,000
Special Features: Music performances in tasting room, barrel tastings

Every winery has its branding, and at Montinore it's the size and scope of their biodynamic efforts. Sure, many wineries in this progressive state are engaged in natural farming, but Montinore (along with

Cooper Mountain) is a forerunner in an increasingly popular approach that some swear by and others deride as voodoo vine-onomics. Rudy Marchesi purchased Montinore and its sprawling 230 acres of grapes in 2001, and started down the natural path two years later. Today, Montinore has earned the lofty tag of "certified biodynamic"—a label with rigorous standards. Be sure to take home some bottles of their specialty chocolate Pinot syrup.

SAKÉONE
503-357-7056
www.sakeone.com
820 Elm Street
Tasting Room: Daily 11–5
Fee: $3–10
Winemaker: Greg Lorenz, sake master
Wines: Momokawa label (silver, diamond, ruby, and pearl), Moonstone label (fruit-infused), G Label (premium)
Special Features: Tours, food-pairing flight

When we were at SakéOne, they were setting up for an event in their parking lot, a limousine was pulling away, and a new batch of tasters arrived in a van. It was a hopping place, ensuring that saké is not just for occasional Japanese dinners. Greg Lorenz is the only American saké master, and is definitely masterful at fermentation of the rice. The fruit sakés are extremely food-friendly. The G label (stands for *genshu*) packs an elegant punch with 18 percent alcohol.

CORNELIUS
ARDIRI WINERY & VINEYARDS
503-628-6060 or 888-503-3330
www.ardiriwinery.com
35040 SW Unger Road
Tasting Room: Daily 10–5 and by appointment
Fee: $10 for four wines and logo glass
Owners/Winemakers: Gail Lizak and John Compagno

Wines: Pinot Noir
Cases: 1,500

Compagno and Lizak purchased the Gypsy Dancer winery site in 2008 from renowned winemaker Gary Andrus, who passed away soon after. But the relationship had begun earlier, with a merging of the Willamette and Napa Valleys. Compagno and Lizak owned a five-acre vineyard of Pinot Noir in Napa and brought their grapes north to Gypsy Dancer, where Lizak had worked and where Andrus made Ardiri's first wine—a 2006 Carneros Napa Valley Pinot Noir. For now, it's all about the Pinot, but plans are in the works for gris and blanc. The new owners also envisioned a spring 2010 opening of a formal tasting room, complete with a welcoming fireplace.

A BLOOMING HILL VINEYARD
503-992-1196
www.abloominghillvineyard.com
5195 SW Hergert Road
Tasting Room: Memorial Day, Labor Day, and Thanksgiving weekends, and by appointment
Fee: $5, refunded with purchase
Owners: Jim and Holly Witte
Winemaker: Jim Witte
Wines: Pinot Noir, white blend
Cases: 1,000

One of the state's newest wineries produced its first commercial vintages in 2008—a Pinot Noir and a Chardonnay–Pinot Gris–Riesling blend that Jim Witte calls, appropriately, Mingle. The operation is small, with the tasting room in the basement of the Wittes' home. As with most small vintners, the Wittes' commitment to their land and vines is a labor of hand. They have steadfastly resisted efforts to subdivide a rapidly growing bedroom community in an effort to keep the land in agriculture. "He's out there every day and touches the vines," Holly Witte says.

The Grand Lodge in Forest Grove is a hot spot.   Courtesy McMenamin's

Lodging in the Forest Grove Area

FOREST GROVE

MCMENAMINS GRAND LODGE
503-992-9533
www.mcmenamins.com
3505 Pacific Avenue
Rates: $40–205
Special Features: Restaurants, pubs, the-ater, heated soaking pool

This historic 77-room hotel with expansive grounds near downtown joined the McMenamins family in 2000. The hotel and surrounding buildings come with enough stories to fill several books—and you might hear a few ghosts whispering from the walls. One of the appeals of such a grand place is that it fits all budgets: You can have a room with a private bath, or for $40 a bunk bed and shower down the hall. There is so much history to absorb, and so many photos on the walls to peruse, that you could lose track of time and forget why you're here—to sip wines on Route 47.

OLD RECREATION INN
Owner: Kim Fox
503-318-2301
www.oldrecreation.com
1718 23rd Avenue
Rates: $70–140
Special Features: Wedding and event facilities

Slip into something comfortable in one of two inns: a 1925 Craftsman-style or a reno-vated 1909 home nearby. Accommodation options include renting entire floors for large groups. Both inns have appealing porches and pretty grounds and are well suited to weddings and special events. Between the two inns, there are 11 rooms and seven baths. Old Recreation Inn's near-future plans include a van for wine touring.

Dining in the Forest Grove Area

GALES CREEK
OUT AZA BLUE MARKET & CAFE

503-357-2900
www.outazablue.com
57625 NW Wilson River Highway
Open: Wed.–Fri. 11.–9, Sat.–Sun. 8 A.M.
–10 P.M.
Credit Cards: Yes
Special Features: Summer outdoor seating
at picnic tables, breakfast served until 5
P.M., dinner reservations recommended

It's a little out-AZA-way, but don't let that
deter you. This is a destination eatery on
your way to anywhere. The menu is
Mediterranean-inspired with a vividly colorful scheme to match. For lunch, grab a
burger, wrap, or the potent Vegenator
sandwich, which the owner and five-star
chef Gabriel—he's so good, he only goes by
one name—claims will halt any desire to be
carnivorous again. Also on the docket are
chicken, salmon, halibut, trout, wild mushrooms, pastas, pizzas, and the specialty:
fresh-baked breads, including focaccia. It's
essential for stop-and-go, or you can sit for
a pleasant surprise in the small full-service
restaurant. Gabriel prides himself on supporting the local wineries; he has some
interesting and hard-to-find domestic and
foreign bottles.

FOREST GROVE
MAGGIE'S BUNS CAFÉ

503-992-2231
www.maggiesbuns.com
2007 21st Avenue
Open: Mon.–Fri. 6:30 A.M.–5:30 P.M.,
Sat. 7–2
Price: Moderate

Credit Cards: Yes
Special Features: Catering services

Maggie's Buns is a breakfast and lunch spot
specializing in unique salads and Thai
dishes, but they're most famous for soups
such as B-52 chili, Hungarian mushroom,
and seafood chowder. You can count on
Maggie's to bake its own sandwich bread
and robust cinnamon rolls daily. The lunch
menu, which varies from season to season,
features up to a dozen entrees and as many
as 10 different salads. The presence of
Stumptown Coffee tells you they cater to
locals and Pacific University students, as
well as lucky visitors.

URBAN DECANTER WINE COLLECTION & BAR

503-359-7678
www.urbandecanter.com
2030 Main Street
Open: Sun.–Mon. 3–7, Tues.–Thurs. 11–9,
Fri.–Sat. 11–10
Price: Inexpensive
Special Features: Wine of the Month Club,
special events featuring music and winemakers, humidor

Winemakers have to eat and socialize, too,
and so Hope Kramer and Danielle French
had this novel idea. With so many winemakers and tourists in the area, why not
bring them together in a non-intimidating
setting where one could learn from the
other? The result is Urban Decanter, where
you're sure to rub shoulders with one of the
many area vintners. Find out more about
Oregon wines over nibbles and such appetizers as paninis, pastas, and salads while
enjoying a glass of local vino. Retail sales
highlight local wines.

Attractions in the Forest Grove Area

Even if you're not staying or dining, there's no movie experience quite like the brew pub
showing independent films at **McMenamins** (503-992-9533, 3505 Pacific Ave.). If you're
in the mood for something live, the **Theatre in the Grove** (503-359-5349, 2028 Pacific
Ave.) offers theater productions throughout the year.

Shopping in the Forest Grove Area

Antiques and other collectibles such as jewelry, china, and pottery are the specialty at **Collections in the Attic** (503-357-0316, 2020 Main St.) near downtown Forest Grove. Right next door, the **Valley Art Association** (503-357-3703, 2022 Main St.) displays juried works by local and regional artists.

Wine Shopping in the Forest Grove Area

The place to pick up a bottle of Oregon wine is **The Friendly Vine** (503-359-1967, 2004 Main St.), which also has wines from Europe, Australia, and South America. The Friendly Vine offers events, private gatherings, and music with tastings every Friday evening. Owner Randy Reeder has been known to say: "If you have a wine emergency, just call me."

Recreation in the Forest Grove Area

For the water-minded, **Henry Hagg Lake** just southwest of Forest Grove is a popular get-away for Portlanders for its boating, Jet Skiing, fishing, swimming, and sailing.

GASTON TO YAMHILL

Between Forest Grove and Carlton, Gaston and Yamhill are just now starting to ride the coattails of the wine industry's success—albeit slowly. With so many wineries and vine-yards calling Gaston home, you'd think this town of 650 would be alive with wine events. Not so, but it's trying.

As recently as 2006, the town began serious discussions about revamping East Main Street to be more attractive to the wine industry, à la Carlton. Meanwhile, Yamhill has retained more of its traditional agricultural aura—timber, wheat, barley, and dairy farm-ing—than its sister city Carlton. But there is no escaping wine's hold on these communities.

Wineries in the Gaston and Yamhill Area

GASTON
PLUM HILL VINEYARDS

503-359-4706
www.plumhillwine.com
6505 SW Old Highway 47
Tasting Room: Mon.–Sat. 11–5, Sun. 12–5
Fee: Complimentary
Owners: R. J. and Juanita Lint
Winemaker: Kramer family
Wines: Riesling, Pinot Blanc, Pinot Gris, Pinot Noir
Cases: Under 1,000
Special Features: Gift shop, picnic area, wedding facility, patio with firepit, special events such as Date Night

The folks at Plum Hill certainly have a sense of humor. R. J. and Juanita Lint were so thrilled to be getting into the business of running their own winery in 2008 that they began naming individual vines in their small vineyard. Our favorites are Cork Douglas, Crush Limbaugh, Wineona Jug, Fermento Valenzuela, and Marilyn Merlot. The Lints first got their hands grapey as volunteers during crush and harvest at Kramer Vineyards. At Plum Hill, they pur-chased a decaying farm and are using the old buildings for processing and a tasting room. A new facility, however, is in the works.

PATTON VALLEY VINEYARDS

503-985-3445
www.pattonvalley.com
9449 SW Old Highway 47
Tasting Room: Mar.–Dec., Thurs.–Sun.
11–5; Jan.–Feb., Sat.–Sun. 11–5
Fee: $5
Owners: Monte Pitt and Dave Chen
Winemakers: Jerry Murray
Wines: Rosé, Pinot Noir
Cases: 3,200

Patton Valley is an unassuming winery in a wealthy neighborhood. There is no artwork, no lavish fixtures, no high-beam ceilings, no expensive furnishings, just Pinot Noir. It's not a name-dropper, just one of those wineries that consistently produces well-made Pinot. One of our favorites, rosé, is here. It sells out quickly—so grab it when you can. Patton Valley helped organize the Sip 47 marketing strategy to start coaxing folks to escape the OR 99W bottleneck and drive into their neck of the woods.

BIG TABLE FARM

503-662-3129
www.bigtablefarm.com
26851 NW Williams Canyon Road
Tasting Room: By appointment only
Owners: Brian Marcy and Clare Carver
Winemaker: Brian Marcy
Wines: Rosé, Pinot Noir, Syrah
Cases: 250
Special Features: Farm-wine dinners for case buyers

You can have your chickens and eat them too at Big Table Farm. The simple concept born in the minds of Californians Carver and Marcy is to raise what they like to eat and drink. Pork, beef, broilers, and laying hens are humanely raised on natural grasses. Some critters have a mobile housing unit called the "Winnebago" for greater access to their 70 acres. Until their vineyard is in the ground, grapes are purchased from Oregon and California for their small lots of wine. Brian's winery experience is grounded in Napa and Australia. Clare's artistic skills round out the multitalented couple's creative world; her art can be seen around Carlton and on several award-winning wine labels—which in turn allows her to buy more animals. The table is set for big things to come.

ELK COVE VINEYARDS

503-985-7760
www.elkcove.com
27751 NW Olson Road
Tasting Room: Daily 10–5, closed major holidays
Fee: $5
Owners: Joe and Pat Campbell
Winemaker: Adam Godlee Campbell
Wines: Pinot Blanc, Pinot Gris, Pinot Noir
Cases: 36,000
Special Features: Winemaker dinners, special events

If you haven't seen an Elk Cove label, you haven't been out of the house enough. The Campbells started their winery in the mid-1970s and have built an established empire—one of the best-known Oregon wineries in and outside the state. It takes outstanding marketing to get there, but it also takes outstanding wine. Two of Elk Cove's 2006 Pinots scored at least 92 from *Wine Spectator,* and *Wine Press Northwest* voted Elk Cove the top winery in the region in 2007. The tasting room is nothing short of astounding—if you can take your eyes off the trophy Roosevelt elk mount over the tasting bar, you'll see sensational views.

KRAMER VINEYARDS

503-662-4545
www.kramerwine.com
26830 NW Olson Road
Tasting Room: Apr.–Oct., daily 12–5,
Nov.–Mar., Thurs.–Sun. 12–5
Fee: Complimentary, except for reserve wines

Owners: Keith and Trudy Kramer
Winemaker: Trudy Kramer
Wines: Chardonnay, Pinot Gris, Müller Thurgau, rosé, Pinot Noir, Merlot, port-style and sparkling wines
Cases: 2,000
Special Features: Picnic area, gift shop

The new tagline at Kramer Vineyards is "The Optimum Wine Country Experience," which is certainly the case the moment you walk in the door. Winemaker Trudy Kramer is frequently in the tasting room and greets visitors with Celebrate, their fittingly named semi-sweet sparkling. Kramer is comfortable, fun, easygoing, and definitely dog-friendly—you're sure to also be greeted by one of their canines. The tasting room is where the affable staff does its best work, generating more than 80 percent of the winery's sales. Kramer produced its 21st vintage in 2009.

THISTLE WINES

503-590-0449

www.thistlewines.com
26830 NW Olson Road
Tasting Room: By appointment only
Owners: Jon and Laura Jennison
Winemaker: Jon Jennison
Wines: Pinot Blanc, Pinot Gris, Chardonnay, Pinot Noir
Cases: 600

Jon does his winemaking at Kramer Vineyards, where Thistle Wines are available for sale. He and Laura still have an occasional party at their vineyard in Dundee, though. About six times a summer, they open their doors to the public, set up a table, drink wine, and "watch the vines grow." Thistle has 27 acres planted in grapes, mostly Pinot Noir, but sells most of the crop to other wineries.

ADEA WINE COMPANY & FISHER FAMILY CELLARS

503-662-4509
www.adeawine.com
26421 NW Highway 47

Kramer Vineyards offers a serene respite along Route 47. |Jeff Welsch

Tasting Room: Memorial Day, Thanksgiving, and Valentine's Day weekends, and by appointment
Fee: $10–20
Owner: Fisher family
Winemaker: Dean Fisher
Wines: Chardonnay, Pinot Noir
Cases: 1,200
Special Features: Taste up to 25 wines on holiday weekends

The collection of winemakers who show off their wares in the ADEA tasting room was once known as the Gaston Five. Bishop Creek, Cancilla, Matello and Twelve were all part of an initial co-op, and they've been joined by Biggio Hamina to make it the "G-6." ADEA winemaker Dean Fisher serves as a consultant. Following are four wineries that jointly host on holiday weekends; see the Bishop Creek listing under Wineries in the Newberg Area.

BIGGIO HAMINA CELLARS
503-737-9703
www.biggiohamina.com
Owners/Winemakers: Todd and Caroline Hamina
Wines: Pinot Gris, Riesling, Pinot Noir, red blend
Cases: 1,500

The primary focus for Todd Hamina: single-vineyard, single-varietal. "If people are wondering what a certain place tastes like, that's what we deliver," he says. The Riesling is from a vineyard pushing its fourth decade. You should also try the red blend called XIV.

CANCILLA
503-985-7327
www.cancillacellars.com
Owner/Winemaker: Ken Cancilla
Wines: Chardonnay, Pinot Noir
Cases: Under 1,000

Ken Cancilla wears all the hats: he is vineyard owner, manager, and winemaker. He also offers tours by appointment at his vineyard five miles west of Gaston.

MATELLO
503-939-1308
Owner/Winemaker: Marcus Goodfellow
Wines: Pinot Noir
Cases: 500

Goodfellow is as renowned on the Portland cuisine scene—if not more so—than he is for his Pinots, which are produced out of a small winery with the help of Westrey's Amy Wesserman and David Autrey.

TWELVE WINE
503-358-6707
www.twelvewine.com
Owner/Winemaker: John Lenyo
Wines: Pinot Blanc, Pinot Noir
Cases: 975

Twelve's small-production wines frequently sell out and are available primarily at the winery. Tours of the vineyard four miles west of Carlton can be arranged by calling.

YAMHILL
ATTICUS
503-662-3485
www.atticuswine.com
20501 Russell Creek Road
Tasting Room: By appointment only
Fee: $5
Owners: Niall and Freda Porter, and Guy Insley and Ximena Orrego
Winemaker: Scott Shull and Ximena Orrego
Wines: Pinot Noir
Cases: 750
Special Features: Pours at Carlton Cellars in summer

Talk about a harmonic convergence. Four people—two couples—from diverse international backgrounds have found their calling in the vineyards of the Willamette Valley. Niall and Freda are from Ireland, lived in England, and moved to Florida before settling in Oregon. Co-owners Guy and Ximena are from Hong Kong and Peru, respectively, and also lived in Florida. Atticus strictly makes Pinot Noir, and if you're looking for a find they have one for $24 that drinks like much more. Their estate vineyard came on in 2008.

ROOTS

503-730-0296
www.rootswine.com
19320 NE Woodland Loop Road
Tasting room: By appointment only
Owners: Hilary and Chris Berg
Winemaker: Chris Berg
Wines: Pinot Gris, Riesling, Viognier, Melon de Bourgogne, Pinot Noir, red blend
Cases: 2,500
Special Features: Roots is the main brand, Racine is the premium label, and Klee is the value wine.

Chris Berg grew up in a Wisconsin town called Racine—which is French for "root." He never imagined the word would take on such meaning in his future. Hilary Berg has her roots firmly planted in the wine industry as editor of the well-read *Oregon Wine Press,* the face and voice of the Oregon wine scene. Together they grow and make small-lot wines that are highly regarded and sought-after. Chris likes to say that he just helps the fruit get into the bottle. Berg's second label, Black Light, pays homage to the Grateful Dead and promotes psychedelic drinking. The Klee Pinot Noir sells for under $20 and is something to dig for. Friends of ours brought the first-release Pinot Noir (2002) to a birthday celebration in Montana—it was exactly what we had been missing.

WILLAKENZIE ESTATE

503-662-3280
www.willakenzie.com
19143 NE Laughlin Road
Tasting Room: Daily 12–5

Handcrafted Pinots . . . Priceless

That $30–90 you're spending for a bottle Pinot Noir isn't about haughtiness or snootiness. Honest. There are practical reasons why Pinot can be one of the most expensive wines.

For starters, most Oregon vintners are devotees of sustainable, LIVE-certified, organic, and even biodynamic vineyards. As with other natural foods, the costs of dealing in non-toxic ways with pests, disease, weeds, and special equipment all add up.

The fickle and fragile nature of Pinot Noir means extra attention in the vineyard, too. Clusters are thinned or "dropped" by hand, giving the chosen fruit more intense flavors. In addition, vineyard hands cut canes, separate shoots, or thin leaves to create optimum growing conditions. All these hands-on practices have proven highly effective, but labor-intensive.

Then there are the vessels used for aging. A French oak barrel is close to $1,000 these days, yet still remains the choice for its gentle way with Pinot. When the label says "30% new oak," that means new barrels and new costs.

Aura certainly might play a role in the price tag. Although Oregon Pinot production was influenced by the movie *Sideways,* few wineries are exploiting buyers with inflated prices. It simply costs more to handcraft than to mass-produce.

We understand why you may wince at the sticker, but considering the effort and expense that went into the bottle in hand, it's still a pretty good deal. We suggest sharing your Oregon Pinot judiciously.

WillaKenzie Estates has 105 acres of sustainable vineyards. Sherry L. Moore

Fee: $5
Owners: Bernard and Ronni Lacroute
Winemaker: Thibaud Mandet
Wines: Pinot Blanc, Pinot Gris, Pinot Meunier, Gamay Noir, Pinot Noir
Cases: 20,000
Special Features: Picnic tables with views

WillaKenzie has as much of an exclusive-club feel as any winery in Oregon, and you can imagine folks sipping wines in the spacious lounge area while discussing lucrative mutual funds or politics. One look at the walls only heightens the realization that this place is in the upper echelon. Most notable are the letters with a presidential seal recognizing WillaKenzie for its contributions to three Clinton administration functions, including a dinner at Camp David with British prime minister Tony Blair. The grounds are beautifully manicured and a sprawling concrete patio with evenly spaced tables looks out over some of the 420 acres of vineyard, forest, and field. Yet there is a down-to-earth respect for the dirt here. WillaKenzie is no symbol of corporate excess: It is one of the most philanthropic wineries in the area and its vineyards have 105 acres of sustainable grapes, leaving about 300 acres untouched for wildlife and serenity.

LENNÉ

503-956-2256
www.lenneestate.com
18760 NE Laughlin Road
Tasting Room: May–Oct., Thurs.–Sun. 12–5
Fee: $5
Owners: Steve and Karen Lutz
Winemaker: Steve Lutz
Wines: Pinot Noir
Cases: 850
Special Features: "If I'm here, I'm open," Lutz says.

Lenné is easy to spot. Look for a tall, linear, all-stone, French countryside barn at the top of a vineyard that owner Steve Lutz describes as "stellar for Pinot." An iron gate beckons visitors up the steep hill to this eye-catching tasting room and winery. There is a quaint patio for drinking in views of hillside vineyards. Lutz certainly likes to talk about his wines, but ask him about the New Mexico clay walls that took him years to finish. All but about 1 percent of the wines—Lutz calls them "vineyard in a bottle"—are sold in the tasting room.

STAG HOLLOW WINES & VINEYARD

503-662-5609
www.staghollow.com
7930 NE Blackburn Road
Tasting Room: Memorial Day, Labor Day, and Thanksgiving weekends, and by appointment
Fee: Complimentary
Owners: Mark Huff and Jill Zarnowitz
Winemaker: Mark Huff
Wines: Muscat, Dolcetto, Pinot Noir, red and white blends
Cases: 1,300

Stag Hollow uses narrow spacing in its vineyard—three thousand plants per acre—in an effort to coax as much flavor intensity as possible out of the grapes, especially the Pinot Noir. In doing so, Mark and Jill strive for low-input viticulture in producing "artistically crafted distinctive" wines. Part of their earth-friendly philosophy includes

setting aside 10 acres of oak forest, wetlands, and creeks for the area's rich wildlife.

Lodging in the Gaston and Yamhill Area

Yamhill
LAKE HOUSE VACATION RENTAL

503-476-2211
www.distinctivedestination.net
Address not listed for privacy
Rates: $325–425 (three-night minimum), $2,000 weekly (Fri. to Fri.)
Special Features: Thomas Kinkade–like setting with large pond, lily pads, frogs, natural landscape, and well-equipped kitchen

Built by an Irishman to fit his dream-house vision, this rental five miles northwest of Yamhill is one of a kind. The house, from the outside, looks as if it was lifted straight out of Disney's Magic Kingdom. High-pitched gable roofs and a red-arched entrance lend to the fairy-tale setting, and there is thoughtful attention to detail and comfort throughout. You might even see Tinkerbell flitting through the graceful flower gardens. If seclusion and quiet are what you're seeking, it's here. Three bedrooms sleep six.

Attractions in the Gaston and Yamhill Area

Equestrian aficionados will appreciate the **Flying M Ranch** (503-662-3222, 23029 Flying M Rd.) six miles west of Yamhill. The Flying M offers camping and horseback rides from an hour to all day, including a steak-fry ride. **Note:** For 15 years, **RD Steeves Imports, Inc.,** was a destination warehouse that sold imported antique furniture from Europe dating to the early 1800s. The huge converted granary in Yamhill closed its doors for good in August 2009, one of the many Oregon victims of the recession.

CARLTON AREA (YAMHILL-CARLTON DISTRICT AVA)

Carlton is the state's epicenter for wine touring—lively, cozy, energetic, compact, intimate, bustling, and a great place to find a bench and people-watch. For decades, this town of about 1,800 was a railroad stop on the seed-and-grain circuit. One of its top employers was a meatpacking plant.

Wine and vines near Carlton. Courtesy Yamhill Vineyards B&B

Today, the community's red-brick and grain-elevator core is alive with wine-tasting boutiques and charming restaurants. No fewer than 11 wineries call Carlton home, and the old railroad station is a tasting room. In 2002, the innovative Carlton Winemakers Studio was built on the edge of town to house up to 10 vintners. The winery is the first in the country to be registered with the U.S. Green Building Council, and the eye-catching building is LEED-certified.

One of the beauties of Carlton is that so many tasting rooms and wineries are within walking distance. A wine shuttle is also available to take you to the Winemakers Studio and anywhere else in town you want to go.

"The Road Less Traveled" notwithstanding, Carlton is no longer a secret. Memorial Day and Thanksgiving weekends are especially a cluster jam—though it merely adds to the excitement of being here.

Wineries in the Carlton Area

CARLTON
CANA'S FEAST
503-852-0002
www.canasfeastwinery.com
750 West Lincoln Street

Tasting Room: Daily 11–5
Fee: $5, refundable with $20 purchase
Owners: Partnership of 14
Winemaker: Patrick Taylor
Wines: Rosato, Sangiovese, Barbera, Nebbiolo, Primitivo, Pinot Noir, Syrah, Bordeaux blends

Cases: 7,500
Special Features: Cucina serves wine-friendly lunch and dinner Friday through Sunday and hosts special events.

Reminiscent of a modest Italian estate, Cana's Feast—formerly Cuneo—offers Northwest and Italian wines, an eatery with piazza seating, and bocce courts (with organized league play in summer), all accentuated by olive and lemon trees. Cucina has a seasonal menu for lunch and dinner, but you can always buy small nibbles. Don't miss the chef's supper on Thursday night—a three-course meal with glass of wine for $25 is a wine-country bargain. One of Cana's more unique and noteworthy wines is the Sangiovese grosso, the same clone used in Brunello di Montalcino. It took some doing, but it was brought over from Italy, quarantined, put through a lengthy certification process, and finally made available in 2007. Cana's other wines for the masses are the Bricco, a red table blend, and the Two Rivers Bordeaux blend—both retail for around $15, a real value. We spent a delightful New Year's Eve here with friends.

CARLTON WINEMAKERS STUDIO
503-852-6100
www.winemakersstudio.com
801 North Scott Street
Tasting Room: Daily 11–5, closed Jan.
Fee: $5–18 for two to four flights

All for one and one for all—that's the innovative and authentically cooperative spirit behind Carlton Winemakers Studio. It's the vision of winemaker Eric Hamacher and Lazy River Vineyard owner Ed Lumpkin—the latter needing a winemaker, the former yearning for a green winery. When the idea of a wine co-op was hatched, an alternating proprietorship was illegal in Oregon. Hamacher and Lumpkin fought the state for years and eventually won. The stunning

building opened in 2002 on the southwest outskirts of little Carlton and, as *Food & Wine* magazine puts it, "is just plain cool." Each of the tenants provides their own fruit and barrels, and they rotate use of the facility. The Golden Rule: You'd better clean the equipment. With so many tenants sharing, things could get testy, but there's a kinship at work here. Case in point: One vintner had to rush home to New York for a family medical emergency in the middle of crush. No worries—everyone signed up for a shift to do his punch-downs. If you want the lowdown on the studio, talk to Barbie, the financial wiz and surrogate mom to all. If you want an education with your pour, talk to Phil, the tasting-room guru.

The list of tenants isn't static, but as of November 2009 the building was hosting the following elite eight:

ANDREW RICH VINTNER
503-852-6100
www.andrewrichwines.com
Owner/Winemaker: Andrew Rich
Wines: Sauvignon Blanc, Roussanne, Cabernet franc, Mourvèdre, Malbec, Pinot Noir, Syrah, Petite Verdot, red and white blends, dessert wine
Cases: 8,000

Andrew Rich is a maestro with single varietals, but also has a respected reputation as a blend master. Rich, listed among the top 100 winemakers in *Wine & Spirits* for 2009, has a devoted following. Who does a Petite Verdot solo? Hardly anyone, except the maverick Rich. One barrel a year, it's funky, spunky, and only available to wine club members. If you happen to catch him at the Studio, you'll see why he is known for his dry sense of humor, quick tongue, and wit. Justin Van Zanten, Rich's longtime assistant, makes his own label (J. Daan) of ultra-high-quality, low-priced Pinot and Syrah.

AYOUB VINEYARD

503-554-9583 or 503-805-2154
www.ayoubwines.com
9650 NE Keyes Lane
Tasting Room: By appointment on weekends at the vineyard
Fee: Complimentary
Owner: Mohamed "Mo" Ayoub
Winemaker: Robert Brittan
Wines: Pinot Noir
Cases: 750
Special Features: Pours at Carlton Winemakers Studio on holidays

Mo Ayoub searched for his dream spot for a vineyard, and as luck or perseverance would have it, he found it in the Dundee Hills. His full focus is on Pinot Noir and he sells fruit to some highbrow neighbors. His wines—the top-shelf Ayoub and budget-minded Memoire— are as elegant as the labels suggest.

BRITTAN VINEYARDS

503-989-2507
www.brittanvineyards.com

Owner/Winemaker: Robert Brittan
Wines: Pinot Noir, Syrah
Cases: 800

Robert Brittan first made wine in his dorm room at Oregon State University— a dorm-tiste, if you will. Brittan was at the famous Stags Leap in Napa for many years, but when the winery wouldn't let him make his Pinot Noir he and his wife, Ellen, returned to Oregon. They have their own vineyard with Pinot and Syrah in the McMinnville AVA. Brittan and Eric Hamacher have history together, and both are dedicated to environmental stewardship. In fact, Robert is taking a role in management to help the Studio elevate its already lofty game. Brittan's Pinot is a winner that flies out the door. His Chardonnay is Chablis-style: bright, crisp, and nuanced with flavors of green apple.

HAMACHER WINES

503-852-7200
www.hamacherwines.com

Memorial Day weekend brings flocks of visitors to Carlton. John Baker

Owner/Winemaker: Eric Hamacher
Wines: Chardonnay, Pinot Noir
Cases: 1,500

Hamacher, the brains and inspiration behind CWS, is a dad first and celebrated winemaker second. Third, he's a recently licensed ski patrol member and plans to spend winter family time in Bend. Oh, and he's married to winemaker extraordinaire Louisa Ponzi, with whom he has four children. That means he comes in at 5 A.M. so he can pick up the kids after school; Louisa works late at Ponzi. He and Louisa could have written the book on Oregon Chardonnay. They've even developed their own clones. Renowned for perfection, elegance, and consistency, Eric was the first Oregon winemaker to score a 95 from Robert Parker Jr. with his Chardonnay.

LAZY RIVER VINEYARD

503-662-5400
www.lazyrivervineyard.com
Owners: Ned and Kirsten Lumpkin
Winemaker: Eric Hamacher
Wines: Pinot Gris, Riesling, Pinot Noir
Cases: 950

There's nothing lazy about Ned and Kirsten, residents of Sun Valley, Idaho, who share equal ownership of the studio with Hamacher and Ponzi. Ed is a champion masters downhill skier and yoga enthusiast, and Kirsten is a master bridge player. Both are into their grandkids and wine. People have been flocking to their Pinot Noir and Pinot Gris since they began producing in 2005. But truth be told, their dry Riesling is perfection in a glass.

MONTEBRUNO

503-852-6100
www.montebrunowine.com
Owner/Winemaker: Joe Pedicini

Wines: Gewürztraminer, Pinot Noir
Cases: 250

Joe Pedicini just might be the next great wine movie. The vagabond chef from Brooklyn, New York, shows up in Oregon for a few weeks each year to turn Willamette Valley grapes into stellar wine. He signed a contract with CWS sight unseen, and arrived in the fall of 2009 with an oak barrel in a Subaru Outback. While he's here, he sleeps on friends' couches. Pedicini is an enigma, but his engaging personality and penchant for feeding everyone have quickly earned him close ties. (When his mother had a stroke, everyone pitched in to do his winemaking.) When he's finished, he packs some bottles, leaves a few, and isn't seen again until the next year.

RETOUR WINES

971-237-4757
www.retourwines.com
Owner: Lindsay Woodard
Winemaker: Eric Hamacher
Wines: Pinot Noir
Cases: 900

The '06 Retour Pinot Noir received a 92 from *Wine Spectator,* which explains why *Food & Wine* describes Retour as a star producer. *Retour* is French for "back to the roots" or "a homecoming that endures." Owner Lindsay Woodard is a sixth-generation Oregonian who lived briefly in Napa Valley before Pinot fever called her back to her native state.

WAHLE VINEYARDS & CELLARS

503-241-3385
www.wvcellars.com
Owners: Mark and Shaghayegh Wahle
Winemaker: Mark Wahle
Wines: Pinot Noir
Cases: 2,000

The Wahle family lays claims to planting Yamhill-Carlton's first commercial vineyard on a 100-acre site in 1974. In a familiar story, after years of watching others produce great Pinots from their grapes, they're now entering the fray with their own label—a recently released 2006 Yamhill-Carlton Pinot Noir. Along the way, they've added another vineyard on Holmes Hill, where they will be producing wines from younger clones.

RAPTOR RIDGE

503-367-4263
www.raptoridge.com
130 West Monroe Street
Tasting Room: May–Nov., Fri.–Sun. 11–4 and by appointment
Fee: $5
Owners: Scott and Annie Shull
Winemaker: Scott Shull
Wines: Pinot Gris, Pinot Noir, Rosé, dessert wines
Cases: 6,500
Special Features: Wine events

Raptor Ridge is so named because of the variety of predators cruising the thermals above the Chehalem Mountain foothills, mostly hawks. In August 2010, visitors will be treated to the vision for the first time because Raptor Ridge is moving into a full-fledged winery on OR 219 about 10 miles north of Newberg. Winemaker Scott Shull has earned his share of awards, most notably for his array of 2006 Pinots.

CARLTON CELLARS

503-474-8986
www.carltoncellarscom
130 West Monroe Street
Tasting Room: May–Nov., Sat.–Sun. 11–4 and by appointment; Dec.–Apr., by appointment on weekends
Fee: $5
Owners: Dave Grooters and Robin Russell
Winemaker: Dave Grooters

Wines: Pinot Noir, rosé
Cases: 2,500
Special Features: Participation in harvest during "crush days"; Raptor Ridge is a coresident at the tasting room

Friendships form the basis of the Carlton Cellars story. A longtime bond between Dave and Army buddy Nick Peirano of Nick's Italian Cafe sparked an interest in Oregon wine. An evolving friendship with Ken Wright led to a vineyard-manager position. Another friendship, formed on a flight from Pennsylvania to Oregon, turned into a romance and eventual wedded partnership between Dave and Robin. Their wine labels reference another strong bond the couple has . . . with the Pacific Ocean. Their flagship Pinot is the Road's End. In 2008, they released an estate Pinot from their Russell Grooters Vineyard, called Cape Lookout. A third wine, Agate Beach, is a dry Rosé of Pinot Noir and only made when the harvest is right. We suggest forming a friendship with any of three.

ZENAS

503-852-3000
www.zenaswines.com
407 West Main Street, #7
Tasting Room: Sat.–Sun. 12–5
Owners: Howard Family
Winemakers: Kevin and Blake Howard
Wines: Riesling, Merlot, Cabernet franc, red blend
Cases: 1,000

The Howards are descendants of early Oregon pioneer Zenas Howard, who came west on the Oregon Trail and landed in southern Oregon. You might say the fruit for their signature blend, Meritage, as well as the Merlot and Cabernet Franc, comes from "home." The Del Rio Vineyard in southern Oregon supplies the grapes for the reds, and the Riesling comes from Montinore.

HAWKINS CELLARS

503-481-9104
www.hawkinscellars.com
407 West Main Street, building #3
Tasting Room: Fri.–Sun. 12–6 and by
appointment
Fee: Complimentary
Owner/Winemaker: Thane Hawkins
Wines: Pinot Gris, Cabernet Sauvignon,
Pinot Noir, Syrah
Cases: 500

Living the dream, young, active, and creative Hawkins, an animator by trade who
once worked for DreamWorks, makes
small-lot wine from vineyards around the
state. And somehow he keeps the prices
reasonable (in the low $20s). He was a cel-
lar rat for a few of the more well-known
wineries in the area when he got his chance
to make his own batch at Methven. The bug
stuck and he's making award-winning wine
for his own label. **Note:** At press time,
Hawkins' tasting room had closed. A new
location was to be determined.

ALEXANA WINERY

503-852-3013
www.alexanawinery.com
116 West Main Street
Tasting Room: Wed.–Sun. 11–6
Fee: Varies
Owner: Madaiah Revana
Winemaker: Lynn Penner-Ash
Wines: Pinot Gris, Pinot Noir
Special Features: Charcuterie and cheese
pairings, private tastings

Alexana has a brand-new tasting room and
hasn't wasted any time making its presence
felt in Pinot country. The 2007 Revana
Vineyard Pinot Noir scored a 92 from
Parker, and the '06 Shea Vineyard Pinot
was right behind with a 91. Alexana is
named for the daughter of owner Madaiah
Revana, a former Houston cardiologist

whose passion for wines first drew him to
the Napa Valley. After producing first-rate
Cabernet Sauvignon in California, Revana
turned his attention to the Willamette
Valley and Pinot Noir. With assistance from
the renowned winemaker Penner-Ash, he
bought 80 acres in the Dundee Hills—16
already planted in Pinot Gris and Pinot
Noir—and produced Alexana's first wines in
2006.

SEVEN OF HEARTS

971-241-6548
www.sevenofheartswine.com
217 West Main Street
Tasting Room: Fri.–Sat. 1–6 and by
appointment
Fee: Complimentary
Owner/Winemaker: Byron Dooley
Wines: Chardonnay, Viognier, Pinot Noir,
white blend
Cases: 500
Special Features: Shares tasting space with
Honest Chocolates, owned by Byron's wife,
Dana

A cat named Seven stole their hearts, and
the same can be said for the heartbreak
grape Pinot Noir. Byron's Pinot is firmly
Burgundian, and so is his Cardonnay fermented in neutral oak. Both exhibit a powerful wow factor. Byron, left in the rubble
of the dot-com boom and bust a decade
ago, says that once he satisfies his challenge
of perfecting Pinot, he will move to
Bordeaux and Rhône varietals and possibly
pursue the perfect Riesling.

TROON

503-852-3084
www.troonvineyard.com
250 North Kutch Street
Tasting Room: Summer, daily 11–6, winter
11–5, closed Jan.
Fee: $5, refunded with purchase
Special Features: Music on Sat.

One of the perks of stopping by Seven of Hearts is the Honest Chocolates counter. |John Baker

This is a second tasting room for this renowned southern Oregon winery (see Wineries in the Grants Pass Area).

KEN WRIGHT CELLARS

503-852-7070
www.kenwrightcellars.com
236 North Kutch Street
Tasting Room: None
Owner/Winemaker: Ken Wright
Wines: Chardonnay, Pinot Blanc, vineyard designate Pinot Noir
Cases: 10,000
Special Features: Thanksgiving open house

Ken Wright Cellars is rarely open to the public, so you'll have to use a bit of imagination when it comes to envisioning the magic woven inside. But don't interpret that to mean Wright is a wine snob. When Sherry was the wine buyer for First Alternative Co-op in Corvallis, the unpretentious and practical Ken would personally deliver his Celilo Chardonnay for the co-op's shelves when he was coming through town. Most of Wright's single-vineyard Pinots are sold as futures, the rest allocated. His Pinots are pricey, but a value considering the meticulous care and expense that go into them. His other label, Tyrus Evan, does have a tasting room in Carlton (see listing).

ANGEL VINE

503-969-7209
www.angelvine.net
258 North Kutch Street
Tasting Room: Memorial Day and Thanksgiving weekends, and by appointment
Fee: Complimentary by appointment, $5 on holidays
Owner/Winemaker: Ed Fus
Wines: Zinfandel, Primitivo, Petite Sirah, Pinot Noir
Cases: 1,600
Special Features: Shares tasting space with Domaine Coteau

Ed Fus started his Three Angels winery in 2007 and was soon told that the name sounded too much like a winery in that southern-bordering state. Rather than face a legal battle, Fus kept the same label design but changed the name to Angel Vine. For now, he's a custom-crush client who wears a lot of hats—"winemaker and head grunt," he claims. His forte is Zinfandel from Washington grapes and Primitivo, though he is expanding. Fus is devoted to sustainable agriculture and serves on the LIVE board.

DOMAINE COTEAU

503-697-7319
www.domainecoteau.com
258 North Kutch Street
Tasting Room: By appointment only
Fee: Complimentary
Owner/Winemaker: Dean Sandifer
Wines: Pinot Noir
Cases: 3,000
Special Features: Hosts local artists, shares tasting room with Troon and Angel Vine

Aside from producing only Pinot Noir, Domaine Coteau touts its attention to the density of its Pinot vines at the vineyard in the Eola-Amity Hills AVA. With nearly 2,500 plants per acre on 17 acres, Domaine Coteau exceeds the standard spacing used elsewhere on the West Coast. The belief is that fewer grapes per plant will enhance quality while still enabling the winery to produce as many tons as a typical vineyard. Sandifer's first Pinot Noir (1998) was voted Best of Class at the San Diego National Wine Competition.

EIEIO & THE TASTING ROOM

503-852-6733
www.onhisfarm.com
105 West Main Street
Tasting Room: Thurs.–Mon. 11–5
Fee: $10–20
Owner/Winemaker: Jay McDonald

Wines: Chardonnay, Pinot Noir
Cases: 1,800
Special Features: The Tasting Room is a converted bank where you can taste EIEIO's wines and other hard-to-find selections

Plucky ol' Jay McDonald was a New York financial wizard who found a way to buy the proverbial farm . . . er, winery. McDonald is a *négociant,* which means he buys juice from other wineries and, with a tweak, tweak here and a blend, blend there, comes up with his own wine. When we asked which one we should try, since we were alcohol-restricted while working, he replied, "None. They're not ready." Taking his personal advice, consider buying and putting it down—and maybe uncorking when the economy turns around. McDonald has big plans: he aims to plant his own grapes and open a winery at an undisclosed location.

TERRA VINA

503-925-0712
www.terravinawines.com
214 West Main Street
Tasting Room: May–Nov., Sat.–Sun. 12–5 and by appointment
Fee: $5
Owners: Karl and Carole Dinger
Winemaker: Karl Dinger
Wines: Cabernet franc, Chardonnay, Riesling, Cabernet Sauvignon, Malbec, Pinot Noir, Sangiovese, Syrah, red blends
Cases: 1,800
Special Features: Vineyard opens for tastings Thanksgiving weekend

The name has changed, but the wines haven't. Two motives precipitated the Dingers' decision to change Dalla Vina Wines to Terra Vina Wines: an occasionally awkward similarity to a California winery and an urge to be more environmentally friendly. Whether they've made progress on the first remains to be seen. On the second, they are determined to walk the talk. Their motto, "Respecting The Earth, Creating Great Wine," applies both professionally and personally. In the vineyard, the focus is on sacrificing high yield for high quality, and the wines reflect the intent.

CLIFF CREEK CELLARS
503-852-0089
www.cliffcreek.com
128 West Main Street
Tasting Room: June–Sept., daily 12–6,
Oct.–May, Sat.–Sun. 12–6
Fee: $5, refunded with purchase
Owner: Garvin family
Winemaker: Joe Dobbes Jr.
Wines: Cabernet Sauvignon, Cabernet franc, Merlot, Syrah, red blend
Cases: 1,600
Special Features: Shares tasting room with Folin Cellars from Gold Hill

The address says Carlton, but everything else about Cliff Creek is southern Oregon—the grapes are grown in the Rogue Valley. The Garvin family is spread out, which explains a tasting room nearly 300 miles from home. The youngest daughter, Ruth, lives in the Portland area and oversees the tasting room. The space was made available by their Gold Hill neighbors at Folin Cellars, who invited them to double the southern Oregon fun in Carlton. The winery is proudest of its Claret and Syrah.

FOLIN CELLARS
503-349-9616
www.folincellars.com
118 West Main Street
Tasting Room: Sat. 1–6, Sun. 1–5
Fee: Complimentary
Wines: Viognier, Grenache, Mourvèdre, rosé, Syrah, Tempranillo, Petite Verdot

Cliff Creek Cellars is based in southern Oregon, but has a tasting room in Carlton.   John Baker

Cases: 1,000

Special Features: Shares space with Cliff Creek Cellars.

If you're Pinoted out, this is your stop; all of the wines are extraordinary. This is a tasting room for Folin's Rogue Valley winery (see Wineries in the Medford Area).

BARKING FROG WINERY

503-702-5029

www.barkingfrogwinery.com

128 West Main Street

Tasting Room: Fri.–Sun. 1–5 and by appointment

Fee: $10–15

Owners: Ron and Cindy Helbig

Winemaker: Ron Helbig

Wines: Cabernet Sauvignon, Pinot Noir, Sangiovese, Syrah

Cases: 1,000

Special Features: Barking Frog uses the Vino Seal, a glass-topped cork substitute

Helbig was an amateur winemaker who won so many awards he decided to enroll in Chemeketa Community College's eonology and viticulture program. Eventually he wound up with an internship/friendship with Soléna's Laurent Montalieu. Humble and softspoken, Helbig relies on grapes from small vineyards and uses earth-friendly, sustainable practices. He makes his ultra-premium wines at the August Cellars facility. He prefers to focus on Columbia Valley grapes instead of competing with hundreds of Pinot Noir producers. The origin of the winery's name is left to the imagination, but the general idea is that the frog is a symbol of prosperity and a barometer of environmental health.

TYRUS EVAN AT THE DEPOT

503-852-7010

www.tyrusevan.com

120 North Pine Street

Tasting Room: Summer, daily 11–6, winter 11–5

Colorful downtown Carlton is an appealing stop at the end of Sip 47. John Baker

Fee: $10, refunded with case purchase
Owner/Winemaker: Ken Wright
Wines: Cabernet franc, Malbec, Syrah, red blend
Cases: 1,500
Special Features: Covered picnic area on a railroad station platform, gift shop

Talented and iconic in the world of vineyard-specific Pinot Noir, Ken Wright branched out into working with warmer-climate grapes under the Tyrus Evan label. The moniker is a blend of his two sons' names. The sophisticated country-leisure tasting room is hard to miss: it's in the town's refurbished train station. In keeping with his commitment to supporting the community that supports him, Wright is instrumental in revitalizing old structures in Carlton, orchestrating community events, and building name recognition for the sub-appellations of the Willamette Valley. He was also one of the first to buy grapes by the acre instead of by the ton, allowing him to keep yields low and quality high in the vineyards he works with.

SCOTT PAUL WINES

503-852-7300
www.scottpaul.com
128 South Pine Street
Tasting Room: Wed.–Sun. 11–4
Fee: $5, refunded with purchase
Owners: Scott Paul and Martha Wright
Winemaker: Scott Paul Wright
Wines: Pinot Noir
Cases: 3,000
Special Features: Hand-selected French Burgundies are available for tasting and purchase

Taking the love of Pinot to an extreme, Scott Paul not only makes fine Burgundian Pinot Noir, but he and his partner Martha started a side business for the sole purpose of importing the French version. You reap the benefits by tasting both side by side in their converted tasting room on the edge of town. Scott goes for what he loves, so he has also purchased the building across the street to renovate into a winery. The rabbit logo and pattern throughout the tasting room is meant to complement the painting Martha bought Scott in California when he was at a precipice in his life and career.

SOLÉNA

503-852-0082 or 503-662-4730
www.solenacellars.com
213 South Pine Street
Tasting Room: Daily 12–5
Fee: $15, refunded with three-bottle purchase
Owners: Steve and Marian Bailey, Laurent Montalieu and Danielle Andrus Montalieu
Winemakers: Laurent Montalieu and Tony Rynders
Wines: Pinot Gris, Cabernet Sauvignon, Merlot, Pinot Noir, Syrah, Zinfandel
Cases: 6,000
Special Features: Wines are showcased at the Northwest Wine Bar (326 NE Davis St.)

You can't go far in the Willamette Valley without hearing of Laurent Montalieu. His imprint is as widespread as the number of labels that list him as winemaker. Wife and business partner Danielle has an impressive pedigree as well—she's the daughter of the late Gary Andrus of Archery Summit and Gypsy Dancer. The couple has been laying the foundation for their small empire since 2000, when they gave each other a wedding present of an 80-acre vineyard they named Domaine Danielle Laurent. What gift did guests bring? Pinot Noir vines, of course. Montalieu received his training through the Institute of Oenology in Bordeaux and was chief winemaker for Bridgeview and a winemaker/partner at WillaKenzie. Besides the Soléna label, the couple has the Northwest Wine Company and a wine bar in McMinnville. And that's not all. The latest for the ambitious couple is Grand Cru Estates winemaking facility, a 13,000-square-foot club outside town where members try their hands at being vintners. Additional feature: high-priced lots are for sale in the acclaimed Hyland vineyard.

CARLO & JULIAN WINERY
503-852-7432
1000 East Main Street
Tasting room: Sat. 12–5
Fee: Complimentary
Owner/Winemaker: Felix Madrid
Wines: Nebbiolo, Pinot Noir, Tempranillo
Cases: Under 1,000

International is the theme. Felix, an enthusiastic organic vegetable farmer on the side, was born in Argentina, moved to the United States as a youngster, and earned a degree in enology at U.C. Davis. He opened his winery in 1996 and produces Spanish, Italian, and French varietals. Carlo and Julian are the names of his two sons.

SOTER VINEYARDS
503-662-5600
www.sotervineyards.com
10880 Mineral Springs Road
Tasting Room: By appointment
Fee: Varies
Owners: Tony and Michelle Soter
Winemaker: James Cahill
Wines: Cabernet Franc, Pinot Noir, sparkling wines
Cases: 1,600
Special Features: Winemaker dinners

Tony Soter made his name in Napa, where he founded Etude Wines. His resume as a consultant reads like a Who's Who of Napa-area wineries. He continues to keep a hand in the Etude operation, but today his focus is on his Mineral Springs Ranch. Winemaker James Cahill is also a busy guy, traveling the country touting Soter's wines at winemaker dinners and opulent events.

BELLE PENTE VINEYARD & WINERY
503-852-9500
www.bellepente.com
12470 NE Rowland Road
Tasting Room: Memorial Day and Thanksgiving weekends, and by appointment
Fee: Varies
Owners: Brian and Jill O'Donnell
Winemaker: Brian O'Donnell
Wines: Chardonnay, Gewürztraminer, Muscat, Pinot Gris, Riesling, Pinot Noir
Cases: 5,000
Special Features: Organic and biodynamic

Belle Pente is French for "beautiful slope," and the way Brian and Jill O'Donnell see it, that includes the grasses and weeds growing naturally between their rows of vines. The O'Donnells strive to produce their Burgundian and Alsatian wines using organic and biodynamic methods, including gravity flow and meticulous handling of the grapes. Their original 16-acre vineyard is lush with Pinot Noir, Pinot Gris, and Chardonnay.

LEMELSON VINEYARD
503-852-6619
www.lemelsonvineyrds.com
12020 NE Stag Hollow Road
Tasting Room: Thurs.–Mon. 11–4
Fee: $10 refunded with two-bottle purchase
Owner: Eric Lemelson
Winemaker: Anthony King
Wines: Chardonnay, Pinot Gris, Riesling, Pinot Noir
Cases: 10,500
Special Features: Tours of organically certified vineyards and expansive facility, with tasting ($15)

No dollar was spared, no corners were cut, and no compromises were made at Eric Lemelson's dream winery. An impressively detailed design was created by Lemelson and fellow winemakers Eric Hamacher and Dean Fisher (ADEA), with the guidance of architect Laurence Ferar. The building is planked with sustainable storm-damaged cedar, and its two 50-yard-long solar panels take care of about half of the building's electricity needs. Melding functionality and beauty and utilizing gravity flow on all levels, Lemelson makes a strong statement: Expect to find a premier product within.

LAUREL RIDGE WINERY

503-852-7050
www.laurelridgewinery.com
13301 NE Kuehne Road
Tasting Room: Jan.–Nov., Mon.–Fri. 12–5, Sat.–Sun. 11–5, and by appointment
Fee: $5 for your choice of six wines
Owner: Susan Teppola
Winemaker: Chris Berg
Wines: Gewürztraminer, Riesling, Sauvignon Blanc, Pinot Noir, Tempranillo, brut, red and white blends, sparkling wines, port-style and dessert wines
Cases: 2,500
Special Features: Wine education classes, wedding facilities, kitchen, gift shop

Laurel Ridge owner Susan Teppola wants you to have a good time, and she loves the idea of wine geeks rubbing shoulders with novices in her recently built tasting room. The winery was incorporated in 1986 on a 240-acre farm site reputedly settled by German immigrants 100 years earlier. The state-of-the-art facility has several custom-crush clients. Today, the vineyards are being replanted and they're starting over, so they have but one estate product. The Laurel Ridge mantra, as Susan puts it: "If we can't find something our customers enjoy or appreciate, we've screwed up."

GHOST HILL CELLARS

503-852-7347
www.ghosthillcellarsllc.com
12220 NE Bayliss Road
Tasting Room: By appointment only at vineyard, but they pour on weekends at Anthony Dell Cellars (845 NE Fifth St., McMinnville)
Fee: Complimentary

Laurel Ridge's tasting room is on the site of an 1880s winery — one of the first in Oregon.
Courtesy Laurel Ridge Winery

Owners: Mike and Drenda Bayliss
Winemaker: Rebecca Sholdis
Wines: Pinot Noir
Cases: 200

Savannah Ridge has seen a lot of activity in the century since the family began farming the 255-acre site. It was a dairy operation in 1920s, and then a sheep ranch followed by 300 head of beef cattle and hay. The idea for planting grapes first arose in 1972, when the family broached the idea with none other than David Lett. Alas, life intervened, and it was another 27 years until 15 acres of Pinot Noir were finally put into the rich ground. The area is called Ghost Hill because a miner camping on the hill was murdered for his gold, and he is said to still be looking for his killers. Plans for a tasting room and winery are on tap.

MONKS GATE VINEYARD
503-852-6521
www.monksgate.com
9500 NE Oak Springs Farm Road
Tasting Room: Memorial Day and Thanksgiving weekends, and by appointment
Fee: Varies
Owners: Ron and Linda Moore
Winemaker: Laurent Montalieu
Wines: Pinot Noir
Cases: 500
Special Features: Pinot Noir brownies for $313 (includes a case of wine)

Since they are a little out of the way, Ron and Linda Moore like to get up close and personal with their guests. They share history on their tours and tastings while offering at least a three-year vertical tasting (three consecutive vintages). You can experience firsthand what a difference a year can make: same grapes, same winemaker, very different wine. Their production is small because they sell most of their grapes, but they do manage to keep some of the

best for their own label. Linda created a memorable Pinot Noir brownie recipe, and with a case purchase and a little coaxing you may just get a batch. Don't bother looking for up-to-date info on their Web site; they're far too busy farming.

ANNE AMIE VINEYARDS
503-864-2991
www.anneamie.com
6580 NE Mineral Springs Road
Tasting Room: Summer, daily 10–5, winter, Fri.–Sun. 10–5, and by appointment
Fee: $5–10, refundable with $50 purchase
Owner: Robert Pamplin
Winemaker: Thomas Houseman
Wines: Riesling, Müller Thurgau, Pinot Gris, Pinot Blanc, Pinot Noir, rosé, white blends, dessert wine
Cases: 14,000

Well-known Portland-area businessman Robert Pamplin bought the Chateau Benoit Winery site in 1999 and did a complete transformation. Anne Amie has turned its attention to making Pinots in an environmentally friendly manner. The eye-popping winery atop a hill is LIVE-certified and Oregon-certified sustainable. Six estate vineyards provide the grapes. The focus is on elegant and balanced Pinot Blanc, Pinot Gris, and Pinot Noir, but there are 30-year-old vines for Riesling and Müller Thurgau as well. Winemaker Thomas Houseman's Pinot Noir is exceptional enough to have earned recognition in *Food & Wine*. A Pamplin Family Vineyards winery was due to come online in 2010.

Lodging in the Carlton Area

Cᴀʀʟᴛᴏɴ
ABBEY ROAD FARM B&B
Owners: John and Judi Stuart
503-852-6278
10501 NE Abbey Road
www.abbeyroadfarm.com

Rates: $210
Special Features: Five suites

Unwind with your new favorite wine among the llamas, sheep, alpacas, donkeys, and chickens on John and Judi's European-style working farm. Despite the definite farm exterior, the "silo suites" are actually quite luxurious. With the Stuarts' careful attention to creature comforts, you'll feel more like you've checked into a resort than a grain silo. View farm life and the famous Guadalupe Vineyard while savoring their Farmstead goat cheese and fresh-baked cookies. Best of all enjoy the culinary treats served for breakfast enhanced by the farm's wide variety of produce.

BROOKSIDE INN

Owners: Bruce and Susan Bandstra
503-852-4433
www.brooksideinn-oregon.com
8243 NE Abbey Road
Rates: $185–350
Special Features: Winemaker dinners, wedding facilities, private events, in-room massage

Brookside's motto is "Catering to the wine & food lover's soul," and it seems to work. Wine tourists are drawn to this 22-acre wooded Shangri-La, with its creek, gardens, and sense of seclusion amid fir trees. There are nine warmly appointed suites surrounding a spacious great room with a stone fireplace. All rooms are themed: four relating to Oregon rivers, two with a Japanese flair, and one leaning Scottish. The Carriage House, not far from the main house, has Egyptian tints, sleeps up to four, and features the two-room Astoria Suite on the second floor. Mornings begin with a Northwest-oriented three-course breakfast featuring a strata, frittata, or French toast. The Brookside's attempts to connect visitors to the area's wine industry have earned frequent plaudits in *Oregon Wine Press.*

THE CARLTON INN

Owners: Edward and Heidi Yates
503-852-7506
www.thecarltoninn.com
648 West Main Street
Rates: $125–190
Special Features: Stumptown Coffee, organic and local products

Back when timber was king in Carlton, this was the baron's home. And you can tell. Wood floors and accents have stood the test of time, and Edward and Heidi Yates have combined turn-of-the-century character with modern amenities. The B&B's three upstairs rooms are named for nearby wine country AVAs: Dundee Hills, Eola Hills, and, of course, Yamhill-Carlton. The gourmet breakfasts made from scratch come with a nod to history as well. The milk and cream are delivered, just as in the old days, by a company whose products are free of hormones and antibiotics.

LOBENHAUS BED & BREAKFAST & VINEYARD

Owners: Joe and Shari Lobenstein
503-864-9173 or 888-339-3375
www.lobenhaus.com
6975 NE Abbey Road
Rates: $160–180

Take your newly purchased bottles of wine, settle back, and view the woods, creek, or vineyard on the huge wraparound deck enveloping Dick and Shari's lodge-style, trilevel home. With experience from previous careers, the owners enjoy emphasizing a healthful, Americana country lifestyle right down to the fresh ingredients they serve in their Oregon Bounty Breakfast. Utilizing their own garden or local farmers' markets they whip up morning delicacies such as hazelnut pancakes, waffles with fresh berries, and their signature Huevos Lobos. The Pinot Noir juice is a nice added touch.

R.R. THOMPSON HOUSE

Owners: Mike and Roselyn Mostafa
503-852-6236
www.rrthompsonhouse.com
517 Kutch Street
Rates: $150–245

Relatively new to the B&B world are Mike and Roselyn, who in 2007 fulfilled their wishes of opening an inn in wine country. The architecture in their 1936 federalist-style home, built by R.R. Thompson—who amassed a fortune in the steamship-navigation industry—reflects its history. The fir and mahogany wood and light fixtures are all original. The five rooms are named for the flora surrounding the two-story home: Rose, Lilac, Magnolia, Lavender, and Garden. The spacious Rose and Lavender suites have European-style bathrooms, including bidets. Breakfast highlights include apple pancakes and brie omelets.

Dining in the Carlton Area

CARLTON
CUVÉE

503-852-6555
www.cuveedining.com
214 West Main Street
Open: Wed.–Sat. 5:30–9, Sun. 5–8, check for seasonal lunch hours
Price: Expensive (on the low side)
Credit Cards: Yes
Special Features: Tarte flambée (French thin-crust pizza) on Wed. and three-course prix fixe dinners Wednesday, Thursday, and Sunday

French cuisine in Pinot country is, of course, the quintessential pairing. Gilbert Henry, who owned the successful Winterborne in Portland, relocated in Carlton and went with his heritage, French country. An understated (much like "G-Bear" himself) storefront, dressed in bisque walls, white linens, black tables, and chairs, is set for special yet unfussy dining.

Classic cassoulet and Couquilles St. Jacques are expertly prepared and served, usually by the gregarious professional server Felippe. Henry's tender sautéed oysters are renowned, but the clams can steal the show (be prepared to find yourself heathenly sipping broth from the bowl). Sauces are not heavy, just there for a wisp of finishing flavor—like the horseradish sauce accompanying the oysters. Add the hand-created bread, delectable desserts, and reasonable markup on local wines and you'll see why this is, hands down, one of our favorite restaurants in the state.

FILLING STATION DELI

503-852-6687
www.fillingstationdeli.com
305 West Main Street
Open: Thurs.–Tues. 7–3:30, closed Wed.
Price: Inexpensive
Credit Cards: Yes
Special Features: Popular with locals

Fill 'er up with soups, sandwiches, and wraps—just what an empty tank needs. There's no wine bar with groovy colors or adornments, just made-to-order down-home goodness. Breakfast sandwiches will start your engine, stacked sandwiches on house-made bread will run your motor, and the Stumptown coffee (paired with a sweet treat) will keep you humming. As in the days when it was a gas station, the eats are good and the goods can be eaten here or got-to-go.

HORSE RADISH CHEESE & WINE BAR

503-852-6656
www.thehorseradish.com
211 West Main Street
Open: Mon.–Thurs. 12–6, Fri.–Sat. 12–10, Sun. 1–6; check for winter hours
Credit Cards: Yes
Special Features: Wine-related gifts, live music on weekends, private parties

The Horse Radish Wine & Cheese Bar has a nice assortment of cheeses, picnic salads, and Italian/Mediterranean antipasti served individually, to go, or family-style on a platter to share with a bottle of local wine. They usually have five to seven bottles open daily for tasting, sometimes more—a great way to sample the local choices before purchasing. There's an inviting garden with seating in the back, just off a small, well-landscaped parking lot.

Shopping in the Carlton Area

Carlton is a great place to browse on a sunny afternoon, though most of the shopping revolves around wine. Oil and acrylic paintings by Steve Taylor are on display at the **Carlton Gallery** (503-435-7107, 250 North Kutch St.). For the do-it-yourselfer, everything from looms and spinning wheels to yarn and how-to books is at **Woodland Woolworks** (503-852-7376, 100 East Washington St.) in Carlton.

Information

Grape Escape Winery Tours, 503-283-3380, www.grapeescapetours.com
Sip 47, www.sip47.com
Willamette Valley Wineries Association, 503-646-2985, www.willamettewines.com
Yamhill Valley Visitors Association, 503-883-7770, www.yamhillvalley.org

4

Willamette Valley East

East of Eden

East of Interstate 5 is the oft-forgotten side of the Willamette Valley. The area between Portland's southeast suburbs and east Salem is characterized by rich farmlands rising gently to meet the forested slopes of the Cascades.

Most of the communities here have no more than a few thousand residents. Economies revolve around agriculture and evolve toward timber the farther east you go. Though wineries are a relatively recent revelation, some established vineyards grow on the south- and west-facing slopes above acres of hazelnuts, loganberries, raspberries, sorghum, and noble-fir Christmas tree farms.

And there is plenty to do here, too. Silver Falls State Park, northeast of Salem, with its 11 breathtaking waterfalls, is one of the state's most popular getaways for hiking and camping. The Oregon Garden complex near Silverton is a spectacularly beautiful snapshot of the state's flora.

Of all the east valley's communities, Silverton and Mount Angel are the most tourist-friendly. Silverton is a leafy, immaculately manicured town astride Silver Creek, with vintage mansions and oak trees for blocks on each side of the boutique shops along Main and Water Streets. A welcoming town that doesn't judge, it has the only openly transgender mayor in America. Another interesting community is Woodburn, which spreads out just east of I-5 about midway between Portland and Salem. Known mostly to Oregonians for its outlet mall, Woodburn has cultural diversity unlike anywhere in the state outside Portland.

Getting Here and Around

Tours of the east Willamette Valley best begin in Portland. Start at the Oswego Hills Winery, just off Interstate 205 in the southeast corner of the metropolitan area. From there, get back on 205 and head east to Oregon City, where you'll take the OR 99E exit across the Willamette River. OR 99E is the highway lifeline of the east Willamette Valley's wine country, much the way OR 99W is west of the interstate.

After pulling over to take a brief peek at Willamette Falls—try to ignore the industrial complex—continue south on 99E along the river into the east valley's wine country. You'll criss-cross the countryside between 99E and OR 213 down to the southernmost winery,

OPPOSITE: *Producing and growing Oregon wine is labor intensive.* Frank Barnett

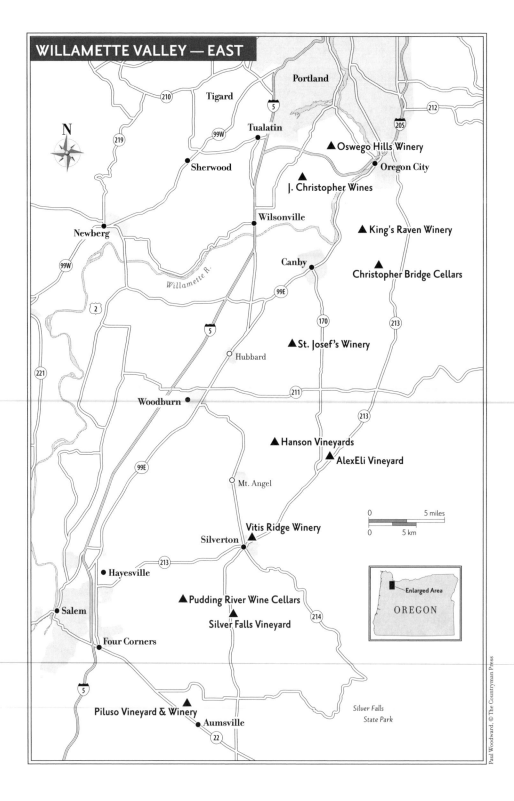

WILLAMETTE VALLEY — EAST

N

Portland

210

Tigard

5

212

99W

Tualatin

205

219

▲ Oswego Hills Winery

Sherwood

● Oregon City

▲
J. Christopher Wines

Newberg

Wilsonville

▲ King's Raven Winery

99W

Canby

▲
Christopher Bridge Cellars

2

Willamette R.

99E

5

170

213

▲ St. Josef's Winery

221

● Hubbard

Woodburn

211

213

99E

▲ Hanson Vineyards

▲ AlexEli Vineyard

○ Mt. Angel

| 0 | | 5 miles |
| 0 | | 5 km |

Vitis Ridge Winery

Silverton ▲

213

● Hayesville

▲ Pudding River Wine Cellars

Enlarged Area

OREGON

● Salem

Silver Falls Vineyard

214

● Four Corners

5

▲
Piluso Vineyard & Winery

*Silver Falls
State Park*

● Aumsville

22

Paul Woodward. © The Countryman Press

Silver Falls, and then return to Portland on I-5. Or you can cross through Salem to tour the dozens of wineries of the mid-Willamette Valley on the other of the river.

THE EAST WILLAMETTE VALLEY

Imagine how Oregon wine history might have turned out if the legendary David Lett had found just one available hillside on which to plant Pinot back in the 1960s. The story goes that when Lett came north from California to look for the perfect Pinot plantation, he stayed in Silverton after temporarily planting his root stock near Corvallis. Lett looked and looked for available land, but every acre was entrenched in existing agriculture—and pricey, to boot. Striking out on the eastern side of the Willamette Valley, Lett went west to Dundee—and the rest is storied Oregon wine lore.

East valley wineries are part of the Willamette Valley, but, like the Sip 47 crew on the west side, they think of themselves as a separate entity. They hope to change this with more marketing and festivals.

Wineries in the East Willamette Valley

WEST LINN
OSWEGO HILLS WINERY

503-655-2599
www.oswegohills.com
450 Rosemont Road
Tasting Room: Sun. 12–5, major holiday weekends, and by appointment
Fee: Complimentary
Owner: Jerry Marshall
Winemaker: Derek Lawrence
Wines: Pinot Gris, Riesling, Viognier, Cabernet Sauvignon, Maréchal Foch, Merlot, Pinot Noir, Syrah, red and white blends, port
Cases: 3,000
Special Features: Events facility

You can't get much closer to Portland and be in an actual commercial vineyard—"A smorgasbord of wines right on the urban-growth boundary," Oswego Hills owner Jerry Marshall describes it. Marshall, a former airline pilot, rehabbed the decaying creamery, pump house, and 1938 barns to create an extraordinary rural environment between the urban hum of Lake Oswego and West Linn. Much of the facility is bathed in white, including the farm home,

which is surrounded by cedar and fig trees as well as a mature vineyard.

J. CHRISTOPHER WINES

503-231-5094
www.jchristopherwines.com
2636 SW Schaeffer Road
Tasting Room: Memorial Day and Thanksgiving weekends, and by appointment
Fee: $10 for 15 wines
Owner/winemaker: Jay Somers
Wines: Sauvignon Blanc, Chardonnay,

It's all hands on deck in the vineyard for many small producers. Courtesy King's Raven Winery

Pinot Noir
Cases: 6,000
Special Features: New tasting room scheduled to open in Newberg in 2010

J. Christopher made headlines in 2008 when owner/winemaker Jay Somers collaborated with the famed Dr. Loosen Estate Winery in Germany to produce a transcontinental Pinot Noir blend. The Two Worlds Pinot is comprised of 90 percent Mosel Valley grapes from Germany and 10 percent Pinot from the Willamette Valley. That partnership is carrying over to a permanent 50–50 relationship that will help J. Christopher move into a new $3 million facility in Oregon. J. Christopher's popular wines include the Zoot Allures, a $20 Pinot with Somers' two dogs on the label, and a pink wine called Cristo Irresisto that's a blend of Grenache, Syrah, and Viognier. Somers got his start with the help of Bill Holloran, a software executive who had a farm perfectly suited for the winemaker. Somers makes about 3,000 cases of Holloran Vineyards Chardonnay, Riesling, Pinot Noir, and Tempranillo.

OREGON CITY
KING'S RAVEN WINERY
503-539-7202 or 503-784-6298
www.kingsravenwine.com
1512 Washington Street
Tasting Room: Thurs.–Fri. 11–6, Sat. 11–4
Fee: Complimentary
Owner: Ingram family
Winemaker: Darin Ingram
Wines: Pinot Gris, Pinot Noir, Maréchal Foch
Cases: 250
Special Features: Wedding facilities, winemaker dinners, private wine tastings, movies

The King's Raven facility is on a small hilltop south of Oregon City where the grapes share space with Angus beef cattle. The tasting room is downtown in the Howden

Art and Framing Gallery, the largest art gallery in Clackamas County. The winery frequently stages special events at the rural vineyard—including movies. The family has owned the property since 1942.

CHRISTOPHER BRIDGE CELLARS
503-263-6267
www.christopherbridgewines.com
12770 South Casto Road
Tasting Room: By appointment, but look for regular hours soon
Fee: To be determined
Owners: Chris and Susanne Carlberg
Winemaker: Chris Carlberg
Wines: Ehrenfelser, Pinot Gris, Muscat, Rosé, Pinot Noir
Cases: 1,000
Special Features: Special-events facility

Chris and Susanne Carlberg not only appreciate what their farm brings them, they have also learned to be tuned to its rhythms. The 15-acre farm, vineyard, and winery has agriculture at its heart: grassfed beef and chickens as well as grapes. Their Sotari Springs Vineyard surrounds the Carlbergs' modest two-level home, as do Christmas tree farms, and hazelnut orchards. A timber-framed building with a bread oven and outdoor fireplace was scheduled to open in 2009. The rare Ehrenfelser wine is a German cross between Sylvaner and Riesling. It tastes similar to a Viognier but "with muscle," Susanne says.

CANBY
ST. JOSEF'S WINERY
503-651-3190
www.stjosefswinery.com
28836 S. Barlow Road
Tasting Room: Sat.–Sun. 11–5 and by appointment; closed Jan.
Fee: $5 for 12 wines
Owners: Josef and Lilly Fleischmann
Winemaker: Josef Fleischmann
Wines: Pinot Gris, Chardonnay,

St. Josef's Winery has Bavarian flair.
Courtesy St. Josef's Winery

Gewürztraminer, Riesling, Cabernet
Sauvignon, Pinot Noir, Merlot, Syrah
Cases: 9,000
Special Features: Winemaker dinners, spe-
cial events, outdoor seating, picnic area

"CAUTION: WINEMAKERS AT PLAY" reads a
sign at the entry to St. Josef's Winery,
revealing the playful nature at this pleasant
country estate. Take equal slices of Italy,
Switzerland, and Oregon, blend them into
a neat package amid rolling countryside—
and you have St. Josef's. Two gold lions atop
brick posts and an iron gate greet visitors,
who then drive a paved lane between nee-
dle-thin Italian cypress and acres of grapes.
Sequoias shade the grounds around the
Swiss-chalet home and winery, which
boasts the Jo-Lily pond out back. The wines
are lively and affordable.

WOODBURN
HANSON VINEYARDS
503-634-2348
www.hansonvineyards.com
34948 South Barlow Road
Tasting Room: Second Sat. of each month,
12–5 P.M., major holiday weekends, and by
appointment
Fee: $1 per taste, waived with purchase

Owner/Winemaker: Clark Hanson
Wines: Pinot Gris, Pinot Blanc, Riesling,
Pinot Noir
Cases: 200

They're tiny now, but with owner/wine-
maker Clark Hanson's first plantings
maturing, look for production to increase
rapidly. The pastoral farm has been growing grapes since the 1920s, when Prohibition forced growers to either shut down,
plant orchards or raise such semi-legal
varieties as Niagara and Concord. The evolution continued when Hanson began making berry and fruit wines in 1968, and has
culminated with the planting of the now-
maturing French and German vinifera.

MOLALLA
ALEXELI VINEYARD
503-829-6677
www.alexeli.com
35803 South Highway 213
Tasting Room: Fri.–Sun. 12–5
Fee: $2 for flight of four wines, waived with
purchase; $8 includes souvenir glass
Owner: Anita Kramer
Winemaker: TBA
Wines: Gewürztraminer, Riesling, Pinot
Noir, white blend
Cases: 1,000
Special Features: Outdoor seating, private
lake

Anita Kramer and her two sons, Phillip
Alexander and Anthony Eli, took over Joe
Dobbes Sr.'s Marquam Hill Winery in April
2008. They renamed it using a combination
of the boys' middle names, and AlexEli bottled its first Pinot Noir in 2008. The tasting
room is an extension of a modest house, as
if remodeled from what was once a garage.
The home, tasting room, and flagstone
patio are tucked away from the highway
amid a mature 18-acre vineyard. The sons
are making quantity-for-quality changes in
the vineyard and have high hopes for their
white wines.

Oregon Wineries Like to Go LIVE

LIVE certification isn't just the trendy thing to do in Oregon; for many vineyard owners, it's the only thing. LIVE is the catchy acronym for Low Input Viticulture and Enology—a non-profit organization that certifies wineries and vineyards based on environmental stewardship.

To many, the most meaningful aspect of LIVE certification is the Salmon-Safe designation that comes with it. Salmon are to Oregon what oranges are to Florida, corn to Iowa, and cheese to Wisconsin. For eons, these itinerant fish annually migrated by the tens of millions between ocean feeding grounds and traditional inland spawning grounds, where they required cool, clean, and brisk waters. Habitat destruction, overfishing, dams, and climate change have conspired to reduce their runs to mere fractions of their historic highs.

In eco-conscious western Oregon, LIVE certification reflects a commitment by vineyard owners to help restore the iconic wild Chinook and Coho salmon runs. Under LIVE's rigorous standards, wineries and vineyards are not allowed to use chemical fertilizers. They also must work to halt erosion by planting trees on or near stream banks. More than 130 of Oregon's vineyards—about one-third in the entire state—are LIVE-certified, including some big hitters: Adelsheim, Cristom, Domaine Drouhin, Ponzi, and Willamette Valley.

SILVERTON
VITIS RIDGE WINERY
503-873-9800
www.vitisridge.com
6685 Meridian Road NE
Tasting Room: Second weekend each month, Sat.–Sun. 12–5
Fee: Complimentary
Owners: Glen Brunger, Chris and Sharon Deckelmann, Bruce and Sally Eich
Winemakers: Chris Deckelmann and Bruce Eich
Wines: Gewürztraminer, Chardonnay, Riesling, Pinot Gris, Muscat, Merlot, Syrah, Cabernet Sauvignon, Pinot Noir, Maréchal Foch, Petit Vordot, dessert wine
Cases: 2,800
Special Features: Picnic area

Vitis Ridge began as a hobby in the Deckelmanns' garage in the mid-1990s and has evolved to produce a dozen wines, about half from the grapes they grow in an 80-acre vineyard. Look for the Eich family at tasting events throughout the region. Perhaps their most unique offering is the Petit Verdot, a rich and colorful red from grapes that ripen later than most.

SUBLIMITY
SILVER FALLS VINEYARDS
503-769-5056
www.silverfallsvineyards.com
4972 Cascade Hwy SE
Tasting Room: Sat.–Sun 11–5 (seasonal)
Fee: Complimentary
Owners: Duane and Gail Defree
Winemaker: Andreas Wetzel
Wines: Chardonnay, Pinot Gris, Riesling, Pinot Noir, rosé, white blends, dessert wines
Cases: 3,000
Special Features: Indoor/outdoor wedding and events facility, picnic area, small selection of wine accessories

Looking for value wines? Silver Falls is the place. Of the 12 wines sold here, only the Reserve Pinot Noir is more than $16—and it's not exactly out of sight at $25. Pinot Noir is the biggest seller, although Silver Falls wines do well across the board and the owners are happy to have it that way.

SALEM
PUDDING RIVER WINE CELLARS

503-365-0391
www.puddingriver.com
9374 Sunnyview Road NE
Tasting Room: Apr.–Dec., Sat.–Sun. 11–5;
weekdays and Jan.–Mar. by appointment
Fee: Complimentary
Owners: Sean and Stacey Driggers and John
and Karen Bateman
Winemaker: Sean Driggers
Wines: Chardonnay, Pinot Gris, Viognier,
Riesling, Pinot Noir
Cases: 1,500
Special Features: Kid- and dog-friendly

There are family-owned wineries and there
are family-run wineries. Pudding River is
definitely run by family—with family of all
ages and sizes running around, sometimes
underfoot. The winery was a poultry farm in
the days of yore, and the rooster on the
country label is a nod to the farm's previous
life. The tasting room is on the second floor
of a small converted barn behind a 100-
year-old Victorian farmhouse. The home,
barn, and vineyard are along the meandering Pudding River. The winery has a fan base
for its barrel-fermented Chardonnay, but
an equal number like the un-oaked version.

AUMSVILLE
PILUSO VINEYARD & WINERY

503-749-4125 or 866-684-9463
www.pilusowines.com
6654 Shaw Hwy SE
Tasting Room: Apr.–Nov., second weekend
of the month, Sat.–Sun. 12–5, and holiday
weekends
Fee: Complimentary
Owners: Sandee and Pinky Piluso
Winemaker: Sandee Piluso
Wines: Gamay Noir, Pinot Noir, Dolcetto,
Maréchal Foch, Tempranillo, white blend,
dessert wine
Cases: 600
Special Features: Picnic area, outdoor
patio, and gardens

Piluso made its big splash when it scored a
90 in *Wine Spectator* with its 2006 Pinot
Noir. Practice makes perfect: Another winner is the 2006 Bianco Dolce, a sweet
dessert wine with a German flair. Sandee
Piluso went back to school at a ripe age to
become a winemaker, and after a stint as an
intern at Airlie Winery she's running her
own show.

Lodging in the
East Willamette Valley

SILVERTON
OREGON GARDEN RESORT

503-874-2500
www.oregongardenresort.com
895 West Main Street
Rates: $95–119
Special Features: Heated outdoor swimming pool, hot tub, pet-friendly rooms,
restaurant highlighting Northwest wines
and cuisine, romance packages

The Oregon Garden has proven such a popular tourist attraction that it seemed only
natural to build accommodations to match.
They've done it with a state-of-the-art,
eco-oriented, attractive 103-room facility
that features a main lodge and six outbuildings that blend well with the lush surroundings. All of the rooms have a
fireplaces, patio, fridge, and microwave,
and rates include admission to the Oregon
Garden. The Moonstone Spa is the ideal
place to relax with a massage after a day of
wine touring.

WATER STREET INN

866-873-3344
www.thewaterstreetinn.com
421 North Water Street
Rates: $125–165
Special Features: Summer specials

The Water Street Inn is a Victorian-style
1890s house that blends seamlessly into the
leafy streets of this appealing community.

Silver Falls near Silverton is Oregon's most popular state park. Travel Oregon

One room has a fireplace and whirlpool tub for two; another room features a double shower. All five rooms have private baths. The yard and patio are well manicured and peaceful, a great place for a respite.

WHITE OAKS BED & BREAKFAST

503-873-1474
www.whiteoaksbedandbreakfast.com
629 Kloshe Lane
Rates: $125–145
Special Features: Artist and interior-design studio open to guests

White Oaks is a decided departure from the Victorian homes dotting Silverton, though it certainly has an English country feel—especially with the wild strawberries growing on the roof. It is home to interior designer and artist S. K. Sartell, whose cheerful studio overlooks the valley. Views are a selling point at White Oaks, particularly in the Strawberries and Champagne Suite. The Red Garden Suite has an outdoor patio with views. Inside, you'll luxuriate in a unique soaking tub filled from a waterfall. As bed-and-breakfasts go, White Oaks has a personality as unique as any.

Dining in the East Willamette Valley

SILVERTON
SILVER GRILLE CAFÉ & WINES

503-873-8000
www.silvergrille.com
206 East Main Street
Open: Wed.–Sun. 5–9
Price: Inexpensive to moderate
Credit cards: Yes
Special Features: Wine dinners

Acclaimed chef Jeff Nizlek came back to the Silver Grille in August 2009 and has refocused on regional fare, ranging from locally picked mushrooms and shrimp harvested from the Pacific to Oregon cheeses and Northwest wines. The ambiance is relaxing and the food a cut above anything on the east side of the Willamette Valley.

Attractions in the East Willamette Valley

Most likely, you'll be starting your wine tour at the end—the End of the Oregon Trail, that is. The **End of the Oregon Trail Interpretive Center** (503-657-9336, 1726 Washington St.) in Oregon City features exhibits from families that actually made the trip west in the nineteenth century. Along the road to wineries, take a few minutes at **Swan Island Dahlias** (503-266-7711, 995 NW 22nd Ave.) in Canby, the **Wooden Shoe Bulb Company** (503-634-2710, 33814 S. Meridian Ave.), about seven miles east of Woodburn, and **Cooley's Iris Garden** (503-873-5812, 11553 Silverton Rd. NE), just outside Silverton. All three have massive fields of color and shops selling flowers, seeds, and bulbs.

If there was a single defining moment for tourism in the east Willamette Valley, it was the opening of the **Oregon Garden** (503-874-8100, 879 Main St.) in Silverton. The one-time lumber town was already on its way to successfully reinventing itself as a classy Sunday drive destination when this 80-acre area with 20 specialty gardens began luring visitors by the thousands.

Before the Oregon Garden, the prime attractions were **Silver Falls State Park** (503-873-8681) and the **Mount Angel Abbey** (503-845-3030) just outside Mount Angel. Oregon's largest state park, Silver Falls has 11 waterfalls, ranging from the 177-foot South Falls to 27-foot Drake Falls. The Abbey is one of Oregon's most beautiful buildings, and has a famous library and a retreat house. Built in 1882, it hosts a **Festival of Arts & Wine** every June, three months before Mount Angel's raucous end-of-summer **Oktoberfest** (503-845-9440), held every September.

Recreation in the East Willamette Valley

The east side of the valley offers a little bit of everything, from salmon and steelhead **fishing** on the Willamette and Clackamas rivers, Class IV **whitewater rafting** on the Clackamas, and **camping** and **hiking** in Silver Falls State Park. For duffers, the public **Evergreen Golf Course** (503-845-9911, 11694 West Church Rd. NE) in Mount Angel offers a modestly challenging nine holes.

Shopping in the East Willamette Valley

Wankers Country Store (503-638-0606, 19995 SW Stafford Rd.) in Lake Oswego, a classic mom-and-pop corner store and an area icon, is a good place to stop and get picnic supplies for your wine tour. If you're in need of a traditional shopping fix, **Woodburn Company Stores** (503-981-1900) is perhaps Oregon's best-known outlet mall. It has all the regional big hitters like Nike, plus name-brand national stores. For antiques, boutiques, and other 'tiques the best bet is Main Street in Silverton, where you could easily spend a day.

Wine Shopping in the East Willamette Valley

Wine enthusiasts won't want to miss the **Howard Hinsdale Cellars Wine Bar** (503-873-9463, 119 North Water St.) in Silverton. Howard Hinsdale touts itself as a fun place to do wine. Exhibit A: Movie night at 7 P.M. every Wednesday.

Information

Silverton Chamber of Commerce, 503-873-5615, www.silvertonchamber.org, 426 South Water St.

East Valley Wine Group, www.eastvalleywines.com

Willamette Valley Central

Head for the Hills

Before the Willamette River punches through the hills southeast of Portland and plunges over the falls at Oregon City, it serpentines through a broad valley between the Coast and Cascade Ranges, from Eugene north some 100 miles to Wilsonville. About halfway, just south of Salem, the river is forced to detour to the west around another set of undulating hills.

If the countryside around Dundee and Carlton are Oregon Wine Country's A team, then surely the Eola Hills and their neighbors between the capital city of Salem and the increasingly charming college town of McMinnville are A-1 and A-2. The heart of this region is Salem, which boasts the oldest college west of the Mississippi River in Willamette University. The soul is McMinnville, a classy place where a fraternity of winery workers gathers most evenings to sip, toast, and share tales from the vineyard. In-between, spaced along pastoral country roads, are such folksy *Petticoat Junction*—esque agricultural villages as Amity, Dayton, and St. Paul.

The Willamette glides through this country almost unnoticed despite the fact that 80 percent of the state's population lives within 20 miles of its banks. This phenomenon arose more out of survival than neglect. Until the river was controlled by dams and straightened by engineers, it braided like so many corkscrews and flooded widely, sometimes leaving steamboat-port towns permanently high and dry.

Getting Here and Around

Though Salem is Oregon's third-largest city behind Portland and Eugene, air service is on-and-off. Horizon Air no longer serves Salem, and Delta Airlines bailed out in October 2008. The **Hut Shuttle** (888-257-0126) serves Salem and Corvallis/Albany with bus service every two hours. In addition, **Amtrak** has one Salem stop daily in each direction on the Coast Starlight.

To get the full flavor of your central Willamette Valley wine tour, you'll want to start in McMinnville. From the Portland airport, the best route is I-205 south to the junction of I-5. The fastest way to McMinnville from there is to head north on I-5 three miles to Exit

OPPOSITE: *Panther Creek Cellars is located in McMinnville's Pinot Quarter.* Ron Kaplan

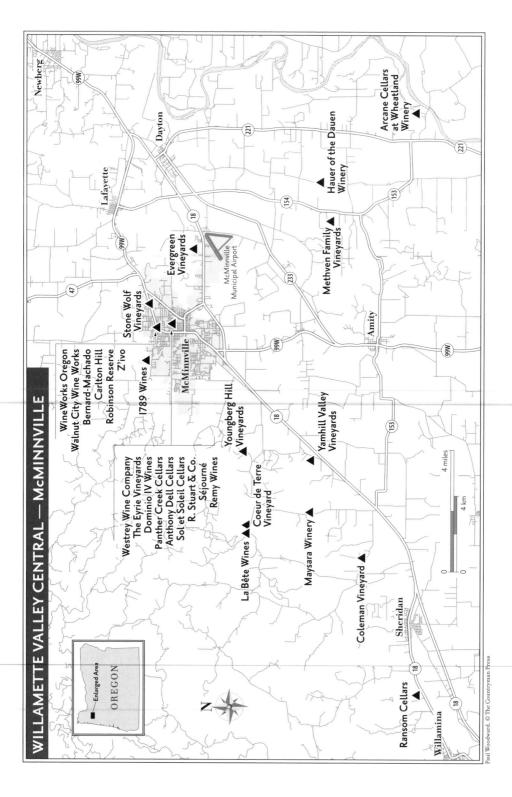

WILLAMETTE VALLEY CENTRAL — McMINNVILLE

Newberg

Dayton

Lafayette

Arcane Cellars
at Wheatland
Winery

Hauer of the Dauen
Winery

Evergreen
Vineyards

Methven Family
Vineyards

Stone Wolf
Vineyards

McMinnville
Municipal Airport

Amity

WineWorks Oregon
Walnut City Wine Works
Bernard-Machado
Carlton Hill
Robinson Reserve
Z'ivo

1789 Wines

McMinnville

Westrey Wine Company
The Eyrie Vineyards
Dominio IV Wines
Panther Creek Cellars
Anthony Dell Cellars
Sol et Soleil Cellars
R. Stuart & Co.
Séjourné
Remy Wines

Youngberg Hill
Vineyards

Yamhill Valley
Vineyards

Coeur de Terre
Vineyard

La Bête Wines

Maysara Winery

Coleman Vineyard

Sheridan

Ransom Cellars

Willamina

OREGON

Enlarged Area

N

4 miles

4 km

Paul Woodward, © The Countryman Press

289, then go west through Sherwood to OR 99W. That route will take you through Newberg and Dundee to McMinnville. However, to avoid OR 99W's traffic and take a more scenic route, go south on I-5 to Exit 283. Wilsonville Road follows the Willamette past Champoeg State Park to Newberg and a meeting with OR 99W.

McMinnville Area (McMinnville AVA)

Once upon a time, McMinnville was an afterthought between Portland and Salem. Then wine happened. Give McMinnville credit: It knew what to do with a phenomenon occurring in its backyard. Few downtowns capture the essence of the new and old Oregon like this vibrant community of thirty-two thousand.

Though McMinnville has a diverse assortment of wine bars, tasting rooms, boutiques, and terrific eateries led by Nick's Italian Cafe, it has retained some of its quirks. Most notable are the annual Turkey Rama and UFO Festival. Turkey Rama began in 1938, when turkey farms were driving the area's economic engine. Once upon a time, live domestic turkeys were raced down Main Street, with the mayor presiding over the festivities. Today, in a more sophisticated McMinnville, the turkey races have given way to "Who's on Third"—a more gentrified festival on Third Street showcasing local wineries, art, and music.

The UFO Festival's genesis is traced to 1950, when the local paper published a photo of a flying saucer hovering over an area farm. More than a half-century later, the authenticity of the photo has neither been verified nor debunked, and now McMinnville hosts the country's largest gathering of UFO junkies this side of Roswell, New Mexico.

Wineries in the McMinnville Area

McMinnville has become Oregon's wine hub, with spokes pointing north to Dundee, west to Yamhill-Carlton, and south to the Eola Hills. It was here that the world's first International Pinot Noir Celebration was staged in July 1987. Dundee is renowned as the place where Lett planted his first Pinot vineyard, but it was in McMinnville, at an abandoned turkey-processing plant, that he perfected the wine.

Though it isn't readily apparent, the foothills stretching for 20 miles southwest of McMinnville—where there are 14 wineries and about 750 acres of vineyards—are notably different from the Red Hills of Dundee, Amity Hills, and Eola Hills just a few miles away. The rain shadow and 1,000-foot elevation make for a warmer, drier, and more frost-free climate. Good thing, because the marine sedimentary soils are shallower here than in nearby grape-growing regions. Though the predominant wines are the expected Pinot Noir, Pinot Gris, and Pinot Blanc, their flavors are distinctly different.

McMinnville
STONE WOLF VINEYARDS

503-434-9025
stonewolfvineyards.com
2155 NE Lafayette Avenue
Tasting Room: Daily 12–5, closed in winter
Fee: $4–8
Owners: Lindsay family

Winemaker: Linda Lindsay
Wines: Pinot Gris, Chardonnay, Müller Thurgau, Pinot Noir, Merlot, Cabernet Sauvignon, dessert wine
Cases: 20,000

There are no wild wolves in western Oregon, but Art "Papa Wolf" Lindsay and his wife, Linda, like the old Kipling saying,

"For the strength of the pack is the wolf, and the strength of the wolf is the pack." With some pack work, skill, and what they describe as "a lot of luck," the Lindsays planted their vineyard in 1985. Today, they are reaping the fruits of their affordable wines. Their Pinot Gris was touted by TV chef Rachael Ray in 2008.

1789 WINES

503-857-0225
www.1789wines.com
2610 NW Riesling Way
Tasting Room: By appointment only
Fee: Varies
Owner/Winemaker: Isabelle Dutartre
Cases: 175

We met the charming Isabelle at the 2009 Indie Festival. When we asked her what set her apart, she replied, "I'm the only winemaker here from Burgundy." Right she was. Her style is not revolutionary; it's old-world traditional reflected in Pinot that is elegantly complex, with infinite finesse and finish. We were enamored. Isabelle started making wine in 1982, came to Oregon in '89, and, after 25 years under someone else's label (currently DePonte), she wanted her own. As you have probably figured out, her brand is a reference to the French Revolution, because she wanted to make a life change for the better.

WINEWORKS OREGON

503-472-3215
www.walnutcitywineworks.com
475 NE 17th Street
Tasting Room: Thurs.–Sun. 11:30–4:30
Fee: $5

As the name implies, there's some nutty history and current activity here. WineWorks Oregon is yet another complicated amicable arrangement for wineries. It's a vineyard management company with long-term relationships. It's also a consortium for boutique producers—Carlton Hill,

McMinnville has one of Oregon's most vibrant downtowns. Courtesy McMenamin's

Bernard-Machado, Robinson Reserve, and Zivo—to be tasted in one location, along with host label Walnut City WineWorks. This isn't a co-op that winemakers can simply buy into; the ticket in is having a vineyard planted or managed by its owners. Founders John Davidson and John Gilpin have formed a clubhouse of sorts for like-minded farmers and wine nerds. Davidson and Gilpin are an odd couple married through their work and love of the heart-break grape: Pinot Noir. They formed a vertically integrated company 25 years ago that includes managing orchards, vineyards, running greenhouses with rootstock, designing vineyards, and winemaking. They now oversee 300 acres of Pinot Noir in the valley, including 80 of their own. Based in a historic red-brick building, the winemaking area and tasting room were once the Willamette Valley Walnut Company. The tasting room now features bright colors, directors' chairs, and many options for sampling from the following wineries:

WALNUT CITY WINEWORKS

Owners: John Gilpin and John Davidson
Winemaker: Davidson and Miguel Lopez
Wines: Pinot Gris, Viognier, Pinot Noir
Cases: Under 1,000

Davidson is the older half of the wine-making team and also happens to be Miguel Lopez's godfather, keeping the ties tight. Miquel's father has worked for the company for years, so Miguel grew up in the family. WineWorks Oregon is WCWW's home facility, and space is also leased to the following Pinot nuts.

BERNARD-MACHADO

Owner/Winemaker: John Davidson
Cases: 500

Ahhh . . . old-world-style burgundy for Burg-hounds. Davidson's private label pinots are all about the grapes and twenty-five years of crafting experience. His label is named for his grandparents. Priced right at around $30 retail, it's a good choice.

CARLTON HILL

www.carltonhillwines.com
Owners/Winemakers: David and Dan Polite
Wines: Pinot Noir
Cases: 400

Carlton Hill Vineyard (11511 NW Cummins Rd.) looks to be right out of a Grandma Moses painting and should be on your list of places to see before you leave Oregon. The Polites grow classic Yamhill-Carlton AVA Pinot, with strong raspberry and earthy characteristics. Tours can be arranged by calling 503-852-7060.

ROBINSON RESERVE

Winemaker: Miguel Lopez
Wines: Chardonnay, Pinot Noir
Cases: 950

Robinson's two wines are from the pretty Robinson Vineyard in the West Hills of the Willamette Valley. Most of the production is Dijon-clone Pinot Noir (800 cases), with a bit of Chardonnay.

Z'IVO

www.zivowines.com
Owners: John and Katherine Zelko
Winemaker: John Zelko
Wines: Pinot Noir, white blends
Cases: 1,900

Zelko vodka didn't want to share a name, so John took the high road and went for a Slovak patchwork. Take Ivo (Johnny) and add the Z and you get something like "life of Johnny" in Slovak. Zelko's wines are as complicated as his story, which is a good thing. These Pinots are meant for cellaring—he's just released his '04 and '06 ('05 didn't work out) and feels his 2000 is almost ready for drinking. Persnickety and meticulous, he dumped 1,700 cases of his Pinot when a "brett bloom" appeared, because he won't deliver less than he promised.

WESTREY WINE COMPANY

503-434-6357
www.westrey.com
1065 NE Alpine Street
Tasting Room: Memorial Day and Thanksgiving weekends, and by appointment
Fee: $15
Owners/Winemakers: Amy Wesselman and David Autrey
Wines: Chardonnay, Pinot Gris, Pinot Noir
Cases: 4,000

The name is combination of a wife and husband's names, reflecting a team that shares all the work and the glory. Since 1993, Wesselman and Autrey have taken a philosophical approach to winemaking, which seems natural given that both have philosophy degrees from progressive Reed College in Portland. Waxing philosophic, they say, helps them deal with the whims of Mother Nature. They now have their own 49-acre vineyard of old vines, Oracle, in the Dundee Hills. Oracle Pinot Noir is one of the best for quality and low price.

THE EYRIE VINEYARDS

888-440-4970 or 503-472-6315
www.eyrievineyards.com
935 NE 10th Avenue
Tasting Room: Wed.–Sun. 12–5
Fee: $5, waived with two-bottle purchase
Owner/Winemaker: Jason Lett
Wines: Chardonnay, Pinot Blanc, Pinot
Gris, Muscat, Pinot Meunier, Pinot Noir
Cases: 7,500
Special Features: The birthplace of Pinot
Noir in the Willamette Valley

No trip to Oregon Wine Country is complete without a visit to Eyrie, where you can "taste the history"—an apropos statement for the winery that started it all. In 1966, before it was considered a sane idea, California transplants David and Diana Lett planted Pinot and Chardonnay in their newly acquired Willamette Valley property. History took shape, the vineyard is now in the Dundee Hills AVA, and Eyrie has provided the affirmation that Oregon belongs on the worldwide wine map. Yet pretension is noticeably absent in the tasting room. David Lett died in 2008 but left matters in the competent hands of his son Jason, who had taken over in 2005. Jason has worked by the side of his famous farmer dad since he was four. Eyrie now has four vineyards that offer diversity and flexibility in producing some of the most acclaimed Pinot Noir in the world, and matriarch Diana is still involved. As for the name, an eyrie (or eyre) is a high and remote but commanding place. How appropriate.

REMY WINES

503-560-2003
www.remywines.com
845 NE Fifth Street
Tasting Room: By appointment only
Owner/Winemaker: Remy Drabkin
Fee: Varies
Wines: Remy label: Rosé, Lagrein, Syrah;
Three Wives label: Pinot Gris, Cabernet
Sauvignon, red blend
Cases: 2,000

Remy Drabkin is a one-woman show creating wine under two labels. Her old-world style is reflected in both. Remy is Oregon's sole producer of Lagrein (60 cases), which hails from northern Italy near the Austrian border. The varietal comes from one acre at Illahe Vineyards and the wine has enough cachet to have earned a select spot among Oregon wines at the posh Bandon Dunes Resort. For updates on tasting room plans, check the Web site.

DOMINIO IV WINES

503-474-8636
www.dominiowines.com
845 NE Fifth Street
Tasting Room: By appointment only
Fee: Varies
Owners: Patrick Reuter and Leigh
Bartholomew
Winemaker: Patrick Reuter
Wines: Viognier, Tempranillo, Syrah Pinot
Noir, blends
Cases: 2,500

Robert Louis Stevenson once said wine is poetry in a bottle—a fitting description for Patrick Reuter's wines. Reuter and his wife, Leigh Bartholomew, journeyed across the world and ultimately landed in the tiny hamlet of Mosier in the Columbia Gorge. He was a friendly fixture—affectionately known as the "madman"—at the Carlton Winemakers Studio until recently, when he moved his operations to the Pinot Quarter. Dominio IV has plans to open a tasting room soon. Patrick isn't only known for his standout wines; a veggie sandwich is named for him at the Filling Station in Carlton.

PANTHER CREEK CELLARS

503-472-8080
www.panthercreekcellars.com
455 NE Irvine Street
Tasting Room: Daily 12–5

Inviting tasting decks await your arrival in Oregon Wine Country. Courtesy Trinity Vineyards

Fee: $5 refunded with purchase
Owner: Liz Chambers
Winemaker: Michael Stevenson
Wines: Pinot Gris, Chardonnay, Pinot Noir
Cases: 7,500
Special Features: Wine dinners, garden arbor, gifts

The three giant diesel generators at Panther Creek Cellars provided all of the electricity for McMinnville in the late 1930s, which gives you an idea of the building's age. Panther Creek bought the building from the city in 1989 have retained much of its character. Liz Chambers now runs Panther Creek, which was founded by Ken Wright. Winemaker Michael Stevenson started here under Wright in 1992 and has been at the helm ever since. The winery is certified biodynamic, organic, and LIVE, and even recycles corks. Panther Creek also can stake a claim to having the most famous wine dog in Oregon: Zoe, a golden lab who turned 6 in 2009, was profiled in Wine Dogs USA 2

and is featured in the 2010 Calendar of Dogs of Willamette Valley Wine Country. Despite all the fame, Zoe is not a wine snob, and she happily greets anyone who graces Panther Creek's entryway.

ANTHONY DELL CELLARS

503-910-8874
www.anthonydell.com
845 Fifth Street, No. 300
Tasting Room: May–Nov., Fri.–Sun. 12–5
Fee: $5
Owners/Winemakers: Douglas Anthony Drawbond and Joy Dell Means
Wines: Pinot Gris, Baco Noir, Pinot Noir, Syrah, red blend
Cases: 800
Special Features: "Brews and BBQs" event in parking lot in mid-June

"Wine will get you through times with no money better than money will get you through times with no wine." They are words to live and work by for owners

Drawbond and Means. Located in the granary district, or "wine ghetto," the ambitious couple does it all by hand, from de-stemming the grapes to bottling the fermented juice. Their food-friendly wines show the promise of getting us through hard economic times.

SOL ET SOLEIL CELLARS

503-925-5328
www.soletsoleil.com
777 NE Fourth Street
Tasting Room: Memorial Day and Thanksgiving weekends, and by appointment
Fee: Varies
Owners: Andrew and Laurel Mason
Winemaker: Andrew Mason
Wines: Pinot Gris, Pinot Noir, Syrah, Cabernet Franc, Merlot
Cases: 550

New in 2005, Sol et Soleil is French for "soil and sun," a name the Masons chose because, after all, great wines start from soil and sun. The wine careers started as a home-brewing passion before they took classes at U.C. Davis. Their Burgundian reserve Pinot is their superstar. The Masons have young children, so give them a couple days' notice.

R. STUART & CO.

503-472-4477
www.rstuartandco.com
528 NE Third Street
Tasting Room: Wed.–Sat. 12–7, Sun. 12–5
Fee: $10 for white flight, $12 for red
Owners: Rob and Maria Stuart
Winemaker: Rob Stuart
Wines: Chardonnay, Pinot Gris, rosé, Pinot Noir, sparkling wines
Cases: 20,000
Special Features: Wine bar with micro-brews and small plates of cheese, nuts, olives, pâté, and fish

R. Stuart has approachable wines with an approachable wine bar to match. In a familiar story in these parts, Rob Stuart took an old granary and converted it into a winery. They don't own any vineyard acreage themselves, but buy select fruit from elsewhere and make it downtown. They're especially proud of the 2007 Big Fire Red, which earned acclaim from the *Wall Street Journal* as one of the country's best wine buys.

SÉJOURNÉ

503-474-4499
www.sejournewines.com
444 NE Third Street
Tasting Room: Fri.–Sun. 1–6
Fee: $15, includes Riedel Oregon Pinot glass
Owner/Winemakers: Kevin and Robyn Howard
Wines: Chardonnay, Pinot Gris, Rosé, Pinot Noir, Syrah
Cases: 1,000
Special Features: The estate vineyard (7700 NE Cooper Ln., Yamhill) is open Memorial Day and Thanksgiving weekends

Séjourné is French for "place of rest," and that's what the Howards have at their foothills hideaway. The vineyards are accented with fruit trees and there's a distinct aroma of lavender in the air. The Howards produce Pinots from the Willamette Valley and Syrah from southern Oregon grapes. Along with Séjourné wines, the wine bar and tasting room in downtown McMinnville also features small plates. Kevin also has a hand in the making of Zenas wines, which are available in Carlton.

EVERGREEN VINEYARDS

503-434-4297 or 866-434-4818
www.evergreenvineyards.com
500 NE Captain Michael King Smith Way
Tasting Room: Daily 11–5
Fee: Complimentary
Owner: Delford M. Smith

Rolling out the Barrels

Oregon grows grapes. Oregon makes wine. Oregon even recycles its bottles, pallets, and corks. These days, Oregon can even claim it makes barrels.

Rick DeFerrari, a Scholls native, has carved a niche by opening Oregon Barrel Works in McMinnville. It is the first and only barrel-making operation, or wine cooperage, in the Pacific Northwest. DeFerrari and his five coopers have created a thriving business out of an art form that many in the industry say is dying. They carefully handcraft between 30 and 40 custom barrels per week, compared to four or five times that many mass-produced daily on assembly lines in California. As far as DeFerrari knows, his is the smallest commercial cooperage anywhere in the world.

Some of his barrels come from Oregon white oak nurtured on privately owned Willamette Valley stands. Other "staves" are imported from six different oak forests in France, each as nuanced in their differences as vineyards.

Though a half-century-old machine purchased in France provides an assist, most of the work requires careful handcrafting reminiscent of another era on another continent. Once the barrels are completed, the interiors of the 60-gallon barrels are "toasted" to the winemakers' wishes to coax tannins and impart subtle flavors. The barrels sell for about $1,000.

DeFerrari didn't come by his business out of pure happenstance. During college, while earning a forest engineering degree from Oregon State University, he worked at Ponzi Winery as a cellar rat. After college, he took an apprenticeship at a cooperage in the France's Burgundy region, and upon returning to Oregon in the mid-1990s he stayed with the same company to market Napa Valley–made barrels in the Pacific Northwest.

Only after local winemakers told him of their desire to see a cooperage in the Northwest did DeFerrari get serious about starting his own business, finally opening his warehouse in 2002. With his eye to detail, he must be on to something—his business is thriving while California's mechanized competitors have watched sales dip in a foundering economy.

Winemaker: Laurent Montalieu
Wines: Pinot Gris, Pinot Noir
Cases: 13,000
Special Features: Two tasting rooms in the Evergreen Aviation and Space Museum, which features an IMAX theater, gift shop, and restaurant

During crush many a visitor has exclaimed: "This is good enough to bottle as it is" when tasting freshly pressed wine grape juice. Spruce Goose label sells a frizzante version, sans alcohol, that takes advantage of that intensely flavored juice. Just for posterity, you'll want to try the Howard Hughes Pinot Noir and Rosey the Riveter Rosé. Along with wine grapes, Evergreen Agricultural Enterprises grows a few other crops in the shadows of the Spruce Goose wing at the Evergreen Aviation Museum: organic blueberries, raspberries and blackberries; walnuts, peaches, pears, cherries, and wheat. Evergreen also is the largest U.S. grower of hazelnuts.

HAUER OF THE DAUEN WINERY

503-868-7359
16425 SE Webfoot Road
Tasting Room: Sat.–Sun. 12–5
Fee: Complimentary
Owners: Carl and Lores Dauenhauer
Winemaker: Carl Dauenhauer
Wines: Chardonnay, Gewürztraminer, Pinot Gris, Riesling, rosé, Gamay Noir, Pinot Noir, Lemberger

Cases: 5,000
Special Features: Occasional tastings at the Wooden Shoe Tulip Farm in Woodburn

Carl Dauenhauer, a quintessential Farmer Bob, has an enthusiasm for life and wine that bubbles forth in the form of a deep, booming belly laugh. While working at Airlie, Sherry would listen to Karl and Mary Olson share their farming woes—all the while waiting for Karl to uncork his laughter. It's a sound not soon forgotten. Hauer of Dauen has a fun roster of wine, all meant to be enjoyed young, with mirth and joy.

METHVEN FAMILY VINEYARDS

503-868-7259
www.methvenfamilyvineyards.com
11400 Westland Lane
Tasting Room: May–Oct., daily 11–5; Nov.–Apr., Fri.–Sun. 11–5
Fee: $5
Owners: Allen and Jill Methven
Winemaker: Chris Lubberstedt
Wines: Pinot Gris, Riesling, Pinot Noir
Cases: 1,800
Special Features: Winery tours upon request, patio, concerts, wedding facilities, special events, and rental of tasting room

Methven is much more than a winery and tasting room. The facilities feature a full commercial kitchen that allows for big events, including summer weekend concerts and Valentine's picnics. Weddings, birthday parties, and class reunions are frequently booked at Methven, and one breathtaking look at the views of the Cascades reveals why. Don't miss Methven's holiday open houses, where the food is positively potent: Joel Palmer House mushroom risotto, barbecued pork made in their kitchen, rich chocolates paired with their Pinots. Valentine's Day serves up Methven's Extreme Chocolate event, featuring Dana Dooley's Honest Chocolates.

YOUNGBERG HILL VINEYARDS

503-472-2727
www.youngberghill.com
10660 SW Youngberg Hill Road
Tasting Room: Apr.–Nov., daily 11–5; Dec.–Mar. by appointment only
Fee: $5
Owner/Winemaker: Nicolette Bailey
Wines: Pinot Gris, Pinot Noir
Cases: 1,800
Special Features: Eight-room B&B ($180–350), wedding and outdoor event facilities

There is no place quite like Youngberg Hill, largely because of its opulent eight-room bed-and-breakfast. Even without the inn, this place would be special. The winery overlooks an expansive 20-year-old organic vineyard that has produced acclaimed wines. If you're into total relaxation, the inn allows you to appreciate the essence of Oregon Wine Country without having to leave the premises—though owner/winemaker Nicolette Bailey's feelings won't be hurt if you venture out to visit some of her winery neighbors. You won't want to be gone long, though: There's complimentary wine tasting from 4 to 5 P.M. and the sunsets are incomparable.

COEUR DE TERRE VINEYARD

503-472-3976
www.cdtvineyard.com
21000 SW Eagle Point Road
Tasting Room: Wed.–Sun. 11–5
Fee: $5
Owners: Lisa and Scott Neal
Winemaker: Scott Neal
Wines: Riesling, Pinot Gris, Pinot Noir, dessert wine
Cases: 2,000
Special Features: Organically farmed; private tours of vineyard and winery; owners run Pinot Quarters in the "wine ghetto" section of McMinnville (see Lodging, below)

Lisa Neal once sold vineyard real estate. Then she found her perfect piece of countryside in the foothills of the Coast Range. The Neals, with the help of friends and family, planted their modest three-acre Pinot Noir vineyard in 1998. We met the Neals in 2000 when they were part of the Airlie Winery tasting group. Lisa claims that Suzy Gagne (then winemaker at Airlie) taught her everything she knows about grafting vines onto rootstock. Coeur de Terre translates to Heart of the Earth, which is exactly what the Neals have done: put their hearts into their earth. Each of their wines reflects their firm belief "that wine is made in the vineyard."

LA BÊTE WINES

503-977-1493
www.labetewines.com
21000 SW Eagle Point Road
Tasting Room: Memorial Day and Thanksgiving weekends, and by appointment
Fee: Varies
Owner/Winemaker: John R. Eliassen
Wines: Aligoté, Pinot Gris, Melon, Pinot Blanc, rosé, Gamay Noir, Pinot Noir, red and white blends
Cases: 2,000

As the name implies, La Bête is all about French Burgundian varietals. Owner John R. Eliassen trained at two famous Domaines in France and also earned a degree in a viticulture program there—one of few Americans to accomplish the feat. Eliassen's dream was to produce Chardonnay and Pinot Noir in the traditional French way, and the results are reflected in his rare wines. Of note is the Aligoté. La Bête is the only winery in Oregon and one of three in the nation to produce this fruit-forward white made from grapes grown in Washington's hot and dry Yakima Valley.

YAMHILL VALLEY VINEYARDS

503-843-3100
www.yamhill.com
16250 SW Oldsville Road
Tasting Room: May–Dec., daily 11–5
Fee: $5 for six wines
Owner: Denis Burger
Winemaker: Stephen Cary
Wines: Pinot Blanc, Pinot Gris, Riesling, Pinot Noir
Cases: 16,000
Special Features: Outdoor deck and fish pond

Yamhill devotes its energies to the three amigos of Pinot: blanc, gris, and noir, all grown on 150 acres of classic Willamette Valley wine country landscapes. The tasting room overlooks the vineyard and visitors with a good sense of timing might get a glimpse of the winemaking. Yamhill Valley has been called an "up-and-coming star" by none other than Robert Parker Jr.

MAYSARA WINERY

503-843-1234
www.maysara.com
15765 SW Muddy Valley Road
Tasting Room: Mon.–Sat. 11–5
Fee: $7
Owners: Moe and Flora Momtazi
Winemaker: Tahmiene Momtazi
Wines: Pinot Gris, Pinot Blanc, rosé, Pinot Noir
Cases: 12,000
Special Features: Vineyard and winery both certified biodynamic; ponds stocked with rainbow trout

Maysara is an ancient Persian term for "House of Wine." At the Momtazi house you will find a true-to-the-land philosophy. You won't find a monoculture here, or chemicals, fertilizers, or other harmful additives to the natural environment. You will see biodiversity in the making. On the family's 538 acres, 250 are planted in vines. The rest is forest and pasture for 50 sheep, two

Maysara takes sustainable farming in its vineyards seriously. Courtesy Maysara Winery

dozen beef cattle, and horses. The animal manure is composted and used for fertilizer in the vineyard. The tasting room is rustic, though there are plans for an expansion.

COLEMAN VINEYARD

503-843-2707
www.colemanvineyard.com
22734 SW Latham Road
Tasting Room: Memorial Day and Thanksgiving weekends, and by appointment
Fee: $8, waived with purchase
Owner/Winemaker: Randy and Kim Coleman
Wines: Pinot Gris, Pinot Noir
Cases: 4,000
Special Features: Wine charms by Savannah for sale

Coleman is a small, sustainable estate where winemaking is a family affair. Their '06 Pinot Noir estate reserve scored a 92 from *Wine Spectator,* but the Colemans are more likely to talk about their label called Racy Red. "The Racy Red is a pretty large wine with fruity flavors and big tannins that are not bitter or rough," the winemaker told *Wine Press Northwest.* The architect of the Racy Red label was none other than the Colemans' son Ryan, age 10 at the time. The cartoonish race car on the label looks like something that would have been on his bedspread. Ryan, who was 12 in 2009, only had to wait nine more years to drink his own wine. Daughter Kristin is no wine slouch, either: She's a CIA-trained culinary chef and makes her own red called Vive.

SHERIDAN
RANSOM CELLARS

503-876-5022
www.ransomspirits.com
23101 Houser Road
Tasting Room: By appointment only
Fee: Varies

Owner/Winemaker: Tad Seestedt
Wines: Pinot Gris, Cabernet franc,
Grenache, Gewürztraminer, Riesling, Pinot
Noir, white blend
Cases: 6,500
Special Features: Gin and whiskey production

The reclusive Seedstedt and assistant Julia
Cattrall have moved to the country southwest of McMinnville, where Ransom Cellars
makes single-vineyard Pinots and other
distinguished wines. They also produce
such distilled spirits as gin, grape-based
brandies with Muscat and Gewürztraminer,
and grappa that comes from Pinot Noir
grapes. Ransom uses a hands-off approach
to the wines and gets most of the fruit from
organic or biodynamic vineyards.

WHEATLAND
ARCANE CELLARS
AT WHEATLAND WINERY
503-868-7076
www.arcanecellars.com
22350 Magness Road NW
Tasting Room: Sat.–Sun. 12–4 and by
appointment
Fee: $5
Owner: Jeffrey Leal Silva
Winemaker: Jason Leal Silva
Wines: Chardonnay, Pinot Blanc, Pinot
Gris, Riesling, Viognier, Cabernet
Sauvignon, Merlot, Pinot Noir, Syrah, red
blend
Cases: 3,000
Special Features: Picnic area

In a sense, this is two wineries in one: The
corporate-scale Wheatland Winery produces large quantities of Chardonnay and a
red blend from grapes hauled in from elsewhere; Arcane Cellars focuses on single-
vineyard estate wines—including three
Pinots and a Riesling from their own vineyards. It's all a family affair for the Silvas,
most notably owner Jeffrey and his winemaker son Jason. The setting is unique as
well: The winery and vineyards are in the
low country on the west bank of the
Willamette River, a short drive from the
Wheatland Ferry.

Lodging in the McMinnville Area

MCMINNVILLE
A'TUSCAN ESTATE B&B
Owners: Jacques and Liz Rolland
503-434-9016
www.a-tuscanestate.com
809 NE Evans Street
Rates: $135–235
Special Features: Coffee room for early ris-
ers, custom gourmet dinners, wine tastings, food books in the library

The name says Tuscany, but the look is an
American-Italian-French medley.
Regardless, it works. A'Tuscan Estate has
three lavishly decorated rooms and mounds
of Italian pottery and cloth in the home-
away-from-home suites. The well-kept
neighborhood property is a sensory feast
with scented plants, mini flower and herb
gardens outside, and extravagant decor of
art and collectibles inside. But it's the
meals that stand alone—not surprising,
given that owner Jacques Rolland is coau-
thor of *The Food Encyclopedia*. Along with
the kind of scrumptious breakfast you'd
expect from a culinary genius, you can also
order dinner. Call it a B&B&D. For $75,
Rolland will prepare a five-course dinner
for which recipes are published in his massive book.

BAKER STREET INN
Owner: Cheryl Hockaday
503-472-5575 or 800-870-5575
www.bakerstreetinn.com
129 SE Baker Street
Rates: $89–159
Special Features: Gift shop, long-term
stays, pet-friendly cottage

Hunker down in one of four rooms, each featuring a private bath, or rent the Petite Château, a two-bedroom house on the property. Centrally located in vibrant downtown "Mac," the comfortably stylish 1900s Craftsman exudes a welcoming aura the owners call "the Aloha spirit." Customizing your stay is their specialty, whether it's quiet and respite you seek, adventure and excitement, or just such thoughtful amenities as a fridge, coffeemaker, and air-conditioning in your room. A 10-minute walk will lead you to one of three top-notch breakfast joints.

JOSEPH MATTEY HOUSE
Owners: Jack and Denise Seed
503-434-5058
www.josephmatteyhouse.com
10221 NE Mattey Lane
Rates: $140–175
Special Features: Orchards of cherries, apples, plums, walnuts, and hazelnuts provide breakfast ingredients; small event and gathering facilities

The Joseph Mattey house, a registered historic Queen Anne Victorian, was built for the Englishman in the 1870s. Mattey, a successful butcher, was an orphan, and after his second wife died, the funds from his estate went to his orphanage in England. Coincidentally, the current owners and innkeepers are a British couple. In the four wine-named rooms, all with private bath, the Seeds have put comfort over decor, choosing eclectic antique furnishings to pamper rather than hinder. The Riesling room has an original clawfoot tub, just what a body needs after an active day. Denise serves up a hearty breakfast that might have you waddling to the porch, upstairs to the balcony, or into an armchair in the parlor. The balcony gets our vote, with its view of the 10 acres of Müller Thurgau grapes, sold to neighboring wineries.

MCMENAMINS HOTEL OREGON
503-472-8427
www.mcmenamins.com
310 NE Evans Street
Rates: $50–135
Special Features: Lounge, restaurant, and rooftop bar

Of all of the McMenamins' restoration projects, the Hotel Oregon might be the closest to traditional. Unlike many of the other projects, this four-story red-brick building with 42 European-style guest rooms *looks* like a hotel—even though it was never known for its accommodations. In its century of existence, the building has been a Western Union office, Greyhound Bus depot, dance hall, soda fountain, and beauty salon. The hotel offers four types of rooms, some with private bath. As with all McMenamin properties, the artwork adorning the halls is one-of-a-kind and every pore of the building oozes history. A bonus: the rooftop bar, with magnificent views of McMinnville and the Yamhill River valley.

OREGON WINE COTTAGE
503-883-1974
www.oregonwinecottage.com
515 NW Birch Street
Owners: Mike and Valerie Rogers
Rates: $185
Special Features: Three-night minimum required on wine holidays; no pets, kids or smoking.

Black leather furniture, a modern gourmet kitchen, king-sized beds, and sophisticated elegance in warm earth tones are trademarks for this deceptive little brick cottage. A soaking tub for two adds to the romantic nature—or the romance of nature. The Oregon Wine Cottage provides the ultimate in privacy. There are no housekeeping intrusions during your stay and you will have the luxury of dining without others. Bring your own food and wine. Don't wait to

The rooftop bar at the Hotel Oregon offers a bird's-eye view of McMinnville.   Courtesy McMenamin's

make your reservation: The cottage books up quickly, especially in summer.

PINOT QUARTERS
Owners: Lisa and Scott Neal
503-883-4115
www.pinotquarters.com
533 NE Davis Street
Rates: $200–225, two-night minimum
Special Features: Private winery tours can be arranged

A 100-year-old Victorian home, handsomely restored and within blocks of downtown, puts you in the center of McMinnville's wine world while still giving you a sense of seclusion. With such neighbors as Panther Creek, Dominio IV, and Sol et Soleil, you'll have great company when you want it. The two nicely furnished bedrooms overlook a lush yard bathed in colorful rhododendrons and other Oregon flora. Some of McMinnville's best restaurants and wine bars are a short stroll from your room, but the kitchen is fully stocked if you prefer dining in. Forgot the wine? The Neals have

every detail down, with an honor bar stocked with local selections for purchase.

LAFAYETTE
KELTY ESTATE
Owners: Bill and Joava Good
503-560-1512 or 800-867-3740
www.keltyestatebb.com
675 Third Street
Rates: $129-179
Special Features: Classic Lincoln stretch limo and driver available for touring, intimate wedding facilities for up to 80

Manager Nicci Stokes loves everything about her family's estate of business: the century-old oak trees, 150-year-old firs, trim hedges, perfect porches, even the semi-hidden pond stocked with koi. Who wouldn't? It's the quintessential movie image of a grandparents' country estate. Pristine white paint sets off the 1872 restored and registered historic home while the dark-green trim blends into the abundant flora. Once the country home of *Oregonian* senior editor Paul Kelty, the property has changed hands at least 14 times. Since 2004 the Good family has brought their style of hospitality, putting it in the capable hands and direction of their daughter. They plan to keep it that way. Five guest rooms furnished tastefully with antiques—no doilies or teddy bears—make for sweet dreams. Complimentary local wine and cheese at 3 P.M. daily sets the mood for exquisite dining nearby.

Dining in the McMinnville Area

McMINNVILLE
BISTRO MAISON
503-474-1888
www.bistromaison.com
729 NE Third Street
Open: Wed.–Fri. 11:30–2, Fri.–Sat. 5–9, Sun. 12–2 and 3–8
Price: Expensive
Credit Cards: Yes
Special Features: Pre- and post-theater dining near the Gallery and Mack theaters

A French bistro in Burgundy country? But of course! Chef Jean-Jacques and Deborah Chatelard transport you to Paris, sans passport and jet lag, with their amazing and authentic cuisine. Classic numbers such as *coq au vin, steak au poivre,* and *confit de canard* are prepared and presented with an experienced hand. Don't pass on the hors d'oeuvres, especially the pâtés, champignons, or truffle cheese fondue. A wide selection of "Orgundian" Pinot Noirs top the wine list for the pièce de résistance to a sublime meal.

CAFÉ UNCORKED
503-843-4401
www.freshpalatecafe.com
19706 SW Highway 18
Hours: Daily 11–3, Fri.–Sat. 5–7:30
Price: Inexpensive
Credit Cards: Yes
Special Features: Catering services

Formerly Fresh Palate, Café Uncorked is an oasis 18 miles outside McMinnville, above the Lawrence Gallery (formerly the Oregon Tasting Room). It's a great place to have a sit-down break or takeaway lunchables for wine touring. The art of food mingles with the art of the hand here. Sit inside or out and choose from a menu that touts its homegrown products. Virginia Murphy has been running and expanding her successful restaurant since 1993. Rumors are that she's planning to grow again, into the former wine-shop space.

CRESCENT CAFÉ
503-435-2655
526 NE Third Street
Open: Wed.–Fri. 7 A.M.–1:30 P.M. , Sat.–Sun. 8 A.M.–1:30 P.M.
Price: Moderate
Credit Cards: Yes
Special Features: Breakfast served all day

This breakfast fave with visitors and residents alike is widely considered a best bet for early-morning food in McMinnville. Using local products and ingredients is their banner and they wear it well. Carlton Farms provides the pork, local farmers the eggs and produce. Grab a cup of Joe on the way for your wait in line.

LA RAMBLA RESTAURANT & BAR
503-435-2126
www.laramblaonthird.com
238 NE Third Street
Open: Daily 11:30–2:30, Mon.–Fri. 5 P.M.–close, Sat.–Sun. 11:30 A.M.–close
Price: Moderate to expensive
Credit Cards: Yes
Special features: Happy hour 4–6 with half-off tapas and discounted beverages; flights of one-ounce tastes; live music on Sat.

During Kathy Stoller's travels in Spain, she fell in love with the buzz of the tapas bars and wanted to create the same kind of place in her own wine-savvy town. Many dollars and several peacock feathers later (she collects them), she and husband Chet have created the real deal in the oldest brick building in downtown "Mac." The light globes—custom-made in peacock-feather patterns—a colorful array of fruit soaking in spigoted glass jars, live floral arrangements, squeezed-together tables, and long two-tiered copper bar in a narrow space emulate the bars of Barcelona. And so does the food. Using as many farmer's market ingredients as possible, creative and traditional tapas are served *fria* and *caliente*. Familiar favorites: Paella, Serrano ham, grilled artichokes, and, for the more daring, garlic chili prawns. Although you can sip cocktails made from house-infused spirits, the place has a huge wine cellar. She has more than 350 offerings from Oregon and, naturally, Spain. The list earned the coveted *Wine Spectator* Award of Excellence in 2008 and 2009. La Rambla, named for the famous pedestrian mall in Barcelona, follows tradition by closing between lunch and dinner on weekdays.

NICK'S ITALIAN CAFE

503-434-4471
www.nicksitaliancafe.com
521 NE Third Street
Open: Tues.–Sat. 11:30–2:30, Tues.–Sat. 5:30–9, Sun. 11:30–6
Price: Moderate to expensive
Credit Cards: Yes
Special Features: Back Room bar (Tues.–Sun. 5 P.M. to close) has condensed menu of inexpensive soup, pasta, pizza, and light bites.

Nick's was a Willamette Valley legend even before the wine phenomenon arrived in McMinnville. When it opened in 1977, the restaurant was one of the few reasons to come downtown after dusk. McMinnville has changed dramatically, and the restaurant competition is fierce, but the Peirano family continues to deliver with five-course prix fixe Italian fare. Now in its second wave, with daughter Carmen and her husband, Eric Ferguson, at the head of the wood-fired oven, Nick's has gained a youthful appeal. Like so many of the region's top restaurants, Nick's has hopped on the fresh-is-best bandwagon. The pork, lamb, eggs, and produce are all local and sustainable. Dinners are $49, or can be ordered à la carte.

RED FOX BAKERY & CAFÉ

503-434-5098
328 NE Evans Street
Open: Mon.–Sat. 7–4, Sun. 7 A.M.–1 P.M.
Prices: Inexpensive
Credit Cards: Yes
Special Features: Next door to McMenamins Hotel Oregon

Laurie and Jason Furch start their days early, usually around 2 A.M. Laurie bakes the bread and Jason is the chef at their specialty breakfast and lunch place. You will find an appealing array of fresh-baked goods, as you might expect, but lunch takes center stage at Red Fox. The turkey, apple, and smoked gouda sandwich is served on golden raisin bread and is rich with flavor. Prosciutto, salami, and fontina on a baguette is manager Melissa's favorite, and makes for great wine-pairing fare. Soups are equally fresh and fabulous, and are creatively made with organic produce from Oak Hill Organics in Amity. If you have trouble locating the bakery, just follow your nose. The aromas waft through downtown starting around 5 A.M.

THISTLE

503-472-9623
www.thistlerestaurant.com
228 NE Evans Street
Open: Tues.–Thurs 5:30–10, Fri.–Sat. 5:30–11
Prices: Moderate
Credit Cards: Yes

Special Features: Ten Pin dinners on occasional Sundays

Well-known chef Eric Bechard and partner Emily Howard have moved out of Portland to become the new kids on the burgeoning downtown McMinnville restaurant block. Bechard's reputation as a chef was honed at the Oyster Bar in Portland and Acquerello in San Francisco, and he uses a six-burner range to create culinary delights from foods provided mostly by local producers and fishermen. The menu changes nearly every day, and almost all of the entrées are under $20. Try the hangar steak with wild mushrooms, carrots, and smoked salt butter or the rabbit loin wrapped in bacon and accompanied by turnips and mustard. Choose from one of about 20 seats in the dining area or six at the kitchen counter. Wines come from around the globe, but there's a distinctly local flavor.

Attractions in the McMinnville Area

You could easily lose track of time in McMinnville, with its seemingly endless array of art galleries, wine shops, boutiques, restaurants, and theaters. On the east edge of town is the **Evergreen Aviation Museum** (503-434-4180, 500 NE Capt. Michael King Smith Way), a massive glass building filled by the equally massive Spruce Goose, a.k.a., the Flying Boat. For a respite from wine touring, drive into the heart of the Coast Range to **Spirit Mountain Casino** (800-760-7977, 27100 SW Salmon River Hwy.) in Grand Ronde. Despite the seemingly remote locale, the casino books big-name entertainment and offers dining and lodging.

Recreation in the McMinnville Area

Golfers will feel a little as if they're at Augusta playing in The Masters at **The Bayou Golf Course** (503-472-4651, 9301 SW Bayou Drive), a nine-hole par-3 layout with a plantation-like mansion on the grounds.

Shopping in the McMinnville Area

The **McMinnville Farmers Market** (503-472-3605) takes place from 2:30 to 6:30 every Thursday from June to October on Cowls Street between Second and Third Streets. For anything and everything organic, visit **Harvest Fresh** (503-472-5740, 251 NE Third St.), where even food for Fido is natural. Pack a few pounds of Oregon hazelnuts and other locally produced snacks for your wine touring from **Evergreen Orchards** (866-434-4818, 3850 Three Mile Ln.). McMinnville also has a handful of antiques shops, including the **McMinnville Antique Mall** (503-474-9696, 1030 East First St.) and **Granny's Touch** (503-843-7811, 17850 SW Highway 18). Every third Saturday of the month, McMinnville has the **Art & Wine Walk** downtown.

Wine Shopping in the McMinnville Area

McMinnville seemingly has a wine shop on every corner. **Wednesday Wines** (503-857-5665, 250 NE Third St.) emphasizes "wines you would drink during the week," with choices from around the globe priced between $7 and $15. **Noah's—A Wine Cellar** (503-434-2787, 525 NE Third St.) is two doors down from the Hotel Oregon and has a food menu. **NW Wine Bar** (503-435-1295, 326 NE Davis St.) is all about Oregon wine and has a solid list of appetizers. **NW Food & Gifts** (503-434-6111, 445 NE Third St.) has everything you need for a picnic, including wines from 80 boutique wineries, and has daily tastings. It also has a varied selection of artisan-made gifts and treasures. The innovative **Willamette

There's always a flurry of activity at McMinnville's Farmer's Market.   Courtesy Creative Commons

Valley Vineyards Wine Center (503-883-9012, 300 NE Third St.)—opened just before Thanksgiving 2009 in a renovated historic building downtown—is more than just a place to taste WVV's wines. It is also a classy and intimate wine-education center designed to shine a spotlight on the industry locally. Sip complimentary wine while viewing wine-related images on a giant screen or perusing the interesting exhibit about area soils.

SALEM AREA (EOLA–AMITY HILLS AVA)

For whatever reason—maybe it's the heavy government influence—when personality and charm were distributed to Oregon communities, Salem was largely ignored. It isn't that the capital city is seedy, unattractive, or unappealing. It's just, well . . . *there*. Yes, there's the state capital and museums and historic homes and music and theaters and parks and the Willamette River, all creating a pleasant enough atmosphere. And there's plenty to do. More likely, though, after a few hours or days here, you'll depart thinking that Salem was nice, but it also could've been Anytown, U.S.A.

Maybe it's something in the water in the heart of the Willamette Valley. Neither Monmouth nor Independence offers much to draw tourists, either, even though they border wine country. Monmouth was in fact a dry town until 2002.

Wineries in the Salem Area

A few miles south of McMinnville, OR 99W straightens for its journey south, bordered by the towering firs of the Coast Range to the west and oak savannahs of the Amity and Eola Hills to the east. This is fertile country, known for its nurseries, Christmas tree farms, orchards, and vineyards.

This is Pinot country with a twist. Because of a slight difference in soil composition and climate, the Pinot grapes grown in the Eola Hills especially are darker, spicier, and tend to bring more acidity and brightness to the wines. The wineries in this region are in picturesque locations, many with stunning views of either the Coast or Cascade Range.

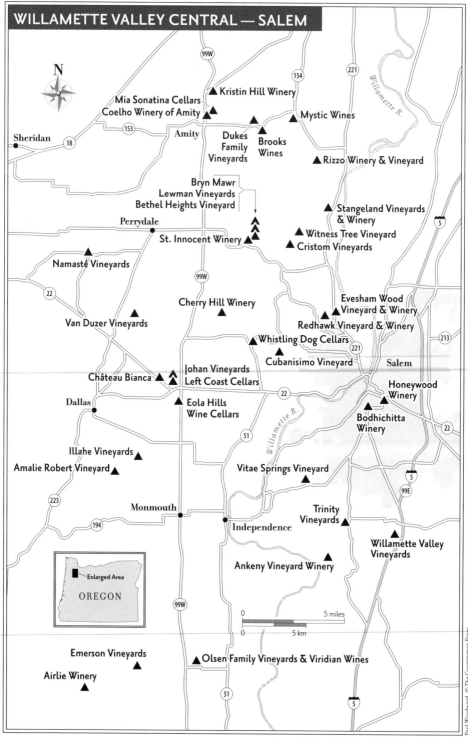

WILLAMETTE VALLEY CENTRAL — SALEM

N

99W

154

221

Willamette R.

Kristin Hill Winery

Mia Sonatina Cellars
Coelho Winery of Amity

Mystic Wines

Sheridan

18

153

Amity

Dukes
Family
Vineyards

Brooks
Wines

Rizzo Winery & Vineyard

Bryn Mawr
Lewman Vineyards
Bethel Heights Vineyard

Stangeland Vineyards
& Winery

Perrydale

5

Witness Tree Vineyard

St. Innocent Winery

Cristom Vineyards

Namasté Vineyards

99W

22

Cherry Hill Winery

Evesham Wood
Vineyard & Winery

Van Duzer Vineyards

Redhawk Vineyard & Winery

213

Whistling Dog Cellars

221

Cubanisimo Vineyard

Salem

Château Bianca

Johan Vineyards
Left Coast Cellars

22

Honeywood
Winery

Dallas

Eola Hills
Wine Cellars

51

Willamette R.

Bodhichitta
Winery

22

Illahe Vineyards

Amalie Robert Vineyard

Vitae Springs Vineyard

5

99E

223

194

Monmouth

Trinity
Vineyards

Independence

Willamette Valley
Vineyards

Enlarged Area

OREGON

Ankeny Vineyard Winery

0   5 miles

0   5 km

99W

Emerson Vineyards

Olsen Family Vineyards & Viridian Wines

Airlie Winery

51

5

Paul Woodward. © The Countryman Press

Touring Wineries in the Salem Area

Start your tour in Amity and curl east to Rizzo before coming down Spring Valley Road toward Zena. From Spring Valley Road, you can hit the wineries off Bethel Heights Road.

AMITY

KRISTIN HILL WINERY

503-835-0850

3330 SE Amity-Dayton Highway

Tasting Room: Mar.–Dec. 12–5, Jan.–Feb. Sat.–Sun. 12–5

Fee: Complimentary

Owner/Winemaker: Eric Aberg

Wines: Pinot Gris, Chardonnay, Müller Thurgau, Gewürztraminer, rosé, port-style and sparkling wines

Cases: 1,000

Special Features: Picnic area with old-fashioned country charm

Spending time in Germany and France while serving in the Armed Forces cinched Eric Aberg's affinity for wine and bubbly. While stationed in San Francisco, he took classes at U.C.–Davis to learn how to make the nectar he loved. When he landed in Yamhill County and started his winery (named for one of his four daughters) he was one of just 22. How the times have changed! Eric holds court in his *Weinstube* (tasting room) and shares his labor of love with a small dose of wine education. Kristin Hill is best known for Fizzy Lizzy, a cherry-infused sparkling wine made in the traditional way (*methode champenoise*).

COELHO WINERY OF AMITY

503-835-9305

www.coelhowinery.com

111 Fifth Street

Tasting Room: May–Dec., daily 11–5 and by appointment

Fee: $5–15

Owners: Dave and Deolinda Coelho

Winemaker: Brian Marcy

Wines: Pinot Gris, Chardonnay, rosé, Pinot Noir, Petite Sirah, Maréchel Foch, dessert wines

Cases: 3,000

Special Features: Local art and gifts, picnic area, Portuguese varietals

Patience is the guiding force behind the operation at Coelho, which is Portugeuse for rabbit (and the surname of co-owners Dave and Deolinda). Many of the wines have Portuguese monikers: Divertimento (fun), Renovãçao (renewal), and Serinidade (serenity). The addition of Amity to the winery's name is in line with their commitment to the friendly spirit of the community—and you feel it in a spacious tasting room with fireplace, artwork, and unique gifts. The Portuguese wines are Iberian varietals trucked up from California.

MIA SONATINA CELLARS

503-449-0834

www.miasonatina.com

101 SE Nursery Street

Tasting Room: Feb.–Dec., Fri.–Sun. 11–5, and by appointment

Fee: $5, refunded with $20 wine purchase

Owners: Vern and Jo Spencer

Winemaker: Vern Spencer

Wines: Pinot Gris, Chardonnay, Riesling, Allegro, Pinot Noir, Cabernet Sauvignon, Merlot, Cabernet franc, red blend, white blends, dessert wine

Cases: 1,500

Special Features: Gift shop

Mia Sonatina is Italian for "My Little Song," and the tagline for the winery is "a song for the palate." Vern and Jo Spencer are up-and-comers, with a relaxed and comfortable facility that matches the ambiance of the quiet countryside. The old-world wines can be had for a song, with most priced between $10 and $20.

DUKES FAMILY VINEYARDS

602-770-1671
www.dukesfamilyvineyards.com
7845 SE Amity Road
Tasting Room: By appointment only
Fee: Complimentary
Owners: Patrick and Jackie Dukes
Winemaker: Patrick Dukes
Wines: Pinot Noir
Cases: 800

Pat Dukes' new-world wines are made for food. No surprise there: Pat is a foodie by trade. The Dukes bought 16 acres in 2005 and replanted half in wine grapes. They live in Scottsdale, Arizona, but are able to keep a close eye on the vineyard through hired help. They suggest you double-decant the Pinot and let it breathe for two hours; you'll then know why it earned a spot at the Indie Festival in 2009.

BROOKS WINES

503-435-1278
www.brookswines.com
9360 SE Eola Hills Road
Tasting Room: Summer, Sat.–Sun., and by appointment
Fee: Varies
Owner: Pascal Brooks
Winemaker: Chris Williams
Wines: Riesling, white blend, Pinot Noir
Cases: Under 1,000
Special Features: New tasting room in an orchard and vineyard setting

Jimi Brooks was an organic and biodynamic advocate and all-around great guy when he died of a heart attack at age of 34 in 2004. "He left a big hole," Harry Pederson-Nedry of Chehalem Wines said, adding, " . . . we are all vulnerable and smaller when a strength, kindness, and intelligence like Jimi exits." Brooks's young son, Pascal, inherited the winery while his sister, Janie Brooks Hauek, took over the operations. Brooks Wines now has a permanent wine-making facility and tasting room in a good-vibes place in the Eola Hills, previously used by Cuneo Cellars and Francis Tannahill wineries. Although Brooks is famed for its Runaway label—named after an accident involving a forklift and futile effort to move a barrel late one night—do not miss the Riesling.

MYSTIC WINES

503-581-2769
www.mysticwine.com
11931 SE Hoodview Road
Tasting Room: May–Nov., Sat.–Sun. 12–5
Fee: Negotiable
Owner/Winemaker: Rick Mafit
Wines: Merlot, Cabernet Sauvignon, Zinfandel, Syrah, Barbera, Pinot Noir
Cases: 1,500

Take a breather in Pinot country and stop by the Mafits' place to savor big reds. What's the mystique of Mystic? Sourcing the right grapes, choosing the right French oak barrels, and giving more time in the barrel—the Cab and Merlot spend at least two years. Mafit is a very particular, hands-on guy with plenty of opinions and the experience to back them; he cut his teeth at Fetzer after attending U.C. Davis. His wines initially sold out before the next release. He now has production where he wants it, with enough to supply his loyal fan base and the restaurants to which he personally delivers. The award-winning abstract label design was created by one of Mafit's sons, Duncan.

SALEM
RIZZO WINERY & VINEYARD

503-577-5741
www.rizzowinery.com
13005 Jerusalem Hill Road NW
Tasting Room: By appointment only
Fee: Complimentary
Owner/Winemaker: David Rizzo
Wines: Muscat, Viogner, Cabernet Sauvignon, Pinot Noir, Tempranillo, Zinfandel
Cases: 1,200

The famous witness tree stands guard over the vineyard. Courtesy Witness Tree Vineyard

Higher-end Pinots and Cabernet Sauvignons ($34–90) are Rizzo's forte. The grapes come from such diverse places as Sonoma County in northern California and near Echo in arid eastern Oregon, and the wines are made in small lots. In 2006, David planted eight acres of Pinot Noir and one each of Muscat Canelli and Viognier at his new vineyard near Hopewell, with an eye on diversifying the winery's output.

STANGELAND VINEYARDS & WINERY

503-581-0355
stangelandwinery.com
8500 Hopewell Road NW
Tasting Room: Fri.–Sun. 12–5,
Mon.–Thurs. by appointment or chance
Fee: $5
Owner/Winemaker: Larry Miller
Wines: Pinot Gris, Chardonnay,
Gewürztraminer, Saignée (some years),
Pinot Noir, Tempranillo
Cases: 2,500–3,000
Special Features: winemaker dinners and special events, barrel tastings, intimate concerts, seasonal wedding and events facility

The Millers are gracious hosts who make it their mission to befriend customers and live up to the motto "There are no strangers at Stangeland." Now a full-time winemaker, Larry Miller has vinifera dating back to 1978 and he's won international awards for his Pinots. The cool—in both senses of the word—climate-controlled winery and tasting room, gracefully terraced gardens, and views of rolling hills make this a winner. And it's a welcome stop on Bike Oregon.

WITNESS TREE VINEYARD

503-585-7874
www.witnesstreevineyard.com
7111 Spring Valley Road NW
Tasting Room: Summer, Tues.–Sun. 11–5;
fall and spring, Sat.–Sun. 11–5; closed
Jan.–Feb.
Fee: $5
Owners: Dennis and Carolyn Devine
Winemaker: Steven Westby
Wines: Chardonnay, Pinot Blanc, Viognier,
Dolcetto, Pinot Noir, dessert wine
Cases: 6,000
Special Features: Picnic area, historic oak tree in vineyard

Coming to Witness Tree feels like visiting your country cousins. An attractive double-wide serves as tasting room, and a narrow wraparound porch adorned with bistro tables has groupies whenever we visit. If Jackie is pouring, you're in for a treat! The ancient oak tree towering above the vineyard like a sentinel is a designated Oregon Heritage Tree suitable for photo ops. Every one of their wines comes from the 51 acres of vineyard surrounding the stately old tree.

CRISTOM VINEYARDS

503-375-3068
www.cristomwines.com
6905 Spring Valley Road NW
Tasting Room: Apr.–Thanksgiving, Wed.–Sun. 11–5, Dec.–Mar. by appointment Fee: $5, refunded with purchase
Owners: Paul and Eileen Gerrie
Winemaker: Steve Doemer
Wines: Pinot Gris, Chardonnay, Viognier, Pinot Noir, Syrah
Cases: 12,500
Special Features: Gift items for sale

Walking past manicured gardens through the covered entry and antique mahogany

Spent vines in the vineyard mean harvest is complete. Courtesy Witness Tree Vineyard

doors into Cristom makes you think of a hoity-toity tasting room—smaller, but with similar attitude. It's not a place where smiles abound, but exquisite Pinot Noirs do. Cristom has two fine northern Rhône varietals—Syrah and Viognier—that were some of the first to be planted in the valley. Once only distributed and sold out of state, Cristom joins the ranks of Oregon wineries dependent on tasting-room sales as well. Cristom is a combination of the names of the Gerries' two children, Christine and Tom, so it's pronounced "chris-*tom*." Six of the family's matriarchs comprise the feminine names on the labels; Marjorie is prized most because it's from the oldest vines.

ST. INNOCENT WINERY

503-378-1526
www.stinnocentwine.com
5657 Zena Road NW
Tasting Room: Tues.–Sun. 11–4
Fee: $5, refunded with purchase
Owner/Winemaker: Mark Vlossak
Wines: Chardonnay, Pinot Gris, Pinot Blanc, Pinot Noir, sparkling wines
Cases: 8,000
Special Features: Separately owned and operated events facility

St. Innocent's name honors Mark Vlossak's father, John Innocent Vlossak, who taught him wine appreciation at an early age. This early education included the belief that wine was meant to go with food, and Vlossak's talents shine as chef as well as winemaker. Open houses at St. Innocent are not to be missed, especially in their new digs. Exquisite Pinot Noirs and a killer cassoulet, leg of lamb, or grilled salmon have flavors that saints—and we mere mortals—would deem heavenly. And the hard-to-get-hold-of sparkling wines . . . doubly divine. The experience is enhanced by the new tasting room completed in 2008.

BRYN MAWR

503-581-4286
www.brynmawrvineyards.com
5955 Bethel Heights Road NW
Tasting Room: Sat.–Sun. 11–5
Fee: Complimentary
Owner/Winemaker: David Lloyd-Jones
Wines: Chardonnay, Pinot Noir,
Tempranillo
Cases: 600

To some, Pinot Noir is poetry in a glass.
That's certainly the case at Bryn Mawr,
which celebrates Oregon's premier grapes
with odes to Pinot. David Lloyd-Jones, a
former yoga and stress-management
instructor, fashions his Pinot Noir from
four acres of grapes in the hills northwest
of Salem. In doing so, his family makes
every effort to be earth-friendly. Their
vineyards are sustainable and they raise
much of their food.

LEWMAN VINEYARDS

503-365-8859
www.lewmanvineyard.com
6080 Bethel Heights Road NW
Tasting Room: Memorial Day, Labor Day,
and Thanksgiving weekends, and by
appointment
Fee: Complimentary
Owner/Winemaker: Dennis Lewman
Wines: Pinot Noir
Cases: 100
Special Features: Gifts, chocolate infused
with cherries, fruit spreads, honey, Oregon
country gourmet products

You might notice that Lewman's Web site
and Facebook pages are sprinkled with
Japanese lettering. That's because owner
Dennis Lewman's wife, Kaoru, is Japanese.
A former schoolteacher, Lewman himself
has lived in some exotic locales, and his
labels reflect these travels. Of particular
note in the gift shop is the honey, gathered
from on the property.

BETHEL HEIGHTS VINEYARD

503-581-2262
www.bethelheights.com
6060 Bethel Heights Road NW
Tasting Room: Tues.–Sun. 11–5
Fee: $5
Owners: Ted and Terry Casteel, and family
Winemakers: Ben and Terry Casteel
Wines: Chardonnay, Pinot Gris, Pinot
Blanc, Gewürztraminer, rosé, Pinot Noir
Cases: 11,000
Special Features: Picnic area with
panoramic views of area vineyards, Eola
Hills, and volcanic Cascade peaks

By establishing Bethel Heights in 1977, the
Casteel brothers were on the forefront of
the Oregon vineyard and wine scene. Today,
an entire Casteel clan owns and runs the
place, and they remain instrumental in the
development of the industry on many levels. In 2008, their wines were the first to be
labeled "Oregon Certified Sustainable." It
was here that we were first introduced to
the minute differences and subtleties of
vineyard-block Pinot. The affable and
patient pourer explained eloquently the
subtle differences in flavor profiles for each
Pinot, depending on where the grapes came
from in a specific section of their 51-acre
acre vineyard (maps included). We just
knew it was well made and we could drink
any one of them and be happy. The Casteel
style is to go for transparency and not try to
manipulate the grapes. Bethel Heights
Pinot Noir is easily purchased or enjoyed in
restaurants across the state and nation.

EVESHAM WOOD VINEYARD & WINERY

503-371-8478
www.eveshamwood.com
3795 Wallace Road NW
Tasting Room: Memorial Day and
Thanksgiving weekends, and by appointment
Fee: Varies

Owners: Mary and Russ Raney
Winemaker: Russ Raney
Wines: Chardonnay, Pinot Gris, Gewürztraminer, rosé, Pinot Noir, white blend
Cases: 4,500

Maybe it's the simple dogwood on the understated label. Maybe it's the contents. Or maybe it's the setting where we first tasted Evesham Wood's Chardonnay—an intimate dinner on the Oregon Coast. Owner and winemaker Russ Raney was trained in Europe and is very much in the Burgundian camp when it comes to making Pinot. Evesham Wood walks the talk when it comes to being sustainable and stewards of the soil. They don't irrigate their certified organic, 13-acre Le Puts Sec ("dry-farmed") vineyard, believing that terroir-driven wines are best expressed with little intervention.

REDHAWK VINEYARD & WINERY

503-362-1596
www.redhawkwine.com
2995 Michigan City Lane NW
Tasting Room: Daily 11–5
Fee: $5, refunded with purchase
Owners: John and Betty Pataccoli
Winemaker: John Pataccoli
Wines: Pinot Gris, Chardonnay, Riesling, Pinot Noir, Dolcetto, Cabernet Sauvignon, Syrah, Gamay Noir
Cases: 4,500
Special Features: Picnic area in park setting with panoramic view, barrel tasting festival three times a year

The winery began in 1988 and was best known for a good-time and -value Pinot named Grateful Red. The Grateful Red is still there, with the same low price any Deadhead fan would appreciate, but the rest has changed dramatically. New owners John

Inviting spaces to taste are the norm in Oregon Wine Country. Courtesy Trinity Vineyards

and Betty Pataccoli revitalized the vineyard and revamped the tasting room. They exploited their limitless views of the valley—who wouldn't?—and added a breath of fresh air to the scene. Enjoy their wines and a hawk's view without spending a fortune. It was previous owner Tom Robinson who had such satirical labels as Chateau Mootown. John and Betty have gone with more sophisticated names, but we're, uh, grateful they did keep their iconic red blend.

HONEYWOOD WINERY

503-362-4111
www.honeywoodwinery.com
1350 Hines Street SE
Tasting Room: Mon.–Fri. 9–5, Sat. 10–6, Sun. 1–5
Fee: Complimentary up to five wines
Owners: Paul and Marlene Gallick
Winemaker: Marlene Gallick
Wines: Pinot Gris, Pinot Blanc, Chardonnay, Gewürztraminer, Müller Thurgau, Riesling, Maréchal Foch, Pinot Noir, Cabernet Sauvignon, Merlot, Syrah, fruit wines
Cases: 30,000
Special Features: Patio, large gift shop

This is the oldest continuously operating winery in Oregon. OK, so you may have noticed a lot of "oldest this" or "oldest that" in Oregon." They're all accurate in their own way, but this is the real deal—dating back to 1933 and post-Prohibition, when Ron Honeyman and John Wood formed Columbia Distillers and made fruit brandies and liquors. When they branched into making wine, they renamed the company Honeywood. They're not just about fermenting tree fruit and berries; they also make decent varietal wines, too. The Müller Thurgau and Maréchal Foch are crowd pleasers. The urban setting with a large gift shop features Oregon food products from cheese to nuts and wine accessories.

BODHICHITTA WINERY

503-580-9463
www.bodhichittawinery.com
1885 Commercial Street SE
Tasting Room: None
Owner/Winemaker: Mark Proden
Wines: Pinot Gris, Chardonnay, Chenin Blanc, Cabernet Sauvignon, Pinot Noir, red blend, honey wines, apple wine
Cases: 600
Special Features: Organic lavender products are also for sale

Get your new age on at the Oregon's first and only (intentionally) nonprofit winery, pronounced "bo-da-chee-ta." Proden's mission: Service to others comes first. Bodhichitta, Sanskrit for "inner self or soul," donates to charities close to home—and not so close. Under his "Three Glasses of Wine" campaign he is raising funds for the Central Asian Institute, started by Greg Mortensen of "Three Cups of Tea" fame. "Passion for wine, compassion for others" seems to us a like a good thing to toast. Better yet, drink and donate. In August 2009, Proden started another journey on the Hawaiian island of Kauai. Until further notice, Bodhichitta products are available only online.

CUBANISIMO VINEYARD

503-588-1763
www.cubanisimovineyards.com
1754 Best Road NW
Tasting Room: Apr.–Dec., daily 12–5
Fee: $4
Owner: Mauricio Collada
Winemaker: Rob Stuart
Wines: Pinot Gris, Pinot Noir, rosé
Cases: 1,200
Special Features: Salsa dance lessons third Saturday of each month

Transport yourself to a place far away from the green and gray of Oregon. White sand, Floridian beach colors, and Cuban music are the hallmark of Havana native Mauricio Collada's winery tasting room. And it's not your imagination—there is something extra in their Pinot that makes it go better with spicy food. A dash of pepper? Who knows? And they're not saying. Come to one of the more unique wineries in the state for a Latin mood swing. Sherry and a friend tried the salsa dance lessons on the patio one warm Memorial Day weekend a few years ago. It was fun, but they are none the better Latin dancers!

WHISTLING DOG CELLARS

503-329-5114
www.whistlingdogcellars.com
1915 Oak Grove Road NW
Tasting Room: Tues.–Sun. 11–4 at St. Innocent
Fee: Complimentary
Owners: Tom and Celeste Symonette
Winemaker: Tom Symonette
Wines: Pinot Noir
Cases: 400

Whistling Dog is a two-person operation where the focus is heavily on the vineyard. The Pinot Noirs come from three Eola Hills vineyards, and are made and poured at nearby St. Innocent. Owner/winemaker Symonette earned a viticulture/enology degree at Fresno State while running Whistling Dog. He describes himself as "a minimalist winemaker who just lets the vintage and site speak for themselves."

CHERRY HILL WINERY

503-623-7867 (winery) or 503-623-9745 (tasting room)
www.cherryhillwinery.com
9867 Crowley Road
Tasting Room: May–Oct., Mon.–Fri. 11–4 (but call first), Sat.–Sun. 11–5
Fee: $10, waived with purchase
Owners: Mike and Jan Sweeney
Winemaker: Chris Luby
Wines: Pinot Gris, rosé, Pinot Noir

Cases: 7,000
Special Features: Barrel tastings, wine-maker dinners, dark chocolate–covered cherries from the orchard

Cherry Hill has just opened a sparkling new winery and tasting room, which means the old tasting room in the little blinking-light community of Rickreall is no longer necessary. Wild cherries once were prolific on the hill—thus the name—and then the domestic variety were planted in the 1960s. Thirty years later, Pinot Noir was put into the Jory soils. The owners kept the orchard, so you can buy cherries covered in dark chocolate—a treat with their Pinot Noir.

DALLAS
VAN DUZER VINEYARDS

503-623-6420 or 800-884-1927
www.vanduzer.com
11975 Smithfield Road
Tasting Room: Mar.–Dec., daily 11–5, and by appointment
Fee: $10, refunded with purchase
Owners: Carl and Marilyn Thoma
Winemaker: Jim Kakacek
Wines: Pinot Gris, rosé, Pinot Noir, estate Syrah, sparkling wines, port-style wines
Cases: 15,000
Special Features: Picnic area, wine club dinners, near wildlife refuge.

Van Duzer has one of most enticing labels for depicting a sensuous sense of place and taste. Zephyr is a Greek symbol for the gentle afternoon west wind. In this case it's Zephyra, her curly, swirling locks making her an inviting grape goddess we'd all like to get to know. She embodies what the vineyard manager and winemaker embrace—those cool breezes funneling east through the Van Duzer Corridor from the Pacific Ocean. The new winery and hilltop tasting room were completed in 2006, and are inviting as Zephyra. Take in the landscaped surroundings and have a taste-off between the Homestead and Flagpole Pinot

Noirs (The Flagpole usually wins for Sherry). Thanks to former tasting room staffer Ray for explaining the *methode champenoise* process repeatedly.

NAMASTÉ VINEYARDS
503-623-4150
www.namastevineyards.com
5600 Van Well Road
Tasting Room: Mar.–Dec., Sat.–Sun. 12–6, and by appointment
Fee: $5, refundable with purchase
Owners: Dave Masciorini, Chris and Sonia Miller
Winemaker: Andreas Wetzel
Wines: Gewürztraminer, Riesling, Pinot Noir, white blend, white port
Cases: 2,500
Special Features: Wedding and events facility, picnic area with views, Vino and Vinyasa outdoor yoga program in summer, occasional concerts

"The spirit of the wine, honors the spirit of the vine." The motto at the winery is a twist on the Hindu greeting *namaste,* meaning: I honor the spirit in you. Three friends, all California transplants, found their peace in a 200-acre piece of property where they planted vines and put together a winery—one piece at a time. Their philosophy may be simple, but their wines are not and have garnered honors. Drink in the peace, tranquility, and serenity—literally.

RICKREALL
CHÂTEAU BIANCA
503-623-6181
www.chateaubianca.com
17485 Highway 22
Tasting Room: Daily 10–5
Fee: $5, waived with two-bottle purchase
Owners: Helmet and Liselotte Wetzel
Winemaker: Andreas Wetzel
Wines: Pinot Blanc, Pinot Gris, Chardonnay, Gewürztraminer, Riesling, Pinot Noir, Syrah, Maréchal Foch, brut, port-style and dessert wines

Cases: 15,000
Special Features: Two bed-and-breakfast rooms available year-round ($145 first night, $110 thereafter) except October; gift shop; English and German spoken

If you can't find the varietal you like in the country casual atmosphere at Château Bianca, you won't find it anywhere. The tasting room has anywhere from 20 to 23 bottles uncorked at a time, and none are budget-busters. To get that many wines, Château Bianca trucks in tons of grapes to complement the production from their own vineyard. Winemaker Andreas Wetzel is definitely Pinot-centric—Pinot Noir, Pinot Gris, and Pinot Blanc—but the winery virtually runs the gamut of cool-climate offerings. And for those frequent blustery days, a mulled red wine spiced with cinnamon sticks, called Glühwein, will surely warm you all over.

JOHAN VINEYARDS
866-379-6029
www.johanvineyards.com
4285 North Highway 99W
Tasting Room: Mar.–Dec., Daily 12–5, closed Jan.–Feb.
Fee: $5, refunded with purchase
Owners: Dag Johan Sundby and Nils Dag Sunby
Winemaker: Dan Rinke and Don Cooper
Wines: Estate Chardonnay, Pinot Gris, rosé, Pinot Noir, Vin Gris
Cases: 1,750
Special Features: Newly completed winery and tasting room opened in 2009

Johan produces Willamette Valley classics from a biodynamic vineyard that winemakers Dan and Don describe as a peaceful "worry-free zone" adjacent to the Van Duzer Corridor. Owner and Norway native Dag Sundby, who is relatively new to these parts (2004), has a firm belief in high-quality fruit. It shows. He sells almost 90 percent of the grapes on his 65 acres, but manages to keep enough for the Johan label. The label is a representation of a Viking pleasure cruiser and is a reminder to Dag that quality first is the goal. The Oseberg ship can be viewed at the Viking Ship Museum in Oslo, Norway, if you happen to be there.

LEFT COAST CELLARS

503-831-4916
www.leftcoastcellars.com
4225 North Highway 99W
Tasting Room: Daily 12–5 (except Dec. 23–Jan. 31) and by appointment
Fee: $5, refunded with purchase
Owners: Suzanne Larson
Winemaker: Luke McCollom
Wines: Pinot Gris, Pinot Blanc, Chardonnay, Pinot Noir, Syrah
Cases: 5,500
Special Features: Picnic area

A stop at Left Coast means passing through a fanciful gate, an artist's representation of the vino-scape ahead. Follow the copper sculpted arrows, make a few left turns, and be prepared for a most appealing setting

among old-growth oak. A true sense of "pride in place" greets your every sense. In an effort to go green, Suzanne received one of the largest USDA grants in the state for installation of solar panels that serve the winery's electrical needs. The signature wine is the approachable and food-friendly Cali's Cuvée, a Pinot Noir blended with all barrels of the vintage.

EOLA HILLS WINE CELLARS

503-623-2405 or 800-291-6730
www.eolahillswinery.com
501 South Pacific Highway (OR 99W)
Tasting Room: Daily 10–5
Fee: Complimentary
General Manager: Tom Huggins
Winemaker: Steve Anderson
Wines: Chardonnay, Gewürztraminer, Pinot Gris, Cabernet Sauvignon, Riesling, Viognier, Sauvignon Blanc, Maréchal Foch, Merlot, Pinot Noir, Sangiovese, Syrah, Zinfandel, dessert wines
Cases: 60,000
Special Features: Sun., Easter, Mother's and Father's Day brunch; winemaker and

Biking through Oregon Wine Country with Eola Hills Wine Cellars has become an August pastime.
Courtesy Eola Hills Wine Cellars

holiday dinners; Oregon State University and Seattle Seahawk football, and Seattle Mariners baseball trips; European wine tours; supported cycling tours; gift shop; events facility

There are as many wines to taste as there are events sponsored by Eola Hills Wine Cellars. Founder and general manager Tom Huggins was an Oregon State long-distance runner and protégé of Oregon legend Steve Prefontaine until an injury forced him to switch avocations. He has an affinity for all things Beaver or Pacific Northwest (except the Ducks), and loves to organize bus trips combining athletics and wine for a best-of-all-worlds good time. Amid all that fun and joy, they have some mighty fine wines. With 24 open bottles to sample at the newly remodeled tasting bar, you can pace yourself with an intermission in the extensive gift shop. Such special events as brunch and winemaker dinners regularly take place in the barrel room, where the aroma and atmosphere provide an unparalleled mix. But our favorite event is Bike Oregon Wine Country, held every weekend in August.

AMALIE ROBERT VINEYARD

503-831-4703
www.amalierobert.com
13531 Bursell Road
Tasting Room: Memorial Day and Thanksgiving weekends, and by appointment
Fee: $5, refunded with purchase
Owners/Winemakers: Dena Drews and Ernie Pink
Wines: Chardonnay, Syrah, Pinot Noir
Cases: 1,300
Special Features: Annual Earth Day celebrations

What was once a cherry orchard quickly evolved into a premium grape vineyard for some of the bigger names in the industry. Even today, Pinot Noir from Amalie Robert Vineyard is appreciated worldwide in bottles carrying such labels as Elk Cove, Beaux Frères, and Cristom. Today, Amalie Robert is sharing the wealth with some credible wines of its own. The first estate crush came in 2006, about a decade after techno-geeks Dena Drews and Ernie Pink began drawing up their dreams on cocktail napkins over glasses of wine.

ILLAHE VINEYARDS

503-831-1248
www.illahevineyards.com
3275 Ballard Road
Tasting Room: Summer, Fri.–Sat.11–5, and by appointment
Fee: Complimentary
Owner: Lowell Ford
Winemaker: Brad Ford and Michael Lundeen
Wines: Viognier, Riesling, Pinot Gris, Grüner Veltliner, Pinot Noir
Cases: 4,500
Special Features: WildAire Cellars wines are also poured

Winemakers Michael Lundeen and Brad Ford bring with them years of working with some of the big hitters of the Oregon wine industry, so they know what they're doing. And they get to do it in an 8,000-square-foot winery that's as eco-friendly as they come. The winery produces nearly as much power as it uses with solar panels, temperatures are managed because much of the winery is underground, rainwater is collected, and the vineyards are LIVE-certified. Illahe is especially proud of its reserve and grand reserve Pinot Noirs.

MONMOUTH
EMERSON VINEYARDS

541-838-0944
www.emersonvineyards.com
11665 Airlie Road
Tasting Room: Sat.–Sun. 12–5
Fee: $5
Owners: Tom, Jane, Elliott, and Jenny Johns
Winemaker: Elliott Johns

Wines: Chardonnay, Pinot Gris, Riesling, Pinot Noir
Cases: 2,500
Special Features: Concerts

Great people just go with great wine. Genuinely friendly and caring, Tom Johns is retired—on paper, anyway—from his day job as a biotech executive. Now he works days and nights keeping the vineyard, winery, and business duties in line. Son Elliott has a degree from Oregon State University in fermentation science and did a stint at Elk Cove. At his family's winery, he crafts the wine and is doing some experimental growing of such hybrids as Maréchal Foch, Baco Noir, Leon Millot, and Oberlin Noir. The wines are as friendly as the people.

OLSEN FAMILY VINEYARDS & VIRIDIAN WINES

888-344-2022
www.viridianwines.com
8930 Suver Road
Tasting Room: May–Sept., Sat.–Sun. 11–5, Thanksgiving weekend
Fee: Complimentary
Owners: Robin and Jamie Olsen
Winemaker: Bill Kremer
Wines: Pinot Gris, Chardonnay, rosé, Pinot Noir, dessert wine
Cases: 15,000
Special Features: Music on holiday weekends

The Olsen family knows soil. They've been farming grass seed, berries, hazelnuts, and other crops on their Willamette Valley acreage (twelve thousand) for five generations. The most recent inhabitants of their soil are vinifera. They carefully staked out the best sites and planted five distinct vineyards covering 500 acres. The family is dedicated to research and experimentation in the vineyard, and like sharing what they've learned with local viticulture students. Enter winemaker Bill Kremer, a third-generation farmer from South Dakota

who made a name at King Estate, and you have the right components for something grand. The tasting room, called a pavilion, is an oversized white tent that gives the feeling of proximity to the vineyards.

AIRLIE WINERY

503-838-6013
www.airliewinery.com
15305 Dunn Forest Road
Tasting Room: Mar.–Dec., Sat.–Sun. 12–5, and by chance and appointment
Fee: Complimentary
Owner: Mary Olson
Winemaker: Elizabeth Clarke
Wines: Pinot Gris, Chardonnay, Gewürztraminer, Müller Thurgau, Riesling, Pinot Noir, Maréchal Foch, white blend
Cases: 8,000
Special Features: Covered pavilion with picnic grounds and pond, dog-friendly, especially lively Memorial Day weekend

Airlie Winery embodies the essence of Oregon wineries: raw determination. Owner Mary Olson long dreamed of owning a winery and went for it in 1996. Pooling her life savings, she bought her 32 acres of heaven and hard work. Not one to rely on others, she quickly learned how to operate a John Deere, manage a vineyard, and run a winery. If she could, she would make the wine as well, but she has turned that job over to two talented and creative women. Suzy Gagné was her first winemaker and took the wines to award-winning levels. Liz Clarke has carried on the tradition while adding her own imprint. The Pinot Gris has been voted one of the Top 10 of the Year in *Wine & Spirits* several times, and the Dunn Forest Pinot is one of the best-priced "Oregundian" Pinot Noirs around.

SALEM

VITAE SPRINGS VINEYARD

503-588-0896
www.vitaesprings.com
3675 Vitae Springs Road South

Tasting Room: Sat.–Sun. 12–5, and by appointment
Fee: $5, applied to purchase
Owners: Earl and Pamela VanVolkinburg
Winemakers: Earl and Joel VanVolinburg, Joe Dobbes (consultant)
Wines: Riesling, Grüner Veltliner, Pinot Noir
Cases: 1,000
Special Features: Reputedly first in U.S. to grow and produce Grüner Veltliner

The elder VanVolkinburgs were stationed at Hahn Air Base in the Mosel Valley of Germany when they fell in love with wine. Their son, Joel, and his wife, Michelle, carry the same passion and are an integral part of operations. The VanVolkinburgs had been making Grüner for more than 30 years for personal consumption, and added it to their line five years ago. It flies out of the tasting room. The wine is great, they say, with turkey, Oregon razor clams, oysters, whitefish, chicken, pork, and even pasta dishes.

ANKENY VINEYARD WINERY
503-378-1498
www.ankenyvineyard.com
2565 Riverside Road South
Tasting Room: Wed.–Sun. 11–5
Fee: $5, refunded with purchase
Owners: Joe Olexa and Kathy Greysmith
Winemaker: Andy Thomas
Wines: Chardonnay, Pinot Gris, rosé, Pinot Noir, Maréchal Foch, red blend, dessert wine
Cases: 2,000
Special Features: "Wine-Downs"—extended hours on the deck on Fridays in summer

Andy does what some winemakers only do in secret: blend a small amount of another red to color the Pinot Noir. He comes out of the winery closet with a Pinot Noir and Maréchal Foch blend called Crimson that's friendly and approachable (Foch) with some acidity for backbone (Pinot). The

Maréchel Foch by itself is popular and often sells out, as does the Hershey's Red, named for the resident chocolate lab. With its warm hospitality and interesting surroundings that include views of Ankeny National Wildlife Refuge's migratory birds, you may decide to stay a while.

TRINITY VINEYARDS
503-371-6977
www.trinityvineyards.com
1031 Wahl Lane South
Tasting Room: Sat.–Sun. 12–5 and Memorial Day and Thanksgiving weekends
Fee: $5
Owners: Steve and Cindy Parker
Winemaker: Joe Dobbes Jr.
Wines: Pinot Gris, Viognier, Pinot Noir, Syrah
Cases: 1,800
Special Features: Super-low-impact sustainable vineyard, views of Mount Jefferson

Starting from scratch was more than Steve and Cindy Parker bargained for when they purchased their plot of the Oregon wine dream. The native Oregonians bought an existing vineyard and fantasized about drinking their own wine. After untangling and pruning, the Parkers discovered the vines were planted east to west, the trellis system was rotting, and they found self-rooted Riesling and Gewürztraminer vines. It took five years of undoing before they could start doing. They built their home, replanted the seven-acre vineyard, and constructed a tasting room. The completed package is nothing short of spectacular.

TURNER
WILLAMETTE VALLEY VINEYARDS
503-588-9463
www.willamettevalleyvineyards.com
8800 Enchanted Way SE
Tasting Room: Daily 11–6
Fee: Complimentary for five wines, $6 for six reserve wines, $10 for six Pinot Noirs
President: Jim Bernau

Pressing juice the old-world way at Willamette Valley Vineyards' annual Grape Stomp.

Courtesy Willamette Valley Vineyards

Winemakers: Forrest Klaffke and Don Crank III
Wines: Chardonnay, Gewürztraminer, Müller Thurgau, Pinot Gris, Riesling, Viognier, Cabernet Sauvignon, Merlot, Pinot Noir, Syrah, dessert wine
Cases: 120,000
Special Features: Special events every month, public grape stomp in September

Willamette Valley might just be Oregon's most visible winery because of its massive distribution and its location off I-5 just south of Salem. The vineyards blanket the South Salem Hills and beckon weary interstate travelers to stop and sip. One of the state's top three producers, along with King Estate and Rex Hill (A–Z), Willamette Valley is publicly owned and traded, and has a corporate feel. Despite a big-business air, they have done a creditable job of making the tasting room an entertaining place to spend time. They host myriad events, one of the most popular being the annual grape stomp where you get your feet squishy and purply—just like in the Old Country.

Dining in the Salem Area

SALEM
GRAND VINES
503-399-9463
www.grandvines.com
195 High Street NE
Hours: Mon.–Thurs. 11–8, Fri.–Sat. 11–11
Price: Inexpensive to moderate
Credit Cards: Yes
Special Features: Music every Tues., Cascade Bakery bread, Oregon cheeses, Extreme chocolates

Maggie Crawford and 11 close friends were simultaneously celebrating a new president and lamenting their failing 401Ks when the topic of purchasing a for-sale bottle shop came up. Conversation halted and ideas started to ferment. A few months later, Crawford and her gaggle of not-so-silent partners are the proud owners of Grand Vines. Congenial Crawford plans live music two to three nights a week, pourings by guest wineries once a week, and a small but pleasing menu to complement wines by the taste, glass, or bottle. She has already shifted focus by doubling the Oregon and Northwest wine section. Grand Vines is a place to linger or catch your breath with comfy corner seating and lots of windows to see downtown happenings, including some colorful characters.

LA CAPITALE

503-585-1975
www.lacapitalesalem.com
508 State Street
Hours: Tues.–Fri. 11–2 and 5–9, Sat. 12–3 and 5–9
Price: Moderate
Credit Cards: Yes
Special Features: Happy hour 2–6, house-made charcuterie, hard-to-find Oregon microbrews

Salemites are excited, with good reason. "The new place in town" features upscale bistro dining utilizing local farmers and ranchers to set the table. Jazzy notes mingle with clanking plates, tinkling glassware, and kitchen buzz. Dropped lighting and tall bistro tables dot the bar area, where you can watch chefs David Rosales (the owner) and Ricardo Antunez co-create in a completely open kitchen. Two flat-screens showing old French-American flicks, Julia Child episodes, or *Ratatouille* symmetrically flank the mirrored back bar. Favorite foods are the *pommes frites* (mix the two sauces for divine dipping), *tarte flambé* (French pizza), and fish and seafood specials. Farmer's-market salads are complete enough to be a meal, but save room for yummy desserts.

OLD EUROPE INN

503-588-3639
www.oldeuropeinn.com
3195 Liberty Road South
Open: Mon.–Fri. 11–2 and 5–9, Sat.–Sun. 5–9
Price: Inexpensive to moderate
Credit Cards: Yes
Special Features: Winemaker dinners, wine for retail purchase

Owners Hans and Hely Afshar are persnickety (Hely) perfectionists (Hans) who create food that actually surpasses its presentation. A tiny, one-room dining room with a low ceiling and dark decor has a dozen tables—after you squeeze past a baby grand piano eating up space in the entry. If you question your choice, one look at the plates passing through the open kitchen, where you can see the top of Hans's head, tells you something special is about to come your way. The night we dined, the soup du jour was cream of sauerkraut. When we threw questioning looks, Hely brought us two tiny bowls to sample. Needless to say we were hooked, and she threw us an "I told you so" look. Pasta made fresh daily, house-baked bread, and French-influenced entrees go beyond the norm. Lunches of paninis, pasta, pizzas, and salads are extraordinary. For the portions (soup or salad is included at dinner), prices are reasonable. Some Oregon reds and whites are available by the glass, and there are plenty by the bottle.

WILD PEAR RESTAURANT & CATERING

503-378-7515
www.wildpearcatering.com
372 State Street
Open: Mon.–Sat. 10–5:30
Price: Inexpensive to moderate
Credit Cards: Yes
Special Features: Happy hour appetizer menu daily 3:30–5:30

Wild Pear built its reputation on catering—they always had the longest lines at wine events. By popular demand, they opened for lunch and dinner serving soup, sandwiches, salads, wraps, and pizzas with flair in an artsy bakery-like setting where flavors run with wild abandon. Take the starters list: white-truffle sweet-potato French fries, maple bleu cheese and candied pecans, mushroom-and-cheese strudel. Entrées are so scrumptious and satisfying you might not want dessert, but we doubt it. The key lime tartlet will be calling your name. Only Oregon wines are served at Wild Pear.

INDEPENDENCE

RAGIN' RIVER STEAK CO.

503-837-0394
154 S. Main St.
Open: Tues.–Fri. 11:30–2 and 4–10,

Sat. 4–10, Sun. 4–8
Price: Inexpensive to moderate
Credit Cards: Yes
Special Features: Happy hour 4–6

Ragin' River is a bit of a misnomer, given that the meandering Willamette River across the street is anything but ragin.' The restaurant is in a 110-year-old building in placid downtown Independence, a fine place to stop for a quiet dinner en route to the southern Willamette Valley wineries. The ambiance is relaxing, and chances are the owner himself will stop by to make sure everything is prepared to your wishes. Ragin' River, known for steaks, not only makes its own bread and salad dressings, it churns its butter as well. The restaurant offers many Northwest wines, big reds to go with big steaks.

Attractions in the Salem Area

Between touring the wineries of the Amity and Eola Hills, take a brief detour at the whistle-stop community of Hopewell to cross the Willamette on the **Wheatland Ferry** (503-588-7979). Cars are $2 each way. In 1844, the ferry was the first to carry a covered wagon across the river to what is now **Willamette Mission State Park** (503-393-1172), which was first occupied by settlers in 1834. A highlight is a 250-year-old black cottonwood tree, the country's oldest. Back on the west side of the river, **Wings of Wonder** (503-838-0976, 5978 Willamette Ferry St.) in Independence is a nonprofit organization with exhibits and live butterflies from all over the world.

In Salem, the **Mission Mill Museum** (503-585-7012, 1313 Mill St. SE) is a tribute to an old woolen mill and the community built around it, including an original water-powered turbine. History also seeps from every creaky pore of the **Deepwood Estate** (503-363-1825, 1116 Mission St. SE), a four-acre Shangri-La near the heart of downtown. The restored Victorian home features a variety of events and was once chosen by *Sunset* magazine as one of the top historic homes in the West.

For one more step into history, consider taking in a performance at the **Elsinore Theatre** (503-375-3574, 170 High St.). The Gothic Elsinore opened in 1926 with a Cecil B. DeMille silent movie and for a quarter-century was the most exquisite theater between Portland and San Francisco. Classic films, concerts, and other acts fill the calendar today.

For a watery perspective of Salem, the **Willamette Queen** (503-371-1103) riverboat at Riverside Park is an authentic sternwheeler in the mold of those that ran up the Willamette as far south as Corvallis in the 1800s. Choose between a gourmet dinner or Sunday brunch cruise for $48, or a lunch float for $22. Just north of Salem, off the I-5 exit at Brooks, are the **Northwest Vintage Car and Motorcycle Museum, Pacific Northwest Truck Museum,** and **Oregon Electric Railway Museum**, all in the same **Western Antique Powerland** complex (503-393-2424).

It rarely snows in the Willamette Valley, but somehow the only museum in the western United States dedicated to the Arctic has found a home in Monmouth. The **Jensen Arctic Museum** (503-838-8468, 509 West Church St.) at Western Oregon University focuses on the indigenous peoples of that region. For more locally oriented museums, there's the **Oregon Heritage Museum** (503-838-4989, 112 South Third St.) in Independence and the **Polk County Museum** (503-623-6251) at the Polk County Fairgounds, just south of the junction of OR 99W and OR 22 in Rickreall.

Recreation in the Salem Area

If you're looking for the ideal place to go **hiking, bicycling, roller-blading**, or **running** around Salem, try **Minto-Brown Island Park** along the Willamette. At just under 900 acres, it is a sea of tranquility on the fringe of the urban hum. **Golf** fans won't lack for options: There are no fewer than 12 public courses in the area. If the salmon are running from the Pacific to their traditional spawning grounds, the **North Santiam River** is one of the best streams in Oregon to land a burly Chinook.

Shopping in the Salem Area

The name notwithstanding, the **Salem Saturday Farmer's Market** (503-585-8264) is open for business every Wednesday from May to October on the corner of High and Market Streets. The capital city also has the year-round **Salem Public Market** (503-623-6605, 2140 Rural St.) on Saturdays. Oregon's oldest farmer's market features food, crafts and other events in a heated indoor facility between 12th and 13th Streets. The downtown **Independence Farmers Market** (503-838-5424) is open Saturday with local art and produce. On the way through the valley on OR 99W, stop at the **Amity Antique Mall** (503-835-0412, 418 North Trade St.) for a peek at a selection of old furniture and other items.

Wine Shopping in the Salem Area

The **Santiam Wine Company** (503-589-0775, 1930 Commercial St. SE) offers wines from around the world and stages tastings every Wednesday, Friday, and Saturday. Sole proprietor Debbie Rios has a crammed-to-the-gills bottle shop with over 100 Oregon bottles, and a large Washington section. Specializing in hard-to-find and custom orders, she's also a pink freak and has arguably one of the largest selections of rosés in the state, many from Oregon producers. **Papá di Vino** (503-364-3009, 1130 Royvonne Ave. SE #104) is Tusc-Oregon-y, with Italian-tableclothed tables, vases of sunflowers, a cozy corner with over-stuffed stuffed leather chairs, and a small bar with three stools. Enjoy five tastes for $5 every Thursday. Add a simple antipasto platter, and you have the ideal date night or a post-touring wind-down.

Information

McMinnville Area Chamber of Commerce, 503-472-6196, www.mcminnville.org, 417 NW Adams St.

Salem Convention and Visitors Association, 503-581-4325 or 800-874-7012, www.travelsalem.com, 1313 Mill St. SE

Oregon Wine Country: The Willamette Valley, 866-548-5018

McMinnville AVA, wwwmcminnvilleava.org

6

WILLAMETTE VALLEY SOUTH

Heart of the Valley

When you arrive in the broad, mostly flat, U-shaped plain that is the southern Willamette Valley, you'd best choose sides. And we don't mean reds versus whites or Pinots versus Chardonnays. Two of the three most prominent communities in this rural region, Eugene and Corvallis, also happen to be home of the state's two major universities: bitter rivals Oregon and Oregon State.

Indeed, area tasting rooms can be quiet even during the autumn crush because many of the state's fans are packed into a football stadium or cloistered around a television, wearing either the green and yellow of the Oregon Ducks or the black and orange of the Oregon State Beavers.

As you drive south from Salem on either I-5 or the prettier route, OR 99W, you'll notice subtle changes to the landscape. The Coast and Cascade ranges are as much as 30 miles apart, the foothills of both a blend of Douglas fir and oak savannah. It is drier here, the summers warmer. Pinot still prevails, but grapes that don't care for the north's bluster have a fighting chance here.

Eugene and Corvallis are the most diverse communities in the southern end of the valley. The other towns were built around either timber or agriculture or both, though the hum of many sawmills has gone quiet as the supply from both mountain ranges dried up. The table-flat fields are mostly planted with grass; the region rightly touts itself as the grass-seed capital of the world, and there's a decent chance the sod in your front yard had its genesis here.

GETTING HERE AND AROUND

If your focus is purely the home-style wineries at this end of the valley, you can fly into Eugene's Mahlon Sweet Field. Typically more expensive than flying into Portland, it is served from only nine western cities by **Delta Connection/SkyWest** (800-221-1212), **United Airlines** (800-241-6522), **Alaska/Horizon Airlines** (800-547-9308), and **Allegiant Air** (702-705-8888). All the major rental car agencies serve Mahlon Sweet Airport.

OPPOSITE: *Vineyards mesh with Coast Range foothills in the south Willamette Valley.* John Baker

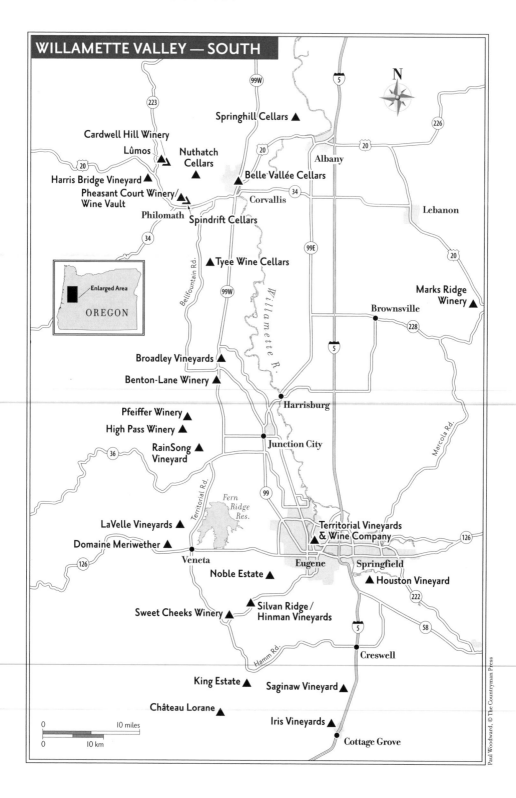

WILLAMETTE VALLEY — SOUTH

Springhill Cellars ▲

Cardwell Hill Winery
Lûmos ▲
Nuthatch Cellars ▲

Albany

Harris Bridge Vineyard ▲
Belle Vallée Cellars ▲

Pheasant Court Winery/ Wine Vault ▲
Corvallis

Philomath
Spindrift Cellars

Lebanon

Bellfountain Rd.

Enlarged Area
OREGON

▲Tyee Wine Cellars

Willamette R.

Marks Ridge Winery ▲

Brownsville

Broadley Vineyards ▲

Benton-Lane Winery ▲

Harrisburg

Pfeiffer Winery ▲
High Pass Winery ▲

Marcola Rd.

RainSong Vineyard ▲

Junction City

Territorial Rd.

Fern Ridge Res.

LaVelle Vineyards ▲
Territorial Vineyards & Wine Company ▲

Domaine Meriwether ▲
Veneta
Eugene
Springfield

Noble Estate ▲
Houston Vineyard ▲

Sweet Cheeks Winery ▲
Silvan Ridge / Hinman Vineyards ▲

Hamm Rd.
Creswell

King Estate ▲
Saginaw Vineyard ▲

Château Lorane ▲
Iris Vineyards ▲

0   10 miles
0   10 km

Cottage Grove

Paul Woodward, © The Countryman Press

If you're coming by car from the north or south, I-5 is the fastest and most direct route, but it's also the least interesting. Highways arriving from the east and west are slower but scenic. US 20 and OR 34 bisect Corvallis and Albany from both directions, and OR 126 is a beautiful drive along the McKenzie River.

Amtrak (800-872-7245) has daily stops in Albany and Eugene on the Coast Starlight. **Greyhound** (800-231-2222) has bus stations on a north–south route in Albany, Corvallis, and Eugene and limited service on an east–west route through Albany and Corvallis that includes Philomath en route to Newport on the coast.

ALBANY/CORVALLIS AREA

Time was when the science for growing grapes in Oregon was provided by the University of California Davis, whose viticulture and enology program celebrates its 130th year in 2010. Today Oregon State University's Viticulture and Enology School—essentially raised from its infancy in the early 1970s by a U.C. Davis graduate named Barney Watson—offers under-graduate and graduate degrees, manages its own vineyard (Woodhall), and has extension agents in the Columbia Gorge, Walla Walla region, and the Rogue and Umpqua valleys.

Corvallis might just be the best hub for Oregon Wine Country touring. It is in easy prox-imity to all Willamette Valley wineries, southern Oregon is about a two-hour drive, and the coast (Newport) is over the hill about an hour away. Historic Albany is equally well placed, though it's not quite as appealing. The city has nearly every style of Victorian home, some dating to the 1850s. Just a few miles west of Corvallis is Philomath, a onetime timber town that has become more of a bedroom community surrounded by numerous wineries.

Wineries in the Albany/Corvallis Area

The southern portion of the Willamette Valley has a more gentrified feeling than the trendy north. Wineries here are places where friends like to meet and newcomers are welcomed into laid-back atmospheres. These are vintners who eschewed the rush of the north and preferred the farm-centric region of the valley. It was our home for many years, and we still cherish the so-called Heart of the Valley.

From Salem, head south on I-5 to the US 20 exit at Albany. Go west toward Corvallis. Cross the river and turn right on Springhill Road toward Springhill Cellars. After visiting wineries in Corvallis and Philomath, we suggest making a side trip across the valley east to Marks Ridge Winery before doubling back to Tyee south of Corvallis.

ALBANY
SPRINGHILL CELLARS
541-928-1009
www.springhillcellars.com
2920 NW Scenic Drive
Tasting Room: May–Nov., Sat.–Sun. 1–5, or by chance
Fee: Complimentary
Owners: Mike and Karen McLain
Winemakers: Mike and Karen McLain
Wines: Pinot Gris, rosé, Pinot Noir
Cases: 1,200

Special Features: Fedeweisser Festival on Thanksgiving weekend, picnic area

When pouring duties were finished Saturday night on Thanksgiving weekend, we used to change our shoes and head to Springhill for brats and barn dancing. The Fedeweisser Festival is a German tradition featuring young, still-fermenting Riesling for consumption (by the pitcher in some cases). The crammed red and white barn holds a lot of folks, and a good time is had by all. But that's not all that's exceptional about Springhill. The Pinot Noir often scores awards and is frequently a staff pick at local shops.

CORVALLIS
BELLE VALLÉE CELLARS
541-757-9463
www.bellevallee.com
151 NW Monroe Avenue (tasting room)
Tasting Room: Tues.–Sat. 11–8, Sun. 11–6
Fee: $3–7 per flight
Owners: Mike Magee and Steve Allen
Winemaker: Joe Wright
Wines: Pinot Gris, Pinot Noir, Cabernet Sauvignon, Merlot, Syrah, red blend, port-style wines
Cases: 7,000
Special Features: The remarkable label designs are reproductions of Claire Magee's glass art; special formats with actual glass label are available

If you favor a lighter Pinot that's more Beaujolais-like, the whole-cluster Pinot Noir might be your ticket. It's a style Joe brought to Belle Vallée from his training grounds at Willamette Valley Vineyards. The grapes are fermented as whole clusters and vinified in stainless steel, sans oak. The rest of his Pinots do see oak, 60 to 100 percent of it new French oak—adding more complexity and expense to the Pinot. At our former home in Corvallis, many a birthday celebration concluded with Belle Vallée's seductive Pinot port.

NUTHATCH CELLARS
541-754-8483
www.nuthatchcellars.com
8792 NW Chaparral Drive
Tasting Room: Memorial Day, Labor Day, and Thanksgiving weekends, and by appointment
Fee: Complimentary
Owners: John Bacon and Jane Smith
Winemaker: John Bacon
Wines: Tempranillo, Syrah, Malbec, red blend
Cases: 250

There's more than one way to tour Oregon Wine Country. Courtesy Eola Hills Wine Cellars

A nuthatch is a small passerine, or perching songbird, an appropriate name for the tiny winery perched on the edge of sweet success. It's also the avian friend with whom John and Jane share their countryside home. Although production is small at Nuthatch, there is nothing small about the big red wines. Full-bodied reds with grapes from eastern Washington and southern Oregon are blended with the help of many hands, barn-raising style. The hand-bottled and -labeled wines are available in shops and restaurants in the area.

PHILOMATH

SPINDRIFT CELLARS

541-929-6555
www.spindriftcellars.com
810 Applegate Street
Tasting Room: Summer, Tues.–Fri. 1–6, Sat.–Sun. 12–5, Thanksgiving weekend, and by appointment
Fee: $4–6
Owners/Winemakers: Matt and Tabitha Compton
Wines: Pinot Blanc, Pinot Gris, Riesling, rosé, Pinot Noir, Syrah
Cases: 3,500
Special Features: Special events, screw-cap tops on all wines

The Comptons have made the most of their space by creating a splashy tasting room full of wine warmth inside a warehouse turned green winery. Their philosophy extends to their bottle closures as well. Sensitive to the plight and low sustainability of cork trees, they chose the more expensive but environmentally sensitive path. Non-cork closures also ensure that your wine won't suffer from cork "taint"—that wet, musty cardboard smell or flat taste you sometimes find after popping a cork. Out of the gate, Spindrift has earned media attention by scoring 90 from *Wine Spectator* for a Pinot and Best Buy from *Wine Enthusiast* for a Pinot Gris. Best of all, their prices are in the reasonable range.

PHEASANT COURT WINERY/ WINE VAULT

541-929-7715
www.winevault.biz
1301 Main Street
Tasting Room: Sat.–Sun. 12–6
Fee: Complimentary
Owner/Winemaker: Charlie Gilson
Wines: Pinot Gris, Chardonnay, Maréchal Foch, Pinot Noir, Merlot, Syrah, port-style and dessert wines
Cases: 750
Special Features: Other local wines are poured

The Wine Vault serves up its own line as well as neighboring wines. Pheasant Court is located in a century-old former bank building on Main Street in this small bedroom community. Your pourer will most likely be Charlie, the face and hands of Pheasant Court. The vineyard for Pheasant Court is just north of town.

HARRIS BRIDGE VINEYARD

541-929-3053
www.harrisbridgevineyard.com
22937 Harris Road
Tasting Room: May–Nov., Sat.–Sun. 12–5
Fee: $5–10
Owners/Winemakers: Nathan Warren and Amanda Sever
Wines: Dessert wines
Cases: 400
Special Features: Picnic or meander along the river next to a covered bridge. The front of the wood and ribbed-metal structure opens to fresh-air sipping in warmer weather.

Nathan and Amy have filled a niche with their sensuous and scintillating dessert wines. The winery is near the community of Wren, adjacent to a covered bridge over the Mary's River. On a recent holiday weekend, we found Amanda pouring, cleaning, and refilling nut bowls, toting the couple's wee one, and deferring questions to Nathan.

A covered bridge over the Mary's River is not far from Harris Bridge's front door. John Baker

He's the visionary, and writer of the short stories encapsulated and attached to the top of each elegant bottle. We savored our sips while thoroughly entertained by the Doggone Divas, a local female musical group. In front of the overflow-parking area is a 300-year-old section of a Douglas fir. Try counting those rings after tasting Harris's sweet treats made from Pinot Noir and Pinot Gris.

LÛMOS

541-929-3519
www.lumoswine.com
24000 Cardwell Hill Road
Tasting Room: Memorial Day and Thanksgiving weekends, and by appointment
Fee: $5
Owners: Dai Crisp and PK McCoy
Winemaker: Dai Crisp
Wines: Gewürztraminer, Pinot Gris, Pinot Noir
Cases: 1,800

Special Features: Picnic area, volleyball, badminton, croquet, goats, beehives

If you're lucky enough to be in this neck of the woods on one of the big holiday weekends, plan to hang a while with Dai and PK. Their retreat-like cabin in the woods serves as the tasting room, a place where friends come to gather, imbibe, converse, and linger, usually with a local musician providing ambiance. Dai was manager of the highly regarded Temperance Hill and Logsden Ridge vineyards before making the leap to his own label in 2002. With the honeybees, goats, and croquet, it's a fun place for kids, too.

CARDWELL HILL WINERY

541-929-9463
www.cardwellhillwine.com
24241 Cardwell Hill Road
Tasting Room: Mar.–Thanksgiving, daily 12–5
Fee: $5, waived with purchase
Owners: Dan and Nancy Chapel

Winemaker: Dan Chapel
Wines: Pinot Gris, rosé, Pinot Noir
Cases: 5,000
Special Features: Wedding and event facilities

Sit and sip at vineyard level on the deck in a relaxed, classic Oregon setting and reflect upon days gone by. The Chapels, California transplants, learned through a few hard knocks and bumps in the road what it takes to run with the big dogs. Dan loves to show off his estate facility, where everything's done on site, including bottling and labeling. Speaking of showing off, Cardwell's 2006 Pinot Noir made *Wine Spectator's* Top 100 list in 2009—quite a coup for a small producer in the southern Willamette Valley.

720 WINE CELLARS
541-929-4562
www.720cellars.com
Tasting Room: None
Owners/Winemakers: Chris and Kirsten Heider
Wines: Pinot Noir

Cases: 1,000
Special Features: Secret location—don't even try

We haven't included wineries that aren't open to the public, but 720 Wine Cellars is an exception. Literally a garagiste, Chris has been making wine as a hobby since 1995. What's special about 720 Pinot Noir? Chris starts with old-vine, organically farmed grapes, gives extended barrel time, and doesn't release for at least two years. On rare occasions the Heiders open their house for events, but generally they prefer privacy and good standing with their neighbors. You can e-mail them for shipments, or support a local shop such as Avalon Wines in Corvallis.

SWEET HOME
MARKS RIDGE WINERY
541-367-3292
www.marksridge.com
29255 Berlin Road
Tasting Room: Sat.–Sun. 12–5
Fee: $3, applied to purchase

Homespun fun is a holiday highlight at Lumos, west of Philomath.   John Baker

Owners: Jay and Janet Westly
Winemaker: Jay Westly
Wines: Gewürztraminer, Riesling, Pinot
Noir
Cases: 1,000
Special Features: Picnic area with outstand-
ing views of the valley and Cascades, sum-
mer concerts, art shows spotlighting local
talent

Marks Ridge is definitely out of the way, but
the Westlys are making it work. They purchased an established vineyard at 1,200 feet
and, still not sure what to do, took over
nurturing the Riesling, Gewürztraminer,
and Pinot Noir. They quickly enrolled in
vineyard-management classes at Salem's
Chemeketa Community College while
simultaneously pulling in the 2006 fruit.
The following year, now almost experts,
they harvested and produced estate wine.
The Westlys are best known for their
Gewürztraminer, so take the drive to see
why and tip your cap to novices who are
livin' the dream.

BELLFOUNTAIN
TYEE WINE CELLARS
541-753-8754
www.tyeewine.com
26335 Greenberry Road
Tasting Room: Apr.–Dec., Sat.–Sun. 12–5;
June–Aug., Fri.–Mon. 12–5
Fee: Complimentary
Owners: David and Margy Buchanan
Winemaker: Merrilee Buchanan Benson
Wines: Chardonnay, Gewürztraminer, Pinot
Gris, Pinot Noir
Cases: 1,300
Special Features: Beaver Pond loop trail,
wedding facility, outdoor stage, covered
picnic area, special events such as comedy
evening with Neal Gladstone and Co.

You can learn a lot about a winery through
its labels. Tyee, a Native American name for
"chief," has Haida art symbols such as the
raven on theirs. It's their tribute to those

who came before and served as stewards of
the land. The Buchanan Family Century
Farm was recently recognized for their
leadership as land stewards by the Oregon
Wildlife Society. A visit to the winery is
similar to convening with nature, especially
when walking their trail with a glass of their
Gewürztraminer in hand.

Lodging in the Albany/ Corvallis Area

ALBANY
THE PFEIFFER COTTAGE INN
Owners: Ray and Debbie Lusk
541-971-9557
www.thepfeiffercottageinn.com
530 Ferry Street SW
Rates: $105-185
Special Features: Local, organic and
farmer's market goods served; walking distance to dining, shopping, and riverfront
park

Albany's blossoming historic district
received a boost in 2006 when newcomers
Ray and Debbie Lusk bought the 1908
Charles Pfeiffer bungalow and opened it as
a B&B two years later. There are three
rooms named after prominent volcanoes in
the Cascades—one of them a small single
room, the others are two-bedroom suites.
The inn is an ideal stop for bicyclists pedal-
ing between Salem and Eugene. If you don't
get your fill during a day of wine tasting, the
Lusks open at least one bottle per evening
for guests.

CORVALLIS
AT HOME IN OREGON
541-929-3059
www.athomeinoregon.com
6120 SW Country Club Drive
Rates: $50–395
Special Features: One-night to one-year
stays, some pet-friendly properties

Want to make centrally located Corvallis
your base while touring Oregon wine coun-

try? Talk to the Ohlens, who have a niche in the lodging market. When they started 20 years ago as a B&B, guests just didn't want to leave. One property led to another and now, with 30 unique accommodations, they'll find you "your own little cave." Whether it's a one-bedroom in a historic downtown home, a small country cottage, or a 3,000-square-foot log home on the Willamette River, they'll fix you up. The Ohlens believe in full disclosure and undersell their guest housing, preferring to see the "thrilled responses," says Ruth.

HANSON COUNTRY INN

Owner: Pat Covey
541-752-2919
www.hcinn.com
795 SW Hanson Street
Rates: $145–165
Special features: Pets welcome for $10 per night; two rooms have balconies well suited for enjoying an aperitif and taking in pastoral views

Four guest rooms in an authentic country home (circa 1928) on the edge of town are filled with the personal treasures and antiques of owner Pat Covey. The inn is perfectly situated as a quiet or romantic place to rest, and although it has an out-of-town look and feel, it is still within walking distance to Oregon State. A hearty country breakfast sets you up for a day of wine imbibing.

HARRISON HOUSE

Owners: Allen Goodman and Hilarie Phelps
541-752-6248 or 800-233-6248
www.corvallis-lodging.com
2310 NW Harrison Boulevard
Rates: $129–149
Special Features: Discounts available

Located near campus on a leafy street, the Harrison House has more than a little Ivy League collegial feel to it. The four rooms each have a private bath. For a little extra

privacy with all the same amenities, rent Hannah's Cottage, off the main entrance. Book early if you're staying during a busy university weekend.

SALBASGEON SUITES

541-753-4320
www.salbasgeon.com
1730 NW Ninth Street
Rates: $120–210
Special Features: All rooms are suites with sitting area, microwave, and mini fridge; complimentary hot breakfast buffet; restaurant and bar; indoor swimming pool

Beautifully and gracefully remodeled in a Northwest motif, this family-owned larger hotel has paid attention to detail and comfort. Each of the 95 large suites features sleeping quarters and a separate living room with pullout queen bed, and some have full kitchens. The hotel's name is a tribute to three common fish (salmon, bass, and sturgeon) in the Umpqua River, where the family acquired their first property. The restaurant serves regional cuisine and Oregon wine. The Anthony's PDX airport shuttle is on site.

Dining in the Albany/ Corvallis Area

ALBANY
CLEMENZA'S ITALIAN AMERICAN CAFÉ

541-926-3353
www.clemenzacafe.com
236 First Avenue West
Open: Tues.–Fri. 11:30–2, Tues.–Thurs. 5–8, Fri.–Sat. 5–9
Price: Inexpensive to moderate
Credit Cards: Yes
Special Features: To-go menu, reservations recommended (required for groups of five or more)

Although not emphasizing Oregon wine, this clever café has home-style, real-world Italian food that you can order to take to the next winery with a picnic table. The unpretentious meals and welcoming style are meant to emulate the working-man lunch or the loud clamor of a family dinner of yesteryear. Dishes center on tomatoes shipped from Naples, and portions are meant to fill and satisfy. Clemenza translates to "merciful," a definition of hospitality that in turn translates to "inclusive and warmly accepting." Don't forget a cannoli, slice of tiramisu or chocolate hazelnut tart—especially delicious paired with Pinot Noir.

SYBARIS

541-928-8157
www.sybarisbistro.com
442 First Avenue SW
Open: Tues.–Thurs. 5–8, Fri.–Sat. 5–9
Price: Moderate
Credit Cards: Yes
Special Features: Wine dinners; local artist featured monthly; charitable events for the community

Innovative and attractive cuisine that heightens your senses is the intent behind Matt and Janel Bennett's successful bistro. The monthly menu is a treat just to read. With such starters as local tomatoes drizzled with basil oil and 30-year-old sherry vinegar or house-smoked black cod with shrimp guacamole, where do you begin? The choices get tougher as you enter the main courses: Pamplona bull shoulder, vegetarian bouillabaisse, and house-made sausage and porcini-stuffed pierogis were recent choices. The wine list is Northwest-centered, and thoughtfully conceived. The culinary duo has been so well-received that they opened a second restaurant (Clemenza's).

WINE DEPOT & DELI

541-967-9499
www.winedepotdeli.com
300 Second Avenue SW
Open: Mon.–Tues. 9–6:30, Wed.–Fri. 9–7:30, Sat. 11–5:30
Price: Moderate
Credit Cards: Yes
Special Features: First Friday wine tastings accompanied by live music, informal Wed. wine tasting, free wine advice

Italy native Matt Morse, a longtimer on the wine and food scene, is the brains and brawn behind the Wine Depot. After running a high-end dinner restaurant, he decided to dial it back and simplify. His popular lunch and late-afternoon hangout serves above-average deli fare with dashes of Italian seasoning. Matt enjoys hosting monthly wine tastings (lots of fun) and occasional wine and food classes. His bottle shop emphasizes Pacific Northwest and Italian wines, and his heartfelt mission is to taste the bad wine so his customers don't have to. Stop in and say hello for us.

CORVALLIS
AQUA SEAFOOD

541-752-0262
www.aquacorvallis.com
151 NW Monroe Avenue (Water Street Market)
Open: Tues.–Sat. 4:30–close
Price: Expensive
Credit Cards: Yes
Special Features: Aloha Happy Hour 4:30–6 with bar menu and drink specials; family-friendly, with kids' menu

Bringing their island tastes to fresh seafood, Ian and Tonya Duncan have created a destination dining spot with aloha spirit. Located on "Restaurant Row," along the river front esplanade, Aqua has a gentler motif that gives it an edge. Aquariums of tropical fish swim for your enjoyment while seemingly imploring you to make up your mind. With so many fascinating options, you may opt to try them all. Faves and raves are the appetizers, especially the crabbed-stuffed Lokelani's prawns, teriyaki wahoo sliders, and ahi tartar. Not so hungry after apps? Go for a cup of Aqua's unique clam chowder and the grilled fish salad. Yum-a-lo-ha.

BIG RIVER RESTAURANT & BAR

541-757-0694
www.bigriverrest.com
101 NW Jackson Street
Open: Mon.–Fri. 11–2, Mon.–Thurs. 5–9:30, Fri.–Sat. 5–11:30
Price: Expensive
Credit Cards: Yes
Special Features: Happy hour menu 5–6:30, summer outdoor dining across from the river, live jazz on weekends

For almost a decade, Big River has been the go-to restaurant in a town that, until recently, seemed to offer little more than pizza and Mexican. It's fair to say this restaurant started the food scene in a university town that should have been more culinary-current. Nuevo Italian is served under a tall ceiling with exposed pipes and beams on a concrete floor. It can get a tad noisy, but clamor aside, the pasta and pizza are usually well above average, the desserts

Big River Restaurant has a large selection of Oregon wines. Courtesy Big River Restaurant

supreme. But then again, so are the prices. Our advice: Split an appetizer, salad, and entrée but order two or three desserts.

CLOUD 9 BISTRO

541-753-9990
www.dinecloud9.com
126 SW First Street
Open: Tues.–Sat. 11:30–2, Mon.–Thurs. 5–9, Fri.–Sat. 5–10
Price: Moderate
Credit Cards: Yes
Special Features: Improv comedy Wed. at the connected Downward Dog Bar, live music, arts

Cloud Davidson opened the bistro-style Cloud 9 in 2007 and followed a year later with the adjacent Downward Dog Bar. The food is slow-cooked, hand-made American fare. The wines come from all over, but the emphasis is regional and especially local. Or, as Davidson puts it, "I like to be able to throw a rock and hit the winery from my restaurant." Cloud 9 has been pairing its cuisine at wine dinners hosted by Wineopolis. The restaurant is quiet by day and livelier at night.

LE BISTRO

541-754-6680
www.lebistrocorvallis.com
150 SW Madison Avenue
Open: Tues.–Sat. 5 P.M.–close
Price: Expensive
Credit Cards: Yes
Special Features: Vegetarian dishes, exceptional service

The Duncans reveal Hawaiian roots at Aqua, but actually began their mainland culinary journey with the purchase of Le Bistro in 2006 after living on Maui for 15 years. Continuing with the French menu and raising the bar while still keeping it approachable, they've seen nothing but success— even in a downturned economy. All meats or fish come from within a 50-mile radius and look particularly appealing plated as lamb osso bucco, filet mignon with port and mushroom sauce, or champagne-poached fish du jour. Desserts are on par, but we'd choose the cheese plate and another glass of Burgundy. The wine list is mostly French, but gives Oregon its due.

PHILOMATH
GATHERING TOGETHER FARM
541-929-4270
www.gatheringtogetherfarm.com
25159 Grange Hall Road
Open: Apr.–Sept., Tues.–Fri. 11–2,
Thurs.–Fri. 6–9, Sat. 9–2
Price: Moderate
Special Features: Farm stand (Tues.–Sat. 9–6), monthly wine dinners featuring local wineries

John Eveland and Sally Brewer have been organic farmers since 1987. Their spread and helping-hands crew has grown and now includes farm-to-fork eating in a thrown-together dining room, once a vegetable sorting room and loading dock. Great flavors are coaxed from the farm's organic produce and local natural meats by chef J. C. Mersmann and pastry chef Bobbie Lee Woutersz. Roasted meats and thin-crust, wood-fired pizzas are baked in an earth oven built by regionally renowned sculptor Kiko Denzer. If you miss the limited dining windows, get some grab-and-go from the farm stand, which includes seasonal produce, eggs, pastries (try their signature potato donuts), and frozen organic and hormone-free meats. It's a terrific sustenance stop while winery-hopping, and a destination for cyclists from Corvallis—part of the Peak Experience Local Loop. Check out the alpaca farm across the road.

Attractions in the Albany/Corvallis Area

In Albany, the **Oregon Covered Bridge Festival** (541-752-8269) every August celebrates the eight covered bridges in the Albany area with timber competitions, arts and crafts, and food booths. For a pleasant summer evening on a grassy riverfront, the **River Rhythms** (541-917-7772) concert series, at the confluence of the Willamette and Calapooia Rivers, lures nationally renowned bands to Albany's Monteith Riverpark every Thursday evening in July and August.

The **Northwest Art and Air Festival** (541-917-7772) fills the Albany skies with hot-air balloons and draws forty thousand people to Timber Linn Park each August. Albany also is justifiably proud of its two historic districts. Stop at the 1849 **Monteith House Museum** (541-967-8699, 518 Second Ave. SW) from June to September to see perhaps the most authentic example of Oregon's pioneer-era history.

Two festivals not to miss in Corvallis are the annual **Da Vinci Days** (541-757-6363), an event for the science- and art-minded in July, and **Corvallis Fall Festival** (541-752-9655), where regional artists set up their booths in Central Park.

If you're around Corvallis in the fall, take in an **Oregon State Beavers** (541-737-4455) football game, or just wander the pastoral campus. Interesting fact: The men's basketball coach in 2010 was Craig Robinson, President Obama's brother-in-law. For the moviegoer looking for something a little offbeat, try the **Darkside Theater** (541-752-4161, www.dark sidecinema.com, 215 SW Fourth St.) in Corvallis, which offers independent films in a casual setting. Philomath has the **Benton County Historical Museum** (541-929-6230, 1101 Main St.) featuring the culture and history of the area.

Recreation in the Albany/Corvallis Area

Corvallis-ites love their hiking, biking, and paddling. The **McDonald-Dunn Research Forest** (541-737-4452) on the northwest edge of town is a favorite for hikers and mountain bikers. Walkers might enjoy the easy trails in the **William L. Finley National Wildlife Refuge** (503-588-2701) about 10 miles south of Corvallis off OR 99W.

Between them, Corvallis and Albany have three full-size public golf courses: **Trysting Tree** (541-752-3332, 34028 NE Electric Rd., Corvallis), **Marysville** (541-753-3421, 2020 SW Allen, Corvallis) and **Golf Club of Oregon** (541-928-8338, 905 NW Springhill Dr., Albany). **Golf City Par-3** (541-753-6213, 2115 NE Highway 20, Corvallis) is a fun little nine-hole chip-and-putt course.

Fishing is another favored pastime, though most ignore the placid Willamette and head for the salmon runs on the nearby Alsea, Santiam, and Siletz rivers. Foster and Green Peter reservoirs east of Albany in the Cascade Range foothills offer **boating, swimming,** and **fishing. Skiing** enthusiasts appreciate the intimate **Hoodoo Ski Bowl** (541-822-3799) just off US 20 in the Cascades, about an hour east of Albany.

Shopping in the Albany/Corvallis Area

Corvallis features many specialty shops, ethnic restaurants, bakeries, coffeehouses, and wine shops on its four-block-wide and half-mile-long downtown area. The riverfront street is particularly pleasant to stroll, with park benches, sculpture, and a fountain some find refreshing enough to dip into.

Corvallis and Albany both have **farmers' markets** (541-752-1510) under the same umbrella from April to November, both offering area produce from 9 to 1 every Saturday—at First and Jackson streets in Corvallis and at SW Ellsworth Avenue and Fourth Street in Albany. The Corvallis market also opens from 3 to 7 every Wednesday at Second and B streets.

First Alternative Food Co-op has two locations (541-753-3115, 1007 SE Third St.; 541-452-3115, 2855 NW Grant Ave.). The south store has the original hippie-style co-op feel, with a cheese cutter and full-service deli of delectable foods from their own commercial kitchen. The remodeled north store offers much of the same. Both have extensive wine sections, with many Oregon bottles and complimentary tastings once a week with food pairings. Thirsty Thursday at the north store alternates between beer and wine; the south store hosts predomi-nantly wine sampling (started by Sherry).

Avalon is one of the state's premier wine shops.
Courtesy Avalon Wine Co.

Wine Shopping in the Albany/Corvallis Area

At **Avalon** (541-752-7418 201 SW Second St., Corvallis), Jean Yates started with a small gourmet food and gift shop and then tipped her hand toward wine retail. The next step was to build her online store, which was tagged one of the "10 Best Online Wine Shops" by *Food & Wine*. The shelves are filled with "cherry-picked" selections from hard-to-find Oregon boutique producers such as Brick House, Ken Wright, Westry, and 720 Cellars. They pride themselves on the unusual and reasonably priced. Don't miss the 15-percent discount on all food and wine on the 15th of every month. **Wineopolis** (541-738-1600, 151 NW Monroe) is a snappy bottle shop owned by self-taught wine geek Jerry Larson. You're bound to take home new knowledge with your purchases. Complimentary tastings are on Saturday, sometimes Sunday. **Corvallis Brewing Supply** (541-758-1674, 119 West Fourth St.) is more into the brew side of life, but sells wine and hosts tastings.

Information

Corvallis Chamber of Commerce, 541-757-1505, www.corvallischamber.com, 420 NW Second St.

Philomath Area Chamber of Commerce, 541-929-2454, www.pioneer.net, 2395 Main St.

Albany Area Chamber of Commerce, 541-926-1517, www.albanychamber.com, 435 First Ave. NW

Benton County Winery Association, www.bentoncountywineries.com

Corvallis Tourism, 541-757-1544 or 800-334-8118, www.visitcorvallis.com

EUGENE AREA

This is a tale of two cities at the confluence of the workmanlike Willamette and pristine McKenzie rivers. Eugene is the Berkeley or Madison of the Pacific Northwest, with sandal-clad University of Oregon students and refugees from the '60s protesting anything and everything. Eugene seemingly has natural foods on every street corner, its Saturday Market was the first of its kind in America, and it remains the only city in the country with a volunteer-run food co-op. This older Eugene is epitomized by the annual Oregon Country Fair in nearby Veneta, an unvarnished and uninhibited display of arts, crafts, music, and in some cases human bodies.

The state's second largest city (155,000), Eugene is an active place that has always had a high opinion of itself while being self-deprecating at the same time. The Emerald City calls itself the "World's Greatest City of the Arts and Outdoors." City fathers once boasted, with some justification, that Eugene was both Track Town USA and Gymnastics Capitals of the World. Yet the town's citizens also freely admit Eugene is the planet's allergy capital, and an exasperated mayor once dubbed it "Anarchist Capital of the United States."

Wineries in the Eugene Area

The wine scene around Eugene is a microcosm of the city itself. You have the rich and opulent, you have husband-and-wife duos, and you have the downright eclectic. Initially, the focus was more on growing grapes than on making wine. The first vineyard in the area was planted at on Silvan Ridge in 1979 on a low-elevation soil called Bellpine.

Reflecting extremes at the southernmost end of the Willamette Valley are the internationally renowned King Estate and the colorful Territorial Vineyards and Wine Company.

King Estate has all the aura of royalty the name implies; Territorial's tasting room is a warehouse on a busy city street in a neighborhood known for its tie-dye, dreadlocks, and sandals. Whatever your taste in wine, be prepared for a taste of the unusual.

MONROE
BROADLEY VINEYARDS

541-847-5934
www.broadleyvineyards.com
265 South Fifth Street
Tasting Room: Some holiday weekends and by appointment
Fee: Varies
Owners: Craig and Claudia Broadley
Winemakers: Craig and Morgan Broadley
Wines: Pinot Noir
Cases: 5,000
Special Features: Case "futures" available

Claudia and Craig Broadley did what many Californians enamored with wine and the vintner lifestyle dreamed of doing. In the '80s they found an affordable piece of land in the "new wine country." Working within the confines of a limited budget and raising a family, the Broadleys achieved what they sought: premium Pinot Noir and a lifestyle they love. Their signature wine is Claudia's Choice, a Pinot from older estate vines (planted in '83) that once rated a 97 from Wine Spectator. Their son and daughter-in-law are now integrated into the lifestyle; Morgan assists in the winemaking and Jessica handles special events. Broadley wines typically sell out, so buying futures is a good way to ensure your allotment.

BENTON-LANE WINERY

541-847-5792
www.benton-lane.com
23924 Territorial Highway
Tasting Room: Apr.–Nov., Sat.–Sun. 11–5, Mon.–Fri. 11–4:30
Fee: Complimentary
Owners: Steve and Carol Girard
Winemaker: Chris Mazepink
Wines: Pinot Blanc, Pinot Gris, rosé, Pinot Noir
Cases: 30,000
Special Features: Outdoor patio, transitioning to screw-cap tops

A rare open house at Broadley, on the main drag through Monroe. John Baker

Steve Girard and his vineyards at Benton-Lane are full of surprises. John Baker

On a recent visit to Benton-Lane, our small group sat on the flagstone patio enjoying the 2007 estate Pinot Noir while Steve Girard held court, giving us the sordid and colorful history of his vineyard and winery. When Girard was making Cabernet at his California winery, the lure of Pinot called to him. Looking for vineyard property, he found his ideal place: a sheep farm that wasn't for sale. And the owner, who had a penchant for growing marijuana, wasn't budging. Offers went back and forth, but it was still out of range—until the owner wound up in legal trouble (imagine). As Girard cultivated his plots and blocks (with grapes), he lettered them. Turns out grapes from the L block—the former pot field—curiously elicit "the munchies" during harvest. Girard is also proud of his LIVE certification, though he wasn't initially a believer. Using sustainable farming practices, he noticed dramatic improvements,

and others noticed. Benton-Lane wines have made top-100 lists more than once. Benton-Lane is a gotta-stop on any south Willamette Valley winery tour.

JUNCTION CITY
PFEIFFER WINERY
541-998-2828
www.pfeiffervineyards.com
25040 Jaeg Road
Tasting Room: Wed.–Sun. 11–5
Fee: $5–20 per taste, includes Riedel glass
Owners: Robin and Danuta Pfeiffer
Winemaker: Robin Pfeiffer
Wines: Chardonnay, Pinot Gris, Viognier, Muscat, Merlot, Pinot Noir
Cases: 1,200
Special Features: Picnic area, wine events, hors d'oeuvres that include a rave-worthy gorgonzola cheese torte

Tunneling into this tasting room feels like entering the catacombs. Candlelight altars in the walls enhance the sensation. The Pfeiffers have one of the few solar-powered wineries in the state, with panels that supply the winery and entire property—including their home. The couple are industry leaders in environmentally friendly business practices. Danuta also likes to educate visitors and offer tasting tips at no charge.

HIGH PASS WINERY

541-998-1447
www.highpasswinery.com
24757 Lavell Road
Tasting Room: May–Nov., Sat.–Sun. 12–5
Fee: Complimentary
Owner/Winemaker: Dieter Boehm
Wines: Pinot Gris, Riesling, rosé, Pinot Noir, dessert wines
Cases: 750–1,000
Special Features: Small picnic area, annual barrel tour

Dieter Boehm's heritage is German, so it makes sense that he is known for unusual German varietals. Another rarity is that his wines are priced at $20 or less. While visiting the Bavarian-style tasting room, be sure to try the dessert wine. Boehm alternates vintages between two dessert wines, made with Huxelrebe or Scheurebe grapes. He also makes just enough wine to supply local retail markets and his tasting room. And that's how he likes it.

CHESHIRE
RAINSONG VINEYARD

541-998-1786
www.rainsongvineyard.com
92989 Templeton Road
Tasting Room: Memorial Day and Thanksgiving weekends, and by appointment
Fee: Complimentary
Owners: Mike and Merry Fix
Winemaker: Mike Fix
Wines: Pinot Gris, rosé, Pinot Noir, Pinot meunier, sparkling wines
Cases: 1,500
Special Features: Buy-a-barrel program

Pfeiffer is a solar-powered winery northwest of Eugene. John Baker

On the New Oregon (Country) Trail

Once abuzz with the whine of chainsaws and the hum of lumber mills, Oregon's timber industry hit the wall in the 1990s, putting communities perilously close to perishing. Enter Oregon Country Trails. In an effort to reinvigorate local economies, the company Vertical Rush reached out to area businesses to create four "trails" near the southern Willamette Valley towns of Corvallis and Eugene.

The "trails" are actually road trips that coax visitors into scenic farms and forests, with tantalizing offerings en route as the proverbial carrot. You'll be introduced to creative folks with a wide range of products. On most trails, wineries are the cornerstones.

The Alsea Valley Country Trail starts in Philomath and winds through the Coast Range to the village of Waldport. Stops include Tyee Wine Cellars, The Wine Vault, and Spindrift Cellars. Other "trail destinations" lead to sheep, alpaca, and goat farms, and a mountain sanctuary for white wolves.

The alluring Alsea River is a famous salmon stream cloaked in Douglas fir, vine maple, and alder and flanked by misty mountains shrouded in fog. The midway point is the snug community of Alsea, population 1,007, a local Sunday-drive favorite with Thyme Garden, John Boy's Mercantile, and a lengthy list of valley artisans.

The Fern Ridge Trail is closer to Eugene and includes LaVelle Vineyards, along with many businesses in Veneta. The Long Tom trail primarily hugs OR 99 north of Eugene to Monroe and is the most wine-centric of the four. Pfeiffer Vineyards, RainSong Vineyards, High Pass Winery, and Benton-Lane Winery are highlights. The River Road Trail consists primarily of farms around Junction City.

Oregon Country Trails is an agri-tourism business that has franchised its self-guided scenic byways. For more information, go to www.oregoncountrytrails.com. A similar tour—the Oregon Farm and Wine Tour (www.oregonfarmandwinetour.com)—has been created in southern Oregon.

Let's say a group of your closest friends, 30 or so, want to buy a barrel of wine and bottle it yourselves—even put your own clever label on the front. For $1,500 a barrel (about $5 a bottle) or $2,500 for an estate barrel ($8.60 a bottle), RainSong will make it happen. It's actually a popular program, and most weekends are spent catering to the hands-on crowd. With remaining barrels the Fix family, including daughters and boyfriends, make small lots of the listed wines. RainSong is one of the few wineries in Oregon to grow and bottle Pinot Meunier, a cousin to Pinot Noir. Some is used in their sparkling wine along with Chardonnay and Pinot Noir, similar to traditional champagne. Their bubbly is very dry; not even at disgorging is sugar added.

The Fix family might emulate the elite French region, but they are most definitely a homespun operation and they plan to keep it that way.

ELMIRA

LAVELLE VINEYARDS
541-935-9406
www.lavellevineyards.com
89697 Sheffler Road
Tasting Room: Daily 12–5
Fee: Complimentary
Owners: Doug and Matthew LaVelle
Winemaker: Matthew LaVelle
Wines: Pinot Gris, Riesling, Gewürztraminer, Viognier, Chardonnay, rosé, Pinot Noir, Gamay Noir, Cabernet Sauvignon, Merlot, Syrah
Cases: 10,000

Special Features: A labyrinth to calm chaos of the mind, club room in Eugene for tastings with light fare

Originally, LaVelle was into custom crushing wine for clients. Today, they are busy enough just making their own. The wines earn their share of awards, but the Riesling, both dry and sweet, seems to win the most. Known for catering to customers, LaVelle has 1,500 club members in the capable hands of Jill Cury. BYOP (bring your own picnic) and hike to the deck overlooking the vineyards and beyond. LaVelle Vineyard also has the Club Room at the Fifth Street Market in downtown Eugene (541-338-9875, Wed.–Fri. 3–9 and Sat.–Tues. 12–6).

VENETA
DOMAINE MERIWETHER
541-521-9690
www.meriwetherwines.com
88324 Vineyard Lane
Tasting Room: By appointment only
Fee: Varies
Owner: Ed "Buzz" Kawders
Winemaker: Ray Walsh
Wines: Chardonnay, Pinot Gris, Pinot Meunier, Pinot Noir, rosé, sparkling wines
Cases: 500

Domaine Meriwether has a new home. After many years at the Carlton Winemakers Studio, owner Buzz Kawders moved onto the site of the whimsical Secret House winery, now defunct. Meriwether has three categories of wine: sparkling, still, and heritage. The *methode champenoise* wines were originally made by a French winemaker before Ray Walsh (King Estate) took over. Look for updates and hours on the Web site.

EUGENE
SWEET CHEEKS WINERY
541-349-9463
www.sweetcheekswinery.com
27007 Briggs Hill Road
Tasting Room: Daily 12–6

Fee: Complimentary
Owner: Daniel Smith
Winemaker: Mark Nicholl
Wines: Chardonnay, Pinot Gris, Riesling, Pinot Noir, Syrah, Tempranillo, red blends, sparkling wines
Cases: 15,000
Special Features: Friday twilight tastings featuring Oregon cheeses year-round; other fun events such as October Masquerade Ball and Summer Solstice celebration

Dan Smith is a resourceful guy. A longtime grape grower (since 1978), he decided it was time to make his own wine. He rescued a doomed building in Junction City, dragged it home, and reassembled it for his winery. Now he needed a winemaker. Fond of the Australian wines, he looked Down Under for his master and came up with young and ambitious Mark Nicholl. Now for a name. Hmmm. The vineyard has a catchy moniker: Sweet Cheeks. Seems the road between the rounded vineyard hills presents itself as the name implies, at least in Dan's mind. Scrumptious views from the patio, wrought-iron tables, and fanciful water features create an inviting setting. The affordable wines and loyal clientele provide the fun. The sparkler, or "fizz," as Nicholl calls it, is popular—as is the sweet Rosy Cheeks, a multi-ethnic blend of Syrah, Tempranillo, Pinot Noir, Merlot, and Pinot Gris.

SILVAN RIDGE WINERY/HINMAN VINEYARDS
541-345-1945
www.silvanridge.com
27012 Briggs Hill Road
Tasting Room: Daily 12–5
Fee: Complimentary for seven wines (three reds, three whites, and dessert), fee for reserve wines
Owner: Liz Chambers
Winemaker: Jonathan Oberlander

*Silvan Ridge was one of the first wineries estab-
lished near Eugene.* Courtesy Silvan Ridge Winery/Hinman
Vineyards

Wines: Chardonnay, Muscat, Pinot Gris,
Riesling, Viognier, Cabernet Sauvignon,
Merlot, Pinot Noir, Syrah, red dessert wine
Cases: 30,000
Special Features: Wedding and event facil-
ity, various picnic settings, movie nights
during summer months

Silvan Ridge has been around since 1979, a
long time in Oregon wine history. Dotted
by rhododendrons and mature landscaping,
it's the kind of place that makes you feel
special just for visiting. And there is no
intimidation factor here: all questions are
welcomed. Bring your own lunch or snacks
for various picnic settings: a fireside nook,
a large dining room with small tables, and a
vineyard-level patio with terraced gardens.
Tons of weddings, reunions, family gatherings, and benefit concerts with local talent
are held throughout the year. We've enjoyed
many a bottle of the sparkling Muscat as an
aperitif or finish to a rich meal. Note:
Winemaker Jonathon Scott has his own
label, J. Scott Cellars.

NOBLE ESTATE
541-338-3007
www.nobleestatevineyard.com
29210 Gimpl Hill Road

Tasting Room: Sat.–Sun. 12–5
Fee: $5, refunded with purchase
Owners: Mark and Marie Jurasevich
Winemaker: Mark Jurasevich
Wines: Chardonnay, Pinot Gris, Riesling,
rosé, Pinot Noir, Syrah, Merlot, Cabernet
Sauvignon, sparkling wines, dessert wines
Cases: 2,000
Special Features: Wine accessories for sale,
two picnic areas (on a deck with covered
area and in the vineyard)

Mark may be the winemaker, but Marie is
in charge of important matters like "cap-
turing the sun" in the vineyard. The lion's
share of the work is done by the couple—
growing, picking, de-stemming, even bottling and labeling so that they can ensure
the quality of each and every bottle. They do
purchase grapes for the bigger reds. The
usually not-too-crowded tasting room
emits a relaxing aura. There is a picnic area
built around a blue-tiled, Mediterranean-
style soaking pool complete with pergola;
another is in the vineyard. One of the
crowd-pleasing wines is the semi-
sparkling Muscat—what every picnic needs.

TERRITORIAL VINEYARDS
& WINE COMPANY
541-684-9463
www.territorialvineyards.com
907 W. Third Avenue
Tasting Room: Thurs. 5–11, Fri.–Sat. 5–9
Fee: $7 for seven wines
Owners: Alan and April Mitchell, and Jeff
Wilson and Victoria Charles
Winemaker: John Jarboe
Wines: Chardonnay, Pinot Gris, Riesling,
rosé, Pinot Noir
Cases: 5,000
Special Features: Live music Thurs. night,
poetry slams, picnic area, outdoor seating

This winery is all-urban, with a combination tasting room/wine bar attached.
Centered in the eclectic Whiteaker neighborhood, and done in Ralph Lauren colors,

Territorial is city-funk meets Burgundy. We're fond of all their wines, but the Rosé of Pinot Noir is exceptional. Alan said his favorite way to serve it was with vanilla Häagen-Dazs. (It works!) By the way, their first release of the rosé was served at a James Beard dinner—not a bad beginning.

HOUSTON VINEYARD

541-747-4681
www.houstonvineyards.com
86187 Hoya Lane
Tasting Room: By appointment only
Fee: Complimentary
Owner/Winemaker: Steve Houston
Wines: Chardonnay
Cases: Under 1,000
Special Features: Picnic area

Steve Houston is a one-wine man—at least when it comes to making it. The Houston family grew table grapes near Lodi, California, for more than a century. Then Steve broke with tradition by coming north in the late 1970s. He planted a vineyard in 1981 and now has two Chardonnay labels: the Houston Vineyard and the Coast Fork. The Houston Vineyard Chard is slightly sweeter than the Coast Fork, which is named after a branch of the Willamette River. Feel free to drop by for an informal visit, but give him plenty of notice, as the Houstons don't live on the property.

LORANE
KING ESTATE

541-942-9874
www.kingestate.com
80854 Territorial Road
Tasting Room: Daily 11–8; check for seasonal changes
Fee: Complimentary for two current releases, or $5 for four wines
Owners: King family
Winemaker: Jeff Kandarian
Wines: Chardonnay, Pinot Gris, Riesling, Vin Gris, Cabernet Sauvignon, Pinot Noir, Syrah Vin glace, dessert wines
Cases: 120,000
Special Features: Lunch and dinner (11–9) daily, several wedding and event venues including entire restaurant

A hillside estate groomed and fit for a king is indeed owned by a family of Kings. Ed King Jr., founder of King Radio, and wife

Visitors enjoy a sunny day on the patio at King Estate.   Courtesy King Estate

Caroline wanted to grow organic hay for the family's horses on a large scale. Their son, Ed King III, already lived in Oregon and owned two small vineyards. After buying their 1,033-acre ranch in the Lorane Valley, they couldn't help noticing the quality of the soil, hillside exposure, and a neighbor who grew grapes (Château Lorane). They still grow organic hay, but 465 of the acres are planted in organic Pinot Gris and Pinot Noir. An additional forty-five acres are orchards and organic vegetable, flower, and herb gardens that supply minutes-old ingredients for the restaurant. Not only do they grow organic ingredients, they bake and cure on site. Indulge in smoked chicken paired with Pinot Noir or seared scallops and a glass of their highly regarded Pinot Gris. Equally superb is the pear and berry crisp with Vin glace. Reservations are recommended at the restaurant (541-685-5819).

CHÂTEAU LORANE

541-942-8028
www.chateaulorane.com
27415 Siuslaw River Road
Tasting Room: June–Sept., daily 12–5, Oct.–May, weekends 12–5, and by appointment
Fee: Complimentary
Owners: Linde and Sharon Kester
Winemaker: Dave Gruber
Wines: Chardonnay, Gewürztraminer, Pinot Gris, Huxelrebe, Melon de Bourgogne, Sauvignon Blanc, Viognier, Baco Noir, Cabernet Sauvignon, Malbec, Maréchal Foch, Merlot, Petite Sirah, Pinot Noir, Gamay Noir, Syrah, Tempranillo, Zinfandel, dessert wines, fruit wines
Cases: 5,000
Special Features: Picnic areas, large redwood deck overlooking the lake, two event facilities, wine club dinners, charity events

Winemaker Dave Gruber gets into his work at Château Lorane. Courtesy Château Lorane

Linde Kester never met a grape he didn't like—or couldn't ferment into wine. In fact, it's said that Château Lorane makes more types of wine than any other Oregon winery, specializing in small lots of the unusual. Output ranges from the traditional Pinot Noir and Chardonnay to such fruit wines as boysenberry, marionberry, and apricot. New to this winery, but not to winemaking, is Dave Gruber, a willing accomplice to Linde's affection for trying anything new. He walked in just days before the grapes came in. "It's all good," he says. Château Lorane also has picture-perfect grounds, so plan to sip a while.

COTTAGE GROVE
SAGINAW VINEYARD

541-942-1364
www.saginawvineyard.com
80247 Delight Valley Road
Tasting Room: Daily 11–5, closed major holidays
Fee: Complimentary
Owners: Scott and Cheryl Byler
Winemaker: Scott Byler
Wines: Chardonnay, Müller Thurgau, Pinot Gris, Rosé, Maréchal Foch, Pinot Noir, fruit wines
Cases: 2,000
Special Features: Picnic area, gift shop with Oregon foods

Saginaw's century-old barn serves as the tasting room and center of authentic country ambiance, thanks partly to the presence of sheep in the pasture. The Bylers provide the homespun hospitality. Pinot Noir and Maréchal Foch are two wines that customers can't get enough of. The Bylers also have a following for their fruit wines, including one made from blueberries grown on the farm.

IRIS VINEYARDS

541-942-5993
www.irisvineyards.com
195 Palmer Avenue

Saginaw produces the French-American hybrid Maréchal Foch.   Courtesy Newport Chamber of Commerce

Tasting Room: In the works
Owner: Pamela Frye
Winemaker: Aaron Lieberman
Wines: Chardonnay, Pinot Gris, Pinot Noir
Cases: 8,000
Special Features: Older Heritage wines available through the Web site

Iris Vineyards—formerly Iris Hill—has a fresh, hip look and label to match a new winery. Iris Hill once had its wine custom-crushed, but when that proved too costly they bought their new digs in Cottage Grove. Now it's simply Iris, with an eye-catching label—an eye followed by the letters "ris." The wines still get attention, especially the Pinot, but are easier found out of state than inside. They do participate in the annual Lane Country Barrel tour; other than that, you'll have to wait until their tasting room opens.

Lodging in the Eugene Area

EUGENE

THE CAMPBELL HOUSE INN

Owners: Jeffrey Parker and Myra Plant

541-343-1119

www.campbellhouse.com

252 Pearl Street

Rates: $99–349

Special Features: Weddings, meeting
rooms, private dinner parties

An established Victorian home on Skinner
Butte near downtown is the setting for a
boutique lodging chosen by *American
Historic Inns* as one of the country's top 25
in the genre. The Campbell House touts
more amenities than most bed-and-breakfasts. All guest rooms have private bathrooms, and some come with fireplaces.
Though the Campbell House restaurant,
known for its fine dinners, is closed, a
warm breakfast buffet with the inn's
famous buttery scones, seasonal fruit,
honey granola, and egg dish is still offered.
In the late afternoon, a complimentary
glass of local wine is served. Wine by the
glass or bottle may be purchased in the
parlor from 5 to 9 P.M. The inn schedules
regular parties, including a Victorian
Holiday Tea Party. The owners also run
Tolly's Restaurant and soda fountain in
Oakland.

VALLEY RIVER INN

541-743-1000

www.valleyriverinn.com

1000 Valley River Way

Rates: $149–209

Special Features: SweetWaters on the River
Restaurant and Bar on the river; covered
riverfront deck

In a town surprisingly bereft of quaint and
intimate lodging, the Valley River Inn is a
fairly traditional hotel with resort-like
touches amid its setting along the

*Myra Plant serves afternoon wine at the Campbell
House Inn in Eugene.*   Courtesy Campbell House Inn

Willamette River. With all of necessary
amenities on site, most notably a restaurant, it's probably the top place to stay in
Eugene. There are 245 rooms and 12 suites,
many with private balconies overlooking
the river.

SPRINGFIELD

MCKENZIE ORCHARDS
BED & BREAKFAST

Owner: Ellie de Klerk

541-515-8153

www.mkobb.com

34694 McKenzie View Dr.

Rates: $150

Special Features: Cooking school, local art

Seclusion and serenity with close-in proximity are the prime features of McKenzie
Orchards, a new B&B along the banks of the
McKenzie River. After a day of touring,
wind down with hors d'oeuvres paired with
southern Willamette Valley wines. Five substantial rooms are named for prominent
watercourses or features in the area. They
are spread out between three floors, top-
ping out with the Sahalie Falls room overlooking the river.

Dining in the Eugene Area

EUGENE
B2 WINE BAR
541-505-8909
2794 Shadow View Dr.
Open: Mon.–Sun. 12–10, later Fri.–Sat.
Price: Moderate
Credit Cards: Yes
Special Features: Serves as tasting room for
Eugene Wine Cellars; family-friendly; live
music on Saturday

B's run rampant in the Beihl family.
Founder Bruce Beihl, former wife Bettina,
and brother Brad, formed Eugene Wine
Cellars. With Brad's untimely death in
2007, their sister Beverly, a retired elementary teacher with plenty of work left in
her, joined the team. They formed another
family business, a wine bar named B
Squared—or B2, for Bruce and Beverly. It's
an inviting place without an intimidation
factor and showcases a the family wines
crafted across town by Greg Sothas: Eugene
Wine Cellar Pinot Noir, Pinot Gris, and
Viognier (labeled B2). Executive chef
Garrett Kirsch has your food fix with a
compact menu offering everything from
tapas to full dinners, using fresh farmer-
and fish-market ingredients. Eugene Wine
Cellars (255 Madison St., www.eugenewine
cellars.com) produces ten thousand cases
per year. Look for the winery to open a tasting room in the near future.

MARCHÉ
541-342-3612
www.marcherestaurant.com
296 E. Fifth Ave.
Open: Daily 11:30–2:30, Sun.–Thurs.
5:30–9, Fri.–Sat. 5:30–10
Price: Inexpensive to moderate
Credit Cards: Yes
Special Features: Outdoor seating,
catering

Locally raised and gathered foods are the
mantra at Marché, a boutique-chic restaurant in the Fifth Street Market. All ingredients are organic or free-range. As the name
implies, the menu has a French tint, and if
you sit outside in the summer you'll be surrounded by the small garden where herbs
are grown. Owner Stephanie Pearl Kimmel
has a wine pedigree—she wrote both the
King Estate Pinot Gris Cookbook and the *King
Estate Pinot Noir Cookbook*. Kimmel's adjoining Marché Provisions emporium includes
a substantial wine shop and the casual
Marché Café.

OREGON ELECTRIC STATION
541-485-4444
www.oesrestaraunt.com
27 E. Fifth Avenue
Open: Daily 5–10, Mon.–Fri. 11:30–2:30
Price: Expensive
Credit Cards: Yes
Special Features: Large groups up to 75–80
can be accommodated in dining cars; separate bar and lounge with bar menu; easy
parking

Billed as Eugene's finest continental dining, Oregon Electric Station is more pre-
dictable than ingenious, but it'll have what
everyone wants from a steak-and-seafood
place. Meals have been well prepared here
under executive chef Tom Smith's watchful
eye for more than twenty years. Oregon bay
shrimp Caesar is a good beginning; Jeff
prefers the French onion soup. Then wrap
your fork and knife around a choice prime
ribeye, crab and rock shrimp cakes, or the
legendary seafood fettuccine. As the name
implies, the restaurant is housed in a vintage brick building that once was a station
that powered an electric train. Some 250-
plus wines are cellared in a train car, and
dining is available in rail cars or in the
main seating area amid photos of Old Town
and the railroad. The restaurant boasts 30

Oregon Pinot Noirs, eight Pinot Gris (sensational with seafood), and at least eight by-the-glass choices. You can also order a bottle of southern Oregon red.

VENETA
OUR DAILY BREAD RESTAURANT
541-935-4921
www.ourdailybreadrestaurant.com
88170 Territorial Road
Open: Mon.–Thurs. 7 A.M.–8 P.M., Fri.–Sat. 7 A.M.–9 P.M., Sun. 10–1 (brunch) and 4–8
Price: Moderate
Credit Cards: Yes
Special Features: Musicians, artists, catering, southern Willamette Valley wines

You might be more inclined to think of eating and sipping as a holy experience after a stop at Our Daily Bread. After all, the restaurant is in a renovated country church. The menu is heavy on the Pacific Northwest side—meaning Pacific halibut, ocean-caught salmon, oysters, and shrimp from the coast, and organic locally raised beef. Five separate dining areas afford small clusters or groups privacy. For a walk on the international side, try the Moroccan tofu with an Oregon microbrew. We confess, we partake in the wine service, which is almost exclusively made in Oregon.

Attractions in the Eugene Area

Once a bastion of alternative-lifestyle folks, the aforementioned **Oregon Country Fair** (541-343-4298) in Veneta every July now draws people of all stripes and has been a local staple for 40 years. **University of Oregon** (541-346-4461) football games are an autumn spectacle as well; be sure to get your tickets early. The Nike juggernaut was created by Duck alum Phil Knight, and you can learn how it all began, as well as how Eugene became known as Track Town USA, at the **Nike Store and Museum** (541-686-4131, 135 Oakway Road.

The **Lane County Historical Museum** (541-682-4242, 740 W. 13th Avenue) traces the state's roots to the first arrivals on the Oregon Trail. If you want to dig deeper into the region's history, visit the **University of Oregon Museum of Natural and Cultural History** (541-346-3024, 1680 E. 15th Ave.), which has a 9,000-year-old—yes, 9,000—pair of shoes. Art aficionados will appreciate the **Jordan Schnitzer Museum of Art** (541-346-3027), a collection of more than 12,500 primarily Pacific Northwest and Asian pieces located on campus. The **Oregon Air and Space Museum** (541-461-1101, 90773 Boeing Dr.) near the airport has a remarkable collection of military fighter jets and more.

For the flora-minded, the **Owen Rose Garden** along the Willamette River features more than 4,500 varieties of roses and a 150-year-old black cherry tree. The lush countryside around Eugene is also renowned for its 20 covered bridges, more than any county west of the Mississippi River. A major event for several weeks each summer is the **Oregon Bach Festival** (541-457-1486), which brings more than 40 concerts to the downtown Hult Center and the Beall Concert Hall.

Recreation in the Eugene Area

Eugene might get an argument from a hundred other communities when it proclaims itself the Outdoor Capital of the World, but there's no question it's ideally suited for doers. The **Adidas Amazon Running Trail** is a well-marked wood-chip course where you could easily find yourself sharing turf with a world-class distance runner doing interval training.

Eugene is rather modest about its **bicycling** opportunities—it merely rates among the top 10 nationally in this category. **Mountain biking** trails crisscross the hills in three directions and road cyclists will find miles of lonely pavement.

When not in their running shoes, locals can usually be found on the water. The clear and cold McKenzie River offers some of the state's best **whitewater rafting** and trout **fishing**. A more placid experience can be had 15 miles west of town on Fern Ridge Reservoir, the best place in the state for **sailing** because of its reliable northerly winds in the summer.

Skiers generally go for the credible powder of **Willamette Pass Resort** (541-393-1436), about 70 miles southeast of Eugene on OR 58. If you like it hot, try a soothing soak in one of the many hot springs in the Cascades. **Belknap Hot Springs** (541-822-3512) has two mineral swimming pools, camping, comfortable lodging, and a serene garden about 60 miles east of Eugene on OR 126.

Shopping in the Eugene Area

Shoppers will quickly discover there's no **Saturday Market** (541-686-8885) in the country quite like Lane County's, in the downtown Park Blocks. Open every Saturday from April to November, the diverse and bustling collection of about 150 booths with artisans, vendors, and musicians is more of a celebration than a market. The **Fifth Street Public Market** (541-484-0383, 296 East Fifth St.) is a laid-back place to shop, cruise on foot, and people-watch in a historic part of town. For the more tradition-minded, the **Valley River Center** (541-683-5513) has the usual assortment of chain stores, theaters, and restaurant fare.

Wine Shopping in the Eugene Area

Oenophiles can get their regional wine needs met at **Sundance Wine Cellars** (541-687-9463, 2441 Hilyard St.), which claims to have the world's largest collection of Pinot Noirs. Sundance has themed wine tastings from 5–7 P.M. every Friday and Saturday.

Information

Eugene Chamber of Commerce, 541-484-1314, www.eugenechamber.com, 1401 Willamette St.

Eugene Visitor and Convention Bureau, 541-484-5307 or 800-547-5445, www.travellanecounty.org, 115 West Eighth, suite 190

Springfield Chamber of Commerce, 541-746-1651, www.springfield-chamber.org, 101 South A St.

Eugene, Cascades and Coast Travel Center, 541-484-5307, www.travellanecounty.org, 3312 Gateway St., Springfield

Wineries of Lane County, www.wineriesoflanecounty.com

7

Southern Oregon

Fly Over No More . . .

Take Oregon's Willamette Valley and California's Napa/Sonoma region, mix vigorously, and then toss the ingredients onto a jumbled landscape. That's southern Oregon.

Beginning at rough-hewn Roseburg, about 80 rugged miles south of the Willamette Valley, the terrain becomes more mountainous, sunnier, warmer, and drier. Douglas fir and vine maple are still the rule at Roseburg, but as Interstate 5 winds through the South Umpqua River Valley toward Grants Pass, Pacific madrone, prolific oak savannah, and sugar pine enter the picture. And by the time the freeway reaches the broad Rogue River Valley at Medford, it has turned east to avoid the wild Klamath Mountains, taking it 30 significant miles farther from the moist marine-air influence of the Pacific Ocean.

Blue-collar Medford is the region's hub and is Oregon's hottest city on average, with temperatures frequently rising above 100 in the summer. Fortunately, wine tourists don't have to go far to beat the heat. The artsy outdoors community of Ashland is 10 miles and a world away to the south, where its location at the foot of the Siskiyou Summit spares it from the heat.

Grants Pass and Roseburg are one-time timber-industry giants that have reinvented themselves around wine in the last decade. Both are a long way from being full-fledged tourist destinations, though Grants Pass has always had the benefit of being the gateway to the mighty Rogue River of Zane Grey fame, with its splashy whitewater rafting and salmon fishing. Ashland is renowned for its acclaimed annual Shakespeare Festival, the powdery Mt. Ashland Ski and Snowboard Area, and a vibrant city center. Jacksonville, a National Historic Landmark, is a delightful foothills village, five miles over the hill from Medford.

Getting Here And Around

Medford has one of the two commercial airports in the long 480 miles between Eugene and Sacramento, California, and is the third busiest in the state behind Portland and Eugene. It is really the only place to arrive by air for wine tours in the Southern Oregon AVA, including the Umpqua region.

Some 60 flights a day come and go on four airlines from Rogue Valley International–

OPPOSITE: *Abacela's rolling vineyards produce Spanish varietals such as Grenache and Albariño.* M. Kim Lewis

Medford Airport, all of them coming from western hubs. **Delta Connection** (800-221-1212) serves Salt Lake City; **United Express** (800-241-6522) departs to Portland, San Francisco, and Denver; **Horizon Air** (800-252-7522) connects to Eugene, Portland, Los Angeles, and Seattle; and **Allegiant Air** (702-505-8888) arrives from Las Vegas, Los Angeles, and Phoenix.

For anyone wanting the romance of a train, **Amtrak** (800-872-7245) roughly follows I-5 from the north, but it veers over the Cascade Range just southeast of Eugene and stops in Klamath Falls—about two hours to the east across the Cascades. A chartered bus takes passengers from Amtrak's Front Street Transfer Station in Medford to Klamath Falls. **Amtrak California** (800-872-7245), which partners with the Caltrans commuter lines, serves Medford and Ashland from the south. **Greyhound** (800-231-2222) has stops in Medford, Jacksonville, and Ashland.

For those behind the wheel, I-5 is the primary artery through the region, bisecting the four largest towns—Roseburg, Grants Pass, Medford, and Ashland. As is typically the case, wine touring requires taking back roads. The Umpqua and Red Hill Douglas County wineries around Roseburg are roughly in the I-5 corridor, but off the beaten path. OR 238 connects Medford with Grants Pass and includes Jacksonville plus the pastoral Applegate Valley. To reach the Illinois Valley, take US 199 southwest from Grants Pass toward Cave Junction.

Umpqua Region
(Umpqua and Red Hill Douglas County AVAs)

Few places better epitomize Oregon's evolution than the wooded valleys where the North and South Umpqua Rivers join for their final 70-mile march through the Coast Range to the sea. The densely forested "100 Valleys of the Umpqua" were once timber country—an area that has long bred bruising football players and leathery men as tough as their hickory shirts. Sawmills hummed by day, the taverns of Roseburg, Myrtle Creek, and Yoncalla rumbled by night, and Roseburg was little more than a refueling stop on I-5 between Portland and Sacramento.

Today, with the sawmills quieted, steep hills and lush valleys covered in fir, sugar pine, and Pacific madrone are also leafing out in a wide range of grapevines reflecting the confluence of northern and southern Oregon climes. It is all part of Douglas County's recent economic diversification from one-sawhorse towns to more inviting settings.

Wineries in the Umpqua Region

The rolling hills and pastures of southern Oregon are where the state's modern-day wine industry truly began a half-century ago, and yet the area remains, as vintners wistfully and optimistically put it, "the last great undiscovered wine region in America."

Oregon's first bonded winery, HillCrest, is here. HillCrest founder Richard Sommers is considered the father of the state's contemporary wine industry. He was, after all, the one who planted 35 varieties of grapes just northwest of Roseburg beginning in 1961, and who later advised David Lett and other Pinot pioneers on the nuances of this crazy notion of growing grapes in the Beaver State. Sommers even produced the state's first Pinot Noir at his fledgling winery just northwest of Roseburg.

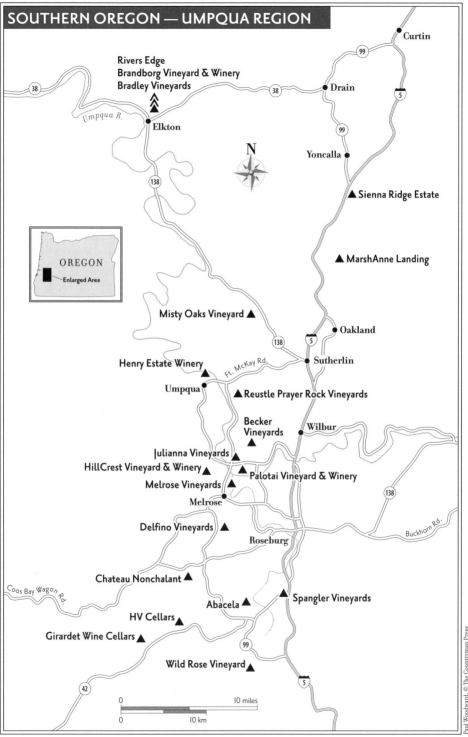

SOUTHERN OREGON — UMPQUA REGION

Curtin

99

Rivers Edge
Brandborg Vineyard & Winery
Bradley Vineyards

38

38

Drain

5

Umpqua R.

Elkton

99

138

N

Yoncalla

▲ Sienna Ridge Estate

OREGON

Enlarged Area

▲ MarshAnne Landing

Misty Oaks Vineyard ▲

138

5

Oakland

Henry Estate Winery

Ft. McKay Rd.

Sutherlin

Umpqua

▲ Reustle Prayer Rock Vineyards

Becker
Vineyards
▲

Wilbur

Julianna Vineyards ▲

HillCrest Vineyard & Winery ▲

▲ Palotai Vineyard & Winery

Melrose Vineyards ▲

Melrose

138

Delfino Vineyards ▲

Buckhorn Rd.

Roseburg

Chateau Nonchalant ▲

Coos Bay Wagon Rd.

▲ Spangler Vineyards

Abacela ▲

HV Cellars ▲

Girardet Wine Cellars ▲

99

Wild Rose Vineyard ▲

5

42

0   10 miles

0   10 km

Paul Woodward, © The Countryman Press

Start your tour by exiting I-5 onto OR 38 toward Elkton. To continue on to Roseburg's wineries, double-back on OR 38 to Drain and head south on OR 99 to Yoncalla. Note: We have not included Anindor Winery in Elkton because they closed their tasting room in 2009; at press time the owners had plans to reopen in 2010 at the vineyard.

ELKTON
BRANDBORG VINEYARD & WINERY
541-584-2870
www.brandborgwine.com
345 First Street
Tasting Room: Daily 11–5
Fee: $5, refunded with purchase
Owners: Terry and Sue Brandborg
Winemaker: Terry Brandborg
Wines: Pinot Gris, Riesling, Gewürztraminer, Pinot Noir, Syrah
Cases: 6,000
Special Features: Street-side patio seating, live music on random occasions (local and headliners), small gift shop, art for sale

This is your first winery stop on the main drag in Elkton, the largest Umpqua Valley community between Roseburg and the coast, featuring exactly zero stoplights. The sweet, light, and airy tasting room has a U-shaped bar and a sprinkling of tables and chairs. Brandborg's tagline is "the coolest" because the vineyard is notably cooler than elsewhere in southern Oregon—hence their Pinot Noir. Brandborg is an up-and-coming winery to watch.

RIVERS EDGE
541-584-2357
www.riversedgewinery.com
1395 River Drive
Tasting Room: Thurs.–Sun. 11–5; summer, daily 11–5
Fee: Complimentary
Owners/Winemakers: Michael and Yvonne Landt
Wines: Chardonnay, Gewürztraminer, Pinot Gris, Pinot Noir
Cases: 3,800

The new kids on the block, of sorts, are Michael and Lavonne Landt, who purchased one of the northernmost vineyards in the Umpqua region in 1996. Half of the grapes used are estate while the rest come from within three miles. Some of the Landts' own vines were planted nearly four decades ago. Tastings are held in the winery on a makeshift table under three used barrels. No need for anything fancier, as the winery and wines speak to the old ways and traditions.

BRADLEY VINEYARDS
541-584-2888
www.bradleyvineyards.com
1000 Azalea Drive
Tasting Room: May–Nov., Wed.–Sun. 11–5, or by appointment
Fee: Complimentary
Owners: John and Bonnie Bradley
Winemaker: John Bradley

Bradley Vineyards cover 25 acres near Elkton.
Courtesy Bradley Vineyards

Wines: Riesling, rosé, Baco Noir, Pinot Noir, dessert wine
Cases: 500
Special Features: RV access, deck, picnic pavilion under old oak trees, small events venue

"Down home and comfy" best describes the style of the Bradleys' little farm and winery. Once you turn onto their driveway, signage leads the way to their equipment shed turned tasting room. Signs announcing "Here are the vines" and "Row after row" make you smile and appreciate their fun-loving approach and attitude. Small production and the fact that they sell 95 percent of their grapes mean you can only get their wines in their tasting room. There is no hard sell here because it's not needed.

OAKLAND
SIENNA RIDGE ESTATE
541-849-3300
www.siennaridgeestate.com
1876 John Long Road
Tasting Room: Daily 12–6
Fee: $5, refunded with purchase
Owner: Wayne Hitchings
Winemaker: Terry Brandborg
Wines: Pinot Blanc, Pinot Gris, Riesling, Gewürztraminer, Cabernet Sauvignon, Merlot, Pinot Noir, dessert wines
Cases: 2,000
Special Features: Historic tasting room, hors d'oeuvres served, picnic area

Sienna Ridge is so special, it has its own AVA. The south-facing slopes and rich, volcanic Jory soils east of Interstate 5 are so unique to the area that the vineyard earned its own designation. The Red Hill Douglas County AVA is one of four in the entire country comprised of one vineyard—in this case the 300-plus-acre Red Hill Vineyard owned by Sienna Ridge. The owners are rightfully proud of the designation, and feel the same way about the 1906 tasting room Hitchings renovated. Most notable among

the wines is their "ice vine," a dessert-style blend of Riesling and Gewürztraminer.

MARSHANNE LANDING
541-459-7998
www.marshannelanding.com
381 Hogan Road
Tasting Room: May–Oct., Wed.–Sun. 11–5; Mar.–Apr. and Nov.–Dec., Sat.–Sun. 11–5; and by appointment
Fee: $5, refunded with purchase
Owners: Greg Marsh Cramer and Frances Anne Cramer
Winemaker: Greg Cramer
Wines: Chardonnay, Viognier, Tempranillo, Cabernet Franc, Cabernet Sauvignon, Merlot, Pinot Noir, Syrah, red blends
Cases: 1,200
Special Features: Gift shop, picnic area, art exhibits in tasting room, concerts

When you're off the beaten wine path, you need to get clever in your marketing. The Interstate 5 billboard with a UFO on it is MarshAnne Landing's first attempt to coax drivers off the freeway to their hidden gem. Once in the tasting room, you'll be captivated by the setting and the wines. In the summer, you'll be amazed to find events that might include the Eugene Opera, a piano/violin concert, jazz musicians, or an Elvis impersonator. "A cultural Mecca here in the wilderness," Fran Cramer calls it. And what about the name? When you say it quickly, it sounds a little like . . . *martian.* Hence, the Red Planet wine. Coming soon: A blend called Southern Cross. It's just one more way to expand on the otherworldly theme. The real story behind the name MarshAnne? It combines the Cramers' middle names.

MISTY OAKS VINEYARD
541-459-3558
www.mistyoaksvineyard.com
1310 Misty Oaks Lane
Tasting Room: May–Nov., Fri.–Sun. 11–5

Fee: $4 for three whites and three reds, refunded with purchase
Owners/winemakers: Steve and Christy Simmons
Wines: Gewürztraminer, Pinot Blanc, Pinot Gris, Cabernet Franc, Pinot Noir, red blends
Cases: 800
Special Features: Colorful and chatty servers who have aged gracefully

The dryness and hilly terrain are apparent as you make your way through the madrones, oaks, and layers of tall grasses up to the winery. Once you're out of your car, the tranquility of Steve and Christy's spot on the rise is even more discernible. The setting is simple, the wines not so much. Ask about the stories behind the labels (Stuck Again Heights, Joan's Road, Friendswood, etc.). Julio's Hill has to do with the Pinot Gris vines that arrived before the owners or equipment did, so Julio planted all 2,100 by hand. The signature wine is a blend of Cabernet Sauvignon, Merlot, Cabernet Franc, and Malbec. This is a winery on the way up.

ROSEBURG
HENRY ESTATE WINERY
541-459-5120 or 800-782-2686
www.henryestate.com
687 Hubbard Creek Road
Tasting Room: Daily 11–5, closed major holidays
Fee: Complimentary
Owner: Scott Henry III
Winemaker: Calvin Scott Henry IV
Wines: Chardonnay, Gewürztraminer, Müller Thurgau, Pinot Gris, Riesling, Merlot, Pinot Noir
Cases: 16,000
Special Features: Large picnic areas in the vineyard and gardens, gift shop, tours by appointment, RV parking

Henry Estate might be southern Oregon's best-known winery, in part for its wide distribution and in part because Scott Henry III created one of the industry's best-known modern-day inventions. The vineyards were first planted on 12 acres in 1972, but the winery didn't earn international acclaim until Henry developed a two-tiered trellis system. Henry Estate is near the

Pinot grapes bask in warm southern Oregon sunlight. Courtesy Bradley Vineyards

Henry System Gets a Rise out of Grapes

In some ways, the Oregon's Umpqua Valley represents the best of all worlds for wine growers. The region blends the cool climate of the Willamette Valley with the Mediterranean climes of California, and some of the richest soil in Oregon is here. The result is rapid, verdant vine growth that can quickly get out of hand and create dense canopies that lead to grape rot and other diseases.

This was an ongoing challenge for Scott Henry III after Henry Estate planted its first vines outside Roseburg in 1972. His solution, after years of experimenting, is an international success story: the Henry Trellis System.

In essence, Henry added a second story, or tier, for his vines. Years earlier, he had figured out he could slow growth by increasing the number of vine shoots from two to four. Trouble was, while having four shoots slowed the plant's growth, it also created greater leaf density that in turn led to delayed ripening and other problems.

With Henry's trellis system, two shoots are trained to grow downward and horizontally on the first story. The other two shoots are guided upward and out. Leaves and clusters are spread out and receive optimum sun exposure. The canopy is reduced overall, decreasing the risk for disease and enhancing grape quality.

While the trellis system requires more management, it can contribute to higher yields, more vivid color on the skins, and higher sugar content (known as Brix), making the effort fully worth the trouble. In fact, it's so worthwhile that many vineyards around the world have implemented Henry's system.

confluence of the North and South Umpqua Rivers, where the family has savored the landscape through three generations. The spacious tasting room is usually an event in the making, so plan to stay a while.

REUSTLE PRAYER ROCK VINEYARDS

541-459-6060
www.reustlevineyards.com
960 Cal Henry Road
Tasting Room: Mon.–Sat. 10–5
Fee: $10 (includes light food pairing)
Owners: Stephen and Gloria Reustle
Winemaker: Stephen Reustle
Wines: Pinot Gris, Riesling, Sauvignon Blanc, Viognier, Semillon, Grüner Veltliner, Roussanne, Grenache, Pinot Noir, Tempranillo, Merlot, Syrah
Cases: 5,500
Special Features: Sit-down wine tasting, kid-friendly, RV parking

The mammoth carved cement block and cedar planked structures will leave you rubbing your eyes in disbelief after coming out of the backcountry. A lower parking lot gives you the advantage of taking in the entire grandeur on the hill. Paths with such scriptural signs as "Drink your wine with a happy heart, God approves of this" on benches and rocks lead you through to the huge, Tuscan-style piazza and carved entrance doors. A miniature forest of bonsai, sculpture, and potted trees builds your anticipation while varying levels of patios, water features stocked with lilies, and goldfish add adornment. Inside, the fantasy continues as you are greeted in the lobby and led to one of four chambers in a chandelier-clad cave, passing barrels, and walls frescoed with scripture and angels. The Reustle family works closely with church and youth groups in a sort of labor exchange program. Volunteers provide free hands for harvest; the money they would have spent on field hands is donated to missions in Romania. The concept of uniqueness carries over to the sit-down tasting, where nibbles of food enhance the wines. The Reustles have garnered many top awards for their wines and are creating quite the media buzz.

BECKER VINEYARDS

541-677-0288
www.beckerwine.com
360 Klahowya Lane
Tasting Room: Daily 11–5
Fee: Complimentary
Owners: Charles and Peggy Becker
Winemaker: Charles Becker
Wines: Müller Thurgau, Pinot Gris, rosé, Cabernet Sauvignon, Pinot Noir, Syrah, dessert wine
Cases: 700
Special Features: Picnic area

Becker Vineyards is as mom-and-pop as it gets, right down to Peggy Becker answering the phone by simply saying, "Hello." By day, she works at a health clinic and he's a painter. Every other waking hour is spent in the vineyard and winery on a pretty ridge above the Umpqua River's Cleveland Rapids. The Beckers are the consummate do-it-yourselfers; they dry-farm the vineyard with no outside help. Come harvest time, they uncork a few bottles of wine, prepare some good food and invite friends, neighbors, and relatives over for the crush. Something's working: The Beckers' 2007 Pinot Noir was voted best red at Oregon's Greatest of the Grape competition.

DELFINO VINEYARDS

541-673-7575
www.delfinovineyards.com
3829 Colonial Road
Tasting Room: Fri.–Sun. 11–5, later on holiday weekends
Fee: Complimentary
Owners: Jim and Terri Delfino
Winemaker: Jim Delfino
Wines: Zinfandel, Syrah, Merlot, dessert wine
Cases: 500
Special Features: Guest cottage includes breakfast, hot tub, and lap pool ($175–250/night), weddings and event facilities

Delfino proudly opened its tasting room in 2009 after tending to 18 acres of grapes for eight years. Their 160-acre farm is pleasing to the eye as you wind through the vineyard to the tasting room. Don't be alarmed by the five dogs that greet you; they're friendly. After you sip and nibble, you can work off the calories on hiking trails that lace their countryside, then watch the sun set from the deck. If you stay at the guest cottage, the resident chickens supply eggs for breakfast.

JULIANNA VINEYARDS

541-672-8060
www.juliannavineyards.com
707 Hess Lane
Tasting Room: Memorial Day through Thanksgiving weekends, Sat.–Sun. 11–5
Fee: $2
Owners: Henry Russel and Debbie Hackler
Winemaker: Henry Russel
Wines: Chenin Blanc, Riesling, Semillon, Sauvignon Blanc, Cabernet Sauvignon, Cabernet Franc, Merlot, Maréchal Foch
Cases: 500
Special Features: Deck overlooking meandering Umpqua River

One of newest wineries in the Umpqua region, Julianna is unique for its location along the Umpqua River. It's also perhaps the first winery on the way south where you won't find Pinot Noir. The vineyard is planted in rich, fertile river soils. Owners Henry and Debbie Russel lived much of their lives in European wine regions, including Spain, Portugal, and Germany, when they were in the Air Force. Julianna is named for Henry's mother. Their wines, featuring the mighty Chinook salmon on the label, are sold only in the tasting room.

PALOTAI VINEYARD & WINERY

541-464-0032
www.palotaiwines.com
272 Capital Lane
Tasting Room: Daily 11–5
Fee: Complimentary
Owner/Winemaker: John and Joy Olson
Wines: Bella Bianca, Chardonnay, Riesling, Baco Noir, Dolcetto, Meritage, Merlot, Pinot Noir, Syrah, Zinfandel, white blend
Cases: 1,300
Special Features: Picnic area, RV turn-around

For years, this was the place to get a double fix: the famous Hungarian Bull's Blood wine, and winemaker Gabor Palotai's one-liners. The gregarious Gabor is now out of the picture, traveling the world, but new owners John and Joy Olson have continued the Bull's Blood tradition. This Hungarian table wine is a unique blend of reds, featuring Baco Noir, and is so popular it's a challenge to keep it in stock. Palotai also produces the classics, and the Olsons say their carefully handcrafted wines taste "like a home-cooked meal."

MELROSE VINEYARDS

541-672-6080
www.melrosevineyards.com
885 Melqua Road
Tasting Room: Daily 11–5
Fee: Complimentary for three wines, $10 for all six wines and glass
Owners: Wayne and Deedy Parker
Winemaker: Cody Parker
Wines: Chardonnay, Pinot Gris, Viognier, Riesling, Sauvignon Blanc, rosé, Merlot, Baco Noir, Dolcetto, Pinotage, Pinot Noir, Syrah, Tempranillo, red blend, port-style
Cases: 4,000
Special Features: Gift shop, gift baskets, picnic area, wedding and event facilities, catering services

There isn't a winemaking facility at Melrose yet, but if anybody can make it happen it's Wayne and Deedy Parker. They arrived in 1996 from Fresno, California, where Wayne had grown grapes, and proceeded to plant vines on 82 acres along the South Umpqua. Alas, that was the winter of massive flooding throughout the West. The result: a loss of five acres and several years of cleanup. After flood-proofing the property to the extent possible, Wayne then turned to the 100-year-old barn on the property. In those rickety old timbers, he saw a tasting room. Rebuilding virtually beam by beam, the Parkers now have a spectacular setting to taste wines and stage special events. Melrose is a bit off the beaten path, but you won't regret the journey—or the results.

HILLCREST VINEYARD & WINERY

541-673-3709
www.hillcrestvineyard.com
240 Vineyard Lane
Tasting Room: Mar.–Dec., Daily 11–5
Fee: Complimentary
Owners: Dyson and Susan DeMara
Winemaker: Dyson DeMara
Wines: Riesling, Valdiguié, Viognier, Cabernet Sauvignon, Pinot Noir, Syrah, Zinfandel, ice dessert wine
Cases: 1,400
Special Features: Tours

"We're No. 1!" Only one winery in the state gets to say it was the first legally bonded facility, and HillCrest is it. History permeates every pore of this winery, which saw its first grapes planted in 1888. A more important date is 1961—when Richard Sommers planted 35 varieties, many seeing Oregon soil for the first time. You'll notice the number, 44, on site, a reference to the state's 44th bonded alcohol producer post-Prohibition. HillCrest produced the state's first Pinot Noir, and noteworthy wines are

Dyson and Susan DeMara, with their children, are starting a new chapter in Oregon wine history at HillCrest, Oregon's first bonded winery.
Courtesy HillCrest

still coming from vines planted in the 1960s. To get these historic wines, you need to stop by the old barn that serves as the winery's home. You might be treated to a barrel tasting by newbie owners eager to show off their Syrah.

SPANGLER VINEYARDS

541-679-9654
www.spanglervineyards.com
491 Winery Lane
Tasting Room: Daily 11–5
Fee: Complimentary, with some exceptions
Owners: Pat and Loree Spangler
Winemaker: Pat Spangler
Wines: Chardonnay, Viognier, Sauvignon Blanc, Cabernet Franc, Cabernet Sauvignon, Merlot, Syrah, Petite Sirah, red blend, sparkling wines
Cases: 3,000
Special Features: Tours, picnic grounds, gift shop, wedding facilities, RV access, kid-friendly

Formerly La Garza, Spangler has made many changes since Pat and Loree took over, not the least of which, she says, is that they "make really good wine now." Spangler's forte is big reds, and they're

especially proud of their Claret and Petite Sirah. The signature grape in the vineyard is Cabernet Sauvignon, which has been dry-farmed in the valley since 1968.

ABACELA

541-679-6642
www.abacela.com
12500 Lookingglass Road
Tasting Room: 11–5 daily (except major holidays)
Fee: $5 for five wines, refunded with three-bottle purchase
Owners: Earl and Hilda Jones
Winemaker: Andrew Wenzel
Wines: Albariño, Viognier, Rosada, Tempranillo, Garnacha, Syrah, Merlot, Malbec, Cabernet Franc, Dolcetto, red and white blends, port-style wine
Cases: 11,000

Hilda and Earl Jones searched the world over to find exactly the right terroir for their beloved Spanish varietals. They found

Bacchus blows his energy into the tasting room at HillCrest. Courtesy HillCrest

it on an early-nineteenth-century home-stead in the Umpqua Valley, where the climate matched the western portion of Spain's famed Ribera del Duero region. They came onto the Oregon wine scene like gangbusters with their favorite grape, Tempranillo, and have been winning barrels of awards ever since. Abacela was also a trendsetter with its Dolcetto and Albariño, both now grown in other Oregon vineyards. Abacela remains one of our favorite stops.

CHATEAU NONCHALANT

541-679-2394
1329 Larson Road
www.chateaunonchalantvineyards.com
Tasting Room: June–Sept., Fri.–Sun. 11–5
Fee: Complimentary
Owners: Weldon and Vicki Manning
Winemaker: Scott Henry Jr.
Wines: Pinot Gris, Pinot Noir, Syrah, Tempranillo
Cases: 1,000

After providing grapes for other wineries in the region, the Mannings decided to raise the stakes and create their own label. When it came to picking a winemaker, they didn't fool around. They secured good friend Scott Henry Jr., of Henry Estate, who began churning out estate Pinot Noir for them in 2005. Another notable sign of Chateau Nonchalant's evolution is a beautifully crafted tasting room framed in wood. The wines are only available in the tasting room. Look for more diversity from Chateau Nonchalant in the future.

HV CELLARS

541-572-0251
116 Haven Lane
Tasting Room: Daily 11–5
Fee: Complimentary

This is a satellite tasting room for HV Cellars & Wild Goose Vineyards in Myrtle Point (see listing under Wineries along the South Coast).

GIRARDET WINE CELLARS

541-679-7252
www.girardetwine.com
895 Reston Road
Tasting Room: Daily 11–5
Fee: Complimentary
Owners: Philippe and Bonnie Girardet
Winemaker: Marc Girardet
Wines: Riesling, Chardonnay, Pinot Gris, Pinot Noir, Baco Noir, Cabernet Sauvignon, red and white blends, dessert wine
Cases: 11,000
Special Features: Picnic and barbecue area, gift shop, tours by appointment

The Girardets are from Switzerland, which doesn't explain their passion for Baco Noir—a white/red hybrid developed a century ago by a Frenchman named François Baco in hopes of finding a grape resistant to phylloxera. Baco Noir was first planted in cool eastern states and did reasonably well, so it's no surprise it thrives in the Umpqua. The Girardets, first Philippe and now his son Marc, have been producing this silky-smooth, colorful, and spicy red with hints of plum and blueberry since 1991. It has become their signature wine, and it's fair to say that if David Lett is Oregon's "Papa Pinot" then Philippe Girardet is "Uncle Baco." The Girardets make some other fine reds and whites, including a Rhône-style value wine called Grand Rouge, a blend of 14 reds intentionally priced at $14 ($1 per varietal).

WINSTON
WILD ROSE VINEYARD

541-580-5488
www.wildrosevineyard.com
375 Porter Creek Road
Tasting Room: Daily 11–5
Fee: Complimentary
Owners: Denise and Carlos Figueroa
Winemaker: Carlos Figueroa
Wines: Pinot Gris, Cabernet Sauvignon, Merlot, Pinot Noir, dessert wine
Cases: 500

Special Features: Picnic area, fundraising for Umpqua Community College culinary-arts program

Carlos Figueroa was an engineering instructor at Umpqua Community College, and his entrepreneurial skills have come in handy at his humble nine-acre vineyard just outside town. He fashioned a Spartan tasting room out of the garage of their two-story home at the end of a gravel road in a small, charming valley. Wild Rose is 100 percent organic, LIVE-certified, and Salmon-Safe—important when you're this close to the salmon-heavy South Umpqua River. At this point Carlos doesn't have winemaking facilities, but he's focusing on that task next.

Lodging in the Umpqua Region

ELKTON
THE BIG K GUEST RANCH
Owners: Kathie Larsen and Linda Parrish
541-584-2295 or 800-390-2445
www.big-k.com
20029 Highway 138 West
Rates: $369–399
Special Features: Winery tours, fishing trips, horseback rides, guide services

"Big" is right. The Big K is 2,500 acres of outdoor wonders along and above 10 miles of a postcard-like bend in the Umpqua River. The ranch is all-inclusive, meaning one price covers all your needs for a day or a week in one of the 20 cabins near the 12,000-square-foot main lodge. Created a century ago by the Kesterson family, the Big K remains a working ranch, with cattle, sheep, and horses grazing in green pastures amid oak and Douglas fir. Owner Kathie Larsen is the daughter of Alvin Kesterson (Big K), who turned a portion of the property into a guest ranch to help offset the rising costs of running a cattle ranch. The cabins are what you'd expect in the country: clean, comfortable, and quiet. The ranch

dining room features Oregon wines, and the staff will point you in the right direction for touring Elkton wineries.

ROSEBURG
C.H. BAILEY HOUSE BED & BREAKFAST
Owners: Jay and Sherry Couron
541-672-1500
www.chbaileyhouse.com
121 Melton Road
Rates: $125–145

Even when it was built in 1909, this white farmhouse in the country east of Roseburg was unique in its construction. More than a century later, the historic C.H. Bailey House is still in the country and still exudes rural charms. Once surrounded by acres of apple, cherry, and prune orchards, it is now a memorable getaway for Umpqua Valley wine tourists and steelhead anglers. The four rooms are beyond comfortable, with warm overtones and European antiques. Play a game of lawn darts or croquet before or after late-afternoon appetizers and wine.

CANYONVILLE
SEVEN FEATHERS HOTEL AND CASINO RESORT
Owners: Cow Creek Band of the Umpqua Tribe
541-839-1111 or 800-548-8461
www.sevenfeathers.com
146 Chief Miwaleta Lane
Rates: $69–89
Special Features: Full-service day spa, large indoor pool, sauna and fitness room, head-line entertainment, cabaret lounge, pack-aged deals, video arcade

The Cow Creek Indians, the first to bring gaming to Oregon, have created a 232,500-square-foot luxury resort and casino with a little bit of everything, from RV spots to 298 spacious and gorgeously appointed higher-end rooms. Feeling lucky? Check into one of 12 suites. The resort hosts the annual Greatest of the Grape festival in March, the oldest wine celebration in Oregon.

STEAMBOAT
STEAMBOAT INN
Owners: Sharon and Jim Van Loan
541-498-2230 or 800-840-8825
www.thesteamboatinn.com
42705 North Umpqua Hwy
Rates: $175-300
Special Features: Cabins, cottages, and houses sleeping up to six, suites sleeping two; breakfast and lunch served until kitchen closes to prepare for dinner

Fall asleep to the sound of the rushing river splashing over rocks and boulders, completely content after savoring some of the best cuisine in Oregon. The Steamboat Inn, long time favorite of wine fans and fishermen, is a quintessential Oregon experience. Dinner ($50 per person) is a ritual and, in keeping with fish-camp tradition, begins with hors d'oeuvres and aperitifs about 30 minutes after rods are put away for the day. The three-course meal, served family-style on a long sugar-pine table, lends itself well to meeting new folk, exchanging information, and sharing the Oregon wine you brought or they sell. By popular demand Sharon and Pat Lee have published the cookbooks *Thyme and the River* and its sequel, *Thyme and the River Too.*

Dining in the Umpqua Region

ELKTON
TOMASELLI'S PASTRY MILL AND CAFÉ
541-584-2855 or 888-285-7834
14836 Highway 38
www.tomasellispastrymill.com
Open: Daily 6 A.M.–8 P.M.
Price: Moderate
Credit Cards: Yes
Special Features: Destination dining or takeaway, hand crafted pastries and bread, Friday night dinners in summer, vegetarian options, local produce for sale during farmer's market season, wine section with local and Italian selections, gourmet cheeses

Owners Marty and Dayna Tomaselli have been serving "good food, not fast food" with a side sense of humor and congeniality in their crowded quarters on the main drag of Elkton for almost 30 years. Breakfast-like foods: three-egg omelets, biscuits or taters and with sausage gravy (good grease loading before wine tasting), or whole-wheat buttermilk pancakes, to name a few. Lunches include—and also depart from—the norm, with deli or grilled sandwiches, burgers made from local grass-fed beef, and a half-dozen sumptuous salads. Dinner entrées lean toward Italian cuisine (no surprise), with fresh, handmade pasta coming from a nearby city. Plan to stay awhile for a sit-down meal, or do as we did: Order food to go, visit a winery, and come back for pickup. Tomaselli's also makes fabulous pizzas from scratch using their own dough.

ROSEBURG
ANTHONY'S ITALIAN CAFÉ
541-229-2233
www.anthonysitalinacafe.com
500 SE Cass Street, Suite 120
Open: Tues.–Fri. 11–9, Sat. 12:30–9
Price: Moderate
Credit Cards: Yes
Special Features: Anthony's Bella Serra wine bar behind the café (Thurs.–Sat. 8 P.M.-midnight), live music that runs the gamut, including classical guitar and violin

Ay, Paisan! Anthony's takes care of its own when it comes to Oregon wine, and so nearly every local winery is represented in this perky restaurant. Anthony's stocks more than 55 wines, and the number continues to grow. Popular dishes are such home-style Italian favorites as chicken, veal or eggplant parmigiana, lasagna, and shrimp scampi. Bella Serra, a separate wine bar behind Anthony's, is a great place to pop a cork with friends. The wine bar has retail sales with discounts for bottles to go.

MARK V GRILL & BAR

541-229-6275
563 SE Main Street
Open: Mon.–Thurs. 11 A.M.–10 P.M.,
Fri.–Sat. 7:30 A.M.–midnight, Sun. 7:30
A.M.–9 P.M.
Price: Moderate to expensive
Credit Cards: Yes
Special Features: Have omelets your way
Sat. and Sun. mornings – five variations for
$5 or build your own.

The Mark V is known for such over-the-
top tapas as blackened ahi tuna, prosciutto-
wrapped asparagus, and parmesan cod.
Lunch soups, dressings, and sauces are
made from scratch, and there are daily
lunch and dinner specials. The prime-
beef rib eye, shrimp pompadour, and
chicken alfredo are crowd-pleasers as well.
Coming soon to the menu: Umpqua Valley
lamb. As for wine, the majority is local.
You'll find some of the region's favorites,
including the Palotai's Bull's Blood,
Girardet's Baco Noir and Riesling, and
Melrose's Pinot Gris.

ROSEBURG STATION PUB & BREWERY

541-672-1934
www.mcmenamins.com
700 SE Sheridan Street
Open: Mon.–Thurs. 11–11, Fri.–Sat. 11
A.M.–midnight, Sun. 11 A.M.–10 P.M.
Price: Inexpensive to moderate
Credit Cards: Yes
Special Features: Patio seating

The McMenamins' tentacles have reached
all the way from the Portland area to
Roseburg. And that's a good thing. The
entrepreneurial and mercurial brothers,
along with a cast of hundreds, have converted the old Southern Pacific railroad
depot into a lively nightspot serving their
wine and microbrews. The menu is classic
pub fare, but there are thoughtful touches.
For instance, the beef is natural and hor-

mone-free. Don't forget a side of hand-cut
fries to complete the meal.

OAKLAND
TOLLY'S RESTAURANT

541-459-3796
115 Locust Street
www.tollys-restaurant.com
Open: Sun.–Thurs. 11–3, Fri.–Sat. 11–8
Price: Moderate to expensive
Credit Cards: Yes
Special Features: Vintage soda fountain,
Umpqua Valley Winegrowers Association
dinners, adjacent antiques store

Tolly's, a calling card for a town once known
for its turkeys, is a major force and anchor
business for this agricultural community of
about one thousand. The current owners,
Myra Plant and chef Jeff Parker, had been
visiting for about 30 years. They jumped at
the chance to simplify and slow their lives
down a notch when they found the brick
landmark for sale. They kept the soda fountain, where they serve hand-scooped cold
classics such as floats, splits, and sundaes
made from Umpqua ice cream. A brick wall
with an open section separates the dining
room, where you can enjoy burgers made
from Oregon grass-fed beef, salads, soups,
and seafood. Dinner entrées are creatively
continental, headlined by a "Mountain Man
USDA Prime" bone-in rib eye that weighs a
hefty 24 ounces. All of the meat is hormone-free, grass-fed, or free-range, and
all wines are from Oregon—mostly the
Umpqua Valley.

CANYONVILLE
CAMAS ROOM

800-548-8461
www.sevenfeathers.com
146 Chief Miwaleta Lane
Open: Tues.–Sun. 5:30–10, Sun.
10:30–2:30 (brunch)
Price: Moderate
Credit Cards: Yes
Special Features: Gambling 24/7, family

Tolly's Restaurant, in Oakland, has a 1910 soda fountain.   Courtesy Tolly's Restaurant

dining at Creekside Restaurant, buffet at Cow Creek Restaurant, sports bar

If you're like us, acres of blacktop parking, windowless buildings, and cigarette smoke filters are not calling you to "Eat here." But it's easy to overlook these few deterrents and actually find an elegant dining experience at the Camas Room. Begin your meal with a taste of the Pacific by choosing from several seafood appetizers, such as a trio of Northwest oysters on the half shell or steamers in a Sauvignon Blanc butter sauce. Salads range from Caesar to Caprese and could be meal enough. But more is in store: roasted Oregon lamb, salmon fillet with blackberry vodka cream, all-natural New York steak with a dollop of Roquefort-horseradish butter, or just roll on to dessert. Odds are, whatever you are dealt, you'll be pleasantly surprised and satisfied.

Attractions in the Umpqua Region

The **Douglas County Museum** (541-957-7007, 123 Museum Dr.) explores the 150-year history of the Umpqua region through more than 7,500 items—the most in the state. Fifteen miles north of Roseburg, the town of **Oakland** was the first in Oregon to establish a historic district. With more than 80 structures at least 130 years old, the entire community made the National Register of Historic Places in 1979.

Lions and tigers and bears in Douglas County? Oh, my! **Wildlife Safari** (541-679-6761, 1790 Safari Rd.) in Winston is a 600-acre drive-through wild-animal park with more than 500 exotic critters from around the globe. Like much of western Oregon, the Roseburg area has **covered bridges**—seven of them. Get a map from the Roseburg Visitors and Convention Bureau (541-672-9731, 410 SE Spruce St.) for a self-guided tour. In Canyonville, the **Pioneer Indian Museum** (541-839-4845, 421 West Fifth St.) features Indian history in the South Umpqua Valley.

Relax after a day of wine touring at the free **Summer Concert Series** (541-677-1708) at 6 P.M. every Tuesday at Roseburg's Stewart Park. Past performers have included the Dixie Chicks and Lyle Lovett.

Recreation in the Umpqua Region

This is hook-and-bullet country, famed for its salmon, steelhead, trout, and smallmouth bass **fishing** on the Umpqua River. The North Umpqua is a blue-ribbon trout stream, but for a unique twist, try casting a dry fly to the ravenous smallmouth bass on the main Umpqua near Elkton. Fishermen have learned to share the North Umpqua with **whitewater rafting** enthusiasts who covet the challenging but forgiving Class III rapids. Nine commercial outfitters offer one-day trips on this river, protected under the National Wild and Scenic Rivers system.

For the consummate **hiking, mountain biking,** or **horseback riding** experience, check out the 79-mile **North Umpqua Trail** (541-440-4930) on the Umpqua National Forest. This gorgeous trail follows the river starting at Stillwater east of Roseburg and is broken into segments.

Bring your sticks for year-round golfing at one of the Roseburg area's three public courses: the woodsy **Myrtle Creek** (888-869-7863, 1316 Fairway Dr.), **Umpqua** (541-459-4422, 1919 Recreation Ln., Sutherlin), or the city's course at **Stewart Park** (541-672-7701, 900 SE Douglas Ave.).

Shopping in the Umpqua Region

Kruse Farms (541-672-5697, 532 Melrose Rd.) is a Roseburg shopping extravaganza offering local produce, dried fruits and nuts, bakery goods, house plants, Umpqua Valley lamb and other local meats, and U-pick fruits and vegetables.

Information

Roseburg Visitors and Convention Bureau, 541-672-9731 or 800-444-9584, 410 SE
  Spruce St., www.visitroseburg.com
Roseburg Area Chamber of Commerce, 541-672-2648, 410 SE Spruce St., www.rose
  burgareachamber.org
Umpqua National Forest, 541-672-6601, 2900 NW Stewart Pkwy.
Oregon Wine Country Tours, 541-677-1906, 5043 Melqua Rd., www.oregonwinecountry
  tours.com

Grants Pass and Illinois Valley Area (Applegate Valley and Illinois Valley AVAs)

Much like Roseburg some 60 miles to the north on I-5, Grants Pass has long been a tough town that first cut its teeth first on the railroad, shifted to gold mining, and finally hosted a booming timber industry. And, much like Roseburg, this pleasant community of 23,000 in a broad bowl has undergone a renaissance as tourists discover a comfortable climate, prolific outdoor recreation and solitude.

Unlike Roseburg, however, Grants Pass has had one enormous advantage for its economic makeover: a world-famous and mighty river. For more than a century, the Rogue has lured fishermen from across the globe, all with visions of monster sea-run Chinook salmon dancing in their heads. For a half-century, it has also been a Mecca for whitewater rafting enthusiasts who know every one of its 88 rapids by name. The legendary Western writer Zane Grey elevated the river to mystical status; rafters pass his cabin in the canyon,

History and charm are woven into a memorable stay at Weasku Inn.   Courtesy Country House Inns

downstream from Grants Pass. The Rogue was among the first rivers in the country to be included in the National Wild and Scenic Rivers Act of 1968.

The catch phrase for Grants Pass—named for the former Civil War general and president—is "It's the Climate." Today, tourism is the predominant industry, thanks not only to the Rogue but also to the wineries that have risen from the rich soils of the Applegate and Illinois valleys to the south and southwest.

Wineries in the Grants Pass Area (Applegate Valley AVA)

One of Oregon's newest AVAs is also home to the state's oldest winery. It was here in 1860 that an adventurous photographer named Peter Britt opened Valley View Winery in Jacksonville, just west of Medford in the Siskiyou Mountain foothills.

For 59 years, virtually right up until his death, Britt produced wines in the moderate climes of the Applegate, a 50-mile south-to-north valley that starts near the California border. Prohibition put a halt to further development of the industry in Oregon and elsewhere, but they reopened for business in the early 1970s, when 26 acres were planted in Pinot Noir, Chardonnay, Gewürztraminer, Merlot, and Cabernet Sauvignon, including 14 acres on the old Valley View site.

The route begins just south of Grants Pass on the Applegate Trail. Follow OR 238 toward Jacksonville and Medford.

GRANTS PASS
BRIDGEVIEW VINEYARDS
541-846-1039
www.bridgeviewwine.com
16995 North Applegate Road
Tasting Room: May–Sept., daily 11–5;
Mar.–May and Sept.–Nov., Sat.–Sun. 11–5
Fee: Complimentary

This is a satellite location for Bridgeview
Vineyards. For more information, see
Bridgeview Winery under Wineries in the
Illinois Valley.

SOLORO VINEYARD
541-862-2693
9110 North Applegate Road
Tasting Room: Apr.–Dec., Sat.–Sun. 1–5,
and by appointment
Fee: Complimentary
Owners: Tim and June Navarro
Winemaker: Linda Donavan and Steve
Anderson
Wines: Grenache Noir, Marsanne,
Roussanne, Syrah, red and white blends
Cases: 350
Special Features: Picnic area

Soloro is Catalan for "Sun Gold," an apt
description for the sun-drenched hillside
where the Navarros raised cattle until 2005.
It's also appropriate for the golden glow in
the tasting room. The neighborhood's
newest winery is laid-back and humble,
with friendly dogs providing atmosphere.
The winery's first release was in 2007.
Among their showcase wines is a white
Rhône blend of Viognier, Marsanne, and
Roussanne. Solid gold.

WOOLDRIDGE CREEK WINERY
541-846-6364
www.wcwinery.com
818 Slagle Creek Road
Tasting Room: Sat.–Sun. 11–5, and by
appointment
Fee: Complimentary for two wines, $5 for
additional flight of four

Owners: Ted and Mary Warrick, Greg
Paneitz, and Kara Olmo
Winemaker: Greg Paneitz and Kara Olmo
Wines: Chardonnay, Gewürztraminer,
Zinfandel, Cabernet Sauvignon, Syrah, red
and white blends, port-style and dessert
wines
Cases: 2,500
Special Features: Picnic area, some wines
available only to club members

Former airline industry employees Ted and
Mary Warrick took off on a new career path
in 1978 when they bought 18 acres within
view of the Applegate River. Over time,
they've expanded to 56 planted acres with
12 varietals. Their expertise in tending to
the vines is complemented nicely by the
winemaking skills of Paneitz and Olmo,
who met doing oenology work at Fresno
State University. With cheerful Adirondack
chairs on the lawn and a picnic area fre-
quented by resident wildlife, Wooldridge is
hardly pretentious. The Warricks might
have the most creative deterrent to bears
and other wildlife munching on the grapes
in the fall: They play AM talk radio through
the night in the vineyard.

SCHMIDT FAMILY VINEYARDS
541-846-9985
www.sfvineyards.com
320 Kubli Road
Tasting Room: May–Dec., daily 12–5;
Jan.–Apr., Fri.–Sun. 12–5
Fee: $5, waived with purchase
Owners: Cal and Judy Schmidt
Winemaker: Bryan Wilson
Wines: Albariño, Chardonnay,
Gewürztraminer, Pinot Gris, Sauvignon
Blanc, Cabernet Franc, Merlot, Zinfandel,
red blends
Cases: 1,700
Special Features: Picnic grounds, weddings,
special events

Picture Steinbeck's *Grapes of Wrath*, only
with wheelbarrows of money. An inviting,

architecturally stunning Sonoma-lux lodge beckons you to relax and linger a while at the 26-acre Schmidt Family Vineyards. An appealing tasting room with Cali-Northwest warmth is surrounded by a large patio, thoughtful landscaping, dozens of young trees, and a pond—all traversed by a gravel pathway with a Siskiyou Mountain backdrop. *Grapes of Wrath*-like images are part of the branding, with paintings of vintage farmers working the fields. The concept is no surprise given that owner Cal Schmidt grew up on a Kansas wheat farm. The winery makes a popular red blend called Soulea, a mix of Cabernet Sauvignon, Merlot, and Syrah.

TROON VINEYARD

541-846-9900
www.troonvineyard.com
1475 Kubli Road
Tasting Room: Daily 11–5
Fee: $5 for five wines, refunded with six-bottle purchase
Owner: Martin family
Winemaker: Herb Quady
Wines: Riesling, Chardonnay, Viognier, rosé, Cabernet Franc, Cabernet Sauvignon, Meritage, Merlot, Syrah, Zinfandel, red and white blends, port-style wine
Cases: 9,000
Special Features: Hors d'oeuvres with wine tasting, picnic areas, summer brunches, winemaker dinners, cooking classes, additional tasting room in Carlton

The name Dick Troon is synonymous with the genesis of southern Oregon's wine industry. The cantankerous former river guide, who first planted wine grapes on this breathtaking knoll in 1972, remains so revered that today he is still called "Mr. Troon." As he did with the grapes he nurtured for three decades, Troon hand-selected the Martin family to carry on his tradition of environmentally friendly wine-making, and the new owners have been

taking it to the next level since 2003. Starting with a spectacular tasting room, Troon has the look of a European villa, a multibuilding complex with all the contemporary accoutrements you can imagine. They have hospitality down pat as well: Cheerful staffers greet you at the door and direct you to bistro tables or a long bar next to a concave picture window looking out on 32 acres of lush vineyards. Outside you'll find a fire oven, five-tiered fountain, and bocce court. And the Martins aren't finished yet: They are the first vineyard in the Northwest to plant a Corsican varietal called Verentino. Of the 25 wines Herb Quady makes for Troon, one of the hottest sellers is the Druid's Fluid—a red blend that, ironically, is the result of a mistake. As a tribute to the still-busy Mr. Troon, Quady produces a blend called River Guide Red.

Troon offers a fountain of afternoon tasting delights.
M. Kim Lewis

ROSELLA'S VINEYARD

541-846-6372
www.rosellasvineyard.com
184 Missouri Flats Road
Tasting Room: Thurs.–Mon. 11–5, and by appointment
Fee: Complimentary
Owners: Rex and Sandy Garouette
Winemaker: Rex Garouette
Wines: Chardonnay, Cabernet Sauvignon, Merlot, Zinfandel, red and white blends
Cases: 600
Special Features: Winery tours

In a well-worn beach-style house that looks as if it came from Santa Cruz—where owner Rex Garouette once was involved in college oenology courses—you'll find Rex or Sandy pouring their grog and spinning a yarn or two. The winery is on the opposite end of pretension and a stark contrast to its neighbors, the Schmidts. Garouette is a chatty sort who describes himself as the "chief cook and bottle washer."

APPLEGATE RED WINERY

541-846-9557
www.applegatered.com
222 Missouri Flats Road
Tasting Room: Sat.–Sun. 12–6
Fee: Complimentary for three wines
Owners: Ferreira family
Wines: Cabernet Franc, Cabernet Sauvignon, Merlot, Syrah
Cases: 900
Special Features: Picnic pavilion, invitation-only wine club

It's hard to miss the watermelon/fuchsia tinted tasting room, deck, miniature aviary, and various outbuildings, but the cute Sicilian donkeys and squawking birds will let you know for certain you've arrived at Frank Ferreira's aloha kingdom. Known through the valley as a "naturalist," Frank didn't believe in any manipulation in the vineyard or the winery. He sold most of his grapes, keeping enough to experiment with in his tasting room and provide for a few nearby restaurants. His signature wine is the Applegate Red, comprised of equal parts Cab Franc, Cab Sauvignon, Merlot, and Syrah. Sadly, Frank died in October 2008, leaving the future of Applegate Red uncertain. In early 2010, the winery was for sale.

Williams
PLAISANCE RANCH

541-846-7175
www.plaisanceranch.com
16955 Water Gap Road
Tasting Room: Wed.–Sun. 2–6, and by appointment
Fee: Complimentary
Owners: Joe and Suzi Ginet
Winemaker: Joe Ginet
Wines: Pinot Noir, Syrah, Cabernet Sauvignon, Tempranillo, Cabernet Franc, Malbec, Mondeuse, Mourvèdre, Petite Sirah
Cases: 500
Special Features: Plaisance organic beef and wines available at farmer's markets in Ashland, Medford, and Grants Pass

Winemaker Joe Ginet describes himself as "winemaker and cow boss," and for good reason. Plaisance is a working ranch where USDA-certified organic beef and organic hay are raised. They also graft 25,000 vines a year. The most interesting grape is Mondeuse Noire, a parent of Syrah that Ginet's grandfather brought from Savoie, France, in 1898 (Plaisance has been a working ranch since 1858). The Mondeuse Noire is dark and highly acidic, which helps with aging. The tasting room is a converted dairy barn that Suzi Ginet describes as "more of the rustic experience" you'd expect at a secluded cattle ranch. Plaisance is tucked into the end of a pastoral valley and worth every mile of the drive.

Wineries in the Illinois Valley (Illinois Valley AVA)

Call it Willamette Valley Lite. The Illinois Valley's cool marine climate, with 60 inches of annual rain punctuated by warm and dry summer days, enables the vintners in this remote, scenic region to produce the same wines as their more renowned brethren 300 miles to the north.

Still, though Bridgeview Vineyards and its Blue Moon label are immensely popular, this remains a relatively undiscovered area. Indeed, Foris Vineyards Winery owner Ted Gerber was only half-joking when he called one of his wines "Fly Over Red," a playful tweak at wine snobs who look down—literally—upon southern Oregon wineries from their jets as they dash between the Willamette and Napa valleys.

There's only one route here: Take US 199 southwest from Grants Pass. You'll come to Selma and Deer Creek Vineyards about 20 miles from town.

SELMA
DEER CREEK VINEYARDS
541-597-4226
www.deercreekvineyards.com
2680 Deer Creek Road
Tasting Room: Summer, daily 11–5; winter, by appointment
Fee: Complimentary
Owner: Gary Garnett
Winemaker: Bryan Wilson
Wines: Chardonnay, Pinot Gris, Pinot Noir
Cases: 8,000
Special Features: Picnic area, gift shop

Though Foris Winery conducts Deer Creek's crushing, all of the wines are strictly from the winery's south-facing vineyard. The sweeping views include two ponds from the tasting room and gift shop. The Garnetts winter in Arizona, but tours of the winery are still available from staff by appointment. In the fall of 2009, the Garnetts were trying to sell their picturesque seventy-acre ranch, including forty acres planted in wine grapes.

CAVE JUNCTION
WINDRIDGE VINEYARD
541-592-5333
www.windridgevineyard.com
2789 Holland Loop Road
Tasting Room: May, Sat.–Sun. 11–5; June–Sept., Wed.–Sun. 11–5; Nov., Sat.–Sun. 11–5; and by appointment

Fee: Complimentary
Owners: Terry and Cate Bendock
Winemaker: Terry Bendock
Wines: Pinot Blanc, Pinot Noir
Cases: 200
Special Features: Picnic area, gift boxes

Pinot Noir and southern Oregon usually aren't mentioned in the same breath, but it's a great fit in this temperate area just a few ridges away from the Pacific. The wines are made under the Bendock Estate label from a vineyard planted on the historic Fort Briggs property. The Bendocks came from Alaska and are now members of the Rogue Appellation Garagiste Society (RAGS), a group of small wineries that celebrate good wine and good food. (*Garagistes* are small producers who literally started making wine in their garages.) The Bendocks also raise organic beef on their 50-acre ranch and orchard, where the Pinot was planted in 1989. Windridge has exclusively produced Pinot Noir, but will release its first Pinot Blanc in the fall of 2010.

BRIDGEVIEW VINEYARDS & WINERY
541-592-4688
www.bridgeviewwine.com
4210 Holland Loop Road
Tasting Room: Daily 11–5
Fee: Complimentary
Owners: Bob and Lelo Kerivan
Winemaker: René Eichmann

Bridgeview is as famous for its Blue Moon Riesling bottle as it is for the wine inside. Brian Prectel

Wines: Gewürztraminer, Riesling, Pinot Gris, Viognier, rosé, Cabernet Sauvignon, Merlot, Pinot Noir, Syrah, early Muscat,
Cases: 85,000
Special Features: Gift shop, picnic area, additional tasting room in the Applegate Valley See listing under Wineries in the Grants Pass area

The Illinois Valley site is the home winery for Bridgeview, which is renowned nationally for its Blue Moon Riesling in a cobalt blue bottle. All Blue Moon wines are $10 or less, and the bottles have become collectors' items. The tasting room is in a large, red hay barn surrounded by 80 acres of vineyards. Combine their easy-drinking wines with a lake and gardens on the grounds, and you can see why Bridgeview is on the docket for just about everybody who passes through this remote neck of the woods.

FORIS VINEYARDS WINERY
541-592-3752 or 800-843-6747
www.foriswine.com
654 Kendall Road
Tasting Room: Daily 11–5, except major holidays
Fee: Complimentary
Owners: Ted and Teresa Gerber
Winemaker: Bryan Wilson
Wines: Chardonnay, Pinot Gris, Pinot Blanc, Gewürztraminer, Riesling, Muscat, Gamay Noir, Pinot Noir
Cases: 55,000
Special Features: Picnic area

Oregon's southernmost winery is one of its oldest and features perhaps the top tongue-in-cheek name for a wine in the state. Fly Over Red is quite popular, suggesting that fewer wine fanatics are flying over southern Oregon's wineries these days. Foris is Latin for "outdoors"—where the first vineyards were planted in 1974. Foris makes some other noteworthy wines, including a 2006 Pinot Noir that the *Wall Street Journal* dubbed Oregon's best buy that year.

Lodging in the Grants Pass and Illinois Valley Areas

GRANTS PASS
THE LODGE AT RIVERSIDE
877-955-0600 or 541-955-0600
www.thelodgeatriverside.com
955 SE Seventh Street
Rates: $125–$325
Special Features: Outdoor pool and spa on banks of Rogue River, plush bedding

Color us simple, but when a bright and welcoming face says, "We've been expecting

It's hard to miss Bridgeview's big, red barn tasting room in the Applegate Valley. Angela Mattey

The Lodge at Riverside provides great access to southern Oregon wine country. Courtesy Country House Inns

you," they have our business. The Lodge at Riverside is adjacent to the OR 99 bridge on the banks of the Rogue River, sporting mature oaks, pines, and aspen that turn golden in the fall. You'll find contemporary comfort in 33 oversized, renovated rooms, most of which have private decks for watching the lazy stretch of river. Traffic noise is surprisingly light. The lodge has a wine reception from 4:30 to 7 nightly, and has an extended continental breakfast served in a separate room or on an outside patio.

THE RIVERSIDE INN
800-334-4567 or 541-476-6873
www.riverside-inn.com
986 SW Sixth Street
Rates: $125–149
Special Features: Pool and spa

This traditional motel is along the Rogue River minutes from city center. The Riverside has small touches that make it feel special. There are 63 rooms with pri-

vate balconies, some with fireplaces. A continental breakfast with fruit, yogurt, and breads is included. The busy Hellgate Jetboats boarding docks are between the inn and the river.

WEASKU INN
800-493-2758 or 541-471-8000
www.weasku.com
5560 Rogue River Highway
Rates: $199–$329
Special Features: Wine tasting every evening from 4 to 7

Pronounced "We ask you in," the Weasku began in 1924 as a destination Rogue River fishing lodge comprised of canvas "tent cabins" for a $1 a day or $6 a week. Thanks to the writings of frequent guest Zane Grey, the inn quickly rose to legendary status with such luminary guests as President Hoover, Gabby Hayes, Walt Disney, and Clark Gable. Gable was a regular, often with his wife, Carol Lombard, and the story goes

The Riverside Lodge in Grants Pass has a pool and overlooks the Rogue River. Courtesy Country House Inns

that the star spent three weeks in a room upstairs after her death in a plane crash. Weasku's charm has persisted through the renovations and remodeling of this compact complex on the river's bank. The original small fishing cabins were razed in the '80s and new cabins with fireplaces and private decks were constructed. The main lodge, which has aged gracefully, has five guest rooms with private baths. Swap fish tales, sip wine, and munch on freshly baked chocolate chip cookies every evening, then awaken to an expansive continental breakfast.

TAKILMA

OUT 'N' ABOUT TREEHOUSE TREESORT

Owners: Michael and Peggy Garnier
541-592-2208
www.treehouses.com
300 Page Creek Road
Rates: $120–250
Special Features: Swimming pool and bathhouse, cooking and barbecue pavilion, tree house building classes

If you're looking to branch out in your overnight experiences, you'll find plentree to like about Out 'N' About—which might be more aptly named Up 'N' Away. In what could pass for a compound for Robin Hood and his Merry Men, you can get your vacation off the ground in one of 15 lodging choices. Included is our favorite, the Forestree, which hugs the trunk of a Douglas fir some 35 feet off the ground. It's accessible only by a swinging rope bridge, and yet has a toilet, sink (affixed to the tree), and a hoist for gear. We spent a dreamy night in the treetops one New Year's Eve. Of course, if heights frighten you, Out 'N' About also has more traditional cabins on terra firma.

Dining in the Grants Pass and Illinois Valley Areas

GRANTS PASS

BLONDIES' BISTRO

541-479-0420
www.blondiesbistro.com
226 SW G Street
Open: Daily 11–8; seasonal hours apply

Price: Moderate
Credit Cards: Yes
Special Features: separate bar, live music throughout the week, late-night dining in summer

Jill Bini and Bobbi Best spent a lot of time, money, and sweat creating the kind of place you wouldn't expect to find in Grants Pass. Think fern bar. The bistro, which is in a strip mall, is wrapped in an array of warm hues and dark wood accents, with walls displaying dramatic art and a stained concrete floor with corresponding hanging track lights. While the appetizers are not typical—Portuguese clams, spiced lamb cutlets, eggplant hummus—the salads are, but still done well. Dinner entrées hit on steak, chicken, and seafood with enhanced flavors that take your palate to other parts of the world. But the best item at Blondies' is the crepes. They come sweet or savory, with many combos of fillings. There is a wonderful selection of Oregon wines, with the spotlight on the Applegate Valley.

THE LAUGHING CLAM

541-479-1110
www.thelaughingclam.com
12 SW G Street
Open: Mon.–Thurs. 11–9, Fri.–Sat. 11 A.M.–10 P.M.
Price: Moderate
Credit Cards: Yes
Special Features: Live music Fri. and Sat. nights with no cover charge

Rock and roll, rough and raucous living, and some good ol' Oregon grub and grog—it's all at The Laughing Clam. It's the kind of place where you can slurp oyster shooters, chow down on chowder, or bite into a sloppy burger without worrying about offending your neighbor. The Laughing Clam is not just about the seafood; you'll also find sandwiches, pastas, and steak to please. It's loud and lively, with communal tables, booths, and the perfect bar to belly

up to for a glass of Druid's Fluid or River Guide White from Troon.

ONE FIFTEEN BROILER

541-474-7115
www.onefifteenbroiler.com
115 NW D Street
Open: Mon.–Fri. 11–3, Mon.–Sat. 5–9
Price: Moderate to expensive
Credit Cards: Yes
Special Features: New York cheesecake from the local Bluestone Bakery

It's a steakhouse with a definite New York style. We love the classic diner look, martini-shaker collection, and eclectic Big Apple memorabilia squeezed as snugly into the interior as their crab is stuffed into mushrooms. The hand-cut steaks from a small ranch in Washington reign supreme, but the seafood and pasta dishes certainly hold their own. For many years, the Musselman family has been dishing up some of their secret recipes, such as creamed spinach, tiramisu, and a tasty Caesar that doesn't hold the anchovies. You can find five or six Oregon wines by the glass, about a dozen labels of Pinot, and 10 or so other Oregon choices.

THE RIVER'S EDGE

541-479-3938
www.riversedgerestaurant.net
1936 Rogue River Highway
Open: Mon.–Sat. 11–3 and 5 P.M.–close; summer, Sun.–Thurs. 11–3 and 4–9, Fri.–Sat. 11–3 and 4–10
Price: Expensive
Credit Cards: Yes
Special Features: Two dining decks overlooking the Rogue, private room for groups

Elegance and blue jeans mesh at The River's Edge, which describes its food as "classic Pacific cuisine." The 36 menu choices pull from states and countries on both sides of the Pacific Ocean and could be called Or-Cali-Mex-Haw-Asian fusion.

This presents some interesting options: macadamia-crusted halibut, Monterey Bay calamari, Baja fish tacos, Hawaiian baby-back ribs, and teriyaki chicken or fish on sticky rice. Beef lovers, never fear: You can order a burger (Kobe, too) or a number of scintillating steaks. The restaurant has a sigh-provoking setting with minimal clutter, clean lines, and a water wall so soothing you'll want to stay a while.

SUMMER JO'S

541-476-6882
www.summerjos.com
2315 Upper River Road Loop
Open: Fri.–Sun. 9:30–2 and 5–8:30
Price: Expensive
Credit Cards: Yes
Special Features: Crops destined for upcoming menu are visible from restaurant windows; adjacent bakery

Summer Jo's is a working farm, orchard, produce stand, events facility, and restaurant just outside busy Grants Pass. In the style and shadow of Alice Waters, the concept here is basic: keep it simple, seasonal, and sensational. Watch the chef and her assistants prepare your food in the narrow open kitchen while the bees buzz, leaves drop, or infrequent snow drifts outside the farmhouse windows. Jo's grows its own ingredients, floral arrangements, and seasonings, bakes its own bread, and creates special menus for holidays. It's a busy place. Local wine is served and there is a special selection of Oregon offerings by the glass or bottle.

TAPROCK NORTHWEST GRILL

541-955-5998
www.taprock.com
971 SE Sixth Street
Open: Sun.–Thurs. 7 A.M.–9 P.M., Fri.–Sat. 7 A.M.–10 P.M.
Price: Moderate
Credit Cards: Yes
Special Features: Deck on the banks of the Rogue River

Dare we say, Grants Pass has long been void of cultural dining experiences but is finally ready to join the foodie circuit. The TapRock Grill embraces what Oregonians and visitors consider important: local and regional ingredients in breakfast, lunch, and dinner plates, scenic views, and Northwest hospitality. The grill is in a ginormous, multilevel timber-framed building with gorgeous grounds for strolling. The park-like setting is a gift to the city from owner and local banker Brady Adams, who spent three years and millions of dollars creating a special place. The intricately detailed hand-carved doors, bars, fixtures, etched stainless steel kitchen doors, mounted wildlife, and tip of the musket to Lewis and Clark give the restaurant a museum feel. The fare is definitely above average, with reasonable pricing. Dungeness crab dip, crispy fried veggies with artisan cheese, halibut fish tacos, a signature clam chowder, and the heart-stopping bison burger with Rogue Creamery blue cheese will stave off the brawniest of appetites. If weather permits, be sure to sit on the deck and enjoy watching ducks playing in the Rogue.

Attractions in the Grants Pass and Illinois Valley Area

The driest way to experience the Rogue River is on one of the famed jetboats that once delivered mail into the wilderness. **Hellgate Jetboat Excursions** (541-479-7204 or 800-648-4874, www.hellgate.com) offers two- to five-hour trips on the Rogue from May through September for $33–58.

Wildlife lovers won't want to miss the **Wildlife Images and Rehabilitation Center** (541-476-0222) in the nearby town of Merlin. Injured or orphaned animals from across the country are brought here to recuperate; call for tours. While visiting Wildlife Images, include a stop at **Pottsville** (541-476-7319), a community near Merlin that's a museum unto itself. Pottsville offers tours of its actual museum plus all of the outdoor exhibits that offer a snapshot of Oregon history. For such a little town, Merlin's a busy place. It also features the **Haines Apple Tree**, which was planted around 1853 and is the second-oldest apple tree in the state.

Speaking of wildlife, wolves were wiped out in this part of the state nearly a century ago, but you can see them live at the **Howling Acres Wolf Sanctuary** (541-846-8962, 555 Davidson Rd.) in Williams, about a half-hour south of Grants Pass in the rugged Siskiyou Mountains.

The **Applegate Interpretive Center** (541-472-8545) in Sunny Valley offers a peek into the area's rich pioneer history, especially gold mining. A unique stop for the art-inclined is **The Glass Forge** (541-955-0815, 501 SW G St.), which fashions Venetian-style wine glasses. The **Josephine County Historical Society** (541-479-7827, 512 SW Fifth St.) operates a museum and offers tours every Tuesday through Saturday at the historic **Schmidt House**.

A strange experience is **The House of Mystery** (541-855-1543, 4303 Sardine Creek L Ford Rd.), otherwise known as the Oregon Vortex, just south of Grants Pass in Gold Hill. Its claim to fame is the inability for visitors to stand upright.

You don't have to be a spelunker to appreciate the **Oregon Caves National Monument** (541-592-2100), about 50 miles south of Grants Pass, but check your claustrophobia at the door. The highlight at the monument, which celebrated its 100th year in 2009, is a lengthy and moderately strenuous walk through a marble cave where the temperature remains a constant 41 degrees. On the way to or from the cave, visit the **Kerbyville Museum** (541-592-2076) in Kerby to get a turn-of-the-century experience highlighting pioneer exhibits and local Native American artifacts.

If you're coming from Roseburg, take a few minutes to duck off I-5 to stretch your legs at the **Wolf Creek Inn** (541-866-2474, 100 Front St.). The historic stagecoach stop was built in 1885 as a luxury hotel for weary travelers; it's now a bed-and-breakfast and restaurant. Several of the fruit trees planted at the time are still alive and producing.

Recreation in the Grants Pass and Illinois Valley Area

Any conversation about recreation in the Grants Pass area starts with the Rogue. Rafters, kayakers, and tubers can enjoy modest day-trip thrills on stretches above and below town. The serious **whitewater rafting** action begins just below the little store and restaurant at Galice, which seems as busy as a metro airport on summer days. No fewer than two dozen guide services offer trips; a permit from the Bureau of Land Management is required for private trips.

There are few locals who don't go **hunting** and **fishing** in these parts, especially if the quarry is a trophy elk or a Rogue salmon or steelhead. Lake Selmac, in the Illinois Valley, is considered the state's top bass fishery. The Rogue is also a favorite for **hiking**. The **Rogue River Trail** follows the north side of the river and includes Zane Grey's cabin; a two-mile trail on the south side of the river ends at Rainie Falls, where you can watch salmon migrate upstream and daring kayakers migrate downstream. Another terrific hike in the works is the **Rogue River Recreational Corridor and Greenway** (541-582-1112), which will connect Grants Pass to Ashland and be geared to **cycling** as well.

Southern Oregon's wine country sets a slower pace.   Courtesy Weasku Inn

The Rogue Valley offers a little bit of everything when it comes to golf, ranging from flat nine-hole courses with few hazards to challenging 18 holes with undulating terrain. The two 18-hole courses are **Dutcher Creek** (541-474-2188, 4611 Upper River Rd.) and the semi-private **Grants Pass Golf Club** (541-476-0840, 230 Espey Rd.).

Winter here generally consists of rain and the occasional snowstorm, but snow enthusiasts will find an outlet at the **Page Mountain Sno-Park** southeast of Cave Junction. Cross-country skiing, snowmobiling, and sledding seem to live in harmony here.

Shopping in the Grants Pass and Illinois Valley Area

ShopRiverRock (541-956-5260, 966 SW Sixth St.), upstairs in Hellgate, has 4,000 square feet of gifts and home decor, a wine bar with regional wines, and a large selection of Vera Bradley, Pandora, and Brighton. The **Outdoor Growers Market** (541-476-5375, Fourth and F Sts.) takes place every Saturday from March through Thanksgiving, highlighting local produce and crafts.

Wine Shopping in the Grants Pass and Illinois Valley Area

Elegance (541-476-0570, 321 SE Sixth St.) sells wine, craft beers, gourmet foods, cheeses, and chocolate next to vintage jewelry, antiques, and collectibles; their motto is "Stuff Is Us." On art nights, the first Friday of the month, wines are usually open and tastes are complimentary. Another attractive shop is **Oregon Outpost** (541-474-2918, 137 SW G St.), which offers terrific picnic baskets with Oregon wine and food. The Outpost also has clothing, wood crafts, and locally made gifts. Every first Friday, an Oregon winery sets up for sampling.

Information

Grants Pass Visitors and Convention Bureau, 541-476-5510, 1995 NW Vine St.,
www.visitgrantspass.org
Southern Oregon Winery Association, www.sorwa.org.
Josephine County Historical Society, 541-479-7827, 512 SW Fifth St.,
www.josephinehistorical.org

JACKSONVILLE AREA

Just over the hill from scorching Medford is a treat, and not just because of its more moderate climes. Jacksonville oozes historic charm in its idyllic setting, and it's the gateway to Applegate Valley wine country to boot. It began as Table Rock City during the 1850s gold rush and eventually grew to be one of the largest towns in the region. When much of the area's commerce moved east to Medford early in the twentieth century, Jacksonville's city fathers had the foresight to recognize the value of what their predecessors had built during the gold boom. It retains much of that character today, so it's little wonder that in 1966 the entire town earned the coveted National Historic Landmark status. More than 100 buildings are on the National Register of Historic Places.

Wineries in the Jacksonville Area

The Jacksonville tour begins at the end of the Applegate Trail, at the country junction of Ruch. Continue on OR 238 into the town of Jacksonville, home for two wineries.

JOHN MICHAEL CHAMPAGNE CELLARS

541-846-0810
1425 Humbug Creek Road
Tasting Room: Fri.–Sun. 11–5, and by appointment
Fee: $5, refunded with purchase
Owners: Michael and Becky Giudici
Winemaker: Michael Guidici
Wines: Champagnes, Chardonnay, Pinot Blanc, Pinot Gris, rosé, Pinot Noir, Merlot, Zinfandel, red and white blends, sparkling saké
Cases 1,000
Special Features: Oregon's only sparkling sake production, picnic area

Talk about a niche. Sure, Michael Guidici has the usual suspects when it comes to wines, but what sets John Michael Champagne Cellars apart—*way* apart—from the neighbors is its champagne and sparkling saké. Guidici learned to make sake from an elderly neighbor 40 years ago, when he was a high school student in California. He kept making the Japanese brew along with small batches of beer in college. Today, the second-oldest winery in the Applegate has some of the best views of the valley, the best champagne, and the *only* saké. An added visual treat is a small studio where Guidici blows glass and makes Asian jewelry.

DEVITT WINERY

541-899-7511
www.devittwinery.com
11412 Highway 238
Tasting Room: Sat.–Sun. 12–5, Mon.–Fri. by chance, and by appointment
Fee: $5, waived with purchase
Owners: Jim and Sue Devitt
Winemaker: Jim Devitt
Wines: Viognier, Chardonnay, Cabernet Franc, Cabernet Sauvignon, Merlot, Shiraz, red and white blends, dessert wine
Cases: 2,500

Special Features: Picnic area with splintery picnic tables (no one complains)

As with most labels bearing a tongue-in-cheek name, there's a story behind Devitt's dessert wine, When Pigs Fly (a.k.a., Le Petite Oink), a blend of Syrah and Gewürztraminer. For years, the Devitts merely sold the grapes they grew. But 2003 brought a regional grape glut, leaving Jim and Sue wondering what to do with the excess. Said Jim, who had made wine in Napa Valley: "Let's make our own again!" Responded Sue, who was perfectly content to merely raise grapes in retirement: "When pigs fly!" It's obvious who won this domestic dispute: in 2004 they produced their first release, a Pinot Gris.

FIASCO WINERY/JACKSONVILLE VINEYARDS
541-899-9645 or 541-899-6923
www.fiascowinery.com
8035 Highway 238
Tasting Room: Summer, daily 11–5; winter, Thurs.–Mon. 11–5
Fee: Complimentary
Owners: David and Pam Palmer
Winemaker: David Palmer
Jacksonville Wines: Cabernet Sauvignon, Merlot, Cabernet Franc, Sangiovese, Zinfandel, Syrah, red blend
Fiasco Wines: Riesling, Zinfandel, Sangiovese, Syrah, Cabernet Sauvignon, red blends
Cases: 2,000 Jacksonville, 1,500 Fiasco
Special Features: Indoor and outdoor eating areas, gourmet foods in gift shop, Fiasco balsamic vinegar

Jacksonville Vineyards is the main player here, and Fiasco Winery is the sister label. The winery is located in the historic William Matney homestead—reputedly the oldest building in Oregon to house a winery. The tasting room is a utilitarian yet multicultural creation, a reflection of the Palmers' 20 years of overseas travel. Most

LongSword's greeting wine is the semi-sparkling Accolade, a bubbly pleasure. M. Kim Lewis

notable is the unusual floor made of decomposed granite, similar to those found in villages in Europe and Australia. David and Pam enjoy making wines they discovered in Italy and France. Jacksonville is known for its Bordeaux blends, and Fiasco for its Zinfandel. The winery sells olive oil and balsamic vinegar made for Fiasco. The name isn't as simple or chaotic as it might suggest; a *fiasco* is one of those old straw-covered glass-blown bottles made for Chianti. It's also a term for a flawed production.

LONGSWORD VINEYARD
541-899-1746 or 800-655-3877
www.longswordvineyard.com
8555 Highway 238
Tasting Room: May–Oct., daily 12–5;
Nov.–Apr., by appointment

Fee: Complimentary
Owners: Maria Largaespada and Matthew
Sorenson
Winemaker: Matthew Sorenson
Wines: Chardonnay, Pinot Gris, Dolcetto,
Syrah, sparkling wines
Cases: 1,500
Special Features: Combined tasting room
with Flying High Vineyards, with two labels
under one license

Picture a wine bar dropped into the middle
of a farmer's field. That's the LongSword
tasting room, which is fashioned out of an
airplane hangar. LongSword is the one winery in Oregon where you could be sitting on
the patio sipping wine and have a
paraglider land in your lap—literally. The
vineyard is a popular landing zone for locals
who like to ride the thermals from Woodrat
Mountain, and once they land, sometimes
within 50 feet of the patio, they'll likely join
you for some tasting. Sparkling wines are
Sorenson's specialty. The congenial
Sorenson and Largaespada, refugees from
pharmaceutical industry jobs in Indiana,
first made sparkling wines in 2003 for their
son's wedding. The labels feature a "long
sword" from Largaespada's family crest.

VALLEY VIEW WINERY

541-899-8468
www.valleyviewwinery.com
1000 Upper Applegate Road
Tasting Room: Daily 11–5
Fee: $5, waived with purchase
Owner: Wisnovsky family
Winemaker: John F. Guerrero
Wines: Chardonnay, Pinot Gris, Viognier,
Cabernet Sauvignon, Merlot, Syrah,
Tempranillo, red and white blends, port-
style and dessert wines
Cases: 10,000
Special Features: Large picnic area with
tables; wedding facility and events pavilion;
extensive gift shop with clothing, ceramics,
and other local art

When it comes to "firsts" in the Oregon
wine industry, you don't often hear about
Valley View. Yet this was indeed the state's
first winery, founded before the Civil War
and operated for a half-century by local
pioneer Peter Britt. The operation ceased
in 1906, and then Prohibition intervened,
but the Wisnovskys resurrected history by
planting 12 acres in 1972. The tasting room
opened in 1978 and John Guerrero soon
took over as winemaker at the winery's
Applegate Valley Wine Pavilion, so named
for its event space. The exceptional and
distinctive Anna Maria wines are named
after the Wisnovskys' mother.

*Valley View, near Jacksonville, has deep roots in
southern Oregon's wine history.* Courtesy M. Kim Lewis

COWHORN VINEYARD

541-899-6876
www.cowhornwine.com
1665 Eastside Road
Tasting Room: May–Nov., Fri.–Mon. 11–4,
and by appointment
Fee: $5 for four wines, refunded with six-
bottle purchase
Owners/Winemakers: Bill and Barbara
Steele
Wines: Viognier, Marsanne, Roussanne,
Syrah
Cases: 1,600
Special Features: Picnic area

Southern Oregon's first certified biodynamic and organic operation is more than a
winery—it's a full-fledged farm. On 117
acres, 11 of which are planted in grapes, the
Steeles grow hazelnuts, cherries, and black
truffles. They are so in tune with the land
that they resist the term "winemakers."
Instead, Bill says, they're "assistants to the
grapes." The two devoted grape assistants
favor Old World–style Rhône varietals. As
for the winery's name, it seems the com-
posting that comes with running a biodynamic operation can be difficult in winter.
So, to generate compost they take a cow
horn, fill it with organic cow manure, and
bury it for up to six months, giving them
rich black soil in the spring. It's actually a
common practice among biodynamic farmers—honest. Bill Steele also had a practical
motive for his company's simple name: He
was the guy always pointing at the wine
names on restaurant menus because he
couldn't pronounce them.

QUADY NORTH

541-702-2123
www.quadynorth.com
255 California Street
Tasting Room: Wed.–Mon. 12:30–6:30
Fee: $5, waived with purchase
Owner/Winemaker: Herb Quady

Wines: Viognier, rosé, Cabernet Franc,
Syrah
Cases: 1,000
Special Features: Tasting room serves and
sells Quady wines from both Oregon and
California

Herb Quady worked his way up to Oregon
after doing quality time at his family's
California winery, stopping for stints at
Bonny Doon, in the Bay Area, and then
Troon, in southern Oregon, before putting
down his own roots. Quady finds cooler-
climate grapes more compelling to work
with. He sources his from high-elevation
vineyards near Ashland as well as the
Applegate Valley. The tasting room and
winery are in a small ivy-covered brick
building with a few tables out front for lin-
gering. Carrying on the Quady tradition of
crafting exquisitely structured dessert
wines, this is a sweet stop for wine lovers.
But with dry wines and blends, Quady
North offers something pleasing for every
palate.

SOUTH STAGE CELLARS

541-899-9120
www.southstagecellars.com
125 South Third Street
Tasting Room: Wed.–Sun. 12–6, Sat.
12–9Fee: $5 for six wines
Owners: Don and Traute Moore
Winemakers: Joe Dobbes and Joe Wright
Wines: Pinot Gris, Sauvignon Blanc,
Viognier, Muscat, Merlot, Cabernet
Sauvignon, Pinot Noir, Syrah, red and white
blends
Cases: 6,000
Special Features: Outdoor patio, reds and
whites from other Oregon wineries sold,
Friday night music with local artists, wine-
maker dinners

After a busy day of touring, there are few
better places to unwind than at South Stage,
especially on a Friday night. The 1865 red-

brick building—the first to be restored in Jacksonville—oozes ambiance and relaxation. Sit around the wrought-iron tables in the Wine Garden and Patio and sip one of South Stage's 27 wines or offerings from many other wines made from the Moores' 10 vineyard sites. The list is lengthy: They supply 29 wineries with grapes.

Lodging in the Jacksonville Area

MCCULLY HOUSE INN AND COTTAGES
800-367-1942 or 541-899-1942
www.mccullyhouseinn.com
240 East California Street
Rates: $135 (house rooms), $195–295 (house suites), $150 (cottages), $175–295 (Reames House)
Special Features: The Garden Bistro is open for dinner Tues.–Sat.

The featured lodging at the McCully House is the Library Suite, which has a private entrance, a fireplace, and a library with a ladder to reach titles on the top shelf. The Kaizen Suite has a Japanese flair, with Asian art and even a Japanese maple just outside. Speaking of outside, two blocks away are the cozy and comfortable C Street Cottages, which are geared toward the budget-minded. Another block away is the Reames House, which offers the choice of the actual home for accommodations or the adjacent Carriage House for $295. The bistro utilizes local wine, cheese, and chocolate.

JACKSONVILLE INN
541-899-1900
www.jacksonvilleinn.com
175 East California Street
Rates: $159–199 (rooms), $270–465 (cottages)
Credit Cards: Yes
Special Features: Full-service restaurant, breakfast included in rate, wine shop, patio

The McCully House Inn was originally the home of Jacksonville's first physician. Courtesy Country House Inns

dining, gift shop, occasional five-star winemaker dinners

Take a journey back to the Rogue Valley's gold-rush era with a stay at the Jacksonville Inn, a national landmark that combines luxury with Civil War ambiance in the heart of this busy little tourist town. The decor is elegant, with shades of red and romance typical of mid-1800s frontier towns. Take a close look at the mortar and you might see a gleaming fleck of gold. The inn has eight rooms above the dining area and four opulent honeymoon cottages a block and a half away. The restaurant menu is continental-inspired and makes use of the state's bounty in its Oregon crab cakes and Rogue Creamery blue cheese crème brûlée with pear caviar. The wine shop, just off the hotel lobby, has some 2,000 selections in an area so snug that all the bottles are almost at your fingertips. The shop has earned *Wine Spectator*'s Award of Excellence more than a few times.

APPLEGATE RIVER LODGE

541-846-6690
www.applegateriverlodge.com
15100 Highway 238
Rates: $130–150
Special Features: Wedding facilities, gourmet restaurant, lounge, special winter rates

The names of the rooms in this spectacular log lodge reflect the diverse frontier history of the valley: Gold Miner's Cabin, Cattleman, Sportsman, Indian, Loggers, Myrtle, and now Vineyard (the honeymoon suite). All rooms look through trees to the Applegate River, but it might be just as appealing to curl up with a book in front of the large stone fireplace downstairs. Four of the guest rooms are in the main house, and there is a separate cottage. The renowned restaurant and lounge serve dinner overlooking the Applegate River.

Dining in the Jacksonville Area

BELLA UNION

541-899-1770
www.bellau.com
170 West California Street
Open: Lunch, Dinner
Price: Moderate
Credit Cards: Yes
Special Features: Britt boxes (to-go food for the festival), live music in summer, oyster and ale pairings

A diverse menu with lite bites, (oyster shooters and steamers), soups, salads, sandwiches, and pizza make a meal at this bustling café worth the typically long wait. Dinner entrées include chicken, beef, fish, but Bella Union is best known for its pasta dishes. The name of this popular social spot supposedly came from a San Francisco gambling house. There are abundant local wines by the glass and bottle.

GOGI'S CAFÉ BRITT

541-899-8699
www.gogis.net
235 West Main Street
Open: Wed.–Sun. 5–9, Sun. 10–2 (brunch)
Price: Expensive
Credit Cards: Yes
Special Features; Britt-nic baskets for festival take-out

Previous owner George Gogi built a solid reputation. Now two brothers are continuing in the same vein, with additional spunk and pizzazz. On a summer stop, we found Jonah and Gabe Murphy wearing most of the hats: greeter, waiter, chef, and busboy to a packed place, all the while patiently answering our questions in good humor. Tagging their cuisine as homegrown European, they grow some of the produce on their family farm. We were completely satisfied by the light-bites menu served on the front patio during Britt Festival season.

Attractions in the Jacksonville Area

Given that Jacksonville itself is a National Historic Landmark, any touring should start with the **Southern Oregon Historical Society** (541-899-8123, 206 N. Fifth St.), with its two museums and five other historic properties. The **Jacksonville Museum**, in what was once the county courthouse, is the society's centerpiece. Next door, in the old county jail, is the **Children's Museum**, featuring lots of hands-on activities for the kids. The **Jacksonville trolley** has five tours a day.

For an indelible night under the stars, the **Britt Festival** (541-773-6077) lures concert-goers from across Oregon and northern California for a wide variety of music and entertainment by some of the biggest names in the industry. The season runs from mid-June to mid-September.

Recreation in the Jacksonville Area

Runners, walkers, and hikers will appreciate the **Jacksonville Woodland Trails**, which were created to help preserve the character of the foothills surrounding the town.

Shopping in the Jacksonville Area

As a historic village, Jacksonville is, naturally, mostly about antique and specialty shops. The **Pickety Place** (541-899-1912, 130 North Fourth St.) is a favorite place to browse. As one might expect in a tourist town, there are numerous galleries featuring art, glassworks, and photography. The **Jacksonville Mercantile** (541-899-1047, 120 E. California St.) is remarkable for its range of imported goods, most notably its international and locally made artisan cheeses. **Llamas & Llambs Boutique** (541-899-9141, 180 N. Oregon St.) is based out of one of Jacksonville's historic cottages; they specialize in weaving, looms, and baskets. The **Ruch Country Store** (541-899-8559, 7350 OR 238) has sundries, groceries, local wine, and a deli that packs wine country lunches on an hour's notice.

MEDFORD AREA (ROGUE VALLEY AVA)

Legend has it that Medford was named for the "middle ford" of Bear Creek, which meanders in relative obscurity toward the burly Rogue River south of town. But the name could also describe its role as an economic, shopping, and transportation hub on Interstate 5, between the distant cities of Sacramento, California, to the south and Eugene to the north. Indeed, many who live in this workmanlike, semi-metropolitan city of more than 200,000 do so either in spite of or because of the isolation.

The city has made an effort to restore its tired downtown, with some modicum of success. Medford is still perhaps best known as home of Ginger Rogers, the Harry & David fruit and vegetable empire, and the Jackson & Perkins rose fortune.

Wineries in the Medford Area

Some like it hot—and that's how best to describe this country. Naturally, the wines here are associated with warm-weather grapes.

Though the 4,200-square-mile AVA is named for the Rogue, few of the region's 20 wineries and 1,100 acres of vineyards are near the river's banks. The borders of this AVA are roughly formed by the Applegate, Bear Creek, and Illinois rivers, and it is in these distinctly different valleys that most of the wineries are found.

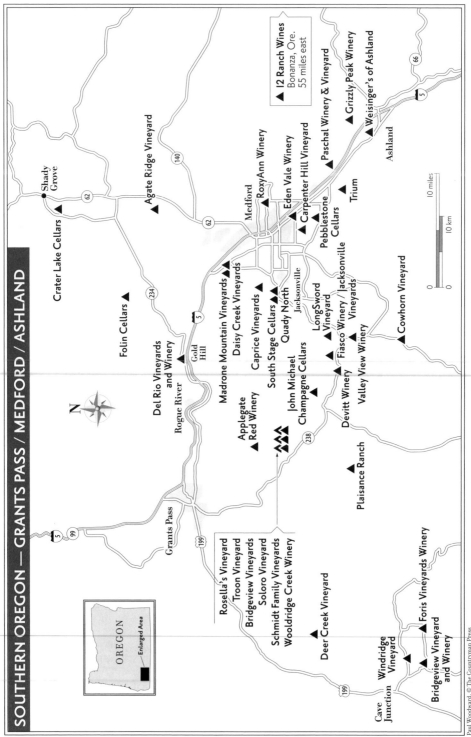

SOUTHERN OREGON — GRANTS PASS / MEDFORD / ASHLAND

12 Ranch Wines
Bonanza, Ore.
55 miles east

Crater Lake Cellars

Shady Grove

Agate Ridge Vineyard

Medford

RoxyAnn Winery

Eden Vale Winery

Carpenter Hill Vineyard

Paschal Winery & Vineyard

Grizzly Peak Winery

Weisinger's of Ashland

Ashland

Trium

Pebblestone Cellars

Folin Cellars

Madrone Mountain Vineyards

Daisy Creek Vineyards

Caprice Vineyards

South Stage Cellars

Quady North

Jacksonville

LongSword Vineyard

Fiasco Winery / Jacksonville Vineyards

Cowhorn Vineyard

Del Rio Vineyards and Winery

Rogue River

Gold Hill

Applegate Red Winery

John Michael Champagne Cellars

Devitt Winery

Valley View Winery

N

Grants Pass

Plaisance Ranch

Rosella's Vineyard

Troon Vineyard

Bridgeview Vineyards

Soloro Vineyard

Schmidt Family Vineyards

Wooldridge Creek Winery

Deer Creek Vineyard

Windridge Vineyard

Foris Vineyards Winery

Bridgeview Vineyard and Winery

Cave Junction

OREGON
Enlarged Area

10 miles

10 km

Paul Woodward. © The Countryman Press

The climate here is similar to that of the Bordeaux region of France. Not surprisingly, the Rogue Valley AVA is known for its Merlot, Syrah, Cabernet Sauvignon, Sauvignon Blanc, and Cabernet Franc, and Malbec.

CENTRAL POINT
MADRONE MOUNTAIN VINEYARD

541-664-1707
www.madronemountain.com
245 A North Front State
Tasting Room: Daily 12–5; check for winter hours
Fee: Complimentary
Owner/Winemaker: Don Mixon
Wines: Dessert wines
Cases: 1,500
Special Features: Picnic area, shared tasting room with Daisy Creek Vineyard

On one side of Madrone Mountain is the famed Rogue Creamery. On the other is Lillie Belle chocolates. In the center is the tasting room, where the theme is "dessert first." Specialties of the house are aperitif and fortified wines, and they aren't made with leftovers: Madrone picks the best grapes to formulate their sweet wines. One of Don's pairing tips: his red-blend dessert wine with Lillie Belle's dark chocolate. Proving that dessert wines aren't just for dessert anymore, his Gewürztraminer, Riesling, and Viognier blend isn't cloying; it has just right amount of sweetness and works well with savory food. The downtown tasting room is in a converted garage.

DAISY CREEK VINEYARD

541-899-8329
www.daisycreekwine.com
245 North Front Street
Tasting Room: Daily 12–5
Fee: Complimentary
Owners: Russ and Margaret Lyon
Winemakers: Kiley Evans and John Quinones

Quail Run, in the Rogue Valley, is one of southern Oregon's most respected vineyards. M. Kim Lewis

Wines: Viognier, rosé, Syrah, Merlot, red and white blends
Cases: 1,200
Special Features: Shared tasting room with Madrone Mountain, $10 Sunday soup suppers Jan.–Mar.

Now this is specialization. Kiley Evans of Agate Ridge makes the whites and John Quinones of RoxyAnn does the reds. In both cases, the grapes come from what was once a 23-acre hay field east of Jacksonville where peaches are still raised. Some 14 years ago, the Lyonses were approached by another winery to grow Merlot in their field. Soon after, those Merlots were winning gold medals. That's when it hit them: Let's make our own wine! The Lyonses haven't sold their grapes since. Daisy Creek—named for the creek bisecting the property—now also makes Rhône varietals. The popular winter soup suppers are sure to take the chill off.

CAPRICE VINEYARDS

541-499-0449
www.capricevineyards.com
970 Old Stage Road
Tasting Room: Thur.–Sun. 11–5
Fee: Complimentary
Owners: Jim and Jeanne Davidian

Winemaker: Jim Davidian
Wines: Cabernet Sauvignon, red blend
Cases: 500
Special Features: Located at Rolling Hills
Alpaca Ranch; tasting room is in corner of
Alpaca Ranch store

Where else can you sit under a grape arbor,
sip wine, and watch a pack of alpacas at the
same time? The Davidians both work in the
medical field, but since 2009 they've begun
to carve a nice wine sideline out of their
ranch. Jeanne also is pretty handy at weaving, and her work with alpaca fibers is on
display in the store on their ranch, about
one mile north of Jacksonville. For now, the
wines are coming from their sister winery
at Jacksonville Vineyard, but Jim is cooking
up a Chardonnay he hopes will be drink-
ready soon.

GOLD HILL
FOLIN CELLARS
541-855-2018
www.folincellars.com
9200 Ramsey Road
Tasting Room: Sat.–Sun. 12–5 (varies by
season), and by appointment
Fee: Complimentary for groups of less than
eight; groups of eight or more require
reservations and may incur tasting fees
Owners: Scott, Loraine, and Rob Folin
Winemaker: Rob Folin
Wines: Viognier, Syrah, Tempranillo, Petit
Sirah, Mourvèdre, Grenache
Cases: 1,200
Special Features: Themed special events,
private dinners, participants in the Upper
Rogue Valley women wine tours (second
Sat.), additional tasting room in Carlton
(see listing under Wineries in the Carlton
Area)

Everyone gets in on the action at this family-owned and operated vineyard, where
the wines are 100 percent estate-grown.
Dad and Mom run the 25-acre vineyard,

while son Rob makes the wine. Although
Rob doesn't look a day over 21, he actually
did a seven-year stint at Domaine Serene.
The winery and tasting room are brand-
new and beautiful, yet highly functional.
Northwest in design, the tasting room has a
20-foot tongue-and-groove cathedral ceiling, stained concrete floors, and granite
countertops that give it a timeless feel. The
three-barrel rooms and main workspace
are 50 percent underground, reducing the
energy footprint. One of the early believers
in "no cork, no worries," Folin uses the
Vino Seal glass closures on all of its wines.

DEL RIO VINEYARDS & WINERY
541-855-2062
www.delriovineyards.com
52 North River Road
Tasting Room: Summer, daily 11–6; winter,
daily 11–5
Fee: $5
Owners: Lee Traynham and Rob and Jolee
Wallace
Winemaker: Jean-Michel Jussiaume
Wines: Chardonnay, Pinot Gris, Viognier,
Muscat, rosé, Cabernet Sauvignon, Malbec,
Merlot, Syrah, port-style wine, red blends
Cases: 3,500
Special Features: Picnic facilities and park;
gift shop with wine-related items, local
cheese and Dagoba chocolate; wedding and
events facility

Rob Wallace has a big job. Del Rio's co-
owner tends to more than 200,000 vines in
the largest vineyard in southern Oregon—a
whopping 205 acres. The vines seem to go
on forever. As you might guess, Wallace is
out there every day, and it shows not only in
the wines but in the beauty of a gorgeous,
meticulously maintained vineyard. The
busy tasting room is in a refurbished portion of the old Rock Point Stage Hotel, built
in 1864 and still one of the oldest structures in southern Oregon.

Getting a Grape Education

Move over U.C. Davis: Here comes UCC. In May 2009, Umpqua Community College in Roseburg planted a five-acre vineyard on the edge of campus. At the same time, the school's Southern Oregon Wine Institute announced plans for a sparkling $7 million winery to enhance its viticulture program. Once completed, it'll be a hands-on working vineyard and winery complete with tastings and community activities as part of the student routine. An incubator will allow area citizens to birth their own wineries. UCC's business program will help new winemakers with the financial and marketing support required for a successful startup. The goal is to see wineries open for business within two to three years of startup.

Students from UCC and area high schools planted the vineyard's first 400 vines in Nebbiolo, a grape renowned in Piedmont, Italy, but rarely grown in Oregon. The reasoning: If the students can grow Nebbiolo in southern Oregon, they should have little trouble with the more familiar varietals. Nebbiolo is viewed as a problematic grape that's as fickle about climate and soils as Pinot Noir.

Farther north, Chemeketa Community College's decade-old program has undergone a $1.4 million expansion and renovation at its Northwest Viticulture Center. The two-year school near Salem offers more than 300 wine-related courses that take students through the entire process, from cultivating vines to selling wine. It also has a commercially bonded and licensed winery.

Further proof of the industry's importance to the state's economy is the beefed-up programs at Linfield University in McMinnville and at Oregon State University in Corvallis, where students can now earn advanced degrees in wine-related studies.

SHADY COVE

CRATER LAKE CELLARS

541-878-4200
www.craterlakecellars.com
21882 Highway 62, Building B
Tasting Room: Memorial Day through Thanksgiving weekend, Thurs.–Mon. 11–5; winter, Thurs.–Sat. 11–5
Fee: Complimentary
Owners: Steve and Mary Gardner
Winemaker: Steve Gardner
Wines: Chardonnay, Muscat, Pinot Blanc, Pinot Gris, Riesling, rosé, Cabernet Franc, Cabernet Sauvignon, Merlot, Pinot Noir, Syrah, Tempranillo, Grenache, red blend, dessert wine
Cases: 1,700
Special Features: Small seating area

You have to wander off the beaten path to find Crater Lake Cellars. In fact, it's the last winery stop on OR 62 if you're on your way to the namesake lake. Though Crater Lake has won its fair share of awards, it's worth taking home a bottle or two, or three, just for the beautiful labels of southern Oregon's most picturesque sites. The '06 Chardonnay has a photo you don't often see in person: Crater Lake and Wizard Island blanketed in snow. A wine to try is the Candy in a Bottle. The name speaks for itself.

EAGLE POINT

AGATE RIDGE VINEYARD

541-830-3050
www.agateridgevineyard.com
1098 Nick Young Road
Tasting Room: Tues.–Sun. 11–5
Fee: $5
Owners: Kim Kinderman and Don Kinderman

Winemaker: Kiley Evans

Wines: Chardonnay, Marsanne, Pinot Gris, Roussanne, Sauvignon Blanc, Semillon, Viognier, rosé, Cabernet Sauvignon, Petite Sirah, Pinot Noir, Primitivo, red and white blends

Cases: 1,500

Special Features: Picnic grounds, concert series, winter fireside Fridays with wine paired to appetizers; tasting tour second Saturday of each month in conjunction with Del Rio, Crater Lake, and Folin

Kim Kinderman wanted to "get the heck out of Alabama" and find her slice of farm heaven in the Pacific Northwest. She has it at Agate Ridge, where a pretty, classic white house that was the hub of a 126-acre farm for more than a century serves as the tasting room. Kim and her father, Don, bought the farm in 2001 and began planting 15,000 vines on 20 acres a year later. The setting, with lightning-magnet Mount McLoughlin as a backdrop, couldn't be more pleasant.

MEDFORD
ROXYANN WINERY
541-776-2315
www.roxyann.com

3285 Hillcrest Road

Tasting Room: Daily 11–6

Fee: Complimentary $3 for five additional wines, credited toward six-bottle purchase

Owners: Jack Day and Day-Parsons Family

Winemaker: John Quinones

Wines: Pinot Gris, Viognier, Merlot, Syrah, Tempranillo, red and white blends, dessert wines

Cases: 16,000

Special Features: Picnic area in gardens, gift shop, wines from other vineyards for sale, artisan foods, concerts, cooking classes, quarterly winemaker dinners

The city of Medford has gradually enveloped RoxyAnn, but that hasn't prevented the Century Farm and Hillcrest Orchard from retaining its aura and charm. The old white barn is on National Register of Historic Places and has been in the same family for 100 years; they've been running the winery for the past 10. The tasting room is a special place with a 360-degree bar that'll help you ignore the suburban east Medford homes springing up around the winery. Don't be surprised if you're joined by locals; RoxyAnn is a popular place to stop on the way home from work.

RoxyAnn is on a small hill where orchards have grown for more than a century. Courtesy RoxyAnn Winery

EDENVALE WINERY

541-512-9463
www.edenvalleyorchards.com
2310 Voorhies Road
Tasting Room: Summer, Mon.–Sat. 11–6,
Sun. 12–6; fall, Sun. 12–4
Fee: $5–10 per flight
Owner: Anne Root
Winemaker: Ashley Campanella
Wines: Pinot Gris, Chardonnay, Viognier,
rosé, Pinot Noir, Grenache, Cabernet
Franc, Cabernet Sauvignon, Syrah,
Tempranillo, Malbec, red and white blends,
port-style and dessert wines
Cases: 10,000
Special Features: Event facility, women's
club dinners, public dinners, winemaker
dinners, holiday events

Though you might be inclined to look over
your shoulder for Rhett and Scarlett at the
Voorhies Mansion, don't let the manor's
antebellum formality deter you. The tasting
room might be dressed to the nines, but it's
still down-home and friendly. The winery
is on the site of some of the oldest orchards
in southern Oregon (planted in 1885),
mostly pears. Indeed, the entire property,
owned by the Voorhies family for more than
a century, is on National Register of
Historic Places. A wide array of well-made
wines doesn't hurt their popularity.

CARPENTER HILL VINEYARD

541-210-8897
www.carpenterhillvineyard.com
928 Carpenter Hill Road
Tasting Room: By appointment only
Fee: Complimentary
Owners: Lee and Vicki Mankin
Winemaker: Lee Mankin
Wines: Petite Sirah, red blend
Cases: 300
Special Features: Wines also poured at
RoxyAnn Winery

Carpenter Hill doesn't do many wines, but
the ones they do, they do well. Case in

point: the estate-grown 2006 Petite Sirah,
which won a silver medal at the *San
Francisco Chronicle* Wine Competition and
gold at the local World of Wine Festival.
They've planted and plan to produce Merlot,
Roussanne, Syrah, and Petite Sirah from 22
acres of what had been a pear orchard.

PEBBLESTONE CELLARS

541-512-1704
www.pebblestonecellars.com
1642 Camp Baker Road
Tasting Room: By appointment only
Fee: $5, refunded with purchase
Owners: Dick and Pat Ellis
Winemaker: Dick Ellis
Wines: Viognier, Pinot Gris, Cabernet
franc, Merlot, Syrah, red blends
Cases: 1,200
Special Features: New tasting room

After more than two decades of harvesting
grapes for others and making wine at their
friends' vineyards in California, Dick and
Pat Ellis came north in 2002 to do their
own thing. Their search for that perfect
piece of vineyard ended a year later when
they found 26 acres of sandy and gravelly
soil—hence, Pebblestone—between
Medford and Ashland. The Ellises don't
have their own winery, instead making tra-
ditional-style wines at various wineries in
the area.

TALENT
PASCHAL WINERY & VINEYARD

541-535-7957
www.paschalwinery.com
1122 Suncrest Road
Tasting Room: Summer, daily 12–6; winter,
Tues.–Sun. 12–6
Fee: $5 for seven or eight wines
Owners: Ron and Donna Tenuta
Winemaker: Ron Tenuta
Wines: Chardonnay, Muscat, Pinot Gris,
Viognier, Dolcetto, Merlot, Pinot Noir,
Sangiovese, Syrah, Tempranillo, red and
white blends, dessert wine

Paschal Winery & Vineyard has lively events and stunning views. M. Kim Lewis

Cases: 2,000

Special Features: Picnic area; wedding and event facilities; live music throughout the year; artists' night first Fri. each month; jazz on Sun.

Coming to Paschal has always been an event, and the Tenudas have kept it that way since buying the winery from Roy and Jill Paschal in 2009. The winery has a distinctly Mediterranean-flavored tasting room that feels more like a boutique coffee shop, with rugs scattered on wood floors, warm colors, and clusters of relaxed seating areas. Ron is a story unto himself. After 30 years in the corporate world, he went back to school at U.C. Davis to learn winemaking and soon became one of the vintners making estate Pinot Noir in California. While Ron gets his footing, vintages from prolific Oregon vintner Joe Dobbes Jr.—who previously made the wines for Paschal—are still in the inventory.

TRIUM

541-535-4015

www.triumwine.com

7112 Rapp Lane

Tasting Room: Apr.–Oct., Thurs.–Mon. 11–5:30; some holiday weekends; and by appointment

Fee: $5–7, refunded with three-bottle purchase

Owners: Laura and Kurt Lotspeich

Winemaker: Peter Rosback

Wines: Pinot Gris, Viognier, rosé, Cabernet Franc, Merlot, Cabernet Sauvignon, red blend

Cases: 1,000

Special Features: Grapes sourced from three LIVE-certified vineyards

Trium is Latin for "of the three"—a reference to the winery's three vineyards and the three classic Bordeaux varietals in Trium's signature blend. Cheery potted flowers and plants give texture to the ivy-covered tasting room. Trium produces high-quality fruit and trusts it to the care of Peter Rosback, of Sineann fame. The result: Trium's wines usually fare well against the competition.

Lodging in the Medford Area

MEDFORD

UNDER THE GREENWOOD TREE B&B

541-776-0000
www.greenwoodtree.com
3045 Bellinger Lane
Rates: $120–140
Special Features: Tea and treats on the patio, hammock, lawn sports

Named for a song in Shakespeare's *As You Like It,* Under the Greenwood Tree is in a prime country location for heading to the Britt Festival in Jacksonville, the Shakespeare Festival in Ashland, and winery hopping in any direction. The rooms—D'Anjou, Comice, Bartlett, and Bosc—are named for pears that remain prolific in the area's orchards. The farm doesn't have any greenwood trees, but there are 300-year-old oaks shading the relatively youthful farmhouse, a mere 125 years old. The lawn is awash in color and the 238-acre farm features Civil War–era buildings, a gazebo, llamas, bicycles to borrow, and hammocks for an evening of lazing after a day of touring.

Dining in the Medford Area

MEDFORD

CAFÉ DEJEUNER

541-857-1290
1108 East Main Street
Open: Mon.–Fri. 10:30–2, Tues.–Sat. 5–8 or 5–9
Price: Moderate to expensive
Credit Cards: Yes
Special Features: Outside dining year-round (with heaters under retractable roof), corkage-free night on Tues.

It takes some sleuthing to find it, but Terry and Louis Swenson's wildly popular café is worth the hunt. The café is in a neighborhood setting, and from the outside looks like a modest residential home with parking on the street. Step inside the cramped rooms and you'll immediately feel the warmth from the wood and stone interior and candlelit tables. White linens, sparkling stemware, and Caesar salads tossed at your table by attentive servers add a touch of class. Expect seasonal menu changes, but you'll usually find lamb osso bucco, wild salmon, and hearty pasta dishes. A majority of the wines are from Oregon, so going local is easy. The café is so popular with the luncheon crowd, reservations are recommended.

ELEMENTS TAPAS BAR & LOUNGE

541-779-0135
www.elememtsmedford.com
101 East Main Street
Open: Tues.–Thurs. and Sun. 4–12, Fri.–Sat. 4 P.M.–2:30 A.M.
Price: Moderate
Credit Cards: Yes
Special Features: Those under 21 welcome until 9; late-night nibbling and imbibing

Channel your inner Spaniard in this relatively new bar with small-plate dining in traditional style. There are plenty of local wines to complement or contrast your meal. Tempt yourself with three versions of paella (the only expensive meal), pastry-wrapped baked Manchego, or the signature grapes rolled in Rogue Creamery blue cheese and pistachios. Flatbreads are dressed in lamb sausage, Serrano ham, or duck breast and heightened with artisan cheeses, just begging for an Oregon Syrah or Pinot Noir. Choose from Oregon and Spanish bottles, with at least 15 glass pours available. Elements encourages sharing small plates, and won't turn you away even near closing time.

POMODORI RISTORANTE

541-776-6332

www.pomodoriristorante.com

1789 Steward Avenue

Open: Tues.–Fri. 11:30–2, Tues.–Sat. 5 P.M.–close

Price: Moderate

Credit Cards: Yes

Special Features: Additional location in Florence, winemaker dinners

As the name indicates, expect to find northern Italian fare in this cheery nook in west Medford. In the windowless back you'll find a more romantic setting with candlelit glass-top tables. In the front, where kids are welcome, the walls are painted in Tuscan red and gold around lots of windows. Every meal is made to order and folks rave about the linguine and jumbo shrimp. Some 95 percent of the wine list comes from the Applegate Valley and the owners are planning more winemaker dinners.

Attractions in the Medford Area

Medford is generally not known for unique attractions. In fact, it bills itself as a cheaper place to stay while you're visiting the more expensive (read: more appealing) Ashland and Jacksonville. Still, Medford has its share of famous alums, which helps explain the **Craterian Ginger Rogers Theater** (541-779-3000). The theater opened in 1924 and has since become the pride of a spruced-up downtown. Rogers, who owned a ranch in nearby Shady Cove and later a home in Medford, appeared there at the age of 15 less than two years after it opened, and returned 67 years later.

There was a time when water-powered gristmills seemed to be everywhere. Now, there is just one—the **Butte Creek Mill** (541-826-3531, 402 Royal Ave. N.) in Eagle Point. The 1872 mill churns out stone-ground flours and other grain products, with the bran and germ preserved by the grinding.

Recreation in the Medford Area

Many people in Medford live for hunting, fishing, and boating on the numerous lakes and streams in the region. Boat rentals are available at **Lost Creek Lake, Lake of the Woods, Fish Lake,** and **Lemolo Lake**. Fly fishermen will see giant rainbow trout cruising the depths in the half-mile-long Holy Waters of the Rogue just below Lost Creek Dam.

Medford's warm weather isn't just suited for river buffs. The valley might just have the best golfing in Oregon. There are no fewer than seven courses, including the renowned **Eagle Point Golf Course** (541-826-8225), 10 miles east of Medford. That course, designed by Robert Trent Jones Jr., was rated among the top 10 public courses in the country by *Golf Week* magazine in 2007. Not to be outdone, the new **Centennial Golf Club** (541-773-4653), designed by former PGA Tour player John Fought, was chosen the valley's top course by readers of the *Medford Mail Tribune*. Medford also has three nine-hole courses: **Bear Creek Golf Course** (541-773-1822), **Stewart Meadows** (541-770-6554), and **Quail Point Golf Course** (541-857-7000).

Wine Shopping in the Medford Area

The **Corks Wine Bar & Bottle Shoppe** (541-245-1616, 235 Theatre Alley) is across from the Ginger Rogers Theater and has the motto "making friends one cork at a time." They offer a single varietal tasting every third Friday of the month.

Shopping in the Medford Area

Everybody who's ever eaten a pear or planted a rosebush knows about **Harry & David** (541-864-2099, 2518 South Pacific Hwy.) and **Jackson & Perkins** (800-292-4769, 2500 Pacific Hwy.). Both of these renowned national shippers are based here and offer prolific shopping opportunities. For 70 years, the **Rogue Creamery** (541-665-1155, 311 N. Front St.) in Central Point has been making famed cheese in the same old building. **Lillie Belle's Chocolates** (541-664-2815, 211 N. Front St.) and their rich, delectable, sometimes-fruity award-winning creations are in a new store next door. The **Rogue Valley Growers and Crafters Market** (888-826-9868), offering locally grown fruits and vegetables, comes to the Medford Armory every Thursday year-round.

Information

Medford Chamber of Commerce,
541-779-4847, 101 E. Eighth St.,
www.medfordchamber.com

The Wine & Farm Tour is a great way to experience Oregon Wine Country, southern-style. M. Kim Lewis

ASHLAND AREA

To Oregonians and Californians alike, Ashland has long been synonymous with Shakespeare. The annual Oregon Shakespeare Festival lures tourists the world over to what has become a trendy, cultured, picturesque community of 22,000 in the forested foothills of the Siskiyou Mountains.

But there's far more to like here: a fresh environment, moderate climate, arts and crafts galore, young energy provided by Southern Oregon University students, a plethora of outdoor activities, and a postcard-perfect Siskiyou Mountains backdrop.

Wineries in the Ashland Area

ASHLAND
GRIZZLY PEAK WINERY
541-482-5700
www.grizzlypeakwinery.com
1600 East Nevada Street
Tasting Room: Sat. 12–4, and by appointment
Fee: Complimentary ($2 for dessert wine)

Owners: Al and Virginia Silbowitz
Winemaker: Andy Swan
Wines: Chardonnay, Cabernet Sauvignon, Merlot, Pinot Noir, Tempranillo, red and white blends, dessert wine
Cases: Under 1,000
Special Features: Wedding and event facilities; Andy Swan's Granite Peak label poured and sold

Al and Virginia Silbowitz had the location. Andy Swan had the winemaking skills. Together, they have formed Ashland's second winery, Grizzly Peak, which sits amid oak savannah at a staggering 2,250 feet above sea level on the flanks of—where else?—Grizzly Peak, a few miles outside of Ashland. The venture began in 2006, the tasting room opened in 2008, and the Silbowitzes are in the process of building a large winery. Both the Grizzly Peak and Granite Peak labels are produced here.

WEISINGER'S OF ASHLAND

541-488-5989
www.weisingers.com
3150 Siskiyou Boulevard
Tasting Room: May–Oct., daily 11–5; Nov.–Apr., Wed.–Sun. 11–5
Fee: Complimentary for one taste; flights $3–8, refunded with three-bottle purchase
Owner/Winemaker: John Weisinger
Wines: Viognier, Chardonnay, Gewürztraminer, Cabernet Sauvignon, Cabernet Franc, Merlot, Syrah, red and white blends, ruby port-style wine
Cases: 3,000
Special Features: Guest cottage in vineyard includes outdoor hot tub, gas barbecue, full kitchen, bottle of wine, cheese and crackers, free wine tasting, and discounts for guests ($135–175).

Last call before California! Grab a glass, pull up a chair and enjoy the views of the Siskiyous from the stunning three-tier deck at Weisinger's. If you're there for the autumn harvest you might even see a resident black bear, which has developed a taste for Gewürztraminer grapes. Though John strives to make world-class wines, he's equally insistent on providing a familiar, comfortable, and inviting place to enjoy a final glass of Oregon wine before you had over the Siskiyou Summit into California on I-5. It's a great place to "get the southern Oregon vibe."

BONANZA
12 RANCH WINES

541-545-1204
www.12ranchwines.com
4550 Burgdorf Road
Tasting Room: Memorial Day and Thanksgiving weekends, and by appointment
Fee: Complimentary
Owners: 12 Ranch Wines Corp.
Winemaker: Ken Masten
Wines: Viognier, Chardonnay, Cabernet Sauvignon, Merlot, Syrah
Cases: 500
Special Features: Periodic open houses

What better to go with a big, juicy steak than a big, juicy red wine? If you're up for an adventure and a diversion, 12 Ranch Wines is the place for both. The nearest town's name, Bonanza, gives you an idea of what to expect from this country drive. The winery is in the arid heart of a cattle ranch and hay fields on the east side of the Cascades, beyond Klamath Falls. 12 Ranch produces 100-percent varietals and nurtures them into big reds that'll complement a rib eye or T-bone. The Mastens, fifth-generation ranchers, were weekend winemakers until Connie suggested to Ken that they get serious, raising the eyebrows of their far-flung neighbors. "It's really a novelty around here," says Connie. The grapes come from the Medford area, 70 miles to the west.

Lodging in the Ashland Area

WINCHESTER INN

Owners: Mike and Lori Gibbs
541-488-1113 or 800-972-4991
www.winchesterinn.com
35 S. Second Street
Rates: $135–295

All's well that begins well, the Bard might say. At the Winchester Inn you begin with a beautifully prepared breakfast followed by a busy day of touring, the most exquisite dining in Ashland, and withdrawal to an amenity-laced room. The elegant, Victorian-style inn has an impressive 11 guest rooms and eight suites. Rates are based on the season, which largely revolves around the Shakespeare Festival. Few wine bars in Oregon have more choices for sipping, and the restaurant's interesting menu includes Vietnamese dishes.

THE INN AT LITHIA SPRINGS

Owner: Duane Smith
800-482-7128
www.ashlandinn.com
2165 West Jackson Road
Rates: $179–299
Special Features: Natural hot springs, spa, English gardens

Once upon a time, Indians from a wide variety of tribes came to what they called the Common Grounds—a site of natural mineral hot springs, or healing waters. That community feeling continues today at Lithia Springs Resort & Garden, which offers European-style rooms in the main lodge, English cottages, and something called the Water Tower. The tower is a contemporary replica of a castle's corner lookout tower, sans turrets. Inside the cozy room is a heart-shaped Jacuzzi suitable for two. Each accommodation has a whirlpool to soak away your cares after an arduous day in wine country.

THE PEERLESS HOTEL

541-488-1082
www.peerlesshotel.com
243 Fourth Street
Rates: $83–269
Credit Cards: Yes
Special Features: Acclaimed restaurant, bar, gardens

Oh, the stories these brick walls could tell. The Peerless, built in 1900, made the list of *1,000 Places To See Before You Die* because of its history, downtown proximity to everything Ashland, and old-world elegance. Even the old Coca-Cola sign on the side, originally painted in 1915, has been brought back to life. The walls in each of the six rooms have eclectic collections of art. Depending on which room you choose, you could be thrust back 100 years to the West Indies . . . or Hawaii . . . or the French Quarter . . . or an Italian garden. Living up to the hotel's standards is The Peerless restaurant, which serves Northwest cuisine and wine, and has earned a *Wine Spectator* Award of Excellence.

Dining in the Ashland Area

CHATEAULIN

541-482-2264
www.chateaulin.com
50 East Main Street
Open: Wed.–Sat. 11–2, Tues.–Sun. 5 P.M.–close, Mon. 5:30 P.M.–close
Price: Expensive
Credit Cards: Yes
Special Features: Acclaimed wine list, champagne and jazz on Tues. starting at 8

Even before Ashland became the artsy recreation hub it is today, Chateaulin was serving up exceptional food, ambiance, and wine selections. The restaurant, opened in 1973 before Ashland's lumber industry began to fade, draws residents and tourists alike for its prix fixe dinner, a three-course supper with two courses of wine ($40). The burgundy carpet, hurricane glass, and glass partitions create a warm French atmosphere inside an ivy-covered two-story building in downtown Ashland.

AMUSE

541-488-9000
www.amuserestaurant.com
15 North First Street
Open: Hours vary by season

Price: Expensive
Credit Cards: Yes
Special Features: Three-course "Sunday Suppers" for less than $30

Amuse features a high-quality organic blend of Northwest and French cuisine. Some examples of main courses that roll off the tongue and tease the palate: Parisienne gnocchi with Fuji apples and chanterelles, wood-grilled Painted Hills Ranch rib eye, black truffle–roasted game hen, and seared Sonoma Liberty duck breast. Their wine list is a blend of regional and international. The hours and cuisine change with the seasons, so it's wise to call ahead. Reservations can be made online.

BEASY'S ON THE CREEK
541-488-5009
www.beasysrestaurant.com
51 Water Street
Open: Daily 5:30–9
Price: Expensive
Credit Cards: Yes
Special Features: Veranda seating above Ashland Creek

If you're looking for something a little more traditional and yet still classy, come upstairs to Beasy's on the Creek. Aged

Oregon steaks, wild sashimi-grade Coho salmon, and lobster tail are just a few of the offerings, each with a wide-ranging choice of special sauces. Most of the wines are from California—a few miles away—but they do make room for southern Oregon faves such as RoxyAnn and Brandborg.

OMAR'S
541-482-1281
www.omarsrestaurant.com
1380 Siskiyou Boulevard
Open: Mon.–Fri. 11:30–2, daily 5 P.M.–close
Price: Moderate to expensive
Credit Cards: Yes
Special Features: Lounge open until 2:30 A.M.

Omar's has an "Ashland's Best Steaks & Seafoods" streak that would make even the greatest dynasties envious—18 years running in *Sneak Preview*'s annual citywide poll. You'll find fresh seafood flown in almost daily, choice steaks, and the popular Jamaican jerk chicken. Lunches are traditional, yet you can also order a turkey burger, oyster po' boy, or curried coconut black mussels. An extensive local wine list often features Abacela, Foris, EdenVale, and RoxyAnn.

Attractions in the Ashland Area

Come any time between February and October, and chances are the town will be abuzz with tourists holding tickets to the **Oregon Shakespeare Festival** (541-482-0446), which began in the 1930s. No theater in the nation sells more tickets for plays or performances. Not surprisingly, art in all forms is a big deal here. The **Ashland Independent Film Festival** (541-488-3823), staged every April, entered its ninth season in 2010. It draws top indie filmmakers from across the globe to show their films at the **Varsity Theatre** downtown. **Oregon Stage Works** (541-482-2334, 191 A St.) offers year-round performances highlighting works from national and local playwrights. If light-and-breezy music or comedy is more to your taste, the **Oregon Cabaret Theatre** (541-488-2902) has been offering a rollicking good time for a quarter-century in a Baptist church that's been refurbished as a nightclub-style dinner theater. Matinee and evening performances include meals featuring wines and beer from the Pacific Northwest. And speaking of music, the **Ashland City Band** is the nation's oldest: It has been playing in what is now Lithia Park since 1876. Locals are justifiably proud of their lush, 100-acre **Lithia Park** (541-488-5340, 59

Winburn Way), which has the band shell, hiking trails, and a Japanese garden. Decades ago, Ashland had visions of becoming a destination spa town, but all that's left of that dream is **Jackson WellSprings** (541-482-3776, 2253 Highway 99 N.), a hot spring with a large swimming pool and private soaking tubs.

Recreation in the Ashland Area

Where to begin? Whatever the time of year, Ashland is another one of Oregon's outdoor-recreation hotspots. Start with winter: **Mt. Ashland Ski Area** (541-482-2897), which sits virtually atop the Oregon-California border, receives more than 300 inches of snow per year. The **Oak Knoll Golf Club** (541-482-4311, 3700 Hwy. 66) offers nine modest holes for the golfer; it's the only course in town. And the dirty—literally—little secret that southern Oregon fat-tire enthusiasts don't want you to share: Moab, Utah, and Jackson, Wyoming, have nothing on Ashland when it comes to **mountain biking**. A network of invigorating single-track trails leads away from town.

Shopping in the Ashland Area

Call it "theme shopping." There's **Shakespeare Books & Antiques** (541-488-1190, 163 East Main St.), **Tudor Guild** (541-482-0940, 15 South Pioneer) gifts, **The Crown Jewel** (541-488-2401, 130 East Main St.) for gifts and jewelry, and **Paddington Station** (541-482-1343, 125 East Main St.) for unique clothing and gadgetry. Even **Portobello** (541-488-0489, 337 East Main St.) antiques is owned by a fellow named Shrewsbury. Fittingly for such a progressive community, there are three farmers' markets: **Rogue Valley Growers and Crafters Market** (541-261-0577) offers locally grown produce on Tuesday mornings in the Ashland Armory and Saturday mornings on Lithia Way and First Street; the **Lithia Artisans Market** (541-535-3733) features music, crafts, and arts on weekends from May to October; and the **A Street Marketplace & Pavilion** (541-488-3433) is open year-round in the Railroad District.

Information

Ashland Chamber of Commerce, 541-482-3486, 110 E. Main St., www.ashland chamber.com

8

The Columbia Gorge

A World of Wines in 40 Miles

Few places in this picturesque state are as spectacularly beautiful as the Columbia Gorge, and nowhere is such a dramatic diversity of terrain packed into such tight geographical quarters.

The western end, which begins abruptly 20 miles from Portland, is all about clouds, mist, Douglas firs, vine maples, blackberry brambles, and close proximity to about 1.5 million predominantly liberal citizens. Just 80 miles to the east, the largely treeless horizon is decidedly rural, arid, sunny, and conservative. Weekend Gorge warriors know not to despair if it's drizzling in Portland. Chances are, the clouds will part by Hood River, about halfway. Along the way, the mighty Columbia River of Woody Guthrie fame—"Roll On, Columbia, Roll On!"—moseys through the Cascade Range to the Pacific Ocean, leaving sheer 4,000-foot basalt cliffs, 77 waterfalls, and an enticing outdoor playground.

The town of Hood River is in the heart of the Gorge, where two distinct climates and topographies meet to provide a blissful setting. This is the end of the line for much of the moist marine air for which western Oregon is renowned. High desert begins one ridgeline to the east. The result is a confluence where lush, colorful valleys and fir-bathed hillsides are supplemented by a plethora of sunny days and productive orchards. If there is a downside to this Eden, it is the gale-force winds that constantly buffet the gorge floor. Then again, the town has turned this nuisance into a hefty and colorful tourist economy.

In the past two decades, this river-oriented town of about 6,700 has emerged as one of Oregon's great outdoor playgrounds. Even more recent is its emergence as a player on the state's wine scene. It has also become a Mecca for foodies and the locavore movement. Some of the best cuisine in the state is served at the local restaurants, many of them set on hillsides overlooking the Columbia River—with no extra charge for the views.

Getting Here and Around

Most adventures into the Columbia Gorge start in Portland. Access is easy from Portland International Airport, which was built along the river on the city's east side and serves no fewer than fourteen domestic and international airlines.

OPPOSITE: *Mount Adams rises above a vineyard at Cathedral Ridge.* John Baker

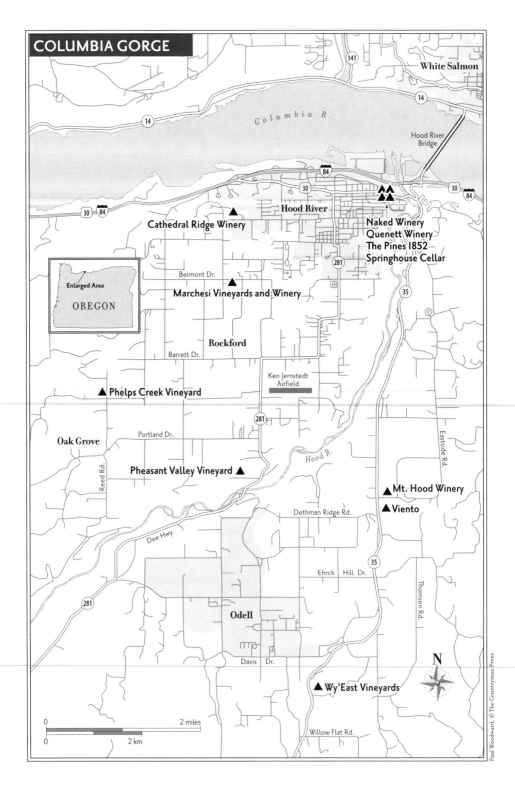

COLUMBIA GORGE

White Salmon

Columbia R.

Hood River Bridge

Hood River

Cathedral Ridge Winery

Naked Winery
Quenett Winery
The Pines 1852
Springhouse Cellar

Belmont Dr.

Marchesi Vineyards and Winery

Enlarged Area

OREGON

Rockford

Barrett Dr.

Ken Jernstedt Airfield

▲ Phelps Creek Vineyard

Oak Grove

Portland Dr.

Hood R.

Pheasant Valley Vineyard ▲

Eastside Rd.

Reed Rd.

▲ Mt. Hood Winery

▲ Viento

Dethman Ridge Rd.

Dee Hwy.

Ehrck Hill Dr.

Thomsen Rd.

Odell

Davis Dr.

N

▲ Wy'East Vineyards

Willow Flat Rd.

0   2 miles

0   2 km

Paul Woodward. © The Countryman Press

Take I-84 through the industrial zones and suburbs of east Portland to Troutdale (home to a mid-sized outlet mall), where the urban hubbub ends when the freeway crosses the Sandy River. Visitors from the east typically descend on the region after lengthy drives across vast wheat fields, empty sage plains and mountains from Boise on I-84 and Spokane on US 395.

The **Amtrak** Empire Builder hugs the Columbia on the Washington side and has Gorge stops—one eastbound and one westbound daily—in Wishram and Bingen. **Greyhound** has six bus stops daily in Hood River, three from each direction.

Wineries in the Columbia Gorge

When spin doctors in the Columbia Gorge AVA say "A World Of Wine In 40 Miles," they aren't overdramatizing. They can legitimately claim that they grow wine grapes from A (Albariño) to Z (Zinfandel).

This phenomenon was made possible in part by a series of colossal dams that harnessed the free-flowing Columbia beginning in the Great Depression. Bonneville, The Dalles, and John Day dams changed the Gorge forever, and have been a boon for grape growing. In fact, it's likely that the wine industry couldn't exist without them. When once the Columbia's waters were rapidly moving and cool, now the river is a series of long, warmer lakes. The vinifera no longer endures wicked bouts of frost that came in on the coattails of ferocious Gorge gales.

Dramatic variances in climate mean fickle Pinot Noir, Gewürztraminer, and Pinot Gris are mainstays at the western end, and the burlier Syrah, Barbera, and Cabernet Sauvignon thrive on the eastern end. Some vines were planted in the 1880s and a few remnants remain today.

Your tour starts in the countryside and finishes with four tightly spaced wineries in downtown Hood River.

HOOD RIVER
CATHEDRAL RIDGE WINERY
800-516-8710
www.cathedralridgewinery.com
4200 Post Canyon Drive
Tasting Room: Daily 1–5
Fee: $5, waived with purchase
Owner: Robb Bell
Winemaker: Michael Sebastiani
Wines: Pinot Gris, Chardonnay, Riesling, Gewürztraminer, rosé, Pinot Noir, Merlot, Zinfandel, Cabernet Sauvignon, Syrah, red blends
Cases: 5,000
Special Features: Small gift shop, expansive gardens, event facilities

Don't tell Robb Bell you can't grow Pinot Noir in this AVA. He has the wine and awards to prove otherwise. Having renamed itself after years as Flerchinger Winery, Cathedral Ridge was chosen Winery of the Year by *Wine Press Northwest* for 2008. Having Sebastiani—a fourth-generation

Cathedral Ridge was named Winery of the Year by Wine Press Northwest in 2007. Courtesy Cathedral Ridge Winery

winemaker from a renowned family—doesn't hurt. Bell is proud to point out that all grapes for their extensive line are grown on the estate or within a 20-mile radius. Expansive gardens and grounds can host many events or an intimate party of two.

MARCHESI VINEYARDS & WINERY

541-386-1800
www.marchesivineyards.com
3955 Belmont Drive
Tasting Room: Spring–fall, daily 11–6
Fee: Varies, waived with purchase
Owner/Winemaker: Franco Marchesi
Wines: Pinot Gris, Barbera, Dolcetto, Pinot Noir
Cases: Under 1,000

Taste a sip of Italy at this small, up-and-coming winery. Born in Piedmont, Marchesi makes wines with Italian passion. His products are true expressions of the northern Italian varietals grown on his estate, and by friends and neighbors in the Cascade foothills. And because he's Italian, he gets a pass for calling it "Pinot Grigio" in a state where it's called "Pinot Gris."

PHELPS CREEK VINEYARDS

541-386-2607
www.phelpscreekwinery.com
1850 Country Club Road
Tasting Room: Nov.–June, Sat.–Sun. 11–5; July–Oct., daily 11–5
Fee: $5 for seven wines, waived with purchase
Owner: Bob Morus
Winemaker: Rich Cushman
Wines: Chardonnay, Gewürztraminer, rosé, Pinot Noir, Merlot, red and white blends, dessert wine
Cases: 6,000
Special Features: "Count Down to Harvest" tour and winery activities in late September

The Phelps Creek tasting room is an extension of the Hood River Golf Course parking lot, located along the valley's Fruit Loop drive and near the winery's 30-acre vineyard. A guest winemaker from France has brought a touch of Old World style to the winery and added a Rosé of Pinot Noir to the line. Mt. Defiance Wines is Phelps Creek's second label. The name is a reference to baseball player turned fire-and-brimstone preacher Billy Sunday, who railed against the evils of alcohol. Sunday settled in the quiet Hood River Valley in the 1920s, long before it became a hot wine region. Hellfire White and Brimstone Red are both affordable blends occasionally bottled in jugs (2,000 cases). Phelps Creek is a pleasant surprise and we consider it one of Oregon's sleeper wineries. We haven't met a wine here we didn't like.

PHEASANT VALLEY VINEYARD & WINERY

541-387-3040
www.pheasantvalleywinery.com
3890 Acree Drive
Tasting Room: Summer, daily 12–6; fall through spring, daily 12–5; closed Jan.
Fee: $5 for six wines
Owners: Scott and Gail Hagee
Winemaker: Garrit Stoltz
Wines: Pinot Gris, Chardonnay, Riesling, Gewürztraminer, Pinot Noir, Syrah, Zinfandel, Cabernet Sauvignon, Tempranillo, red blend, blush, pear wine
Cases: 4,000
Special Features: Guest cottage, organic wine store

After strictly relying on certified organic pear and apple orchards for many years, a third fruit has become a charm for Pheasant Valley—grapes. Organic Pinot Noir and Pinot Gris are grown on 16 acres and reflect the cool, moist marine air that makes its last stand here. Pheasant Valley is at the ready with an assortment of six to fifteen wines typically open for tasting. The

Phelps Creek's tasting room serves as the 19th hole at Hood River Golf Course. |Jeff Welsch

Hagees haven't forgotten their roots: They make a popular organic pear wine as well.

MT. HOOD WINERY
541-386-8333
www.mthoodwinery.com
2882 Van Horn Drive
Tasting Room: June–Oct., daily 11–5
Fee: $5, applied to purchase
Owners: Steve and Don Bickford
Winemaker: Rich Cushman
Wines: Pinot Gris, Chardonnay, Riesling, Gewürztraminer, Pinot Noir, Syrah, Merlot, port-style wine
Cases: 2,500
Special Features: Small gift shop

The owners boast that they have the newest, biggest, and best tasting room in the AVA. You can enjoy a lengthy lineup of wines under 30-foot vaulted ceilings in a Northwest lodge setting, or on the 3,000-square-foot picnic patio that allows for double mountain views (Mount Hood and Mount Adams). The winery is best known for its Pinot Noir and Pinot Gris.

VIENTO
541-386-3026
www.vientowines.com
2265 Highway 35
Tasting room: Under construction at press time
Owner/winemaker: Rich Cushman
Wines: Riesling, Viognier, rosé, Syrah, Sangiovese, Pinot Noir, Barbera, white blend
Cases: 1,500

You frequently see Hood River native Rich Cushman listed as winemaker, but finding his wines under the label Viento is a bit tricky. And after 28 years of making wine for other wineries, he had plans to settle into his own winery on Country Club Road by the fall of 2009. Until then, his wines are available at the Gorge White House tasting room. Regardless of where you find them, the search for Cushman and his wines is definitely worth the effort. Viento is highly recognized for its Riesling, made from grapes planted in 1982 in Cushman's own small vineyard.

WY'EAST VINEYARDS
541-386-1277
www.wyeastvineyards.com
3189 Highway 35
Tasting Room: April–Nov., daily 11–5; Dec., Feb. and Mar., Sat.–Sun. 11–5; closed Jan.
Fee: $5, waived with purchase
Owners: Dick and Christie Reed
Winemaker: Peter Rosback
Wines: Pinot Gris, Chardonnay, Pinot Noir, Syrah, Cabernet Sauvignon, port-style wine
Cases: 2,000
Special Features: Tasting deck with views

The unique character of Wy'East Vineyards' Pinot Noir and Pinot Gris is a result of the 1,600-foot elevation, one of the highest vineyards in Oregon. The combination of elevation and cool, blustery weather forces the grapes to work extra hard, and it shows in the taste. Rosback uses these hardy grapes for his own label: Sineann Reserve Pinot. The name Wy'East comes from an Anglo interpretation of the Native

American name for Mount Hood, which is visible from the picnic deck. Be sure to try the savory and locally made Outrageous Shortbread; its flavors are designed to pair perfectly with wine.

NAKED WINERY

800-666-9303
www.nakedwinery.com
102 Second Street
Tasting Room: Sun.–Thurs. 12–7, Fri.–Sat. 12–11
Fee: $5
Owners: Barringer and Michalec families
Winemakers: Dave Barringer and Dave Michalec
Wines: Pinot Gris, Chardonnays, Riesling, Pinot Noir, Syrah, Sangiovese, Merlot, Cabernet Sauvignon, Barbera, Nebbiolo, Meritage
Cases: 14,000
Special Features: Wine bar setting, live music Mon. nights

Changing the conversation surrounding wine from technical to sensual is the Naked Winery's mission. Although it's technically a Washington winery, the headquarters and not-to-be-missed tasting room/wine bar are in Hood River. A large, sexy lineup of more than 15 wines is poured in a city-chic yet comfortable bar where you can listen to live music. Provocative back labels are great conversation starters with fellow imbibers. If you like big and oaky wines, try the orgasmic: Oh! Barbera, Oh! Nebbiolo, Oh! Meritage, and Oh! Cabernet Sauvignon. Oh, yes!

QUENETT WINERY

541-386-2229
www.quenett.com
111 Oak Street
Tasting Room: Summer, daily 12–6; fall–spring, Wed.–Sun. 12–6 (later Fri.–Sat.)
Fee: $5 for six wines, waived with purchase
Owners: James and Molli Martin
Winemaker: Craig Larson
Wines: Chardonnay, Pinot Gris, Viognier, Cabernet Sauvignon, Sangiovese,

Naked Winery serves more than a tease to your palate. John Baker

Refillable wine bottles at Springhouse Cellar are economical and good for the environment. Courtesy Springhouse Cellar

Zinfandel, Merlot, Syrah, Barbera, red and white blends
Cases: 2,000

This winery's Napa-esque tasting bar is in downtown Hood River, but the winery is 30 miles to the east in The Dalles. A few select varietals are grown along the shores of the Columbia River, not far from where Lewis and Clark camped. The Corps of Discovery would surely list Quenett's Zinfandel as a necessity, but would have also enjoyed their other wines. The name Quenett is a Chinook word for "steelhead", the name for the sturdy rainbow trout that migrates to the ocean and back.

SPRINGHOUSE CELLAR
541-308-0700
www.springhousecellar.com
13 Railroad Avenue
Tasting Room: Mon.–Sat. 11–5, Sun. 1–5
Fee: Complimentary
Owners: James and Lisa Matthisen
Winemaker: James Matthisen
Wines: Chardonnay, Gewürztraminer, Merlot, Sangiovese, Cabernet Sauvignon, Cabernet Franc, red blends
Cases: 2,000

Special Features: Sling-top bottles.

With handcrafted wines named Perpetual Merlotion, Make Cab Not War, and Peace, Love and Chardonnay . . . what's not to love? Springhouse is currently the only winery in the state to offer refillable sling-top bottles for takeaway, using a specifically designed spigot system that allows minimal air exposure. More wine, less packaging: James estimates that thus far the refillables have saved more than 10,000 bottles, labels, corks, and capsules. All of his wines have won at least one medal, but his commitment is to Sangiovese.

THE PINES 1852 TASTING ROOM & GALLERY
541-993-8301
www.thepinesvineyard.com
202 State Street
Tasting Room: Wed.–Sun. 12–6, Thurs.–Sat. 12–9
Fee: $5, applied to purchase
Owners: Lonnie and Linda Wright
Winemaker: Peter Rosback
Wines: Pinot Gris, Viognier, old-vine Zinfandel, Pinot Noir, Syrah, Merlot,

The Pines 1852 combines a tasting room with an art gallery. Courtesy The Pines 1852 Tasting Room & Gallery

Over the River and through the Vines

What in the Sam Hill is this? And why is a Washington winery in a book about Oregon? We'll answer the second question first: Even if we ignore the Maryhill complex, you can't miss the stately buildings on a bluff across the Columbia on the Washington side. It looks as if an English country estate was dropped into the high desert.

As for the question "What in the Sam Hill is this?" . . . the answer lies in none other than Sam Hill himself. The man for whom the question was coined long dreamed of constructing a highway through the daunting Columbia Gorge, and so in 1907 he created a community on a parcel of arid lands at the Gorge's eastern terminus. He named the town for his daughter, Mary, and began building a mansion more befitting his native Minneapolis.

Hill managed to punch a breathtaking highway through the Gorge, but even with the vast Columbia tantalizingly close, he couldn't find a way to get enough water to his remote community. He abandoned construction in 1917. The story might have ended there except a longtime friend of Hill's, a renowned Parisian dancer named Loie Fuller, suggested that he finish the mansion and turn it into an art museum featuring works from France. The museum was dedicated in 1926 and still under construction when Hill died unexpectedly five years later, leaving the building in limbo. Finally, the wife of a San Francisco sugar magnate took it upon herself to finish the project, and on April 13, 1940, Hill's birthday, it opened to the public with a wide array of art.

Today, the museum hosts a variety of summer programs revolving around the arts, ranging from Shakespearean plays to concerts in the amphitheatre on a lush green lawn overlooking the Columbia.

And for curiosities and oddities, the Maryhill Museum of Art and Winery now rates a close second to the full-sized Stonehenge replica three miles to the east on WA 14. Built by Hill and completed just before his death in 1930, the circular concrete creation is his tribute to World War I veterans from Klickitat County.

Oh, and thanks to the modern marvels of irrigation, there's a large winery and tasting room at Maryhill now, too. Highlights include free music every weekend in the summer, and concerts with marquee performers.

Cabernet Sauvignon, red and white blends, port-style wine
Cases: 5,000
Special Features: Live music Thurs.–Sat.

This winery, named for a stately grove of ponderosa pines on a farm plowed out of the Oregon Territory in 1852, might be home to the oldest surviving vines in the state. Photos dated 1911 show Zinfandel vines planted by Italian immigrant Louis Camini, who brought them from his homeland, Genoa. Current owner Lonnie Wright painstakingly revived the vineyard. Family-owned and -operated, this dairy farm turned vineyard turned winery is renowned for its old-vine Zinfandel. All the wines are heavily fruit-driven and complex. The tasting room/art gallery is in downtown Hood River, but the vineyard has a split personality: The line between the Columbia Gorge and Columbia Valley AVAs literally bisects Wright's property.

Lodging in the Columbia Gorge

HOOD RIVER
COLUMBIA GORGE HOTEL
541-386-5566 or 800-345-1921
www.columbiagorgehotel.com

4000 Westcliff Drive
Rates: $129–229
Special Features: 208-foot waterfall on the grounds, patio dining overlooking the river, Simon's restaurant

This Gorge landmark has a country-estate feel, punctuated by extraordinary views of the Columbia River from its perch on a bluff. Built in 1904, it was renovated two decades later when the Columbia Gorge Highway was completed, using leftover stones from the roadway. The new owners envisioned a luxurious retreat for visitors who had navigated the Gorge from the East in their Model T's. Over the years, the hotel has hosted American icons, including presidents Calvin Coolidge and Franklin Roosevelt. Not surprisingly, Women's Entertainment Television rated the hotel among the country's top 10 wedding sites. Surprisingly, the hotel closed in 2009, but by the end of the year the bank had reopened the property, a sale was pending, and wedding bookings were pouring in.

COLUMBIA CLIFFS VILLAS

Owners: Steve Tessmer and others
866-912-8366
www.columbiacliffvillas.com
3880 Westcliff Drive
Rates: $195–395
Special Features: Probably the poshest accommodations in the area

A development company had plans for creating luxury condos adjacent to, and utilizing services from, the Columbia Gorge Hotel. When the economy went into free fall and the hotel closed temporarily, the condo complex needed to reinvent itself and decided to offer a wider range of lodging options. The choices range from European hotel rooms to a penthouse suite with a dining table that seats 22. Private chef service in your condo is available, as well as limited room service from the bistro at the White Buffalo Wine Shop next door.

HOOD RIVER HOTEL

Owners: Brian and Penny Cunninghame
541-386-1900 or 800-386-1859
www.hoodriverhotel.com
102 Oak Street
Rates: $89–159
Special Features: Kitchen suites, $10 breakfast voucher for the indoor/outdoor restaurant

The hotel is on the National Register of Historic Places, but it requires some imagination—or at least a gaze at the old photos adorning the walls—to see it that way. The original hotel, a stately wood Victorian structure, towered above the town on a site next door. That building was demolished in 1913, leaving only an annex where the current hotel sits. Efforts were made to retain the building's old-world European essence when it was renovated. The 32 rooms and nine suites each feature antique furnishings and either four-poster or sleigh beds, some with lace canopies. Riverview rooms are the most coveted.

INN AT THE GORGE

Owners: Frank and Michele Bouche
541-386-4429 or 877-852-2385
www.innatthegorge.com
1113 Eugene Street
Rates: $119–159
Special Features: Discounted lift tickets to Mt. Hood Meadows ski area, in-room DVDs, homemade tarts at breakfast

This classic Queen Anne home near downtown Hood River has five guest rooms, all with private bath. The backyard is lush and private, for those wanting a little quiet time. The rooms and bathrooms are a little cozy, but the suite does have a kitchen. Noise from nearby traffic can be an issue, but the shrubbery and trees dull some of the din. Hearty breakfasts and go beyond the basic eggs, bacon, and pancakes.

LAKECLIFF B&B

Owners: James and Allyson Pate
541-386-7000
www.lakecliffbnb.com
3820 Westcliff Drive
Rates: $150–175
Special Features: Atkins and South Beach Diet meals upon request

Lakecliff feels like an English country cottage tucked into a Douglas fir forest—until you arrive at this 1908 summer home and catch a glimpse of the Columbia from this lofty locale. Each of the four floral-themed rooms features a fireplace, private bath, and river view. Enjoy your breakfast on the deck overlooking the river, and then stroll the inviting three-acre grounds.

SAKURA RIDGE FARM AND LODGE

Owners: John and Deanna Joyer
541-386-2636 or 877-472-5872
www.sakuraridge.com
5601 York Hill Drive
Rates: $150–225
Special Features: Sheep, geese, and the hum of tractors reveal the working character of the place

Want to get away from the hum of Hood River? This stunning 5,000-square-foot lodge in the center of a working pear and cherry farm is on a lush bench above town. It's a little more than four miles from I-84. Three of the five bright and cheery rooms feature views of snow-flanked Mount Hood. All five have private tubs and showers. Breakfast includes produce from the farm, and creatively incorporates organic heirloom tomatoes, berries, pears, and squash. *Sakura* is Japanese for "cherry blossom."

SEVEN OAKS B&B

Owner: Greg Herman
541-386-7622
www.sevenoaksbb.com
1373 Barker Road

Rates: $85–150
Special Features: Discounted Mt. Hood Meadows ski tickets

Seven Oaks has five spacious and tastefully decorated rooms and a separate "cottage" that looks more like a converted shed but has all the creature comforts. The main house was built by French inventor and craftsman August Guignard, and it is on the National Register of Historic Places. The peaceful grounds and gardens, lush and immaculately manicured, include a backdrop of Mount Hood and Mount Adams. It's a place to retreat to the porch swing, contemplate life and the virtues of wine.

VINEYARD VIEW B&B

866-588-8466
www.vineyardviewbnb.com
4240 Post Canyon Drive
Rates: $95–200
Special Features: Private winery and vineyard tours at four area wineries; spa, sport, golf, and romance packages

This B&B is a roll of the dice in terms of hospitality, but there's no denying its connection to wine. Some of the rooms have views of the Cathedral Ridge Winery vineyards. The grounds feature pears, plums, and Himalayan blackberries, all of which find their way to the breakfast table. The Honeymoon Suite has a hot tub, and another suite is set up for families.

MOSIER
THE MOSIER HOUSE B&B

Owners: Koerner family
541-478-3640 or 877-328-0351
www.mosierhouse.com
704 Third Avenue
Rates: $85–125
Special Features: Gardens, creek and pond

Mosier House is an appealing restored 1904 Victorian home—built by town founder Jefferson Newton Mosier himself—that consists of five nonsmoking guest rooms full of antiques. The master suite has a private entrance and views of ponds and a creek. The other four, smaller rooms share a bath with a clawfoot tub. In keeping with Gorge tradition, the baked goods and fruits are locally grown and produced.

Dining in the Columbia Gorge

HOOD RIVER
CELILO RESTAURANT & BAR
541-386-5710
www.celilorestaurant.com
16 Oak Street
Open: Daily 11:30–3 and 5 P.M.–close
Price: Expensive
Credit Cards: Yes
Special Features: Many naturally raised and organic ingredients are grown or acquired within a few miles of the front door

Ben Stenn and Jacqueline Carey place a conscious emphasis on local organic foods, and choose the best of both from foragers' offerings each morning. Enjoy their intriguing cuisine in a casual bistro setting with understated sophistication. Wines and brews are predominantly from Oregon and Washington, and the service is attentive to detail. The emphasis on handmade and sustainable products is consistent down to the tasty flatbread crackers and wooden beams, which are reclaimed castoffs from the Columbia River. Celilo even converts its used vegetable oil into biodiesel that powers the company car.

DIVOTS RESTAURANT AT INDIAN CREEK GOLF COURSE
541-308-0304
www.indiancreekgolf.com
3605 Brookside Drive
Open: Daily 11–9
Price: Inexpensive to moderate
Credit Cards: Yes
Special Features: Happy hour 3–6 daily, outdoor patio dining with views of Mount Hood and Mount Adams

Usually a golf course restaurant doesn't earn first-rate billing, but Divots is distinct. This is a local favorite that serves Northwest cuisine at reasonable prices. The menu ranges from intriguing salads and bento to ahi tartar and Korean short ribs. Don't miss the Peteloaf, the chef's version of meatloaf served with classic sides.

FULL SAIL BREWING COMPANY TASTING ROOM AND PUB
541-386-2247
www.fullsailbrewing.com
506 Columbia Street
Open: Daily 11:30 A.M.–close
Price: Inexpensive to moderate
Credit Cards: Yes
Special Features: Free brewery tours at 1, 2, and 4 P.M. daily

A million bottles of beer on the wall, or at least off the assembly line: That's how many bottles Full Sail produces annually, and then some. Take a break from vino fatigue at one of Oregon's first microbreweries while viewing the river action below. The pub-type food is above average and so is the service. Beer is used as an ingredient in most menu items, from sauerkraut to Imperial Stout brownies. Excellent fish and chips, sustainable local beef, and even a tempeh burger made at the Tofurkey factory next door are menu favorites. CEO and founder Irene Firmat and her husband, executive brewmaster James Emmerson, take environmentally sound business practices seriously. Full Sail pretreats all of its runoff and recycles religiously. It's an employee-owned business and it shows in the service and cheerful attitudes. Their efforts earned the 2008 Oregon Sustainable Tourism Award from the state's governor.

Take a break from vino fatigue at Full Sail Brewery in Hood River.   John Baker

SIXTH STREET BISTRO & LOFT

541-386-5737
www.sixthstreetbistro.com
509 Cascade Avenue
Open: Daily 11:30–9:30 (later Fri.–Sat.)
Price: Moderate
Credit Cards: Yes
Special Features: Green Smart–certified business; celebrates local producers who raise crops and meats in environmentally sensitive ways

Choose from stacked sandwiches, wraps, and a wide variety of mouthwatering burgers in this popular establishment. Dinner options include Pad Thai, pasta, and local, natural pork and beef. Oregon and Washington wines dominate the list, with some California added for balance. Twelve local brews are on tap. Service can be slow.

SOPHIE'S

541-386-1183
www.sophieshoodriver.com
1810 Cascade Avenue
Open: Wed.–Sun. 5:30–close (varies by season)
Price: Moderate

Credit Cards: Yes
Special Features: Small outdoor patio is buffered from street noise by stucco walls that also provide a sense of intimacy.

New to proprietorship are John Helleberg and Marcie Wily, both formerly of Celilo. Their ambitious menu relies upon produce raised on their one-acre home site, including 100 varieties of heirloom tomatoes. The restaurant is named for their young daughter and has the feel of a congenial pub. The compact wine list is strongly local, with some unusual selections added for flair.

STONEHEDGE GARDENS

541-386-3940
www.stonehedgegardens.com
3405 Cascade Avenue
Open: Daily 5 P.M.–close
Price: Moderate
Credit Cards: Yes
Special Features: Wine dinners; voted Best Outdoor Dining in the Gorge by *Best Places Northwest*

Owners Mike and Shawna Caldwell purchased this restored 1898 home in 2000.

Mike was maitre d' at the Columbia Gorge Hotel and cellar master at what is now Cathedral Ridge Winery. The house is divided into four dining rooms, including the Grand Room showcasing the fireplace. The Italian-stone patio has five levels and seats up to 200. Entrées that don't break the bank include fresh Oregon salmon (suggested pairing: Winter's Hill Pinot Noir), Portobello-stuffed ravioli with local pear chutney, and New Zealand rack of lamb. North Oak Brasserie (113 Third St.) is another distinctive Hood River eatery owned by the Caldwells; Stonehedge and North Oak share a Web site.

3 RIVERS GRILL
541-386-8883
www.3riversgrill.com
601 Oak Street
Open: Daily 11–11
Price: Moderate
Credit Cards: Yes
Special Features: Summer outdoor dining

Combine extraordinary views and a renovated historic house with organic, local food and an award-winning wine list, and you can see why 3 Rivers is perhaps Hood River's most popular dining spot. An inspiring mosaic wall borders the property and represents all that Hood River has to offer—a great place for family, recreation, animals, the outdoors, and fruit. The community art project took more than a year. It's the creation of children of all ages, under the direction of two local artists. The grill has as many tantalizing dishes as it has seating options. Bring friends and share while enjoying a spectacular view from

every seat in one of five dining rooms, the deck, or the patio. Choice meals include Columbia River salmon (in season), local beefsteaks, Idaho trout, and fried razor clams from the Oregon coast. The wine list is heavily local; *Wine Press Northwest* rated it "Outstanding."

MOSIER
GOOD RIVER RESTAURANT
541-478-0199
www.goodriverrestaurant.com
904 Second Avenue
Open: Daily 5 P.M.–close, Sun. 9–2 (brunch); winter, Wed. – Sat. 5 P.M.–close
Price: Inexpensive to Moderate
Credit Cards: Yes
Special Features: The Thirsty Woman, next door, is Good River's sister pub and garden.

Sporting 16 local beers on tap, it serves food from the restaurant in a colorful outdoor setting. Cycling enthusiast chef Barry Ramsey and his wife, Zeb, brought their award-winning restaurant experience from back East to this tiny hamlet and created a hidden gem. Situated in a recycled river house, a dozen tables afford personal service by an accommodating staff. A corner bar seats about eight more. Enticing entrées include various all-natural beef burgers, pizzas (smoked bacon, caramelized pears, bleu cheese, and mozzarella is a fave), and pappardelle pasta with oysters, local mushrooms, and tarragon from the herb garden. Brunch has tantalizing choices, but do not pass on the caramelized (local) pear pancakes. Try the basket of fries with three dipping sauces for a decadent treat with a chilled rosé.

Attractions in the Columbia Gorge
You might want to start your journey on the east end of the Gorge in The Dalles, home of the **Gorge Discovery Center** (541-296-8600). Technically it is east of the Columbia Gorge AVA, but it is full of information on geology, geography, wildlife, vegetation, and ancient cultures.

The Mount Hood Scenic Railroad traverses the Hood River canyon. Courtesy Mount Hood Scenic Railroad

To get a grand early perspective on the area's scenic wonders en route to the wineries on the Oregon side, take a side trip up the old **Columbia Gorge Historic Highway** (US 30) to the interpretive center in the octagon-shaped **Vista House** at Crown Point. Rising some 730 feet above the river, the Vista House is perhaps the most-photographed location in the Gorge. Just east of Crown Point is the spectacular **Multnomah Falls**, which plunges 620 feet from a lip directly above a historic lodge.

For relaxing diversions on unique forms of transportation, take the **Mount Hood Scenic Railroad and Dinner Train** (800-872-4661) south up the Hood River Valley. Choose from dinner, brunch, or a ride on the wild side of the rails during a murder mystery dinner show. The train ride terminates at the **Hutson Museum** (541-352-6808), located on a national historic site and chock-full of Native American dolls, arrowheads, rocks, and taxidermy. If you prefer a watery route, the **Sternwheeler Columbia Gorge** (541-374-8427) hosts day, dinner, and charter cruises, and gives another perspective of the Gorge.

Hood River County has been home to the state's most prolific fruit orchards since the 1850s—hence, the **Fruit Loop** (800-366-3530). A 35-mile scenic driving tour of orchards, forests, farmlands, vineyards, wineries, dining establishments, and quintessential B&Bs, the route starts at Hood River and finishes up the valley in the community of Mount Hood.

Recreation in the Columbia Gorge

Any mention of the Gorge and recreation begins with **windsurfing** and **kite-boarding**. Wind is a given, especially around Hood River, where on any given spring or summer day the Columbia is awash with the bright colors of sails skimming, sweeping, and cart-wheeling across the whitecaps in 40-knot breezes.

For landlubbers, **bicycling** has become a favored sport around Hood River, whether it's a casual pedal along Old Highway 30 or a more strenuous climb up the valley along the cascading river for which the town is named. **Mountain biking** is excellent in the summer, but it becomes especially good in the fall after the first rains improve traction.

Even when it's 100 degrees in August, you can windsurf in the morning and ski in the afternoon at **Mt. Hood Skibowl**, site of the only year-round ski area in the U.S. (and largest night-ski area).

Though salmon numbers aren't what they once where, salmon fishing is still a state religion, and it isn't uncommon for fishermen to reel in 30-pound Chinook or feisty 10-pound wild steelhead out of the Columbia as they head for spawning grounds in the river's.

For **golf** enthusiasts, the Gorge has seven courses of varying difficulty. And just when you think you've seen it all, a new sport has come to the Columbia Gorge: **stand-up paddling**. Basically, all it requires is an oversized surfboard, a paddle, a wet suit, and one of those rare days when the Columbia is calm.

The Gorge White House treats you to many tastes from the Gorge.   Jeff Welsch

Shopping in the Columbia Gorge

For shoppers, Hood River's quaint downtown offers a little bit of everything for everyone with its seemingly endless array of boutiques and galleries, bicycle and windsurfing shops, and stores loaded with antiques and nick-nacks.

Wine Shopping in the Columbia Gorge

The **Gorge White House** (541-386-2828, 2265 Hwy. 35), just up the hill from Hood River, offers many local wines to savor by the taste, glass, or bottle, has local beer on tap, and sells fruit, flowers, and other Gorge products. **White Buffalo Wines** (541-386-5534 or 503-753-3134, 4040 W. Cliff Dr.) is a blend of wine shop, tasting room, and lunch spot where about 90 percent of the 250 wines are from the Northwest. **The Wine Sellers** (541-386-4647, 514 State St.), which opened in the historic Smith House in 1985, offers wines that span the globe, including many from the region, and daily free tastings.

Information

Hood River County Chamber of Commerce, 541-386-2000, 405 Portway Ave., Hood River, www.hoodriver.org

Columbia Gorge Wines, 866-413-9463, www.columbiagorgewine.com

9

The Oregon Coast

Sea Breezes and Fruit Wines

By now, perhaps all this talk about Oregon's progressive attitudes might be getting old. But let's give credit where it's due. Not only are Oregonians forward-thinking about the land, they're pretty protective of the sea, too. Unlike neighboring California and Washington, Oregon had the foresight to decide that its stunning coastline—with long strips of beach punctuated by towering capes and jagged rock formations hugged tightly by US 101— belongs to everyone. The result: Every square inch of coastal beaches belongs to the public, a hard-fought right held dear by the state's residents.

The Oregon Coast's geography doesn't change much from north to south, but its climate does. From Astoria down to Coos Bay, clouds, fog, and rain are a common theme, and even in the summer it's not unusual for temperatures to be in the mid-60s at, say, Newport while they're in the mid-90s some 55 miles away in Corvallis. Farther south, Bandon and Brookings are known for warmer temperatures and sunnier days, albeit still blustery, much like the northern California coast.

Getting Here and Around

There's no easy way to navigate this area, but that's part of the beauty. If one of the many twisty, winding drives through the misty Coast Range doesn't take your breath away, the intermittent views of the coastline surely will.

You can fly from Portland to Astoria and Newport: **SeaPort Airlines** (888-573-2767) offers three flights daily to Astoria and two to Newport. In addition, Coos Bay/North Bend is served twice daily by **United Express** (800-864-8331), with flights from Portland and San Francisco.

The Coast Range is bisected by 12 highways, all between 50 and 70 miles long. All are scenic, snaking through verdant narrow valleys with stands of Douglas fir, blackberry brambles, and vine maple, with orange-barked Pacific madrone and sugar pine more prevalent farther south.

To make the coastal wine tour from north to south, take US 30 from Portland along the Columbia River to Astoria. Once on the coast, expect to move slowly along US 101 because of heavy traffic (especially in summer), numerous communities, and frequent cape traver-

OPPOSITE: *Heceta Head is one of the most photographed settings on Oregon's spectacular coast.* John Baker

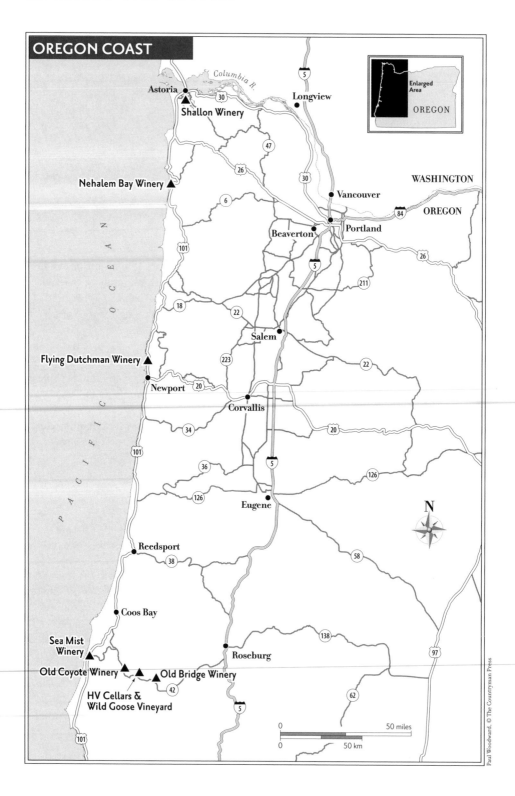

OREGON COAST

Columbia R.

Astoria

Shallon Winery

Longview

Nehalem Bay Winery

WASHINGTON

Vancouver

OREGON

Beaverton

Portland

PACIFIC OCEAN

Salem

Flying Dutchman Winery

Newport

Corvallis

Eugene

Reedsport

Coos Bay

Sea Mist Winery

Roseburg

Old Coyote Winery

Old Bridge Winery

HV Cellars & Wild Goose Vineyard

Enlarged Area

OREGON

N

0   50 miles

0   50 km

Paul Woodward. © The Countryman Press

sals. You'll need more than a day, and preferably three or four, to do justice to the 250 miles of viewing pleasure from Astoria to Bandon.

THE NORTH COAST (ASTORIA TO LINCOLN CITY)

Oregon's north coast is rugged, wet, and windy, with old forests and towering capes separated by the estuaries of well-known salmon streams. The primary working communities are Astoria and Tillamook; Seaside and Cannon Beach are favorite vacation and weekend destinations, particularly for Portlanders.

Wineries along the North Coast

ASTORIA
SHALLON WINERY
503-325-5978
www.shallon.com
1598 Duane Street
Tasting Room: Daily 1–6
Fee: Complimentary
Owner/Winemaker: Paul van der Veldt
Wines: Zinfandel; chocolate, fruit, and whey wines
Cases: Under 1,000
Special Features: Two blocks from Maritime Museum; open 365 days of the year for the past 25 years

In what was once a showroom for Packard cars and later a bicycle shop, Shallon's tasting-room visitors are treated to one-of-a-kind wines and an extraordinary view of the gaping breadth of the Columbia River. The only traditional wine made here is the

Shallon makes a chocolate wine. Courtesy Shallon Winery

Zinfandel, and that's only periodically. Van der Veldt's signature wine is a chocolate orange whey—yes, whey—concoction that he describes as a "liquid chocolate truffle." He uses six different chocolates from four countries. Among his other favorites are his lemon meringue pie, wild Hawaiian mango, and wild evergreen blackberry wines. You get the idea.

NEHALEM
NEHALEM BAY WINERY
503-368-9463 or 888-368-9463
www.nehalembaywinery.com
34965 Highway 53
Tasting Room: Daily 10–6
Fee: $5, refunded with purchase
Owner/Winemaker: Ray Shackelford
Wines: Chardonnay, Gewürztraminer, Pinot Gris, Riesling, Cabernets, Maréchal Foch, Merlot, Pinot Noir, fruit wines
Cases: 4,500
Special Features: Music festivals, barbecues, wedding and events facility

Of all the claims made by Oregon's nearly 400 wineries, Nehalem Bay's is the most abnormal—or should we say paranormal? The moaning, creaking, and shadowy figures going bump in the night here even induced a group of supernatural experts from McMinnville to come check it out. The verdict: Yep, they're *heeerrre.* Who can blame a couple friendly ghosts for hanging around a winery? The living folks at Nehalem Bay are entertaining sorts as well. Owner Ray Shackelford is a Texas emigrant who does philanthropic work domestically and in Africa and Southeast Asia. The winery was opened in 1974 in an abandoned creamery about a mile off US 101, and first produced a blackberry wine. Nehalem Bay does a brisk business, and as far as Shackelford and his managers can tell, the wines are all consumed by the living.

Lodging along the North Coast

ASTORIA
CANNERY PIER HOTEL
503-325-4996 or 888-325-4996
www.cannerypierhotel.com
10 Basin Street
Rates: $189–550
Special Features: Convenient to dining at Bridgewater Bistro; several banquet and meeting rooms

When the Cannery Pier Hotel touts its location *on* the river, they are not exaggerating. Indeed, the swanky five-story boutique hotel sits on a pier 600 feet above the Columbia, with magnificent oceanic views from each room. It's obvious from first glance that the hotel was once an actual cannery, and great care was taken during renovation to ensure that its character was retained. The suites all have balconies and fireplaces, but for a truly memorable stay, rent the exclusive Pilot House penthouse suite on the fifth floor. It has a kitchen, fireplace, and views all around.

CANNON BEACH
ARCH CAPE INN & RETREAT
800-436-2848
www.archcapeinn.com
31970 East Ocean Lane
Rates: $249–389
Special Features: Saturday night Dungeness crab feeds in dining area (reservations recommended)

Start with a spectacularly beautiful castle-like setting overlooking the Pacific from a fir-bathed hillside. Add extra touches in every room, such as a fireplace, bath and spa extras, wine and appetizers, and a three-course gourmet breakfast. Then complement your retreat with a dinner of pan-seared salmon or roasted quail created by one of two master chefs. If you like to be spoiled, the Arch Cape Inn & Retreat is your place.

NEHALEM
NEHALEM RIVER INN & RESTAURANT
503-368-7708
www.nehalemriverinn.com
34910 Highway 53
Rates: $100–185
Special Features: Restaurant with wine bar and outdoor patio (reservations advised)

All you need for a bucolic escape is a few miles inland on the banks of the Nehalem River. The inn has four comfortable rooms, two with private bathrooms. The Champagne Cottage by the river boasts a four-poster bed and an outdoor Jacuzzi. The French-style restaurant uses organic produce and locally caught seafood, and can easily fill your coastal cravings with carefully crafted entrées by chef Ryan Hamic. The wine list is heavily regional.

Dining along the North Coast

ASTORIA
BRIDGEWATER BISTRO
503-325-6777
www.bridgewaterbistro.com
20 Basin Street
Open: Mon.–Sat. 11:30–3 and 5 P.M.–close, Sun. 11–3 (brunch) and 5 P.M.–close
Price: Moderate
Credit Cards: Yes
Special Features: "Afternoon small bites" served Mon.–Sat. 3–5, Happy Hour Mon.–Fri. 4–6, full bar, wedding and party facilities

An extensive wine list is only part of the charm at Bridgewater, which offers all the regional seafood choices you would expect at a restaurant located across the water from a former cannery. The views of the Columbia and the dramatic Astoria-Megler Bridge spanning the gaping river are a treat, especially on one of those rare sunny days where it's comfortable to sit on the patio. Bridgewater, an Astoria institution for three decades, emphasizes Oregon wines from large and small producers alike.

SILVER SALMON GRILLE

503-338-6640
www.silversalmongrille.com
1105 Commercial Street
Open: Daily 11 A.M.–close
Price: Moderate to Expensive
Credit Cards: Yes

Owners Jeff and Laurie Martin embrace all that is Astoria: colorful history, a touristy ambiance, and fresh seafood from a perfect perch. Their traditional seafood, pasta, and steak menu has much to offer and adds uniqueness with low-carb entrées or sandwiches and sugar-free desserts. Silver Salmon has a reasonably priced, extensive, and varied (by the bottle, half bottle, or glass) wine list, and the bottles are cellared for quality control. They also have wine under their own label, which is made from Columbia Valley grapes at Maryhill Winery in Washington.

CLEMENTE'S

503-325-1067
www.clementesrestaurant.com
1198 Commercial Street
Open: Tues.–Sun. 11–3 and 5–9
Price: Moderate to expensive
Credit Cards: Yes
Special Features: Events facility, live music Sun., art gallery, outdoor market Sun. from May to October

Sea-fresh, sustainable cuisine is the name of the game at Clemente's. Copper River salmon tartar, Dungeness crab Caesar salad, Willapa clams steamed with onion and garlic, yellowfin tuna (in season), award-winning chowder made with two kinds of clams . . . it's a seafood lover's nirvana. Love to sample wine with small plates? They do that, too, serving a three-wine flight and two seasonal tapas for a remarkably reasonable price. Speaking of reasonable, the lounge menu has seafood such as a crab or shrimp melt, a halibut or salmon basket, and bacon-wrapped scallops, each for $10 or less. On the green side, Clemente's uses rice oil for frying and then utilizes the spent grease for biofuel. As for wine, they're partial to Oregon offerings.

SEASIDE
YUMMY WINE BAR & BISTRO

503-738-3100
www.yummywinebarbistro.com
831 Broadway Avenue
Price: Moderate
Credit cards: Yes
Open: Thurs.–Mon. 3–close (usually 9 or 10)
Special Features: Several menus, retail wine shop, classes, wine dinners, art gallery

Welcome to the hippest place in Oregon's quintessential tourist town. The name suggests a good time, and that's what you should have. The focus is on the wine

Yummy Wine Bar calls a renovated fire station its home. Courtesy Yummy Wine Bar

experience, and Yummy's offers wine by the taste, glass, flight, or bottle. The wines come from around the world—including the Pacific Northwest—and change seasonally. Bites and bits off the Happy Hour menu include a cheese pizza, shrimp quesadilla, or BLT at a happy $4-5. Move into appetizers and choose from shrimp ceviche, an onion tartlet, or cheese and charcuterie plates for not much more. Stay for dinner and find more regional and seasonal choices: beef kabobs with sweet potato hash, the catch of the day, or pasta with basil, goat cheese, and chicken. Still not satiated? Finish with a light sorbet made from Oregon berries.

Attractions along the North Coast

Astoria

Begin your coast tour at the end—**Fort Clatsop** (503-861-2471), a replica of the rainy place that Lewis and Clark's Corps of Discovery called home in the winter of 1805–06. Among the features is an exhibit of the fort that the 33-member Corps built. Also worth the time is riding the **Astoria Riverfront Trolley** (503-325-6311), which was built in 1913 and used in San Antonio, Texas, until coming to the Pacific Northwest in the 1990s. Before leaving Astoria, visit the **Columbia River Maritime Museum** (503-325-2323, 1792 Marine Dr.). The museum has an eye-catching exhibit before you even get inside—an actual 44-foot Coast Guard boat on artificial waves, rescuing a storm-struck boater from the perilous mouth of the Columbia, a.k.a. the Graveyard of the Pacific.

Tillamook

Down US 101 in cheese country, the **Tillamook Air Museum** (503-842-1130, 6030 Hangar Rd.) is almost impossible to miss because of its colossal size and the 50-foot-high words on its side: "Air Museum." The museum is actually a hangar that once housed blimps to be used in case Japanese submarines showed up offshore during World War II.

Recreation along the North Coast

Don't drive the length of the Oregon Coast without stopping to work off some of the wine and cheese on one of many jaw-dropping hikes. The best are **Cape Lookout** and **Cascade Head**. Cape Lookout is a stunning two-mile walk through towering Douglas firs to the tip of a narrow peninsula that juts into the Pacific south of Tillamook. Cascade Head, named for waterfalls crashing into the ocean, has three moderate trails to meadows that overlook the dramatic Pacific.

Shopping along the North Coast

Astoria

Downtown Astoria is the place to be, with a range of bookstores, antiques shops, boutiques, galleries, and other quaint offerings in view of the dramatic Columbia River on Commercial Street. Try to catch the **Astoria Sunday Market** (503-325-1010) and its flotilla of 200 vendors under white tents every Sunday from May to October.

Seaside

Seaside is a rapidly evolving tourist town with an ever-growing number of boutiques moving in alongside a Coney Island–esque array of souvenir shops, kite merchants, and beach-

More Cheese, Please

It only makes sense that an agricentric state would be at the forefront of the artisan-cheese movement—or at least less than a lap behind California. After all, herds of dairy cows, goats, and sheep traverse Oregon's hillsides, munching on the sweet grasses that provide special flavors much as the soils provide distinct flavors to the wine grapes.

The most renowned cheese company, **Tillamook** (503-815-1300, 4175 Hwy. 101 N.) celebrated its 100-year anniversary in 2009. Tillamook is such a mega-producer that they have most of the state's cow's milk under contract. Now made from rBST-free milk, their dairy products are widely available. The year-round visitor center offers informative self-guided daily tours that include a viewing deck where you can see the curds and whey. It is definitely worth an hour (though it could take two). Plus, they give lots of samples.

Stop by the Tillamook cheese factory for a tour and samples.

Travel Oregon

Tom Vella of Sonoma, California, started southern Oregon's **Rogue Creamery** (541-664-1537, 311 N. Front St., Central Point) during the Great Depression. When jobs were needed most, he voluntarily paid premium prices to small dairy farmers in the Rogue River Valley. During World War II, he also sent millions of pounds of cheddar to soldiers overseas. After permeating the secretive walls of the Roquefort Association in France, Vella built another facility and began making blue cheeses in 1957.

The inspirational man behind the mission died in 1998 (at age 100) and the business was turned over to his son Ignazio. Unable to run Vella in Sonoma and the Oregon creamery, Ignazio sold to co-buyers who promised with a handshake to keep the Rogue plant open and stick to his father's principles. Today, the award-winning cheese is readily available, but it's more fun to buy it from the source.

Juniper Grove (541-923-8353, 2024 SW 58th St., Redmond), one of the earliest farmstead cheese makers in Oregon, produces goat cheese made from livestock that graze on the high-desert grasses, reflecting the terroir of the farm. Juniper Grove's owner and fix-it guy, Peter (now Pierre) Kolisch, started his goat farm in 1985 after training in the art of cheese making in Normandy. His flagship cheese is the Tumalo Tomme, a firm, mountain-style *fromage* rubbed on pine planks during aging, giving it an irresistible and unique flavor. The farm has a self-serve shop that works on the honor system, just like in the good ol' days.

Alsea Acre Alpines began as, and still is, a cottage industry owned by marketer turned goat farmer Nancy Chandler, who started tending her herd of 60 multicolored French and American alpine goats through her son's 4-H project. Chandler learned to make four simpler styles of goat cheese from a friend and continues to cater to the American palate with milder, subtler flavors. Alsea Acres has stuck to the original business plan of "milk to money in four days," resisting the urge and demands to grow the five-acre farm. Alsea Acres is a drive-by and wave on the Oregon Country Trail, but you can buy her "party in a jar" marinated feta cubes and other cheeses at John Boy's Alsea Mercantile.

continued on next page

continued from previous page

Willamette Valley Cheese Company (503-399-5806) produces all-natural farmstead cheese from Jersey milk cows on organic pastures outside Salem. Rob Volbeda is a second-generation dairyman who started cheese production with his wife, Melissa, in 1993. Rob spent a decade perfecting family recipes before putting them on the market. The Volbedas' certified organic family farm is a recognizable name in Oregon, specializing in aged Goudas.

An up-and-comer on the farmstead market is Pat Morford of **River Edge Chèvre** (541-444-1362), who has a sustainable family farm in the pre-coastal community of Logsden near Newport. Her complex fresh and aged goat cheeses are served in top-notch restaurants and sold in many specialty stores across in the state.

Also worth the search, roughly from north to south:

Silver Falls Creamery (415 Myrtle Dr., Monmouth, 503-551-5687): blended soft, spreadable goat cheese

Ancient Heritage Dairy (42067 Hwy. 226, Scio, 503-394-2649): family-run sheep dairy specializing in raw and pasteurized soft and aged cheese and bleu cheese

Oregon Gourmet Cheeses (815 1st Ave., Albany, 541-928-8888): soft and aged cow's milk cheese

Fraga Farm (28580 Pleasant Valley Rd., Sweet Home, 541-367 3891): widely distributed fresh and aged goat cheese using certified organic raw and pasteurized milk

Tumalo Farms (64515 Mock Rd., Bend, 541-350-3718): gourmet, aged goat and cow cheeses, most notably the Pondhopper, made with a local microbrew

Fern's Edge Goat Dairy (39466 Hwy 58, Lowell, 541-937-3506): organic and biodynamic, fresh soft cheeses, aged and bloomy rind cheeses

Pholia Farm (9115 W. Evans Creek Rd., Rogue River, 541-582-8883): raw goat's milk cheese, visits by appointment

gear stores—mostly on the **Seaside Carousel Mall** (503-738-6728, 300 Broadway). For relic hounds, the **Seaside Antique Mall** (503-717-9312, 39 S. Holladay) probably has the widest and most diverse offerings.

Wine Shopping along the North Coast

ASTORIA

Surely the most renowned wine shop on the north coast—probably the entire Oregon coast—is Astoria's **Cellar on 10th** (503-325-6600, 1004 Marine Dr.), called a cellar for good reason: It's underground. The Cellar on 10th has a staggering assortment of wines from around the globe.

CANNON BEACH

A longtime favorite in these parts is **The Wine Shack** (503-436-1100, 124 Hemlock) in Cannon Beach, especially popular on Saturday for afternoon tastings. The Shack has offered a strong cadre of regional wines to go with hard-to-find international bottles for more than three decades. For surprisingly good in-and-out wine shopping nearby, **Surfcrest Market** (503-436-1189, 3140 S. Hemlock) has a large selection and conducts occasional tastings.

PACIFIC CITY

Once basket cases, the folks at Pacific City's lone wine hangout are now merely twisted. The **Twist Wine Company** (503-965-6887, 6425 Pacific Ave.), formerly Basket Case Wine, is an eco-oriented, socially progressive wine-tasting lounge with a flair for the zany.

THE CENTRAL COAST (LINCOLN CITY TO FLORENCE)

Oregon's central coast is much like the north, only it serves as a playground for folks in Salem, Albany, Corvallis, and Eugene. What makes this drive special is that the highway rarely leaves sight of the ocean, whether you're along the beach or high atop a cape. Newport is an authentic harbor town with personality, and state parks come at you one after another.

Wineries along the Central Coast

OTTER ROCK
FLYING DUTCHMAN WINERY

541-765-2553
www.dutchmanwinery.com
Address: 915 First Street
Tasting Room: June–Sept., daily 11–6, Oct.–May, daily 11–5
Fee: Complimentary for some, $5 for others
Owner/Winemaker: Richard Cutler
Wines: Chardonnay, Cabernet Franc, Cabernet Sauvignon, Pinot Noir, Syrah, fruit wines, fruit dessert wines
Cases: 1,800
Special Features: Flying Dutchman currently has a tasting room in Astoria (541-325-8110), in the Red Building next to the Cannery Pier Hotel. Call for hours.

Flying Dutchman began as a "micro-winery" and now occupies a rocky peninsula above the churning sea waters of Devil's Punchbowl. It is the one coastal winery where traditional wines are actually made. After the grapes arrive from the Willamette, Umpqua, Applegate, and Rogue valleys, they are fermented outdoors in the blustery, salty air for up to 10 days—about three times the normal fermentation period. The folks at Flying Dutchman believe the longer fermentation takes, the better the wine. It's then anywhere from 14 months to four years before a bottle is ready to be opened. One more niche: Flying Dutchman is the only producing coastal winery that has a Pacific Ocean view.

Flying Dutchman is the only Oregon winery with a full view of the Pacific.   Courtesy Flying Dutchman Winery

Lodging along the Central Coast

NEWPORT

EMBARCADERO RESORT HOTEL & MARINA

541-265-8521

www.embarcadero-resort.com

1000 SE Bay Boulevard

Rates: $104–269

Special Features: Restaurant, indoor heated pool, hot tubs, sauna, private crabbing and fishing dock, sundries store, gift shop, boat rentals, marina

Even the affordable patio guest rooms have views of Yaquina Bay and all the activities taking place at any given hour. If you want to spread out a little and have more expansive views, the Columbus on the Bay Suite offers two bedrooms and a top-floor view. At the Embarcadero, you're in the heart of the action on Newport's lively bay front.

Dining along the Central Coast

LINCOLN CITY

FATHOM'S RESTAURANT

541-994-1601

www.spanishhead.com/site/restaurant

4009 SW Highway 101

Open: Daily 9 A.M.–1 P.M. (brunch on Sun.)

Price: Expensive

Credit Cards: Yes

Special Features: Located in the Inn at Spanish Head, with phenomenal views of coastline; early-bird menu 4–5:30; Sunday champagne brunch

The penthouse views of the Pacific provide a command performance at Fathom's, which offers a solid array of seafood, steaks, and pasta to complement the setting. In addition, Fathom's has a monthly menu comprised of such treasures as marionberry pink-peppercorn salmon, or a porterhouse pork chop drizzled with aged balsamic and dressed with apple-raisin chutney. Don't skip the soup course, which

Fathoms Restaurant at the Inn at Spanish Head serves ocean views on the side. Courtesy Inn at Spanish Head

is either clam or smoked-halibut chowder. Oregon and Washington wines dominate the list and include Spanish Head's private label of Oregon origin.

NEWPORT

PANACHE

541-265-2929

www.panachenewport.com

614 West Olive Street

Open: Daily 4:30 P.M.–close

Price: Moderate

Credit Cards: Yes

Special Features: Live music occasionally, banquet facilities

We can't tell you how many times we've been in Newport (an hour away when we lived in Corvallis) looking for a fabulous, fresh meal from the sea. We had our favorite fish shacks, but full-dining options were bleak. So welcome, Panache! Bright, light, and airy with floor-to-ceiling windows, it serves up dishes like cranberry- and hazelnut-crusted halibut or pan-seared salmon dressed in pomegranate glaze and served with shitake risotto. With entrées for $20 or less, we've got a definite winner. For less enthusiastic fans of seafood: Organic lamb or pork chops, beef short ribs braised in Rogue Mocha Porter, or a chicken crock pie should suffice. Panache mixes it up with wines from the West Coast states and some popular South American selections, but most notably they have big-name and boutique Oregon producers gracing their wine list. Spindrift, Harris Bridge, and Vitis Ridge can share the spotlight with Elk Cove and Bethel Heights.

SAFFRON SALMON

541-265-8921
www.saffronsalmon.com
859 SW Bay Boulevard
Open: Thurs.–Tues. 11:30–2 and 5–8:30;
closed Nov. 1–Thanksgiving
Price: Expensive
Credit Cards: Yes
Special Features: Dining literally above the ocean, within feet of resident seals

Saffron Salmon is another breath of fresh sea air, with its delicate representations of fresh-caught Northwest cuisine and wines to match. Overhanging the bay at the edge of the pier on Newport's revitalized Bayfront, this spot is a gem for both lunch and dinner. The signature dish saffron salmon is served as either an entrée or a sandwich. There's a solid collection of Oregon wines, from Airlie to Eyrie. The

Newport is the Dungeness crab capital of the world.
Courtesy Newport Chamber of Commerce

atmosphere is laid-back and the space cozy, so reservations are recommended.

NYE BEACH
VILLAGE MARKET BISTRO & DELI

541-574-9393
741 NW Third Street
Open: Daily 11–5
Price: Moderate
Credit Cards: Yes
Special Features: Adjoining wine shop

If you're not in a hurry or on a budget, the Village Market is the place to grab a bite of gourmet fare to pair with an Oregon wine from the market's small shop. Your sense of adventure and patience will be rewarded with tasty treats such as house-made focaccia and dipping sauces, artisan cheeses, and deli sandwiches. You may want to take an hour or two to sniff the sea air and explore the historic Nye Beach area with one of four Sandwich Box selections to go.

APRIL'S AT NYE BEACH

541-265-6855
749 NW Third Street
Open: Wed.–Sun. 5 P.M.–close
Price: Expensive
Credit Cards: Yes
Special Features: Herbs, flowers, and summer produce come from the owners' five-acre farm in Toledo

Fifteen years old and still fresh is April and Ken Wolcott's smallish (38-seat) restaurant by the sea. Don't come for the views of the Pacific; come for the everything-from-scratch, never-deep-fried, Mediterranean cuisine. The Wolcotts' homegrown produce was introduced in 2009, and completes the already attractive package. A longtime favorite with locals for special occasions, it's a great place to celebrate life and the pursuit of the perfect wine and food pairing. A decent smattering of Oregon reds and whites will help you in your quest.

Attractions along the Central Coast

NEWPORT

Two words: **whale watching**. This twice-a-year
phenomenon of watching migrating gray whales is
as long awaited by some Oregonians as the end of
the rainy season. Though spouts are frequently visible from the coast, you can get up close and personal from a chartered whale-watching boat out of
Newport or Depoe Bay. **Marine Discovery Tours**
(541-265-6200, 345 SW Bay Blvd.), on Newport's
busy Bayfront, not only gets you within camera shot
of whales, but they'll also explore other areas of
Oregon's picturesque coastline. Be prepared for wet
weather and seasickness.

*A million gallons of fun can be had at
the Oregon Coast Aquarium in Newport.*
Travel Oregon

For a drier and less bouncy look at Pacific sea
life, visit Newport's **Oregon Coast Aquarium** (541-
867-3474, 2820 SE Ferry Slip Rd.), widely regarded
as one of the nation's finest. A highlight is the
walkway through glass portals where sharks and
other sea creatures are visible underfoot. The
nearby **Hatfield Marine Science Center** (541-867-
0100, 2030 SE Marine Science Dr.) is equally
intriguing for the more academically oriented—young and old alike.

YACHATS

On a coast famed for its lighthouses, none is more photographed than **Heceta Head
Lighthouse** (866-547-3696, 92072 Highway 101 S.), which is carved out of a rocky coastal
bluff about 12 miles north of Florence. The still-active lighthouse, whose fresnel lens can
be seen 21 miles out to sea, is just above the old lightkeeper's house and a reputedly
haunted bed-and-breakfast.

FLORENCE

Sea Lion Caves (541-547-3111, 91560 Hwy. 101 North) is a cavernous rookery for the
Stellar sea lion. A short hike and elevator ride takes you to the cave, where seals are sure to
be lounging, birds squawking, and perhaps even whales spouting in the distance.

Recreation along the Central Coast

NEWPORT

If you're an experienced boatman (or -woman), you can rent your own seagoing craft from
the **Embarcadero Resort Hotel and Marina** (541-265-8521, 1000 SE Bay Blvd.).

YACHATS

Cape Perpetua features 26 miles of hiking and biking trails—some to points overlooking
the sea, some to the beach, and one to a 500-year-old Sitka spruce.

FLORENCE

A favorite beach pastime is to ply the dramatic sand hills at **Oregon Dunes National
Recreation Area** (541-750-7000) in a dune buggy. **Sandland Adventures** (541-997-8087,

85336 Highway 101 S.) and **Sand Dunes Frontier** (541-997-3544, 83960 Highway 101 S.) have buggies for 2 to 10 passengers and also rent ATVs. **Aero Legends** (541-991-6139) offers 20-minute biplane rides along the coast for $130.

Golfers have numerous options on the central coast, ranging from nine-hole **Agate Beach Golf Course** (541-265-7331, 4100 Hwy. 101 N.) in Newport and **Crestview Golf Club** (541-563-3020, 1680 Crestline Dr.) in Waldport to the breathtaking 18-hole **Sandpine Golf Links** (800-917-4653, 1201 35th St.) in Florence and Oregon native Peter Jacobsen's swanky **Salishan Spa & Golf Resort** (541-764-3632, 7760 Highway 101 North) outside Gleneden Beach—one of the top courses in America.

Shopping along the Central Coast

LINCOLN CITY
This town is best known for the **Tanger Outlet Center** (541-996, 5000, 1500 SE Devils Lake Rd.), with more than 60 name-brand discount stores.

NEWPORT
Stroll through a historic district and get your shopping fix at the Cape Coddish collection of shops in the **Nye Beach** area. Your art and wine fix can be sated at the same time at the **Nye Beach Gallery** (541-265-3292, 715 NW Third St.), where tastings are conducted every Saturday afternoon. **Made In Oregon** (541-574-9020, 342 SW Bay Blvd.) offers a classy variety of gifts and other Oregon products. The Newport store is one of eight in the state.

Nye Beach is one of Newport's prime strolling and shopping areas. Courtesy Robert Smith

FLORENCE
A handy way to cover a lot of shopping in a short space is at **Old Town Florence**, a waterfront cluster of more than 60 stores. There are gift shops, galleries, restaurants, antiques, and myriad other stores on the Siuslaw River. And there's the **Organic Farmers Market** (541-997-1794, 1845 Hwy. 126) every Saturday in season.

Wine Shopping along the Central Coast

LINCOLN CITY
If you didn't get a chance to visit **Anne Amie's** winery in Carlton, they have a store—formerly the Chateau-Benoit Wine Food Center—at the Tanger Outlet Center (541-996-3981, 1500 SE E. Devils Lake Rd.).

GLENEDEN BEACH
On the grounds at Salishan Spa & Golf Resort is **Wine and Romance** (541-764-0238, 7760 Hwy. 101 N.), a small but nifty shop where you can peruse a credible assortment of wines while listening to old movies playing on a black-and-white TV.

Crush can be a very manual labor of love.
Courtesy Flying Dutchman Winery

Depoe Bay

If you missed tasting Nehalem Bay's wines, here's your second chance: The **Depoe Bay Winery** (541-765-3311, 22 Highway 101 South) is essentially an outlet store for the home office up the coast. It has the intriguing "Wine Cave" and views of surf crashing over US 101.

Newport

Swafford's Champagne Patio (541-265-3044, 1630 Hwy. 101 N.) has more than 900 wines to pair with smoked salmon, cheeses, and other gourmet fare for your wine tour. You can also pick up gift baskets for the folks you left behind.

Yachats

The Wine Place (541-547-5275, Hwy. 101 and West Fourth St.) is an offbeat retail wine shop that offers regular tastings of its Oregon wines. The newly minted **Yachats Wine Trader** (541-547-5100, 131 Hwy. 101) is both a bottle shop with more than 200 labels and a wine bar with food and specialty beers.

Florence

While in Old Town Florence, check out **Incredible & Edible Oregon** (541-997-7018, 1350 Bay St.), which features a large selection of Oregon wines, and **Grape Leaf Wine Shop & Bistro** (541-997-1646, 1269 Bay St.), where you can get international and regional wine offerings as well as gifts and gourmet foods.

The South Coast (Florence to Bandon)

The state's finest mountains of sand are a magnet for dune-buggy enthusiasts. Farther south is the industrial port of Coos Bay/North Bend. Bandon-by-the-Sea—more commonly known to as Bandon—has become one of the state's top coastal destinations for its rugged beauty.

Wineries along the South Coast

Bandon
SEA MIST WINERY
541-348-2351
www.seamistwinery.com
86670 Croft Lake Lane
Tasting Room: Mon.–Fri. 8–12 and 1–5, Sat.–Sun. by appointment
Fee: Complimentary
Owner/Winemaker: Ray Foster

Wines: Cranberry
Cases: Under 1,000
Special Features: View a working cranberry bog while sipping the fruits of their labor

At Sea Mist, it's all about doing one thing and doing it well: cranberries. Cranberry-blueberry. Cranberry-raspberry. Cranberry . . . period. Naturally fermented wines made from the abundant berry are, in a pure sense, "estate" wines. After all, Sea

Mist is located in a 20-acre cranberry bog just south of Bandon, which is perhaps the sunniest town on the Oregon Coast.

MYRTLE POINT

OLD COYOTE WINERY

541-572-8090
2025 Spruce Street
Tasting Room: Daily 11–6
Fee: Complimentary
Owners: Russell and Tina Barnett
Winemaker: Tina Barnett
Wines: Chardonnay, Interlochen, Pinot Noir, fruit wines
Cases: Under 500
Special Features: Bus tours, events facility (30-40 people), apple and cherry orchards

The story goes that Tina Barnett began making wine for fun after reading a how-to book. Now it's a business she can do from home, after several back surgeries left her work and income challenged. Her co-owner and husband built the stunning tasting room from native maple, myrtle, and tan-oak woods. The decor is Old West. As for the name, Tina was feeling overwhelmed and looking for a sign that she was on the right path. At that moment, a coyote passed in front of her, declaring her destiny, she believes.

HV CELLARS & WILD GOOSE VINEYARD

541-572-0251
46165 Highway 242
Tasting Room: By appointment only
Fee: Complimentary
Owners: Terry and Evelyn Luce
Winemaker: Terry Luce
Wines: Pinot Gris, Chardonnay, Pinot Noir, Baco Noir, red blend, blackberry and cranberry wines
Cases: 3,000
Special Features: Winery tours by appointment; bicycle and motorcycle camping

The home vineyard is located above the South Fork of the Coquille River valley, far enough inland to be spared the dramatic

Dining on the south coast matches bounty from the sea with the fruits of the earth. Courtesy Inn at Spanish Head

coastal weather. Thus, HV is able to grow 19 grape varietals in its Wild Goose Vineyard, making it the first and only estate winery in Coos County. For Baco Noir fans, Mark Girardet, a name synonymous with the hybrid, helped fashion this slightly different version. Don't dismiss the fruit wines, which have cachet among wine drinkers of all stripes. In February 2010, HV Cellars opened a second location near Roseburg with tastings daily from 11 to 5.

REMOTE
OLD BRIDGE WINERY

541-572-0272
50706 Sandy Creek
Tasting Room: May–Dec., Tues.–Sun. 11–5
Fee: Complimentary
Owners: George and Angie Clarno
Winemakers: George Clarno and Janis Clarno
Wines: Chardonnay, Riesling, Viognier, Pinot Noir, Merlot, Zinfandel, port-style wine, fruit wines, sparkling wines
Cases: 2,000
Special Features: Annual barbecue serving bison and tuna steaks along with live music

Ask George and Angie which of their wines they favor and they'll quickly answer, "The one in our hand, of course." And they have a few from which to choose. The couple started winemaking many years ago for fun, friends, and guests who came for their hunting-guide service. Finally convinced to go commercial, they became Coos County's first bonded winery in 2001. The fruit they use to make blackberry, cranberry, and strawberry-rhubarb sweet and dry wines is locally grown. And you have to love their pricing: nothing is over $20. The sparkling cranberry, neither too dry nor too sweet, is a big seller. The winery overlooks the Sandy Creek covered bridge, once on the main road from Roseburg to the coast.

Lodging along the South Coast

NORTH BEND
THE MILL CASINO HOTEL

541-756-8800 or 800-953-4800
www.themillcasino.com
3201 Tremont Avenue
Rates: $97–129
Special Features: Six luxury-view suites, shuttles to Bandon Dunes and Watson Ranch golf courses, casino, restaurant, marquee entertainment, gift shop

The Mill Casino is a shining light in the dreary coastal twin cities of Coos Bay and North Bend. The hotel towers seven stories above the bay, with many of the 92 rooms offering views. Another 115 rooms in the lodge reflect Native American history.

BANDON
A BANDON INN

541-347-4417 or 800-526-0209
www.abandoninn.com
56131 Tom Smith Road
Rates: $150–280
Special Features: Massages, stocked humidor, salmon fishing trips, concierge service

A Bandon Inn is just a long three-iron away from one of the world's most spectacular golf courses, Bandon Dunes, and exploits its proximity with, well, abandon. The two rooms named Crenshaw and Hagen answer any doubts about which former PGA golfers are owner Al Greenfield's favorites. The Top Shelf bar is for toasting birdies or forgetting bogeys. After hitting 'em straight— or not—at Bandon Dunes, there's probably no better 19th hole in the area than the inn's huge deck with expansive views of the coastal foothills.

LIGHTHOUSE BED & BREAKFAST

541-347-9316
www.lighthouselodging.com
650 Jetty Road SW

Rates: $140–245
Special Features: Off-season discounts

There isn't a bad view in the house—some are just more spectacular than others in this ideally located B&B, across the mouth of the Coquille River from Bandon's storied lighthouse. Accommodations range from Karen's Room, with its view of the lighthouse and the Pacific, to the Gray Whale Room, a new addition that rises above it all for a panoramic view of the ocean, lighthouse, and estuary. Though the inn is on the river, it's only a short walk to the beach.

THE LODGE–BANDON DUNES GOLF RESORT
888-345-6008
www.bandondunesgolf.com
57744 Round Lake Drive
Rates: $200–1,800
Special Features: Caddies, free shuttles, several restaurants, three lounges

Tee it up in luxury and intimate style in the 17-room lodge or 39-room inn just off the 18th green at Bandon Dunes. Or bring your golfing team for a stay in an ultra-plush four-bedroom suite situated in The Grove. If you'd like to hit one straight down the middle, go for condo-like accommodations at the Lily Pond or the roomier choices at Chrome Lake. And don't worry about feeling too far from the action: Shuttles can take you anywhere on the grounds, anytime, day or night—including the driving range, where you can hit an unlimited number of practice shots.

Dining along the South Coast

BANDON
ALLORO WINE BAR & RESTAURANT
541-347-1850
www.allorowinebar.com
375 Second Street SE
Open: Spring through fall, daily 4–9;
winter, Mon.–Sat. 4–9 (call to confirm)
Price: Expensive
Credit Cards: Yes
Special Features: Retail wines, enoteca-style wine bar, nightly wine specials

Jeremy Buck and Lian Schmidt bring their great love of Florence to Old Town Bandon. Alloro combines local seafood, meat, berries, and produce with imported Italian goods to create a high-end Tuscanesque sensation. In season, you can find foraged huckleberries, chanterelles, and porcinis adorning their inspired dishes. Alaskan halibut and organic lamb osso bucco are as popular as the Dungeness crab bisque. A selection of two or three gelatos will complete your meal without giving you a too-full feeling. Alloro's lengthy list of wines showcases the best of Oregon and Italy.

THE GALLERY
888-345-6008
www.bandondunesgolf.com
57744 Round Lake Drive
Price: Expensive
Credit Cards: Yes
Special Features: Panoramic ocean views

Wine and seafood are a perfect pair for a meal on the coast. Courtesy Newport Chamber of Commerce

A world-class golf course merits a restaurant to match. The Gallery serves such Northwest-oriented fare as pan-seared steelhead with local forest mushrooms, sea scallops, and a 22-ounce T-bone steak that weighs in at $50. Lunch is on the lighter side, highlighted by Coos Bay oysters. You might find yourself wishing more of the wines came from Oregon (many are from California), but the majority of Pinot Noirs hail from the Willamette Valley and will enhance most entrees.

Attractions along the South Coast

REEDSPORT
One of the best ways to understand the varied history of native tribes along the coast is at the **Umpqua Discovery Center** (541-271-4816, 409 Riverfront Way), where you'll get a feel for how coastal people have lived for centuries near the confluence of the Umpqua and Smith rivers with the sea.

COOS BAY / NORTH BEND
As you're passing through to wineries at Myrtle Point, take a break at the **Coos Historical and Maritime Museum** (541-756-6320, 1220 Sherman Ave.) in North Bend. The museum provides a cultural peek into the history of the most industrial communities on the coast. Timber was king here for a century or more, and this longtime cornerstone of western Oregon's economy comes to life at the exquisite **Shore Acres State Park** (541-888-4902), about 13 miles southwest of Coos Bay. Shores Acres features the colorful gardens and immaculate grounds ringing the former estate of Louis Simpson, one of the state's most notable timber barons.

MYRTLE POINT
The **Coos County Logging Museum** (541-572-1014, 705 Maple St.) houses a wide range of logging artifacts, myrtlewood carvings, and photos. The building was constructed as a sanctuary for Mormons in 1910.

Recreation along the South Coast

BANDON
Only about 160 so-called "links" golf courses exist in the world, and truly one of the most stunning is **Bandon Dunes Golf Resort** (888-345-6008, 57744 Round Lake Rd.). Golfers from the world over travel here to challenge four courses reminiscent of those in Scotland, only with better weather. Barely a decade old, Bandon Dunes is generally rated among the top five courses of any type in the world.

Shopping along the South Coast

REEDSPORT
The southern coastal area is known for two distinct trees: the Port Orford cedar and Oregon myrtlewood. **The Myrtlewood Gallery** (541-271-4222, 1125 Hwy. 101) showcases the beautiful soft grains of the latter tree, a broadleaf evergreen that's said to have biblical significance.

Wine Shopping along the South Coast

BANDON

After playing 18 at Bandon Dunes, drop into the **Oregon Wine Tasting Room** (541-347-9081, 350 Second St.) for a taste of wines from Oregon, California, and points beyond. **Tiffany's Drugs** in the Bandon Shopping Center (541-347-4438, 44 Michigan Ave. NE) has shelves of wine, many from the area.

Information

Oregon Coast Visitors Association, 541-574-2679, 137 NE First St., Newport, www.visit theoregoncoast.com

Oregon Coast Tourism, www.oregoncoasttourism.com

Travel Oregon, 800-547-7842, www.traveloregon.com/explore-oregon/oregon-coast .aspx

Astoria Chamber of Commerce: 503-325-6311, 111 West Marine Dr., www.oldoregon.com

Bandon Chamber of Commerce: 541-347-9616, 350 South Second St., www.bandon.com

Cannon Beach Chamber of Commerce: 503-426-2623, 207 North Spruce St., www .cannonbeach.org

Coos Bay/North Bend Chamber of Commerce: 541-269-0215, 50 East Central, Coos Bay, www.oregonsbayarea.org

Florence Chamber of Commerce: 541-997-3128, 290 Hw. 101, www.florencechamber .com

Lincoln City Chamber of Commerce: 541-994-3070, 4039 Logan Rd., www.lcchamber .com

Myrtle Point Chamber of Commerce: 541-572-2626, 424 Fifth St., www.myrtlepoint chamber.org

Nehalem Bay Chamber of Commerce: 503-368-5100, 13015 Hwy. 101, www.nehalembay chamber.com

Newport Chamber of Commerce: 541-265-8801, 555 SW Coast Hwy., www.newport chamber.org

Reedsport Chamber of Commerce: 541-271-3495, 855 Hwy. 101, www.reedsportcc.org

Seaside Chamber of Commerce: 503-738-6391, 7 North Roosevelt, www.seaside chamber.com

Tillamook Chamber of Commerce: 503-842-2575, 3075 Hwy. 101 N., www.tillamook chamber.org

Yachats Chamber of Commerce: 800-929-0477, 241 Highway 101 South. www.yachats.org

10

Eastern Oregon

High, Dry, and Juicy

Welcome to The Big Empty. Eastern Oregon is the antithesis of the state's rainy west. It is a land of vast sagebrush prairies, rugged mountains, harsh winters, and conservative ideology. Yet even with those attributes as anchors, you can't paint this arid region with one broad stroke of the brush.

The area around booming Bend, which straddles the Deschutes River on the eastern flank of the Cascade Range, is a vibrant, sun-drenched, and snow-kissed outdoor paradise set amid thick ponderosa forests. The Columbia, Umatilla, and Snake River valleys are hot, dry, and renowned for their onions, sugar beets, and wheat—though vineyards are coming on strong enough in all three to receive AVA designations. The northeast and east-central parts of Oregon are mountainous and cold, though even here a few vineyards have taken root. Also inhospitable for grapes is the south-central portion of the state, a dry and remarkably remote basin-and-range region reminiscent of Nevada's deserts.

Because nearly all of the wine produced in eastern Oregon is from the Columbia and Umatilla valleys, our focus will be there. But the Bend/Redmond/Prineville triangle bears some discussion, even though the first vineyards are only now beginning to poke through volcanic rock. With its vigor, money, and progressiveness, Bend is too much of a natural to not be included in the wine industry. The town has three wineries, and vineyards are popping up on the outskirts.

Though Oregon's portions of the Columbia, Walla Walla, and Snake River AVAs are immersing themselves into the wine business, most wineries are in neighboring Washington and Idaho. The Walla Walla AVA has literally been adding by a winery a week on the Washington side.

GETTING HERE AND AROUND

Getting anywhere in eastern Oregon requires some effort, and most definitely includes a car. The Walla Walla (Washington) Regional Airport offers three flights a day from Seattle on **Horizon Air** (800-547-9308); Horizon no longer serves Pendleton. The Columbia Valley is even farther removed from air service. Most visitors come to The Dalles and points east via Portland.

OPPOSITE: *Some grapes love the hot, dry climate of eastern Oregon.* Courtesy The Pines 1852

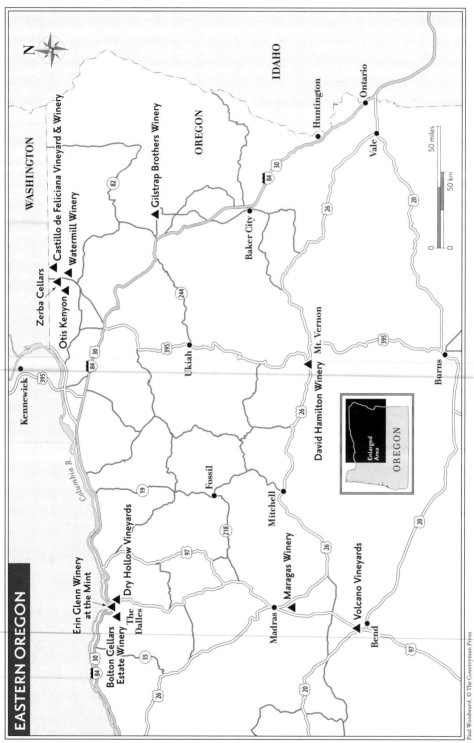

EASTERN OREGON

WASHINGTON

IDAHO

OREGON

N

Kennewick

Zerba Cellars

Otis Kenyon

Castillo de Feliciana Vineyard & Winery

Watermill Winery

Gilstrap Brothers Winery

Baker City

Huntington

Ontario

Vale

Burns

Ukiah

Mt. Vernon

David Hamilton Winery

Fossil

Mitchell

Erin Glenn Winery at the Mint

Dry Hollow Vineyards

The Dalles

Bolton Cellars Estate Winery

Maragas Winery

Madras

Volcano Vineyards

Bend

Columbia R.

Enlarged Area

OREGON

50 miles

50 km

Paul Woodward. © The Countryman Press

Getting to Bend, in central Oregon, is easier as its growth has been matched by air service to Roberts Field in nearby Redmond from **SkyWest** (800-221-1212), **United Express** (800-241-6522), and **Allegiant Air** (702-505-8888). **Greyhound** has a route on I-84 with stations in Ontario, La Grande, Pendleton, and The Dalles. Another route from Ontario goes across the heart of the state to Bend and across the Cascades on US 20. All of the major rental car agencies are available at Portland International Airport. There is no **Amtrak** service to eastern Oregon.

Interstate 84 bisects the Columbia Valley AVA, including The Dalles. This freeway connects Portland with Boise, Idaho. Milton-Freewater is 12 miles south of Walla Walla and 26 miles north of Pendleton on OR 11.

Bend is at a crossroads in central Oregon. From Portland, the best route is to take US 26 over the Cascades to the junction of US 97 at Madras, and then head south another 42 miles. If you're arriving from the east off I-84, exit at Biggs Junction onto US 97 and continue south for 135 miles.

THE DALLES AREA (COLUMBIA VALLEY AVA)

Though only 19 miles east of Hood River and similarly perched on a crescent-shaped slope overlooking the Columbia River, The Dalles couldn't be more different than its sister city in the Gorge—which helps explain the different appellations. A massive dam and industrial zone give this community of 12,500 the feel of a blue-collar shipping port.

People have been conducting commerce of varying sorts here for 10,000 years, and downtown The Dalles is on the National Register of Historic Places. Named for dangerous rapids on the Columbia, which were inundated by The Dalles Dam in 1957, the city is known for its sweet cherries, prolific salmon fishing, and the Fort Dalles Museum—Oregon's oldest history museum.

Wineries in The Dalles Area

Overall, the Columbia Valley AVA covers a vast high-desert area of 11 million acres, though only a fraction is in Oregon; the rest is in Washington. It is hot, dry, and seemingly vine-unfriendly. Nevertheless, there are producing Zinfandel vines here that are more than 100 years old.

This is Oregon's driest AVA, averaging six to eight inches of rain per year—less than Phoenix, Arizona—on the stark Columbia Plateau, meaning irrigation from the Columbia River and its tributaries is crucial. A wide variety of grapes grows well here amid these sunny days and cool nights, most notably Merlot, Syrah, Chardonnay, Pinot Gris, Gewürztraminer, Semillon, Riesling, and Cabernet Sauvignon.

THE DALLES
BOLTON CELLARS ESTATE WINERY
541-298-1285 (farm) or 541-296-7139
(tasting room)
www.boltoncellars.com
306 Court Street
Tasting Room: Mon.–Fri. 3 P.M.–close,
Sat.–Sun. 2 P.M.–close

Fee: Complimentary
Owners: Dan and Mercedes Bolton
Winemaker: Tim Schechtel
Wines: Gewürztraminer, Pinot Noir,
Meristem, Merlot
Cases: Under 1,000
Special Features: Live music Fri. at 5; gift
shop sells wares made by Bolton helpers

Four generations of the Bolton family have farmed the land in the Dufur Valley since 1858. Only the latest crew thought to grow wine grapes. All of Bolton's wines come from their two vineyards, one at the family farm between Dufur and The Dalles, the other across the Columbia at Horsethief Lake. Winemaker Schechtel is the owner of Erin Glenn at the Mint (see below).

ERIN GLENN WINERY AT THE MINT

541-296-4707
www.eringlenn.com
710 East Second Street
Tasting Room: Fri. 12–9, Sat.–Sun. 12–5

(extended in summer and on holidays)
Fee: Complimentary until 5 P.M.
Owner/Winemaker: Tim Schechtel
Wines: Viognier, Chardonnay, Gewürztraminer, rosé, Syrah, Pinot Noir, Barbera, Dolcetto, Tempranillo, Cabernet Sauvignon, red and white blends
Cases: 5,000
Special Features: Live music Fri., wedding and small party facilities

Taste small-lot boutique wines in Erin Glenn's historic building, which was commissioned as a mint by Abraham Lincoln but never completed beyond the second floor. After much excavation, the basement

Erin Glenn's basement barrel room was commissioned as a U.S. mint but never completed.   John Baker

Wind turbines watch over a vineyard on the high desert of eastern Oregon. John Baker

is the optimum space for the winery and barrel room. The tasting room is airy, fashioned in a Mediterranean style, and gives off an aura of fun. The Roosevelt elk mount on the wall is a reminder that you're still in eastern Oregon. Erin Glenn is known locally for its red Tantrum (a blend of Pinot, Merlot, and Barbera), which may be acting out due to an identity crisis. The Mint is a great place to sit a spell and taste away an afternoon or evening. Enjoy live music and small plates on Friday nights.

DRY HOLLOW VINEYARDS
541-296-2953
www.dryhollowvineyards.com
3410 Dry Hollow Lane
Tasting Room: Sat. 1–5 P.M. (extended on holiday weekends)

Fee: $5, waived with purchase
Owner: Bridget Bailey Nisley
Winemaker: Rich Cushman
Wines: Chardonnay, Syrah, Merlot, Cabernet Sauvignon, red blend
Cases: 1,000
Special Features: Horseback tours of 15-acre vineyard by appointment

The tasting room at Dry Hollow is in an area that seems anything but dry. Visitors look out through ponderosa pines over rolling hills to the thirsty Columbia River benches. The lush lawn beckons tasters outside when the wind isn't blowing. Owner Bridget Bailey Nisley is a fourth-generation cherry farmer turned vintner. The Syrah and Merlot are estate; the rest of the grapes are from the Columbia Valley AVA.

Lodging in The Dalles Area

For exploring the Columbia Valley AVA, the lodging options can be summed up in two words: The Dalles. Fortunately, there are plenty of options, particularly if you're into the bed-and-breakfast scene. Many accommodations feature views of the Columbia River and The Dalles Dam.

THE DALLES
CELILO INN MOTEL
541-769-0001
www.celiloinn.com
3550 East Second Street
Rates: $129–200
Special Features: Continental breakfast (pastry and espresso bar), patio and fire pit, fitness room, outdoor pool

Views are the selling point for this 46-room inn, which is on a bluff overlooking The Dalles Dam. The motel mixes the modern with vintage after its complete and recent overhaul. This boutique lodging still has the motel's spine, but has the new flesh of an upscale inn. It's easy to spot from I-84 on the east end of town.

THE DALLES INN
541-296-9107 or 888-935-2378
www.thedallesinn.com
112 West Second Street
Rates: $84–119
Special Features: Complimentary breakfast, Wi-Fi, outdoor pool, dog-friendly rooms

The Dalles is a long, crescent-shaped community where you can be far from downtown, so if you like to be at the heart of it all, this is your place. The inn supplies all the basic needs, and then some. It features six types of suites and studios renovated to a decidedly upscale feel, complete with DVD players and in-room gourmet coffee service.

COURT STREET BED & BREAKFAST
541-350-9850
www.gorgeonline.com/courtbnb
3550 East Second Street

Rates: $40–95
Special Features: Wine tours and packages, dog-friendly

This modest home offers a master bedroom for one or two guests, or the entire home for $200 a night. The bedroom has a private bath with clawfoot tub. Downstairs there's a bed in a recreation room with a TV. A two-night stay and four-hour tour of Hood River wineries is offered at $360.

SHILO INN & SUITES
541-298-5502
www.shiloinns.com
3223 Bret Clodfelter Way
Rates: $129–169
Special Features: Outdoor pool, sauna and spa, restaurant, dog-friendly (fee applies)

Shilo Inns is a regional chain with most of its motels in Oregon. What stands out at this location is the setting on the shores of the Columbia River, with views of the dam and Pioneer Village. Many of the 112 comfortable rooms overlook the river and some have outdoor patios.

Dining in The Dalles Area

THE DALLES
BALDWIN SALOON
541-296-5666
www.baldwinsaloon.com
205 Court Street
Open: Mon.–Thurs. 11–9, Fri.–Sat. 11–10
Price: Moderate
Credit Cards: Yes

Opened in 1876, the Baldwin Saloon hasn't always been a purveyor of food and spirits. The brick building a block away from

In Defense of Fast Food

Seriously? Fast food in a wine book? If you're touring Oregon Wine Country with the kids or just have a hankering for a burger, we know just the place to fill the tanks.

Burgerville looks like a basic burger joint, but they buy fresh, local, and sustainable products whenever possible. And while the food is fast, it isn't *too* fast; no stale, skimpy burgers from the heat lamps here. Your local, hormone-free, beef burger is cooked to order and can be topped with pepper bacon or Tillamook cheddar cheese. For a lower calorie count, make it a free-range turkey burger or veggie burger made from Anasazi beans.

They have the greens covered as well, most notably salads with such locavore ingredients as smoked salmon, Oregon blue cheese, hazelnuts, and pear chutney. Kids of all ages will appreciate smoothies and milkshakes made with seasonal fresh-from-the-farm fruit mixed with hormone-free milk. Other seasonal treats include strawberry shortcake, sweet potato fries, Walla Walla onion rings, Yukon Gold waffle fries, and Oregon beer-battered halibut. Even the coffee is sourced from fair trade roasters.

You can find Burgervilles in the Portland area, Monmouth, The Dalles, and Albany—the latter two cleverly advertised by billboards stating, "Last Burgerville for 27,000 miles." And you gotta love their community-oriented sponsorship of Special Olympics, United Way, and the American Diabetes Association. It's all good.

Seriously.

---

downtown also has been used as a steam-boat-navigation office and a place to store coffins. After renovation, it came full circle in 1991, when it reopened as a restaurant with an eye on its past. Oil paintings adorn the walls around mahogany dining booths, an 18-foot mahogany back bar, and a pendulum clock that dates to the 1870s. The food ranges from steaks and halibut to Coquilles St. Jacques (scallops). Local wines complete the experience.

THE WINDSEEKER RESTAURANT ON THE PORT

541-298-7171
www.windseekerrestaurant.com
1535 Bargeway Road

Open: Mon.–Fri. 11–9, Sat.–Sun. 9–9
Price: Moderate
Credit Cards: Yes
Special Features: Full bar (the Portside Pub)

The Windseeker accurately bills itself as the only riverside dining in The Dalles. Burgers and specialty sandwiches are augmented at lunch by the hum of activity on the Columbia—especially if you eat on the deck. Evening meals consist of the usual steak, seafood, and pasta, accompanied by a solid all-Northwest wine list. Breakfast includes Indian fry bread, sourdough pancakes, and frittatas. Both food and service often get mixed reviews among visitors and locals alike, however.

Attractions in the Dalles Area

Even if you're headed east or south to sip wine, the **Columbia Gorge Discovery Center** (541-296-8600, 5000 Discovery Dr.) is a required stop for an overview of everything Gorge. The expansive facility includes the **Wasco County Historical Museum**. Also on site is the **Discovery Gallery**, which captures the story of the Lewis and Clark Corps of Discovery with detailed displays and exhibits.

Oregon's oldest museum has its roots in a fort built before the Civil War. The **Fort Dalles Museum** (541-296-4547, 500 West 15th St.) is in the old surgeon's quarters at the fort. It opened in 1905 and mostly features military, pioneer and Indian artifacts

Perhaps the most significant historical event for the valley since the arrival of European settlers was the construction of **The Dalles Dam** in 1957, with an accompanying visitor center (541-296-1181).

Recreation in The Dalles Area

It isn't Hood River, and the winds aren't quite as prodigious, but The Dalles holds its own among the board and kite **surfing** crowds. Depending on the time of year, you can always count on boats full of fishermen to be stacked up on the Columbia, angling for the salmon and steelhead making their annual appearances. Bass and walleye fishing are also popular pastimes, particularly in pools where creeks meet the Columbia.

AROUND PENDLETON AND MILTON-FREEWATER (WALLA WALLA AVA)

Walla Walla—it's not just about the sweet onions anymore. This is one of the fastest-growing AVAs in the country in both size and pride. It's only a matter of time before Oregon steals some of the thunder from its deserving Washington neighbor, where most of the vineyards are actually located.

For most of its modern life, this dry, mild, and windswept corner of Oregon has been all about agriculture, ranching, and cowboys. Pendleton is famous for its woolen mill, its rich underground—literally—history, and both real and wannabe cowboys letting 'er buck at the internationally renowned Pendleton Round-Up. While Pendleton is tucked into a deep valley between endless wheat fields, Milton-Freewater has the Blue Mountains for a backdrop. It has an abiding affection for frogs, developed in the past decade as a struggling town's clever attempt to boost tourism. Thus, Milton-Freewater is now "Muddy Frogwater Country," and visitors are invited to find the 40 frog statues scattered about town.

Wineries in the Pendleton/Milton-Freewater Area

For now, there are only four wineries and just over 30 vineyards on the Oregon side of the AVA, all in and around the town of Milton-Freewater. But that's sure to change with the rapid growth of the tiny Walla Walla AVA, a sub-appellation of the larger Columbia Valley AVA to the west.

The terroir here is silt, deposited 15,000 years ago by the Missoula Floods on top of ancient lava left 15 million years ago by one of the largest volcanic eruptions in the earth's history. A final terroir factor is the constant winds, which have coated the Walla Walla Valley with a fine soil called loess. The area is blessed with endless sunshine, warm summers, crisp evenings, mild winters, and limited rainfall (13 inches annually) augmented by irrigation. Most vineyards range from 650 feet above sea level to just under 1,500 feet at the foot of the Blue Mountains. Merlot, Cabernet Sauvignon, and Syrah are predominant, though the range in elevation and soils allows for diversity.

The barrel room at Watermill.   Courtesy Watermill Winery

MILTON-FREEWATER
WATERMILL WINERY

541-938-5575
www.watermillwinery.com
235 East Broadway Avenue
Tasting Room: Thurs.–Sun. 12-4
Fee: Complimentary
Owner: Brown family
Winemaker: Andrew Brown
Wines: Sauvignon Blanc, Viognier,
Gewürztraminer, rosé, Malbec, Syrah,
red blend, dessert wine
Cases: 4,500
Special Features: "Summer Nights on the
Patio" (Fri. 5–9), event facility with com-
mercial kitchen

After running the highly successful Blue
Mountain Cidery and growing grapes for
other wineries, the Brown family started
their own winery in 2005. The tasting room
features a kitchen, dining room, and library
capable of hosting large gatherings. Many
of Watermill's LIVE-certified grapes come
from an area called The Rocks, where the
family once grew apples.

OTIS KENYON

509-525-3505 or 206-463-3125
www.otiskenyonwine.com
52744 Burris Lane
Tasting Room: Thurs.–Mon. 11–5
Fee: $5
Owners: Steve Kenyon and Deborah
Dunbar
Winemaker: Dave Stephenson
Wines: Cabernet Sauvignon, Merlot, Syrah,
Malbec
Cases: 2,500
Special Features: Tasting room at 23 East
Main St., Walla Walla.

Otis Kenyon is one of four Oregon wineries in the Walla Walla AVA.   Courtesy Otis Kenyon Winery

Of all the family winery stories in Oregon, Otis Kenyon is one of the most colorful. The picture on the label is of James Otis Kenyon, a dentist who settled in the valley a century ago and disappeared for 50 years after burning down a competitor's business. His family was eventually reunited with him, and created the label as a tribute after he died at age 101. Steve Kenyon's passion for wine was born while living in the southern Rhône region of France. The Kenyons now produce their reds from Bordeaux and Rhône varietals grown in their two vineyards near Milton-Freewater.

ZERBA CELLARS
541-938-9463
www.zerbacellars.com
85530 Highway 11
Tasting Room: Mon.–Sat. 12–5, Sun. 12–4
Fee: Complimentary
Owners: Cecil and Marilyn Zerba
Winemaker: Doug Nierman
Wines: Chardonnay, Semillon, Viognier, rosé, Cabernet Franc, Barbera, Syrah, Cabernet Sauvignon, Merlot, Malbec, Sangiovese, port-style and dessert wines
Cases: 6,000

Zerba is probably the best-known Oregon winery in the Walla Walla region, in part because of their boatloads of awards. The bulk of their wines come from three LIVE-certified estate vineyards, planted at different elevations in distinct soils. Zerba's tasting room, in a log cabin next to one of the vineyards, is a reflection of its location near the Blue Mountains. You can find the Zerba label at many highly regarded dining establishments throughout the state.

CASTILLO DE FELICIANA VINEYARD & WINERY
541-558-3656
www.castillodefeliciana.com
85728 Telephone Pole Road
Tasting Room: Fri.–Sun. 11–5

Owners: Sam and Deborah Castillo
Winemaker: Ryan Raber
Wines: Albariño, Semillon, Cabernet Sauvignon, Malbec, Merlot, Syrah, Tempranillo
Special Features: Patio with fire pit

Make a visit to southern Spain—without leaving Oregon. Castillo de Feliciana was brand-new on the Walla Walla AVA winery scene in late 2009, opening a Spanish-style winery complete with the requisite red roof and white stucco exterior. *Castillo* means "castle," which is what Sam and Deborah have emulated with their tasting room. Surrounded by vineyards that include Spanish varietals Albariño and Tempranillo, it features a patio where visitors can sit and listen to tango music while fantasizing that the distant Blue Mountains are in Spain's Andalusia region. All they're missing is an ocean.

Cove

GILSTRAP BROTHERS VINEYARD & WINERY
541-568-4646 or 866-568-4200
www.gilstrapbrothers.com
69789 Antles Road
Tasting Room: Wed.–Sun. 11–5, and by appointment
Fee: Complimentary
Owners: Warren Gilstrap and Susan Olliffe
Winemakers: Warren and Ted Gilstrap
Wines: Chardonnay, Cabernet Sauvignon, Merlot, Syrah, Maréchal Foch
Cases: 1,600
Special Features: Wedding facility, winery tours

If Californians thought their expatriates were nuts for thinking they could grow grapes in the Willamette Valley, consider the Gilstraps. They actually believed they could plant a vineyard at 3,000 feet above sea level, on the fringes of the Blue Mountains, and make good wine. They replaced their cherry orchard with cold-resistant French hybrids in 1993, and they have managed to eke out a living making wines in the upper Grande Ronde Valley. The winery is about an hour's scenic drive from Pendleton on I-84. It's worth it, just for the seeing-is-believing factor.

Lodging in the Pendleton/ Milton-Freewater Area

PENDLETON
PENDLETON HOUSE BED & BREAKFAST
541-276-8581
www.pendletonhousebnb.com
311 North Main Street
Rates: $100–135
Special Features: Daily wine and cheese hour, 5–6 P.M.

Don't be looking for a place to hitch your horse here. This historic six-room home is decidedly Italian Renaissance and French neoclassical, with hints of old Pendleton's Chinese presence. In the back are English gardens, which the owners readily admit seem "slightly out of place" in arid cowboy country. The same goes for the home's primary exterior color: pink. The citified rooms are spread among three floors, with a second-floor balcony overlooking downtown. Many of the fixtures are original, including the Chinese wallpaper.

WILDHORSE RESORT & CASINO
541-278-2274 or 800-654-9453
www.wildhorseresort.com
72777 Highway 331
Rates: $70–149
Special Features: Casino, golf course, RV park, teepee village, tent camping, museum

This 100-room hotel was recently renovated to become a more appealing, if still basic, place to put up your feet. The advantages are all the above-mentioned amenities, which help because options are limited in Pendleton. The plain rooms feature a Native American motif.

Dining in the Pendleton/ Milton-Freewater Area

MILTON-FREEWATER
THE OASIS @ STATELINE
541-938-4776
85698 Highway 339
Open: Tues.–Thurs. 11 A.M.–10 P.M., Fri.–Sun. 9 A.M.–10 P.M.
Price: Expensive
Credit Cards: Yes
Special features: Live country music Fri. and Sat., keno.

People come from miles around to eat at this Western roadhouse in the country. It exudes eastern Oregon cowboy ambiance with its Texas Hold 'em card games, thick cuts of prime rib, and platters of seafood. You might not expect to find an extensive wine list at such a place, but the Oasis has just that—and it highlights regional producers. They also use seasonal farm-fresh produce.

PENDLETON
GREAT PACIFIC WINE & COFFEE COMPANY
541-276-1350
www.greatpacific.biz
403 South Main Street
Open: Sun.–Thurs. 10–8, Fri. 10–9, Sat. 8:30 A.M.–9 P.M.
Price: Moderate
Credit Cards: Yes
Special Features: 40 coffee and espresso drinks, Saturday bluegrass jams, live music

Located in the historic Masonic Lodge downtown, Great Pacific has one of Pendleton's most extensive wine selections. The choices heavily emphasize Oregon, and that goes for the beer, too. The eating area is set amid the racks of wine and has an aura that oozes all the history the 120-year-old building has witnessed. The menu is casual, highlighted by sandwiches, soups, gourmet salads, and specialty pizzas that include "One Night in Bangkok," topped with shrimp and peanut sauce.

RAPHAEL'S

541-276-8500
www.raphaelsrestaurant.com
233 SE Fourth Street
Open: Tues.–Sat. 5–9 (closing varies by
season)
Price: Moderate to expensive
Credit Cards: Yes
Special Features: Sushi on Fri. nights

Chef Rob is known for his slightly exotic
touch, from his pan-seared elk medallions
and 24-ounce rib eye to Hawaiian ahi tuna
and crab-stuffed salmon. For a warm up,
try the sautéed wild mushrooms or apple-
wood-smoked rattlesnake and rabbit
sausage. Part of the charm is the setting:
the century-old Raley House, with its seven
gables outside and oak and mahogany
inside. Roy Raley was the founder of the
Pendleton Round-Up rodeo. The wine list
is strictly Northwest, and is selected for its
pairing potential.

STETSON'S HOUSE OF PRIME

541-966-1132
www.stetsonshouseofprime.com
103 SE Court Street
Open: Daily 4:30–close
Price: Moderate to expensive
Credit Cards: Yes
Special Features: Famous for prime rib;
reservations required for six or more

Stetson's is a Pendleton icon, a watering
hole where ranchers and livestock traders
have cut deals over Herculean steaks. The
menu is what you'd expect: prime rib,
steaks, chicken, seafood, and pasta, but the
smoked beef and salmon move it up a belt
notch. Servings are robust and the atmosphere is authentically western. Stetson's
gets its fresh seafood from Astoria on
Friday and Saturday, including Dungeness
crab and salmon. Most of the wines are
from the Northwest, especially the big reds
that go with big steaks.

Attractions in the Pendleton and Milton-Freewater Area

Yes, this is *the* Pendleton—at least when it comes to the famous blankets and other wool
products. See where it comes together at the **Pendleton Blanket Mill** (541-276-6911, 1307
S.E. Court Pl.). Six generations of the Bishop family have watched over the company, which
has thrived for 100 years since it began making Indian blankets in 1909.

You probably won't need a blanket at the annual **Pendleton Round-Up** (541-276-2553)
at the rodeo grounds in September, unless it's to keep the dust off your chaps. The Round-
Up is Carnival meets the frontier, with rowdy crowds of 50,000 partying long into four
starry nights. If you're not in town for the rodeo, stop by the **Pendleton Round-Up and
Happy Canyon Hall of Fame** (541-278-0815, 1114 SW Court St.), which is across from the
rodeo grounds and open every day but Sunday. To give you an idea of the mindset in these
parts: of the first 15 inductees, five were horses.

Few places reveal the seamy underbelly of the American West better than **Pendleton
Underground Tours** (800-226-6398, 37 SW Emigrant Ave.). For a deeper look into the
area's native history, you'll be impressed by the **Tamástslikt Cultural Institute** (541-966-
9748, 72789 Hwy. 331) on the eastern outskirts of town.

After picking up your obligatory frog souvenir in Milton-Freewater, you'll want to visit
the popular **Blue Mountain Cidery** (541-938-5575, 235 E. Broadway), best known for its
award-winning handcrafted hard ciders. The cidery, one of a hundred of its kind in the
United States, shares a tasting room and patio bar with Watermill Winery.

Recreation in the Pendleton/ Milton-Freewater Area

Thanks to a mild climate, golf is almost a year-round pastime in the Umatilla and Walla Walla valleys. The 18-hole **Milton-Freewater Municipal Golf Course** (541-938-7284, 301 Catherine) is economical and moderately challenging. The golf course at **Wildhorse Resort** (541-276-5588) has four sets of tees, so the finesse types can play as short as 5,718 yards and the big hitters can go for 7,128.

For a western-style wine adventure, reserve a place on the **Muscat-Dun Vineyard and Ranch Tour** (541-571-3640), about 15 miles west of Pendleton in the tiny community of Echo. For $250 per person, you'll get lunch and a horseback ride along the Umatilla River through the Echo West Ranch and Vineyard followed by dinner served at the ranch.

Shopping in the Pendleton/Milton-Freewater Area

You'd expect to find fresh fruits and vegetables in the heart of ag country, and indeed roadside stands are common in these parts. To get it all in one place, check out the **Pendleton Farmers Market** (541-969-9466), every summer Friday from 4 P.M. to dusk in the 300 block of Main Street.

Testing barrel contents using a wine thief is all in a day's work.   Courtesy Watermill Winery

BEND AND ELSEWHERE (SNAKE RIVER AVA)

The eastern Oregon country outside of the Columbia and Umatilla valleys is vast and varied, ranging from the ponderosa pines and high desert around Bend to the flat onion fields of Ontario, hard on Oregon's arid eastern border with Idaho.

The Bend/Redmond/Prineville area of central Oregon has become one of the state's premier outdoor summer and winter playgrounds. It is one of the state's most active regions, with every type of recreation imaginable that doesn't involve an ocean. Bend is more cosmopolitan, thanks to its proximity to Mt. Bachelor Ski Resort, and more picturesque thanks to its pines and volcanic Three Sisters mountain peaks looming over town.

Wineries in the Bend Area and Elsewhere

You can't help but root for folks who, being so attached to where they live, have brought the wine industry home with them instead of vice versa. It seems the only place left in Oregon without a winery and/or vineyard is the ultra-remote southeastern desert.

CULVER
MARAGAS WINERY
541-546-5464 (winery) or 541-330-0919 (tasting room)
www.maragaswinery.com
15233 South Highway 97
Tasting Room: Tasting room in Bend, daily 12–5; winery in Culver, May–Sept., Wed.–Sun. 12–5 , Oct.–Dec., Fri.–Sun. 11–4
Fee: $5
Owners: Doug and Gina Maragas
Winemaker: Doug Maragas
Wines: Pinot Gris, Muscat, Merlot, Zinfandel
Cases: 2,300
Special Features: A second tasting room is in a former residence at 643 NW Colorado Ave. in Bend.

What is a longtime California wine family doing with a winery in Bend? It's the biking, hiking, and outdoor recreation for Doug and Gina Maragas, whose grapes travel great distances—from southern Oregon and California—for their high-end wines. The focus is on Bordeaux-style reds and a variety of whites. For sheer ambiance, both tasting rooms rate high, with an edge going to the one at the winery in Culver.

BEND
VOLCANO VINEYARDS
541-390-8771
www.volcanovineyards.com
126 NW Minnesota Avenue
Tasting Room: Fri.–Sat. 12–8, Sun. 12–5, Wed.–Thurs. 2–8, and by appointment
Fee: $5, applied to purchase
Owners: Scott and Liz Ratcliff
Winemakers: Gus Janeway and Scott Ratcliff
Wines: Merlot, Syrah, red blends
Cases: 1,500

Though the name might elicit images of wines produced in this highly volcanic region, the grapes for this small winery come from the Rogue Valley of southern Oregon. The Ratcliffs came from San Francisco, where they developed a passion for wine by waiting tables during the week and driving to Napa or Sonoma on weekends. For those familiar with the Brooks Street tasting lounge, the Ratcliffs moved their tasting room to Minnesota Avenue in trendy old-town Bend.

MOUNT VERNON
DAVID HAMILTON WINERY
541-932-4567
www.davidhamiltonwinery.com
150 North Mountain Boulevard
Tasting Room: Fri.–Sun. 12–5
Fee: Complimentary
Owner/Winemaker: David Hamilton
Wines: Fruit wines

When it comes to wines, David Hamilton goes for a walk on the wild side—literally. David "The Winer" Hamilton makes wine from the bounty the Strawberry and Blue Mountains provide: chokecherry, wild plum, elderberry, raspberry, blackberry, Oregon grape, and more. Hamilton, whose lengthy gray beard gives him the look of a mountain man, goes from border to border throughout the Northwest states seeking the perfect berries. The apricots come from a family orchard along Idaho's wild Salmon River, the plums from Hells Canyon, and cranberries from the Oregon coast. No sulfites are added to any of his wines, so their shelf life is limited. Drink them young.

Lodging in the Bend Area and Elsewhere

SUNRIVER
SUNRIVER RESORT
800-801-8765
www.sunriver-resort.com
17600 Center Drive
Rates: $245–495
Special Features: Part of a residential neighborhood with town amenities

Set in the ponderosa pines about 20 miles south of Bend, this community is so sprawling and the layout so complex that it's easy to get lost—which isn't necessarily a bad thing given the natural scenery. Accommodations at Sunriver Resort range from attractive Lodge Village guest rooms to river condos and full-fledged vacation homes. Sunriver is popular with Oregonians from the western valleys as an escape from the rain and for its plethora of attractions and activities: golf, fishing, bicycling, hiking, and shopping.

BEND

THE RIVERHOUSE

541-389-3111 or 866-453-4480
www.riverhouse.com
3075 North Business Highway 97
Rates: $115–290
Special Features: Complimentary breakfast buffet

Though it looks fairly ordinary from US 97 on the north end of Bend, you'll quickly grasp the appeal of the Riverhouse once inside the complex. The Riverhouse is so named because it straddles the rocky Deschutes River, which runs briskly past the restaurant and many of the rooms. Accommodations range from simple deluxe queens to the Gilchrist Suite, which has two full baths, three TVs, a spiral staircase, and huge living area. It's a mere $10 extra to face the river.

SEVENTH MOUNTAIN RESORT

541-382-8711 or 877-765-1501
www.seventhmountain.com
18575 SW Century Dr.
Rates: $99–639
Special Features: Restaurants, lounge, three outdoor pools with hot tubs, sauna, fitness room, skating rink, tennis, Mt. Bachelor shuttle

Also known as the Inn of the Seventh Mountain, this is one of central Oregon's iconic resorts. Surrounded by towering pines and situated between Bend and Mount Bachelor Ski Resort, the hotel has luxury suites that can be a bit spendy. It also has affordable rooms, and privately owned condos and homes for rent. Whether you're looking for a romantic getaway for two or planning a family gathering, Seventh Mountain has the lodging to fit.

Dining in the Bend Area and Elsewhere

BEND

CROSSINGS AT THE RIVERHOUSE

541-389-8810
www.riverhouse.com
3075 North Highway 97
Open: Daily 11–2 and 5–10
Price: Expensive
Credit Cards: Yes
Special Features: Wine bar, complimentary breakfast for lodging guests

Listen to the murmur of the Deschutes River from the restaurant's patio while dining on prime Angus beef (laced in one of five sauces) and sipping a bold Northwest red. Try the truffle-drizzled potato chips or fresh scallops for an appetizer, and the blueberry almond crisp with Meyer lemon sorbet for dessert. Lunch offerings are equally tempting, such as a prime-rib sandwich, tempura fish with yam fries, or a shrimp and crab Louie salad. *Wine Spectator* has consistently given its Award of Excellence to this usually packed, upscale steakhouse.

JACKALOPE GRILL

541-318-8435
www.jackalopegrill.com
1245 SE Third Street
Open: Tues.–Sat. 5 P.M.–close
Price: Moderate
Credit Cards: Yes
Special Features: Nightly specials reflect seasonal regional ingredients

Jackalope's intensely Northwest cuisine is local, organic, seasonal, and matched well to its wines. Chef Timothy Garling and his wife, Kathy, wholeheartedly believe in sustainable food practices and put their philosophy into action in the kitchen. Wild game, fresh seafood, and Oregon beef headline the menu in a white-linen and good-glassware setting that defies its exterior (next to Blockbuster Video). A *Wine Spectator* Award of Excellence recipient and the "Inexpensive" rating means you can enjoy a select bottle of wine with dinner—and maybe order a second.

PINE TAVERN
541-382-5581
www.pinetavern.com
967 NW Brooks Street
Open: Daily 5:30–9:30, Mon.–Sat. 11:30–2:30
Price: Moderate to expensive
Credit Cards: Yes
Special Features: A 200-year-old ponderosa pine tree grows through the roof in the middle of the dining room

The Pine Tavern has been a Bend stalwart for more than 75 years. The food is plenty good, but everyone leaves talking about the baskets of scones with honey butter. There is also a decent selection of Oregon wines—Argyle, King Estate, DDO, Foris, and Volcano, among many others. For the best experience, sit outside on the patio or near the windows overlooking Mirror Pond.

Redmond
AVERY'S WINE BAR
541-504-7111
www.averyswinebar.com
427 SW Eighth Street
Open: Tues.–Sat. 4–10
Price: Inexpensive to Moderate
Credit Cards: Yes
Special Features: Special wine events

Don't let "wine bar" fool you. Avery's has real food, too, such as rib-eye steak. But the favorite is, of all things, macaroni and cheese. Avery's is intimate and comfortable, and touts itself as a great date-night place or a terrific spot for singles who don't care for the bar scene. In winter, the menu shifts more to such comfort foods as homemade soup. The customers at Avery's aren't afraid to let their hair down once in a while with costume-oriented parties.

Attractions in Bend and Elsewhere

Bend was built on volcanic rock, so it's no surprise that some of the most intriguing attractions are related to the region's volatile geologic history. The **Newberry National Volcanic Monument** and **Lava Lands Visitor Center** (541-593-2421) offer panoramic views of ancient lava flows and an understanding of how it all happened—and could happen again. While you're there, it's worth the walk to the end of the mile-long **Lava River Cave,** one of the longest volcanic tubes in Oregon. It's always 41 degrees, so bring a jacket, and you might want to rent a lantern for $4.

The **Oregon High Desert Museum** (541-382-4754), three miles south of Bend on US 97, covers just about everything there is to know about central Oregon's geology, history, and wildlife. Its interpretive programs are highly educational and entertaining.

Recreation in the Bend Area and Elsewhere

Ask anybody for their favorite outdoor recreation pastime in the Bend area and you'll need more than two hands to count the answers. Though Mount Hood aficionados might argue, the **Mt. Bachelor Ski Resort & Nordic Center** (800-829-2442), in the Cascades about 22 miles southwest of Bend, probably offers the state's best skiing. The powder is prodigious, the runs many and varied, and the weather just right.

When it isn't snowing, much of the recreation in the Bend area revolves around the Deschutes River, which is cherished for its **whitewater rafting** and **fishing** for feisty redsides trout and steelhead.

Among the outdoor wonders, one rises above the rest here. Climbers from around the globe come to test their mettle on the rugged outcroppings at **Smith Rock State Park** (541-548-7501) just outside Terrebonne, about 10 miles north of Redmond. Even if your legs get a little wobbly at the thought of roping up the sheer wall of the aptly named Monkey Face, pull up a lawn chair and watch the experts.

Needless to say, given the climate, **golf** is a favored sport. There are nine public courses in the area, seven of them covering 18 holes and all of them scenic. Three of the public courses are in **Sunriver Resort**.

Shopping in the Bend Area and Elsewhere

Bend's vibrant downtown has lots of boutique shops, and the **Old Mill District** (541-312-0131) has several dozen trendy chain stores such as Banana Republic, Coldwater Creek, Gap, and Orvis.

Wine Shopping in the Bend Area and Elsewhere

For the everyday wine drinker, **Wine Styles** has stores in Redmond (541-526-0489, 249 NW Sixth St.) and Bend (541-389-8889, 1740 NW Pence Ln.). For a taste of Italy in the Oregon mountains, try **The Wine Shop and Tasting Bar** (541-389-2884, 55 NW Minnesota Ave.) in Bend. The store features more than 40 wines by the glass and is distinctly European, with one out of seven bottles from Oregon.

Information

Milton-Freewater Chamber of Commerce, 541-938-5563, 157 S. Columbia, www.mfchamber.com

The Dalles Area Chamber of Commerce, 541-296-2231, 404 W. Second St., www.thedalleschamber.com

Central Oregon Visitors Association, 888-781-7071, www.visitcentraloregon.com

Columbia Valley Winery Association, 866-360-6611, www.columbiavalleywine.com

APPENDICES

A. Festivals and Events Celebrating Oregon wine

January

Oregon Truffle Festival, Eugene, Valley River Inn. Oregon truffles and wines, notable guest chefs, lecture series, grand truffle dinner, and Sunday marketplace with fresh fungi for sale. Sat.–Sun. $15 for admission to marketplace ($20 with Riedel glass), $275–1,000 for various packages that include meals, lodging, and related events. 503-296-5929, www.oregontrufflefestival.com

Oregon Wine and Food Festival, Salem, Oregon State Fairgrounds. 100 booths featuring Oregon wineries, microbreweries, eateries, arts and crafts, and live music. Sat.–Sun. $12/day. 503-390-7324, www.oregonstateexpo.org

February

Newport Seafood and Wine Festival, Newport, South Beach Marina Parking Lot. "The original and still the best" after more than 30 years. Fri.–Sun., last full weekend in Feb. $5–15/day (must have valid ID). 800-262-7844, www.newportchamber.org

Chardonnay runneth over at the Newport Seafood & Wine Festival. Courtesy Newport Chamber of Commerce

Oregon Seafood and Wine Festival, Portland, Convention Center. Celebrating all things Oregon in the middle of crab season. Fri.–Sat. $12/day. www.oregonseafoodfestival.com

Confluence Festival, Reedsport/Gardner, W.F. Jewett School. A wine, beer, and seafood festival on the coast that highlights West Coast bands and includes a Friday night wine-tasting dinner. Fri.–Sun. $8/day. 800-247-2155, http://reeds portcc.org/confluence, 325 High St.

Valentine's Day: Check with your favorite winery for Valentine-themed events, dinners, and galas on and around Cupid's day.

March
Oregon Wine, Cheese, and Pear Jubilee, Turner, Willamette Valley Vineyards. Willamette Valley Vineyards wines matched with Oregon artisan cheeses and pears. Sat.–Sun. $5 includes wine, food, and Riedel glass. 800-344-9463, www.willamettevalleyvineyards.com

Flavors of Carlton, Carlton, Ken Wright Cellars. Works of top valley chefs paired with recent releases from Carlton-area vintners. Auction fundraiser for local kids' programs. Sat. $50/person (must be at least 21). 503-852-4405, www.carltontogethercares.com

Wine glass art is part of the charm at the Newport Seafood & Wine Festival.
Courtesy Newport Chamber of Commerce

Sip Classic (formerly McMinnville Wine and Food Classic), McMinnville, Evergreen Aviation and Space Museum. Wine, food, and art booths, music, and guest chefs—a classic event. Fri.–Sun. $15/day, $30/three-day pass. 503-472-3033, www.sipclassic.org

Gorge Passport Weekend, Hood River, Columbia Gorge Wineries. Special reserve tastings of Gorge wines, discounts at Gorge-area merchants. Hosted by local businesses and Columbia Gorge Winemakers Association, in conjunction with Travel Oregon. Fri–Sat. $15. 866-413-9463, www.columbiagorgewine.com

Greatest of the Grape, Canyonville, Seven Feathers Resort and Casino. A food-and-wine pairing event showcasing southern Oregon wines. Partial proceeds go to Sylvia Henry Scholarship Fund for students studying viticulture or oenology. Sponsored by Umpqua Valley Winegrowers. Sat. $75. 541-673-5323, www.umpquavalleywineries.org

Rhapsody in the Vineyard, Corvallis, downtown. Three-hour wine walk through hosting businesses downtown. Also in September. $5 admission, tastes $0.50–$1.50. 541-754-6624, www.downtowncorvallis.org

April

Barrel Tour, Roseburg, Umpqua Valley Winegrowers Association. Taste wine in the making from up to 20 southern Oregon producers. Three tour options available: North, Central, and South, featuring six or seven wineries. Also held in May. Sat. $50/tour, $90/two tours. 541-672-5701, www.umpquavalleywineries.org

Astoria-Warrenton Crab, Seafood and Wine Festival, Astoria, Clatsop County Fairgrounds. More than 50 wineries, 100 arts and crafts booths, plenty of crab and seafood. Fri.–Sun., last full weekend in April (unless it's Easter). $5–10/day, weekend pass available. Parking and shuttles $1. 800-875-6807, www.oldoregon.com

Dundee Hills Passport, Dundee, various venues. Highlights wineries in the Dundee Hills AVA using a passport facsimile. Stamps earn a chance at prizes from the Dundee Hills. Free seminars hosted by participating wineries. Sat.–Sun. Fees vary. www.dundeehills.org

Mount Angel Fine Wine and Food Festival, Mount Angel, Willamette Valley Events Center, 210 Monroe St. Local and regional wineries, craft and food vendors, live music. Families welcome until 9 P.M. Some proceeds benefit town beautification. Fri.–Sat. $4/day. 503-873-9979, www.woodennickel.com

North Willamette Wine Trail, various locations at 15 wineries starting west of Portland. New release, barrel tastings, food and dessert samples, wine activities. Hours vary. Sat-Sun. $35–40 includes glass. www.northwillamettevintners.org

Tulip Wine Down, Woodburn, Wooden Shoe Tulip Farm. Ten wineries, local cuisine, confections, beer. Sat.–Sun. $5 (must be at least 21). 503-984-3825, www.tulipwinedown.com

Visitors get inside information from the source at the Portland Indie Festival. |eff Welsch

Spring Beer and Wine Fest, Portland, Convention Center. Chef demonstrations, wine tastings, wine competition, cheeses, music from Northwest bands. Sat.–Sun. $5, $8 includes wine glass. 503-238-3770, www.springbeerfest .com

May

Indie Wine Festival, Portland, site TBD. Meet winemakers from small Oregon producers (less than 2,500 cases annually). Forty juried selections out of 175 submissions to sample, along with tasty tidbits by a Who's Who list of Portland-area chefs and a winemakers' dinner. Fri,–Sat. $75 all-inclusive on Sat. www.indiewinefestival.com

Silverton Wine and Jazz Festival, Silverton, various venues. Features east Willamette Valley wineries and jazz concerts. Second Saturday in May. $25.

503-873-9463, www.silvertonwineand
jazz.com

Albany Wine Walk, Albany, First
Avenue. Shops play host to local wineries. Sponsored by Albany Rotary Club to
benefits children's programs. Fri. $5 for
10 wine tickets and glass; additional
tastes $1–2. 541-928-2469, www.albany
downtown.com

Fern Ridge Wings and Wine Festival,
Domaine Meriwether Winery. Activities
at Fern Ridge Reservoir. Guided birding
tours and tastings with local wineries,
interpretive nature walks, canoeing, and
activities for kids. Free, including transportation from winery to reservoir;
some activities require preregistration.
Second Sat. 541-935-8443, www.wings
andwinefestival.com

Seaside Downtown Wine Walk,
Seaside, downtown. Appetizers and live
music, hosted by downtown businesses.
Children welcome if accompanied by
adults. Sat. $5 includes logo glass. 503-
717-1914, www.seasidedowntown.com

*The Indie Festival in Portland brings Oregon's top small
producers together under one roof.*   Sherry L. Moore

Science of Wine, Ashland, ScienceWorks Hands-On Museum. Wine gala, winemakers'
dinner, seminars, tours, live wine auction. Benefits ScienceWorks educational programs.
Fri.–Sun. Fees vary by event. 541-482-6767, www.scienceofwineashland.com

Memorial Day Weekend: The onset of summer after a long winter is marked by festive
celebrations that run the gamut. Anything goes: lively music, salsa dancing, barrel tastings,
classes and seminars, local artisan foods paired (or not) with wine, cheeses, chocolates,
nuts, meats, or chef-made cassoulet. The venues are as varied as the vintners and admission fees apply to most. Check Web sites for details, grab a group and a designated driver,
and party hardy.

June

Best of Oregon Food and Wine Festival, Portland, Convention Center. A collection of
local culinary and wine purveyors under one giant roof. Co-sponsored by Doernbecher
Children's Hospital. Sat. $25. 503-998-9580, www.bestoforegonfoodandwine.com

Canby Wine and Art Festival, Canby, Clackamas County Fairgrounds. Regional culinary
creations from pros and amateurs alike paired with Northwest wines, featuring music and
winery tours. Fri.–Sun. $5 (food, wine, and winery tours not included). 503-266-1136,
www.clackamascountyfairandevents.com

Terra Vina takes an award at the Newport Seafood & Wine Festival. Courtesy Newport Chamber of Commerce

Taste in the Garden, Silverton, The Oregon Garden. Wine and food tasting in stunning setting. Sat. $15 includes glass; additional fees for tastings. 503-874-8100, www.oregongarden.org

Festival of Arts and Wine, St. Benedict, Mount Angel Abbey. Food and wine from Northwest wineries and restaurants plus an auction, art displays, and Civil War exhibit. Sat. Admission TBD. 503-845-3030, www.mountangelabbey.org/festival-arts-wine

Hood River County Fruit Loop Wine Celebration, Hood River, various locations. Wine tasting, winery and vineyard tours, and food tasting along the Fruit Loop. Free. Sat.–Sun. 386-7697, www.hoodriverfruitloop.com

Rockaway Beach Wine, Cheese, and All That Jazz Festival, Rockaway Beach. Rose Festival–sanctioned event features wines and cheeses from all over the state as well as some of the country's most renowned jazz musicians. $20. Sat. 503-355-2496, www.rock awaybeach.net/allthatjazz

Oregon Brews and BBQs, McMinnville, Granary District. Crafts, beer, music, family fun, local wines. $5 includes souvenir mug. Fri–Sat. www.oregonbrewsandbbq.com

July
Who's on Third, McMinnville, downtown. A wine and beer garden and artist village have been added to the 50-year-old Turkey Rama celebration. Once called "Turkey-Trama" by locals, the event has a new look and feel, sans turkeys running down Main Street. Fri.–Sun. Free. 503-472-3605, www.downtownmcminnville.com

SunRiver Sunfest, Sunriver, The Village at SunRiver Resort. More than 30 Oregon wineries and a few outa-staters, artists' booths, food vendors, and children's activities. Sat.–Sun, last full weekend in July. 541-385-7988, www.sunriversunfest.com

Bite of Salem, Salem, Riverfront Park. A beer and wine garden celebrating Northwest foods, bands, and carnival rides for the kids. Proceeds benefit Salem youth. Free ($3 donation suggested), $15 for ride tickets. Fri–Sun. www.biteofsalem.com

International Pinot Noir Celebration, McMinnville, Linfield University. Some of the world's top Pinot producers and Northwest's best chefs convene for an annual celebration of the state's premier grape. Fri.–Sun. $125–975. 800-775-4762, www.ipnc.org

August

Carlton's Walk in the Park, Carlton, Wennerberg Park. A benefit for local charities, with local restaurants and wineries sharing their fare in the center of town. Sat.–Sun. $15. 503-852-6572, www.carltonswalkinthepark.com

Silverton Fine Arts Festival, Silverton, Coolidge McClaine Park. A family-friendly event featuring entertainment, food, beer, and wine from small, east Willamette Valley producers. Sat–Sun. Free. 503-873-2480, www.silvertonarts.org

Gorge Wine Celebration for Hospice, Hood River, Best Western Hood River Inn, 1108 E. Marina Way. Celebrating "A World of Wine In 40 Miles" offering 20 wineries, food from the inn, and entertainment. Proceeds benefit Hospice of the Gorge. Sat. $50 includes glass, tasting, and dinner. 866-413-9463, www.columbiagorgewine.com/celebration

Herb and Veggie Festival, Corvallis, Garland Nursery. Gardening classes and wine tasting. Sun. 541-753-6601, www.garlandnursery.com

The Bite of Oregon, Portland, Waterfront Park. Wine and food booths and wine competition. Purchase wine by the taste, glass, bottle, or case. Proceeds benefit Special Olympics of Oregon. Fri.–Sun. $8. 503-248-0600, www.biteoforegon.com

Oregon State Fair Awards Ceremony & Tasting Event, Salem, State Fairgrounds. Held on the first night of the fair to celebrate and announce the winners of the wine competition. Taste more than 200 different wines and sample Oregon foods. Silent auction benefits Oregon Make-A-Wish Foundation. $45 includes fair admission. 800-992-8499, www.oregonstatefair.org

World of Wine, Gold Hill, Del Rio Vineyard, 52 N. River Rd. Talk with winemakers, experts, and enthusiasts in a famed vineyard. Live music, top-flight food, silent auction, tours, and more. Co-sponsored by Southern Oregon Winery Association. Tends to sell out. Sat. $70. 541-855-2062, www.worldofwinefestival.com

September

Umpqua Valley Wine, Arts & Food Festival, Oakland City Park and Umpqua Community College. More than 40 years old, this is a well-run wine festival highlighting 17 wineries, food vendors, artists, cooking-with-wine demonstrations, and a wine-appreciation class. Sat.–Sun. $10. 541-459-1385, www.umpqua.edu

Wineries make room for all kinds of fun on holiday weekends. |John Baker

Labor Day Weekend: New to the famed holiday wine-weekend scene is Labor Day, an oxymoron of sorts for the industry folk. On *your* days off, come and watch *them* labor. Open houses prevail and an aura of titillation hangs in the air as wineries prepare for the next crush. Admissions and festivities vary. Check winery Web sites for specific details and activities.

November

Holiday Food & Gift Festival, Portland, Convention Center. Arts, crafts, gourmet foods, and wines in a festival holiday atmosphere. Also staged in Eugene and Redmond. Fri–Sun. $8. 888-412-5015, www.hfgf.com

NW Food & Wine Festival, Portland, Memorial Coliseum, Benefits Oregon Food Bank. Food, hundreds of wines to sample, guest winemakers, chef demonstrations Sat. $75, $95 for all-inclusive early entrance. 800-422-0251, www.northwestfoodandwinefestival

¡Salud! Wine Auction. Raises money in partnership with Tuality Healthcare Foundation for health care to vineyard seasonal labor by auctioning top-shelf Oregon Pinot Noir. Fri.–Sat. $395/person includes dinner and auction entry. 503-681-1850, saludauction.org

Thanksgiving Weekend Open Houses: A longstanding tradition in Oregon, after giving thanks and feasting with friends and family, is to get them out of the house (off the video games) and doing something active—like touring. And eating even more. The wineries deck their halls, barrels, and tasting rooms with new and old releases, case discounts, and specialty foods. It's a great time and place to do your holiday shopping. Tasting fees vary. Fri.–Sun. Check wineries' Web sites for details and activities.

Grocery and Specialty Stores That Host Regular Wine Tastings

Bales Marketplace: Cedar Mill, West Linn, Farmington
Fred Meyer: Statewide
Haggen Food & Pharmacy: Beaverton, Oregon City, Tualatin
Lamb's Thriftway: Portland, Lake Oswego, Wilsonville
Made In Oregon: Statewide
Market of Choice: Eugene, Ashland, Portland, West Linn
New Seasons Markets: Portland, Beaverton, Lake Oswego, Hillsboro, Happy Valley
Ray's Food Place: Statewide, excluding Portland
Roth's Fresh Markets: Willamette Valley
Stroheckers: Portland
Whole Foods Market: Portland, Hillsboro, Tigard, Bend
Zupan's Markets: Portland

B. Touring Companies Serving Oregon Wine Country

Want to let focus more on the sipping and less on the driving? Give one of the many touring companies that have materialized with the boom of the wine industry a try. In fact, it's a good idea for many reasons. Oregon Wine Country is full of winding, challenging roads and out-of-the-way wineries. You don't want to take chances with your safety or the state's strict drunk-driving laws.

PORTLAND

BEAUTIFUL WILLAMETTE TOURS

360-904-1402 or 877-868-7295
www.willamettetours.com
Rates: $75–225 per person
Special Features: Premium tours at high-end wineries; free photographs

You can't go wrong with tour drivers named Merlot and Shiraz. OK, they're stage names, but this group is fun and unpretentious. They lean toward smaller boutique wineries where winemakers often give personalized tours. This is possible because most of the five-hour tours anywhere in the Willamette Valley—including the Eugene area—are done in small groups.

ECOTOURS OF OREGON

503-245-1428
www.ecotours-of-oregon.com
3127 SE 23rd Avenue
Rates: $59.50 per person, plus tasting fees

An eight-hour tour focuses on some of the more environmentally oriented wineries in the north Willamette Valley, including Sokol Blosser, Elk Cove, and Erath. Your group could go as far west as Carlton or as far south as the Eola Hills. Lunch is either a picnic or a restaurant meal, depending on weather and group preference. Custom tours are welcome.

GRAPE ESCAPE WINERY TOURS

503-283-3380
www.grapeescapetours.com
77 NE Holland Street
Rates: $75–110 per person
Special Features: Custom packages, three-winery special Friday trips on in summer ($100)

As Pinot Noir is to Oregon wines, Grape Escape is to Oregon wine tours. Tours can be for a group, a couple, or just you. Gourmet lunches, hot-air balloon rides, even a helicopter drop can be arranged with Grape Escape. There are no pre-set itineraries, so the sky (literally) is the limit. Luxury vans called "vimos" sporting a running grape logo are guided by "escape artists." Grape Escape will take you anywhere in the state, including overnight trips, but they specialize in the Willamette Valley. Weeklong trips are also available.

MARTIN'S GORGE TOURS

503-349-1323 or 877-290-8687
www.martinsgorgetours.com
Rates: $85 per person for wine tour, $99 for wine/waterfall tour

Limo services are readily available throughout the state for wine touring. John Baker

Special Features: Tasting fees included; discounts for groups of 10 or more

These four- to six-hour tours in the Gorge and into the Columbia Valley AVA (at The Dalles) usually include stops at three wineries. Special requests are accepted. Group size is limited to 20. Participants are picked up at Portland-area hotels and the Hood River Hotel. Tours range from Edgefield on the west to Maryhill (Washington) on the east.

OREGON WINE TOURS

503-681-9463
www.orwinetours.com
Rates: $75–165 per person, $750–1,000 for VIP private tours
Special Features: Specializing in boutique and Pinot Noir wineries, winemaker dinners

Smaller groups are the focus at Oregon Wine Tours—typically from 2 to 10. Passenger vans takes guests to select Willamette Valley wineries, though custom tours are also available. An all-day tour includes lunch at either a winery or a restaurant. The Ultimate VIP Tour ($1,000) includes transportation, tasting fees, lunch, and the full-day presence of Biggio Hamina Cellars winemaker Todd Hamina.

SEA TO SUMMIT TOURS

503-286-9333
www.seatosummit.net
4128 North Montana Avenue
Rates: $69–119
Special Features: Custom wine tours, 15-percent discount for groups of 10 or more

Choose a tour that includes tasting fees or fend for yourself in the tasting rooms. Ride in a biodiesel 4x4 passenger van that can handle rain, mud, and snow. Let Sea to Summit guides know which north Willamette Valley wineries you want to visit and they'll handle the rest—"Any place, any time" is their motto. Rates are higher for all-inclusive packages.

WINE TOURS NORTHWEST

503-439-8687 or 800-359-1034
www.winetoursnorthwest.com
15714 NW Clubhouse
Rates: $85–125 per person
Special Features: Tours conducted in executive vans; groups of up to 48 accommodated; Washington tours, including Walla Walla AVA

Groups of 4 to 12 are the norm here, with special access to wineries—such as Ken Wright Cellars—normally closed to the public. The owners have been leading tours for a decade and have developed relationships with many of the winery owners through the Oregon Wine Brotherhood. Custom tours are also available. A "deluxe" tour for a couple includes a three-course lunch, a meeting with a winemaker, and tasting fees for $295. Most clients are from local upscale hotels such as the Allison, where special packages are available.

BEAVERTON
JMI LIMOUSINE

503-643-6404 or 800-223-8246
www.jmilimousine.com
3737 SW 117th Avenue
Rates: $65–175 per hour
Special Features: Airport pickup, special packages

Go with 12–14 passengers on the Limo Party Bus, decked out with a bar, TV, DVD player, and sound system. Creative packages include the Fly & Dine helicopter wine tours and game-day tailgaters if you're a Duck or Beaver fan. The owner knows the Portland area well and claims to have the best rates in town.

OREGON WINE TOURS AND TASTING

503-616-1918
www.winetoursandtasting.com

Rates: $125–700
Special Features: Introductory wine tour for novices and a red-wine lovers' tour

"A Beautiful Oregon Wine Tour" focuses on Dundee, Carlton, and Newberg—but they'll go as far south as Salem. A minimum of five wineries appear on the Grand Tour and Red Wine Lovers tour, on which you'll learn about history, soils, and other related topics. Archery Summit is always included so visitors can enter the famous "cave"; an interpretive walk through another vineyard is also included. The 8- to 10-hour tours begin and end at your hotel, and gourmet lunch is included.

MY CHAUFFEUR WINE TOUR COMPANY

503-969-4370 or 877-692-4283
www.winetouroregon.com
Based in Portland
Rates: $59–79 per person or $50–115 per hour
Special Features: Exclusive tours can be arranged

Diversity is the name of the game with My Chauffeur. Tours include the requisite north Willamette Valley winery stops, of course, but also on the menu are Columbia Gorge wineries, the Evergreen Aviation Museum in McMinnville, Spirit Mountain Casino, an Oregon Symphony concert, and hot-air balloon rides. Transportation choices range from a four-door sedan to a 14-passenger limousine or coach bus, with pickup at your door. Check out their lodging packages.

CORNELIUS
EXECUTIVE LIMOUSINE COMPANY

503-992-8481
www.executivelimocompany.com
997 South Fourth Avenue
Rates: $80–100 per hour, depending on the limousine

Special Features: Airport pickup, edible arrangement of chocolate-dipped fruit for an additional $50

Four-hour wine tour packages range from $320 in the Lincoln Town Car stretch limo to $400 in the Ford Expedition stretch SUV. Chauffeured tours are offered daily or nightly (except Sunday) in Yamhill County . Rates are reduced on weekdays.

TIGARD
ECO-WINE TOURS

503-863-7777
www.eco-winetours.com
Rates: $59 per person, $89 including tasting fees
Special Features: Private evening winery tours with dinner

Everything is eco-oriented on these tours, right down to the eco-van that picks you up and drops you off at your hotel or residence. The Willamette Valley wineries you'll visit are certified LIVE and Salmon-Safe, and some are organic and biodynamic. You'll spend five hours visiting three or four "sustainable" wineries, including a picnic lunch or stop at a bistro. Extended tours are available upon request.

MCMINNVILLE
INSIDERS WINE TOUR

503-791-0005
www.insiderswinetour.com
1259 NW Michelbrook Lane
Rates: $75/hour in limo, $60/hour in town car or SUV

Yamhill County's only wine-touring company touts rides in a limousine and/or a helicopter. Insiders has access to wineries offered nowhere else, thanks to relationships developed with area winery owners and winemakers. The chopper takes off from the Newberg Air Park and provides an overflight of the Dundee Hills. Four ground adventures are suggested—OR 99W, the

North End, Carlton, and the Dundee area—but custom tours are also available, including wineries in the Gorge.

EUGENE
SUNSHINE LIMOUSINE SERVICE
541-543-6486
www.sunshinelimoservice.com
193 Wallis Street
Rates: $165–450 for three hours, $275–750 for eight hours
Special Features: Gourmet box lunches and appetizers available for extra charge

Sunshine offers three- to eight-hour tours anywhere in the Willamette Valley as well as the Roseburg area and Columbia Gorge. Rides range from a Lincoln Town Car for four and Cadillac Escalade ESV for 6 to 16 passengers to the 18-passenger Lincoln Navigator. Because of their focus on the region, Sunshine is your best bet if you're interested in touring the central and southern portions of the Willamette Valley.

THE DALLES
HOOD RIVER TOURS
541-350-9850
www.hoodrivertours.com
914 Court Street
Rates: $80–95/person or $600 total for custom van tour for 7–14 people
Special Features: Tasting fees not included

The Hood River Tour hits four or five wineries in four hours, and includes a picnic lunch. They were one of the first to do wine tours in the Gorge and are well acquainted with all of the owners; they even have access to barrel rooms at many wineries. Tours are customized to hit the best wines at the time.

ROSEBURG
OREGON WINE COUNTRY TOURS
866-946-3826
www.oregonwinecountrytours.com
2855 Edenbower Boulevard
Rates: $55/person

Special Features: A maximum of eight people per group

Start your tour with a pickup at the Sleep Inn south parking lot in Roseburg and embark on an adventure that includes a Wine Tasting 101 class, gourmet lunch, four winery stops, possible barrel tastings, and maybe even a meeting with an Umpqua Valley winemaker.

GRANTS PASS
JULES OF THE VALLEY WINE TOURS
541-973-9699
www.julesvalley.com
Redwood Highway
Rates: $75/person

Jules of the Valley does wine tours with flair. Choose a tour of five wineries in the Applegate Valley, or a Rogue Valley wine and cheese tour that features the Rogue Creamery. There's also an Illinois Valley tour that includes a stop at a tree-house lodge, and a tour of three wineries before a visit to Crater Lake National Park.

ASHLAND
MAIN STREET TOURS
541-488-7895
www.ashland-tours.com
17 North Main Street
Rates: $69–89 per person
Special features: Winemaker dinners at Applegate River Lodge and Steamboat Inn, east of Roseburg

M. Kim Lewis's Main Street Tours is the only southern Oregon wine-touring company sanctioned by the Oregon Wine & Farm Tour. The three-hour custom tour includes three wineries of your choice, a snack at a winery, and transportation from your lodging. The company emphasizes wine education and visits artisan food vendors in an effort to pair local fruits and cheeses with southern Oregon's finest. Choose between tours of the Rogue, Applegate/Illinois Valley, or Umpqua AVAs.

C. Great Grape Destinations

2 WILLAMETTE VALLEY NORTH

Portland Area
- ❏ Hip Chicks Do Wine 503-234-3790
- ❏ Boedecker Cellars 503-288-7752
- ❏ Groschau Cellars 503-522-2455
- ❏ Helvetia Vineyards & Winery 503-647-7596

Aloha Area
- ❏ Cooper Mountain Vineyards 503-649-0027

Beaverton Area
- ❏ Ponzi Vineyards 503-628-1227

Hillsboro Area
- ❏ Oak Knoll Winery 503-648-8198
- ❏ Beran Vineyards 503-628-1298
- ❏ Freja Cellars 503-628-0337
- ❏ J. Albin Winery 503-628-2986

Troutdale Area
- ❏ Edgefield Winery 503-665-2992

Sandy Area
- ❏ Wasson Brothers Winery 503-668-3124

Newberg Area
- ❏ Hawks View Cellars 503-625-1591
- ❏ Alloro Vineyard 503-625-1978
- ❏ VX Vineyard 503-538-9895
- ❏ Quailhurst 509-427-5132
- ❏ Barron-Wahl Vineyards 503-625-7886 or 503-544-1957
- ❏ McKinlay Vineyards 503-625-2534
- ❏ J.K. Carriere Wines 503-554-0721
- ❏ Owen Roe Winery 503-678-6514
- ❏ Anam Cara 503-537-9150
- ❏ A-Z Wineworks & Rex Hill Vineyards 503-538-0666
- ❏ August Cellars 503-554-6766
  - ❏ Artisanal 503-537-2094
  - ❏ Barking Frog 503-702-5029
  - ❏ Crowley Wines 971-645-3547
  - ❏ Et Fille 503-853-5836
  - ❏ Laura Volkman Vineyards 503-806-4047
  - ❏ Toluca Lane 971-241-7728

- ❏ Chehalem 503-538-4700
- ❏ Fox Farm Vineyards & Wine Bar 503-538-8466
- ❏ Hip Chicks Do Wine 503-554-5800
- ❏ Bishop Creek Cellars 503-487-6934
- ❏ Dark Horse Tasting Room 503-538-2427
  - ❏ Medici Vineyards 503-538-9668
  - ❏ Sineann Cellars 503-341-2698
  - ❏ Ferraro Cellars 503-758-0557
- ❏ Roco Winery 503-538-7625
- ❏ Anderson Family Vineyards 503-554-5541
- ❏ Prive Vineyard 503-554-0464
- ❏ Natalie's Estate Winery 503-807-5008
- ❏ Vidon Vineyard 503-538-4092
- ❏ De Lancellotti Family Vineyards 503-554-6802
- ❏ Bergström Winery 503-554-0468 or 503-554-0463
- ❏ Lachini Vineyards 503-864-4553
- ❏ Arborbrook Vineyards 503-538-0959
- ❏ Adelsheim Vineyards 503-538-3652
- ❏ Ayres Vineyard 503-538-7450
- ❏ Penner-Ash Wine Cellars 503-554-5545
- ❏ Patricia Green Cellars 503-554-0821
- ❏ Beaux Freres 503-537-1137
- ❏ Whistling Ridge Vineyards 503-554-8991
- ❏ RR 503-706-9277
- ❏ Styring Vineyards 503-866-6741
- ❏ Redman Vineyard & Winery 503-554-1290
- ❏ Trisaetum Winery 503-538-9898
- ❏ Brick House Vineyards 503-538-5136
- ❏ Aramenta Cellars 503-538-7230
- ❏ Utopia Wines 503-298-7841
- ❏ Shea Wine Cellars 503-241-6527

Dundee Area
- ❏ Duck Pond Cellars 503-538-3199 or 800-437-3213
- ❏ The Four Graces 800-245-2950
- ❏ Dobbes Family Estate 503-538-1141 or 800-556-8143
- ❏ Ponzi Wine Bar 503-554-1500
- ❏ Argyle Winery 503-538-8520 or 888-427-4953

❏ Gino Cuneo Cellars 503-949-1992
❏ Sokol Blosser Winery 503-864-2282 or 800-582-6668
❏ Daedalus Cellars 503-538-4400
❏ Winderlea Vineyard & Winery 503-554-5900
❏ Maresh Red Barn 503-537-1098
❏ Torii Mor 503-538-2279
❏ Lange Estate Winery & Vineyards 503-538-6476
❏ Bella Vida Vineyard 503-538-9821
❏ Crumbled Rock Winery 503-537-9682
❏ Erath Winery 800-539-9463

Dayton Area
❏ Winters Hill Vineyard 503-864-4538
❏ Domaine Serene 503-864-4600
❏ Vista Hills Vineyard 503-864-3200
❏ Domaine Drouhin of Oregon 503-864-2700
❏ White Rose Wines 503-864-2328
❏ De Ponte Cellars 503-864-3698
❏ Red Ridge Farms/Durant Vineyards 503-864-8502
❏ Archery Summit 503-864-4300
❏ Stoller Vineyards 503-864-3404
❏ Seufert Winery 503-709-1255

3 ROUTE 47

Forest Grove Area
❏ Apolloni Vineyards 503-359-3606 or 503-330-5946
❏ Purple Cow Vineyards 503-330-0991
❏ Shafer Vineyard Cellars 503-357-6604
❏ David Hill Winery & Vineyard 503-992-8545
❏ Montinore Estate 503-359-5012
❏ SakéOne 503-357-7056

Cornelius Area
❏ Ardiri Winery & Vineyards 888-503-3330 or 503-628-6060
❏ A Blooming Hill Vineyard 503-992-1196

Gaston Area
❏ Plum Hill Vineyards 503-359-4706

❏ Patton Valley Vineyards 503-985-3445
❏ Big Table Farm 503-662-3129
❏ Elk Cove Vineyards 503-985-7760
❏ Kramer Vineyards 503-662-4545
❏ Thistle Wines 503-590-0449
❏ ADEA Wine Company/Fisher Family Cellars 503-662-4509
  ❏ Biggio Hamina Cellars 503-737-9703
  ❏ Cancilla 503-985-7327
  ❏ Matello 503-939-1308
  ❏ Twelve 503-358-6707

Yamhill Area
❏ Atticus 503-662-3485
❏ Roots 503-730-0296
❏ WillaKenzie Estate 503-662-3280
❏ Lenne Estate 503-956-2256
❏ Stag Hollow Wines & Vineyards 503-662-5609

Carlton Area
❏ Cana's Feast 503-852-0002
❏ Carlton Winemakers Studio 503-852-6100
  ❏ Andrew Rich Vintner 503-852-6100
  ❏ Ayoub Vineyard 503-554-9583 X or 503-805-2154
  ❏ Brittan Vineyards 503-989-2507
  ❏ Hamacher Wines 503-852-7200
  ❏ Lazy River Vineyard 503-662-5400
  ❏ Montebruno 503-852-6100
  ❏ Retour Wines 971-237-4757
  ❏ Wahle Vineyards & Cellars 503-241-3385
❏ Raptor Ridge 503-367-4263
❏ Carlton Cellars 503-474-8986
❏ Zenas 503-852-3000
❏ Hawkins Cellars 503-481-9104
❏ Seven of Hearts 971-241-6548
❏ Troon 503-852-3084
❏ Ken Wright Cellars 503-852-7070
❏ Angel Vine 503-969-7209
❏ Domaine Coteau 503-697-7319
❏ EIEIO & The Tasting Room 503-852-6733
❏ Terra Vina 503-925-0712
❏ Cliff Creek Cellars 503-852-0089

❑ Folin Cellars 503-349-9616
❑ Barking Frog Winery 503-702-5029
❑ Tyrus Evan at the Depot 503-852-7010
❑ Scott Paul Wines 503-852-7300
❑ Soléna 503-852-0082 or 503-662-4730
❑ Carlo & Julian Winery 503-852-7432
❑ Soter Vineyards 503-662-5600
❑ Belle Pente Vineyard & Winery 503-852-9500
❑ Lemelson Vineyard 503-852-6619
❑ Laurel Ridge Winery 503-852-7050
❑ Ghost Hill Cellars 503-852-7347
❑ Monks Gate Vineyard 503-852-6521
❑ Anne Amie Vineyards 503-864-2991
❑ Alexana Winery 503-852-3013

4 WILLAMETTE VALLEY EAST

West Linn Area
❑ Oswego Hills Winery 503-655-2599
❑ J. Christopher Wines 503-231-5094

Oregon City Area
❑ King's Raven Winery 503-539-7202 or 503-784-6298
❑ Christopher Bridge Cellars 503-263-6267

Canby Area
❑ St. Josef's Winery 503-651-3190
❑ Hanson Vineyards 503-634-2348

Molalla Area
❑ AlexEli Vineyard 503-829-6677

Silverton Area
❑ Vitis Ridge Winery 503-873-9800

Sublimity Area
❑ Silver Falls Vineyard 503-769-5056

Salem Area
❑ Pudding River Wine Cellars 503-365-0391

Aumsville Area
❑ Piluso Vineyard & Winery 503-749-4125 or 866-684-9463

Aurora Area
❑ Champoeg Wine Cellars 503-678-2144

5 WILLAMETTE VALLEY CENTRAL

McMinnville Area
❑ Stone Wolf Vineyards 503-434-9025
❑ 1789 Wines 503-857-0225
❑ WineWorks Oregon 503-472-3215
  ❑ Walnut City WineWorks
  ❑ Bernard-Machado
  ❑ Carlton Hill
  ❑ Robinson Reserve
  ❑ Z'ivo
❑ Westrey Wine Company 503-434-6357
❑ The Eyrie Vineyards 503-472-6315 or 888-440-4970
❑ Remy Wines 503-560-2003
❑ Dominio IV Wines 503-474-8636
❑ Panther Creek Cellars 503-472-8080
❑ Anthony Dell Cellars 503-910-8874
❑ Sol et Soleil Cellars 503-925-5328
❑ R. Stuart & Co. 503-472-4477
❑ Séjourné 503-474-4499
❑ Evergreen Vineyards 503-434-4297 or 866-434-4818
❑ Hauer of the Dauen Winery 503-868-7359
❑ Methven Family Vineyards 503-868-7259
❑ Youngberg Hill Vineyards 503-472-2727
❑ Coeur de Terre Vineyard 503-472-3976
❑ La Béte Wines 503-977-1493
❑ Yamhill Valley Vineyards 503-843-3100
❑ Maysara Winery 503-843-1234
❑ Coleman Vineyard 503-843-2707

Sheridan Area
❑ Ransom Cellars 503-876-5022

Wheatland Area
❑ Arcane Cellars at Wheatland Winery 503-868-7076

Amity Area
❑ Kristin Hill Winery 503-835-0850
❑ Coelho Winery of Amity 503-835-9305
❑ Mia Sonatina Cellars 503-449-0834
❑ Dukes Family Vineyards 602-770-1671
❑ Brooks Wines 503-435-1278
❑ Mystic Wines 503-581-2769

Salem Area
- ❑ Rizzo Winery 503-577-5741
- ❑ Stangeland Vineyards & Winery 503-581-0355
- ❑ Witness Tree Vineyard 503-585-7874
- ❑ Cristom Vineyards 503-375-3068
- ❑ St. Innocent Winery 503-378-1526
- ❑ Bryn Mawr 503-581-4286
- ❑ Lewman Vineyards 503-365-8859
- ❑ Bethel Heights Vineyard 503-581-2262
- ❑ Evesham Wood Vineyard & Winery 503-371-8478
- ❑ Redhawk Vineyard & Winery 503-362-1596
- ❑ Honeywood Winery 503-362-4111
- ❑ Bodhichitta Winery 503-580-9463
- ❑ Cubanisimo Vineyard 503-588-1763
- ❑ Whistling Dog Cellars 503-329-5114
- ❑ Cherry Hill Winery 503-623-7867 or 503-623-9745
- ❑ Vitae Springs Vineyard 503-588-0896
- ❑ Ankeny Vineyard Winery 503-378-1498
- ❑ Trinity Vineyards 503-371-6977

Dallas Area
- ❑ Van Duzer Vineyards 503-623-6420 or 800-884-1927
- ❑ Namasté Vineyards 503-623-4150

Rickreall Area
- ❑ Chateau Bianca 503-623-6181
- ❑ Johan Vineyards 866-379-6029
- ❑ Left Coast Cellars 503-831-4916
- ❑ Eola Hills Wine Cellars 503-623-2405 or 800-291-6730
- ❑ Amalie Robert Vineyard 503-831-4703
- ❑ Illahe Vineyards 503-831-1248

Monmouth Area
- ❑ Emerson Vineyards 503-838-0944
- ❑ Olsen Family Vineyards & Viridian Wines 888-344-2022
- ❑ Airlie Winery 503-838-6013

Turner Area
- ❑ Willamette Valley Vineyards 503-588-9463

6 WILLAMETTE VALLEY SOUTH

Albany Area
- ❑ Springhill Cellars 541-928-1009

Corvallis Area
- ❑ Belle Vallee 541-757-9463
- ❑ Nuthatch Cellars 541-754-8483
- ❑ Tyee Wine Cellars 541-753-8754

Philomath Area
- ❑ Spindrift Cellars 541-929-6555
- ❑ Pheasant Court Winery/Wine Vault 541-929-7715
- ❑ Harris Bridge 541-929-3053
- ❑ Lûmos 541-929-3519
- ❑ Cardwell Hill Winery 541-929-9463
- ❑ 720 Wine Cellars 541-929-4562

Sweet Home Area
- ❑ Marks Ridge Winery 541-367-3292

Monroe Area
- ❑ Broadley Vineyards 541-847-5934
- ❑ Benton-Lane Winery 541-847-5792

Junction City Area
- ❑ Pfeiffer Winery 541-998-2828
- ❑ High Pass Winery 541-998-1447

Cheshire Area
- ❑ RainSong Vineyard 541-998-1786

Elmira Area
- ❑ LaVelle Vineyard 541-935-9406

Veneta Area
- ❑ Domaine Meriwether 541-521-9690

Eugene Area
- ❑ Sweet Cheeks Winery 541-349-9463
- ❑ Silvan Ridge Winery/Hinman Vineyards 541-345-1945
- ❑ Noble Estate 541-338-3007
- ❑ Territorial Vineyards & Wine Company 541-684-9463
- ❑ Houston Vineyards 541-747-4681

Lorane Area
- ❑ King Estate 541-942-9874
- ❑ Château Lorane 541-942-8028

Cottage Grove Area
- ❑ Saginaw Vineyard 541-942-1364
- ❑ Iris Vineyards 541-942-5993

7 SOUTHERN OREGON

Elkton Area
- ❑ Brandborg Vineyard & Winery 541-584-2870
- ❑ Rivers Edge 541-584-2357
- ❑ Bradley Vineyards 541-584-2888

Oakland Area
- ❑ Sienna Ridge Estate 541-849-3300
- ❑ MarshAnne Landing 541-459-7998
- ❑ Misty Oaks Vineyard 541-459-3558

Roseburg Area
- ❑ Henry Estate Winery 541-459-5120 or 800-782-2686
- ❑ Reustle Prayer Rock Vineyards 541-459-6060
- ❑ Becker Vineyard 541-677-0288
- ❑ Delfino Vineyards 541-673-7575
- ❑ Julianna Vineyards 541-672-8060
- ❑ Palotai Vineyard & Winery 541-464-0032
- ❑ Melrose Vineyards 541-672-6080
- ❑ HillCrest Vineyard & Winery 541-673-3709
- ❑ Spangler Vineyards 541-679-9654
- ❑ Abacela 541-679-6642
- ❑ Chateau Nonchalant 541-679-2394
- ❑ Girardet Wine Cellars 541-679-7252

Winston Area
- ❑ Wild Rose Vineyard 541-580-5488

Grants Pass Area
- ❑ Bridgeview Vineyards 541-846-1039
- ❑ Soloro Vineyard 541-862-2693
- ❑ Wooldridge Creek Winery 541-846-6364
- ❑ Schmidt Family Vineyards 541-846-9985
- ❑ Troon Vineyard 541-846-9900
- ❑ Rosella's Vineyard 541-846-6372
- ❑ Applegate Red Winery 541-846-9557

Williams Area
- ❑ Plaisance Ranch Winery 541-846-7175

Selma Area
- ❑ Deer Creek Vineyards 541-597-4226

Cave Junction Area
- ❑ Windridge Vineyard 541-592-5333
- ❑ Bridgeview Vineyards 541-592-4688
- ❑ Foris Vineyards Winery 541-592-3752 or 800-843-6747

Jacksonville Area
- ❑ John Michael Champagne Cellars 541-846-0810
- ❑ Devitt Winery 541-899-7511
- ❑ Fiasco Winery/Jacksonville Vineyards 541-899-9645 or 541-899-6923
- ❑ LongSword Vineyard 541-899-1746 or 800-655-3877
- ❑ Valley View Winery 541-899-8468
- ❑ Cowhorn Vineyard 541-899-6876
- ❑ Quady North 541-702-2123
- ❑ South Stage Cellars 541-899-9120

Central Point Area
- ❑ Madrone Mountain 541-664-1707
- ❑ Daisy Creek Vineyard 541-899-8329
- ❑ Caprice Vineyards 541-499-0449

Gold Hill Area
- ❑ Folin Cellars 541-855-2018
- ❑ Del Rio Vineyards 541-855-2062

Shady Cove Area
- ❑ Crater Lake Cellars 541-878-4200

Eagle Point Area
- ❑ Agate Ridge Vineyard 541-830-3050

Medford Area
- ❑ RoxyAnn Winery 541-776-2315
- ❑ EdenVale Winery 541-512-9463
- ❑ Carpenter Hill Vineyard 541-210-8897
- ❑ Pebblestone Cellars 541-512-1704

Talent Area
- ❑ Paschal Winery & Vineyard 541-535-7957
- ❑ Trium Winery 541-535-4015

Ashland Area
❏ Grizzly Peak Winery 541-482-5700
❏ Weisinger's Winery 541-488-5989

Bonanza Area
❏ 12 Ranch Wines 541-545-1204

8 Columbia Gorge

Hood River Area
❏ Cathedral Ridge Winery 800-516-8710
❏ Marchesi Vineyards & Winery 541-386-1800
❏ Phelps Creek Vineyards 541-386-2607
❏ Pheasant Valley Vineyard & Winery 541-387-3040
❏ Mt. Hood Winery 541-386-8333
❏ Viento 541-386-3026
❏ Wy'East Vineyards 541-386-1277
❏ Naked Winery 800-666-9303
❏ Quenett Winery 541-386-2229
❏ Springhouse Cellar 541-308-0700
❏ The Pines 1852 Tasting Room & Gallery 541-993-8301

9 The Oregon Coast

Astoria Area
❏ Shallon Winery 503-325-5978

Nehalem Area
❏ Nehalem Bay Winery 503-368-9463 or 888-368-9463

Otter Rock Area
❏ Flying Dutchman Winery 541-765-2553

Bandon Area
❏ Sea Mist Winery 541-348-2351

Myrtle Point Area
❏ Old Coyote Winery 541-572-8090
❏ HV Cellars & Wild Goose Vineyards 541-372-0251

Remote Area
❏ Old Bridge Winery 541-572-0272

10 Eastern Oregon & Elsewhere

The Dalles Area
❏ Bolton Cellars Estate Winery 541-298-1285 or 541-296-7139
❏ Erin Glenn Winery at the Mint 541-296-4707
❏ Dry Hollow Vineyards 541-296-2953

Milton-Freewater Area
❏ Watermill Winery 541-938-5575
❏ Otis Kenton 509-525-3505 or 206-463-3125
❏ Zerba Cellars 541-938-9463
❏ Castillo de Feliciana Vineyard & Winery 541-558-3656

Cove Area
❏ Gilstrap Brothers Vineyard & Winery 541-568-4646 or 866-568-4200

Culver Area
❏ Maragas Winery 541-330-0919 or 541-546-5464

Bend Area
❏ Volcano Vineyards 541-390-8771

Mount Vernon Area
❏ David Hamilton Winery 541-932-4567

There is nothing like a wine-inspired conversation among friends. John Baker

General Index

Lodging by Price

Inexpensive	$75 or less
Moderate	$75 to 125
Expensive	$126 to 199
Very Expensive	$200 and above

Willamette Valley North

Moderate
McMenamins Edgefield, 36

Expensive
Chehalem Ridge B&B, 68
Heathman Hotel/Marble Bar, 35
Lions Gate Inn, 69
Moderate Avellan Inn, 68
Vineroost, 70
Wine Country Farm B&B and Cellars, 86

Expensive–Very Expensive
Dreamgiver's Inn, 68–69
Dundee Manor B&B, 85
University House of Newberg, 69–70

Very Expensive
Allison Inn & Spa, 68
Black Walnut Inn & Vineyard, 84–85
The Governor, 35–36
Hotel Vintage Plaza, 36
Inn at Red Hills, 85–86
Springbrook Hazelnut Farm, 69
Vineyard Ridge, 86

Willamette Valley Route 47

Inexpensive–Expensive
Mcmenamins Grand Lodge, 96
Old Recreation Inn, 96

Expensive
Carlton Inn, 119

Expensive–Very Expensive
Lobenhaus Bed & Breakfast & Vineyard, 119
R.R. Thompson House, 120

Very Expensive
Abbey Road Farm B&B, 118–19
Brookside Inn, 119
Lake House Vacation Rental, 104

Willamette Valley East

Moderate
Oregon Garden Resort, 129

Expensive
Water Street Inn, 129–30
White Oaks Bed & Breakfast, 130

Willamette Valley Central

Inexpensive–Moderate
Mcmenamins Hotel Oregon, 146

Moderate–Expensive
Baker Street Inn, 145–46

Expensive
Joseph Mattey House, 146
Kelty Estate, 147–48
Oregon Wine Cottage, 146–47

Expensive–Very Expensive
A'Tuscan Estate B&B, 145

Very Expensive
Pinot Quarters, 147

Willamette Valley South

Inexpensive–Very Expensive
At Home in Oregon, 178–79

Moderate–Expensive
Pfeiffer Cottage Inn, 178

Moderate–Very Expensive
Campbell House Inn, 194

Expensive
Hanson Country Inn, 179
Harrison House, 179
McKenzie Orchards Bed & Breakfast, 194
Valley River Inn, 194

Expensive–Very Expensive
Salbasgeon Suites, 179

Southern Oregon

Moderate
Seven Feathers Hotel and Casino Resort, 210

Moderate–Very Expensive
Peerless Hotel, 245
Steamboat Inn, 211

Expensive
Applegate River Lodge, 232
C.H. Bailey House Bed & Breakfast, 210
Under the Greenwood Tree B&B, 241
Riverside Inn, 221

Expensive–Very Expensive
Inn at Lithia Springs, 245
Jacksonville Inn, 231–32
Lodge at Riverside, 220–21
McCully House Inn and Cottages, 231
Out 'n' About Treehouse Treesort, 222
Winchester Inn, 244–45

Very Expensive
Big K Guest Ranch, 210
Weasku Inn, 221–22

Columbia Gorge

Moderate
Mosier House B&B, 258–59

Moderate–Expensive
Hood River Hotel, 257
Inn at the Gorge, 257
Seven Oaks B&B, 258
Vineyard View B&B, 258

Expensive
Columbia Gorge Hotel, 256–57
Lakecliff B&B, 258

Expensive–Very Expensive
Sakura Ridge Farm and Lodge, 258

Very Expensive
Columbia Cliffs Villas, 257

Oregon Coast

Moderate
Mill Casino Hotel, 280

Moderate–Expensive
Nehalem River Inn & Restaurant, 268

Moderate–Very Expensive
Embarcadero Resort Hotel & Marina, 274

Expensive–Very Expensive
A Bandon Inn, 280
Lighthouse Bed & Breakfast, 280–81

Very Expensive
Arch Cape Inn & Retreat, 268
Cannery Pier Hotel, 268
Lodge-Bandon Dunes Golf Resort, 281

Eastern Oregon

Inexpensive
Court Street Bed & Breakfast, 290

Inexpensive–Very Expensive
Seventh Mountain Resort, 299

Moderate
Dalles Inn, 290

Moderate–Expensive
Pendleton House Bed & Breakfast, 295
Wildhorse Resort & Casino, 295

Moderate–Very Expensive
The Riverhouse, 299

Expensive
Celilo Inn Motel, 290
Shilo Inn & Suites, 290

Very Expensive
Sunriver Resort, 298–99

Dining by Price

Inexpensive	$10 or less
Moderate	$11 to 20
Expensive	$21 to 30
Very Expensive	$30 and above

Willamette Valley North

Inexpensive–Moderate
Underground Café Coffeehouse, 70–71

Moderate
Café Castagna, 37–38
Dundee Bistro, 86–87
Farm Café, 38
Ken's Artisan Pizza, 39
Mother's Bistro & Bar, 40
Navarre, 40–41

Moderate–Expensive
Higgins Restaurant & Bar, 38
Joel Palmer House, 88
Tina's Restaurant, 88
Veritable Quandary, 42

Expensive
Beast, 37
Bluehour, 37
Farm to Fork, 87
Meriwether's, 39–40
The Painted Lady, 70
Paley's Place Bistro & Bar, 41
Park Kitchen, 41
Red Hills Provincial Dining, 87
Ringside Steakhouse, 41–42
Wildwood, 42

Very Expensive
Jory Restaurant & Bar, 71

Willamette Valley Route 47

Inexpensive
Filling Station Deli, 120
Urban Decanter Wine Collection & Bar, 97

Moderate–Expensive
Out Aza Blue Market & Cafe, 97

Moderate
Horse Radish Cheese & Wine Bar, 120–21
Maggie's Buns Café, 97

Expensive
Cuvée, 120

Willamette Valley East

Inexpensive–Moderate
Silver Grille Café & Wines, 130

Willamette Valley Central

Inexpensive
Café Uncorked, 148
Red Fox Bakery & Café, 149

Inexpensive–Moderate
Grand Vines, 166–67
Old Europe Inn, 167
Ragin' River Steak Co., 168
Wild Pear Restaurant & Catering, 167–68

Moderate
Crescent Café, 148
La Capitale, 167
Thistle Restaurant, 149–50

Moderate–Expensive
La Rambla Restaurant & Bar, 148–49
Nick's Italian Cafe, 149

Expensive
Bistro Maison, 148

Willamette Valley South

Inexpensive–Moderate
Clemenza's Italian American Café, 179–80
Marché Restaurant, 195

Moderate
B2 Wine Bar, 195
Cloud 9 Bistro, 181
Gathering Together Farm, 182
Our Daily Bread Restaurant, 196
Sybaris, 180
Wine Depot & Deli, 180

Expensive
Aqua Seafood, 180–81
Big River Restaurant & Bar, 181
Le Bistro Corvallis, 181–82
Oregon Electric Station, 195–96

Southern Oregon

Inexpensive–Moderate
Roseburg Station Pub & Brewery, 212

Moderate
Anthony's Italian Café, 211
Bella Union, 232
Blondies' Bistro, 222–23
Camas Room, 212–13
Elements Tapas Bar & Lounge, 241
The Laughing Clam, 223
Pompodori Ristorante, 242
Taprock Northwest Grill, 224
Tomaselli's Pastry Mill and Café, 211

Moderate–Expensive
Café Dejeuner, 241
Mark V Grill & Bar, 212
Omar's Restaurant, 246
One Fifteen Broiler, 223
Tolly's Restaurant, 212

Expensive
Amuse Restaurant, 245–46
Beasy's on the Creek, 246
Chateaulin, 245
Gogi's Café Britt, 232
The River's Edge, 223–24
Summer Jo's, 224

Columbia Gorge

Inexpensive–Moderate
Divots Restaurant at Indian Creek Golf
  Course, 259
Full Sail Brewing Company Tasting Room
  and Pub, 259
Good River Restaurant, 261

Moderate
Sixth Street Bistro & Loft, 260
Sophie's, 260
Stonehedge Gardens, 260–61
3 Rivers Grill, 261

Expensive
Celilo Restaurant & Bar, 259

Oregon Coast

Moderate
Bridgewater Bistro, 268–69
Panache, 274–75
Silver Salmon Grille, 269
Village Market Bistro & Deli, 275
Yummy Wine Bar & Bistro, 269–70

Moderate–Expensive
Clemente's Restaurant, 269

Expensive
Alloro Wine Bar & Restaurant, 281
April's at Nye Beach, 275
Fathom's Restaurant, 274
The Gallery, 281–82
Saffron Salmon, 275

Eastern Oregon

Inexpensive–Moderate
Avery's Wine Bar, 300

Moderate
Baldwin Saloon, 290–91
Great Pacific Wine & Coffee Company, 295
Jackalope Grill, 299–300
Windseeker Restaurant on the Port, 291

Moderate–Expensive
Pine Tavern, 300
Raphael's Restaurant, 296
Stetson's House of Prime, 296

Expensive
Crossings at the Riverhouse, 299
Oasis @ Stateline, 295

Dining by Cuisine